DISCARD

SOUND...

FASHION NOW

EDITED BY TERRY JONES

TASCHEN

PHOTOGRAPHY TERRY JONES. RAF SIMONS. AUTUMN/WINTER 2002.

PHOTOGRAPHY TERRY JONES. YOHJI YAMAMOTO.

14 HAIDER ACKERMANN
18 AZZEDINE ALAÏA
22 GIORGIO ARMANI
26 KRIS VAN ASSCHE + DIOR HOMME
30 AGNÈS B.
32 CHRISTOPHER BAILEY • BURBERRY
36 NEIL BARRETT
38 WALTER VAN BEIRENDONCK
42 THOM BROWNE
44 CONSUELO CASTIGLIONI • MARNI
46 DEAN & DAN CATEN • DSQUARED
50 ROBERTO CAVALLI
54 HUSSEIN CHALAYAN
58 MARIA CORNEJO • ZERO
62 FRANCISCO COSTA • CALVIN KLEIN
66 GILES DEACON
70 CHRISTOPHE DECARNIN • BALMAIN
72 ANN DEMEULEMEESTER
76 DOMENICO DOLCE & STEFANO GABBANA • DOLCE & GABBANA
80 ALBER ELBAZ • LANVIN
84 SILVIA VENTURINI FENDI • FENDI
88 ALBERTA FERRETTI
92 LIMI FEU
96 TOM FORD
100 DAI FUJIWARA • ISSEY MIYAKE
102 JOHN GALLIANO
106 JEAN PAUL GAULTIER
110 NICOLAS GHESQUIÈRE • BALENCIAGA
114 FRIDA GIANNINI • GUCCI
118 KATHARINE HAMNETT
120 ANN VALÉRIE HASH
122 DESIRÉE HEISS & INES KAAG • BLESS
124 LAZARO HERNANDEZ & JACK MCCOLLOUGH • PROENZA SCHOULER
128 TOMMY HILFIGER
132 VIKTOR HORSTING & ROLF SNOEREN • VIKTOR & ROLF
136 MARGARET HOWELL
138 MARC JACOBS
142 ROSSELLA JARDINI • MOSCHINO
144 CHRISTOPHER KANE
148 DONNA KARAN
152 REI KAWAKUBO • COMME DES GARÇONS
156 ADAM KIMMEL
158 SOPHIA KOKOSALAKI
160 MICHAEL KORS
162 TAO KURIHARA
166 KARL LAGERFELD + CHANEL
170 RALPH LAUREN

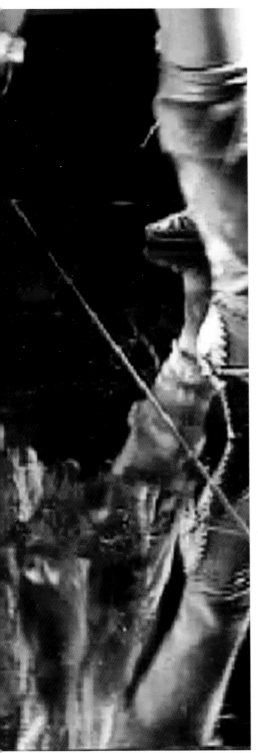

PHOTOGRAPHY TERRY JONES. JOHN GALLIANO AUTUMN/WINTER 2004.

174 CHRISTOPHE LEMAIRE • LACOSTE
178 JULIEN MACDONALD
180 HANNAH MACGIBBON • CHLOÉ
182 TOMAS MAIER • BOTTEGA VENETA
186 MARTIN MARGIELA • MAISON MARTIN MARGIELA
190 ANTONIO MARRAS + KENZO
192 STELLA MCCARTNEY
196 ALEXANDER MCQUEEN
200 ANGELA MISSONI • MISSONI
202 ROLAND MOURET
204 KATE & LAURA MULLEAVY • RODARTE
208 RICHARD NICOLL
210 NIGO® • A BATHING APE
212 DRIES VAN NOTEN
216 LUCAS OSSENDRIJVER • LANVIN
218 RICK OWENS
222 BRUNO PIETERS • HUGO BOSS
224 STEFANO PILATI • YVES SAINT LAURENT
228 ZAC POSEN
230 MIUCCIA PRADA • PRADA + MIU MIU
234 GARETH PUGH
238 JOHN RICHMOND
240 NARCISO RODRIGUEZ
242 SONIA RYKIEL
244 JONATHAN SAUNDERS + POLLINI
248 MARIOS SCHWAB
250 JEREMY SCOTT
254 RAF SIMONS • JIL SANDER
258 MARTINE SITBON • RUE DU MAIL
262 PAUL SMITH
266 ANNA SUI
268 JUN TAKAHASHI • UNDERCOVER
272 OLIVIER THEYSKENS
274 JUSTIN THORNTON & THEA BREGAZZI • PREEN
276 AITOR THROUP
278 RICCARDO TISCI • GIVENCHY
282 JEAN TOUITOU • APC
284 GIAMBATTISTA VALLI
286 AN VANDEVORST & FILIP ARICKX • AF VANDEVORST
288 DONATELLA VERSACE
292 STUART VEVERS • LOEWE
294 ALEXANDER WANG
298 JUNYA WATANABE
302 VIVIENNE WESTWOOD
306 BERNHARD WILLHELM
310 MATTHEW WILLIAMSON
312 YOHJI YAMAMOTO
316 ITALO ZUCCHELLI • CALVIN KLEIN

INTRODUCTION

When Benedikt Taschen first proposed this idea – to make a selection from the highly successful 'Fashion Now' editions – my first reaction was uncertainty. The nature of fashion, a business that naturally changes every season, flagged up various problems. Designers move about, some go out of business. Fashion is constantly reinvented. But on reflection, I realised that after three decades of 'i-D' promoting creativity and ideas, this book's selection from its pages since 2000 would serve as an inspiration for a new generation. The potential of fashion is to create work and jobs in which many people find self-expression. As we approach 2012, the challenges that face the industry are to research fabrics and dyes and improve production techniques in a sustainable way and also to maintain traditional crafts and skills in an increasingly competitive market. In editing this book from the original 160 designers to 95, we have tried to keep a cross section, from the revered titans in the industry to the exciting new talents that are constantly striving to survive. Every season is a new challenge and the global recession, which has hit the fashion industry hard, is forcing re-evaluation, reinvention and the reinterpretation of luxury through necessity. I have always thought fashion communicates who we are. Human priorities are shelter, food and clothing. Clothing is often an expression of your life. After any hardship, whatever war or natural disaster, people have found different ways to express survival. Whether fashion is frivolous, fabulous or functional, the designer's task is to surprise and entertain. Recession is for the brave heart. Ideas are the currency for success along with value for money, innovation not imitation, authenticity and a new ethical awareness. With fashion today the choice is massive: from laser to hand-cut, from stitch to weld, from man-made to nature-made, organic or chemical, sustainability is the new byword, which could see us all recycling our wardrobe within the next decade. Shareware could be the next chic. Travel light – toothbrush and panties in your bumbag and your wardrobe arranged over the Internet with 'fashion family friends' or shareware by clubbing together to buy a fabulous couture creation and timeshare. It's not so far removed from borrowing wellingtons and raincoats when visiting friends in their country home or renting ski boots while on holiday! 2008 saw many collections inspired by resourceful ideas. From Prada and Comme des Garçons to Rodarte and Ralph Lauren, we saw patches, overstitch or overdyeing. The designer's skill is to exploit every idea and retain their individuality, which gives them a sustainable credibility not to be lost or their name depends on it. A decade is equivalent to an era in the world of fashion. The main concern in this game is to create the illusion of change. Look in your wardrobe and the odds are you will be mixing that Spring 2005 piece with an Autumn 2010 with a hot-in-the-shop bargain or another find on eBay.

Fashion has never before produced so much stuff and the current crunch has forced us all to re-evaluate our spending habits. A well-known fashion collector with a banker husband confided in me this spring that he had told her to be more careful. But why? she asked. Her purchases are of more value than the interest she might get from money in the bank. She might buy less Comme des Garçons or Margiela but is interested in Christopher Kane or Antonio Marras at Kenzo. Fashion continues to be variable art for many and placing your

bets on the future is a demanding challenge for every retail fashion buyer. Their survival depends on their nose for the zeitgeist. People don't just want to replace something they already have in their wardrobe. They want to have a fresh input – something unique – and that is what gets these designers out of bed each day.

TERRY JONES

EINLEITUNG

Als Benedikt Taschen vorschlug, aus den überaus erfolgreichen Ausgaben von ‚Fashion Now' eine Auswahl für dieses Buch zu treffen, war ich mir zunächst nicht sicher, was ich davon halten sollte. Die Mode an sich und das Geschäft mit ihr bringt es mit sich, dass jede Saison Veränderung bedeutet, was für zahlreiche Probleme sorgt. Designer suchen sich andere Herausforderungen, manche ziehen sich ganz aus dem Geschäft zurück. Mode erfindet sich ständig neu. Als ich länger darüber nachdachte, wurde mir jedoch klar, dass die Auswahl für dieses Buch aus den Seiten von i-D seit 2000 nach drei Jahrzehnten, in denen ich Kreativität und Ideen gefördert habe, einer neuen Generation als Inspiration dienen könnte. Mode bietet die Möglichkeit, Jobs zu schaffen, in denen viele Menschen sich selbst verwirklichen können. Jetzt, wo wir auf das Jahr 2012 zusteuern, sind die Herausforderungen, denen die Textilindustrie sich stellen muss, die Entwicklung von nachhaltigen Materialien, Farben und Produktionstechniken, aber auch die Bewahrung traditioneller Handwerkstechniken in einem immer stärker umkämpften Markt. Bei der Auswahl der 95 Designer für das vorliegende Buch aus ursprünglich 160 Namen haben wir versucht, einen Querschnitt zu bieten – von hochverehrten Titanen der Branche bis hin zu aufregenden neuen Talenten, die noch ums Überleben kämpfen. Jede Saison bedeutet eine neue Herausforderung, und die weltweite Rezession, die die Modebranche hart getroffen hat, zwingt zur Neubewertung, Neuerfindung und zu einer neuen Interpretation von Luxus im Verhältnis zur puren Notwendigkeit. Ich war schon immer der Überzeugung, dass Mode unsere Umgebung wissen lässt, wer wir sind. Unterkunft, Nahrung und Kleidung sind menschliche Grundbedürfnisse. Kleidung ist oft Ausdruck unseres Lebensstils. Nach Entbehrungen aller Art, ob durch Krieg oder Naturkatastrophen, haben die Menschen schon immer Wege gefunden, ihr Überleben auszudrücken. Ob frivol, fabelhaft oder funktional – der Designer hat die Aufgabe, uns mit seiner Mode zu überraschen und zu unterhalten. Eine Rezession ist etwas für Kämpfernaturen. Ideen sind die Währung des Erfolgs, dazu Wertigkeit, Innovation statt Imitation, Authentizität und ein neues ethisches Bewusstsein. In der gegenwärtigen Mode ist die Auswahl überwältigend, ob per Laser oder von Hand zugeschnitten, ob genäht oder geschweißt, ob von Menschenhand gemacht oder natürlich gewachsen, organisch oder chemisch. Nachhaltigkeit lautet das neue Schlagwort, das dafür sorgen könnte, dass wir im nächsten Jahrzehnt alle unsere Garderobe recyceln. Shareware könnte der künftige Trend sein. Unbeschwert reisen – mit Zahnbürste und Unterhosen in der Gürteltasche, während man sich die Garderobe via Internet über ‚fashion family friends' organisiert. Oder Shareware, bei der man sich zusammentut, um eine fantastische Couture-Kreation zu erstehen, die man sich dann nach dem Prinzip Timesharing

teilt. Das ist schließlich nicht so viel anders, als sich beim Besuch von Freunden auf dem Land Gummistiefel und Regenmäntel auszuleihen oder in den Ferien Skischuhe zu mieten. 2008 waren viele Kollektionen von erfinderischen Ideen geprägt. Angefangen bei Prada und Comme des Garçons bis hin zu Rodarte und Ralph Lauren sahen wir Flicken, Gestopftes oder Umgefärbtes. Hier zählt die Fähigkeit der Designer, jede Idee auszunutzen und so ihre Individualität zu bewahren, um sich die nötige Glaubwürdigkeit in Sachen Nachhaltigkeit zu verschaffen, auf die inzwischen kein Markenname mehr verzichten kann. Ein Jahrzehnt entspricht in der Mode einer Epoche in dem Spiel, bei dem es darum geht, die Illusion von Veränderung zu erzeugen. Wenn Sie in Ihren eigenen Schrank schauen, stehen die Chancen gut, dass Sie ein Teil aus dem Frühling 2005 mit einem anderen aus dem Herbst 2010, einem aktuellen Schnäppchen sowie einer Entdeckung bei eBay kombinieren. Die Mode hat noch nie so viel produziert wie heute, und die Wirtschaftskrise hat uns alle gezwungen, unsere Ausgabenpolitik zu überdenken. Eine bekannte Sammlerin von Mode mit einem Banker als Ehemann gestand mir kürzlich, dass er ihr geraten hätte, zurückhaltender zu sein. Warum?, fragte sie. Denn die von ihr erworbenen Stücke verzeichnen wahrscheinlich mehr Wertzuwachs, als sie im Moment an Zinsen für ihr Geld auf der Bank bekommt. Vielleicht kauft sie weniger Comme des Garçons oder Margiela, interessiert sich aber für Christopher Kane oder Antonio Marras bei Kenzo. Denn Mode gilt weiterhin vielen als veränderliche Kunst, und auf künftige Trends zu setzen ist selbst für den Einkäufer im Einzelhandel eine gehörige Herausforderung. Da hängt das Überleben vom Gespür für den Zeitgeist ab. Die Menschen wollen schließlich nicht einfach nur etwas ersetzen, das sich bereits in ihrem Kleiderschrank befindet. Sie wünschen sich frischen Input – etwas Einzigartiges, und genau das lässt diese Designer jeden Tag aufs Neue motiviert ans Werk gehen.

TERRY JONES

INTRODUCTION

La première fois que Benedikt Tachen m'a fait part de son idée, en l'occurrence réaliser une sélection à partir des deux éditions Fashion Now à succès, je ne savais pas trop quoi en penser. La nature même de la mode, avec son marché qui change à chaque saison, soulevait divers problèmes. Certains créateurs font faillite, d'autres changent de maison. La mode ne cesse de se réinventer. Après mûre réflexion, je me suis pourtant rendu compte qu'avec trois décennies au service de la créativité et des idées, ce livre réunissant une sélection des pages d'i-D depuis l'an 2000 pourrait servir de source d'inspiration à toute une nouvelle génération. La mode a le potentiel de créer des emplois où de nombreuses personnes auront la possibilité de s'exprimer. Alors que l'année 2012 approche, l'industrie fait face à plusieurs défis : innover dans le domaine des tissus et des teintures, améliorer les techniques de production dans le respect du développement durable, préserver le savoir-faire artisanal et la tradition au sein d'un marché de plus en plus concurrentiel. En réduisant le nombre de créateurs de mode de 160 à 95, nous avons cherché à garder un échantillon représentatif de ce métier, entre les géants adulés déjà bien établis et les nouveaux talents prometteurs

qui luttent constamment pour survivre. Chaque saison représente un nouvel enjeu et, nécessité oblige, la crise mondiale qui frappe l'industrie de la mode de plein fouet la contraint à réévaluer, réinventer et réinterpréter le concept de luxe. J'ai toujours pensé que la mode nous permettait d'exprimer qui nous sommes. L'être humain a en priorité besoin d'un toit, de nourriture et de vêtements. La façon dont on s'habille est souvent le reflet d'un style de vie. Après une épreuve, qu'il s'agisse d'une guerre ou d'une catastrophe naturelle, les gens trouvent toujours différentes façons d'exprimer leur idée de la survie. La mode est frivole, la mode est merveilleuse ; fonctionnelle ou fantastique, la mission du créateur consiste à surprendre et à divertir. Seuls les plus courageux survivront à la récession. Les idées sont la condition du succès, tout comme le rapport qualité-prix, l'innovation et non l'imitation, l'authenticité et une nouvelle conscience éthique. La mode d'aujourd'hui nous offre l'embarras du choix ; coupe à la main ou au laser, couture ou soudure, synthétique ou naturel, bio ou chimique, la durabilité est le nouveau maître mot qui, peut-être, nous incitera tous à recycler le contenu de nos placards au cours des dix prochaines années. La culture du partage pourrait devenir le nouveau chic : voyager léger – brosse à dents et culottes dans votre banane –, composer sa garde-robe sur Internet avec les « amis de la famille de la mode », se cotiser à plusieurs pour acheter de fabuleuses créations haute couture et se les partager. En somme, ce n'est pas si différent que d'emprunter bottes de pluie et imperméables quand on part en week-end dans la maison de campagne de ses amis, ou de louer des chaussures de ski pour les vacances à la montagne ! En 2008, de nombreuses collections reposaient sur des idées ingénieuses. Chez Prada, Comme des Garçons, Rodarte et Ralph Lauren, on a vu des patchs, des surpiqûres ou des surteintures. Le talent des créateurs dépend de leur capacité à exploiter la moindre idée tout en conservant la personnalité qui pérennise leur crédibilité ou leur nom. Une décennie de mode, c'est une tranche d'histoire dans le jeu qui consiste à créer l'illusion du changement. En ouvrant votre armoire, il y a de fortes chances que vous combiniez une pièce du printemps 2005 et une de l'automne 2010 avec une bonne affaire ultra tendance ou quelque trouvaille faite sur eBay.

La mode n'a encore jamais produit autant de choses, et les difficultés actuelles nous forcent tous à réévaluer le budget que nous y consacrons. Au printemps dernier, une célèbre collectionneuse de vêtements mariée à un banquier m'a confié que ce dernier lui avait demandé de faire plus attention. Elle ne comprenait pas pourquoi. Ses achats représentent plus d'argent que tous les intérêts qu'elle pourrait gagner en plaçant de l'argent à la banque. Elle achète peut-être moins de Comme des Garçons ou de Margiela, mais s'intéresse à Christopher Kane ou à ce que fait Antonio Marras chez Kenzo. Pour beaucoup, la mode reste un art variable, et miser sur l'avenir représente un risque pour toutes les boutiques. Leur survie dépend de leur flair à capter l'air du temps. Les gens ne veulent pas seulement remplacer un vêtement par un autre. Ils ont besoin de nouveauté, de quelque chose d'unique. Et c'est justement cela qui donne envie aux créateurs de se lever chaque matin.

TERRY JONES

"You can only design what you know"
HAIDER ACKERMANN

One of Antwerp's brightest young stars, Haider Ackermann has seen many more ports than the one fronting the town in which he now lives and works. Born in Santa Fe de Bogotá, Colombia, in 1971, he was adopted by a French family. Due to his father's business obligations, he spent his childhood moving around the globe. After living in Ethiopia, Chad, France, Algeria and the Netherlands, he decided fashion was his vocation. High school finished, he left home in 1994 and headed for Belgium to study at the fashion department of Antwerp's Royal Academy. During his three-year stay (he left the four-year course prematurely because of financial difficulties), he also worked as an intern at John Galliano's Paris office. Taking a job as an assistant to his former academy teacher Wim Neels in 1998, he worked on both the men's and womenswear collections of the Belgian designer. After saving money and taking encouragement from his friends and acquaintances – among them Raf Simons – Ackermann finally took the plunge and presented his first, self-financed women's collection in Paris for Autumn/Winter 2002. His subtle, dignified and sensuous clothes immediately struck a chord with buyers and editors, as they did with Italian leather manufacturer Ruffo. Just two weeks after his debut show, Ackermann was hired as the head designer for Ruffo Research and commissioned to create two collections (Spring/Summer and Autumn/Winter 2003), while continuing to produce his own line. Ackermann is now receiving even wider acclaim, not least in the form of the prestigious Swiss Textiles Award at the 2004 Grand Fashion Festival. Ackermann's sensitivity with drape and textures shows through in every collection. These are modern clothes for strong women who love the subtle colour palette that adds to Ackermann's seasonal collections.

Haider Ackermann gilt als einer der vielversprechenden Jungstars von Antwerpen und hat schon einiges mehr von der Welt gesehen als nur die Stadt, in der er jetzt lebt und arbeitet. Geboren wurde er 1971 im kolumbianischen Santa Fe de Bogotá und kurz darauf von einer französischen Familie adoptiert. Aufgrund der geschäftlichen Verpflichtungen seines Vaters kam er schon als Kind in der ganzen Welt herum. Nachdem er in Äthiopien, dem Tschad, Frankreich, Algerien und den Niederlanden gelebt hatte, erkannte er in der Mode seine Berufung. Als er 1994 die Schule abgeschlossen hatte, machte er sich auf den Weg nach Belgien, um an der Königlichen Akademie in Antwerpen zu studieren. Während seines dreijährigen Aufenthalts (er musste die an sich vierjährige Ausbildung wegen finanzieller Schwierigkeiten vorzeitig abbrechen) jobbte Ackermann bereits als Praktikant im Pariser Atelier von John Galliano. Nachdem er 1998 eine Assistentenstelle bei seinem ehemaligen Dozenten Wim Neels bekommen hatte, arbeitete er sowohl an Herren- wie an Damenkollektionen des belgischen Designers mit. Als er etwas Geld gespart hatte, wagte er mit Unterstützung seiner Freunde und Bekannten – darunter Leute wie Raf Simons – schließlich den Sprung ins kalte

Wasser. In Paris präsentierte Ackermann seine erste selbst finanzierte Damenkollektion, und zwar für Herbst/Winter 2002. Seine raffinierten, würdevollen und sinnlichen Kreationen kamen bei Einkäufern und Journalisten wie auch beim italienischen Lederwarenhersteller Ruffo auf Anhieb gut an. So wurde Ackermann nur zwei Wochen nach seinem Debüt Chefdesigner von Ruffo Research und erhielt den Auftrag für zwei Kollektionen (Frühjahr/Sommer und Herbst/Winter 2003). Nebenbei entwarf der Designer noch für seine eigene Linie. Heute erhält er mehr Zuspruch denn je, nicht zuletzt 2004 mit dem angesehenen Swiss Textiles Award im Rahmen des Grand Fashion Festival. Ackermanns Gespür für Drapierungen und Texturen ist in jeder einzelnen Kollektion sichtbar. Dabei handelt es sich um moderne Kleider für starke Frauen, die die dezente Farbpalette lieben, die Ackermann für seine saisonalen Kollektionen verwendet.

Célébré comme l'une des étoiles montantes d'Anvers, Haider Ackermann a fait étape dans bien d'autres ports que celui qui borde la ville dans laquelle il travaille et vit aujourd'hui. Adopté par une famille française, il est en fait né en 1971 à Santa Fe de Bogota en Colombie. En raison des obligations professionnelles de son père, il passe son enfance à parcourir le monde. Après avoir vécu en Éthiopie, au Tchad, en France, en Algérie et aux Pays-Bas, il se rend compte que la mode est sa véritable vocation. En 1994, il termine le lycée et part pour la Belgique afin d'étudier la mode à l'Académie Royale d'Anvers. Pendant son cursus de trois ans (il abandonnera prématurément la quatrième année en raison de problèmes financiers), il fait un stage dans les bureaux parisiens de John Galliano. En 1998, il devient l'assistant de son ancien professeur à l'Académie, le styliste belge Wim Neels, travaillant sur les collections pour homme et pour femme. Il réussit sagement à mettre de l'argent de côté et, encouragé par ses amis et relations, parmi lesquels Raf Simons, Ackermann fait finalement le grand plongeon et présente une première collection féminine autofinancée aux défilés parisiens automne/hiver 2002. Grâce à leur style subtil et voluptueux néanmoins empreint de dignité, ses vêtements séduisent immédiatement les acheteurs et les rédacteurs de mode, ainsi que le maroquinier italien Ruffo qui, deux semaines après son premier défilé, nomme Ackermann styliste principal de Ruffo Research et lui demande de créer deux collections (printemps/été et automne/hiver 2003) tout en lui permettant de continuer à travailler sous sa propre griffe. Aujourd'hui, la réputation d'Ackermann n'est plus à faire. Il a notamment reçu le prestigieux Swiss Textiles Award décerné au Grand Fashion Festival en 2004. Toutes ses collections témoignent d'un grand sens du drapé et de la texture : autant de vêtements modernes destinés aux femmes de caractère qui adorent la palette de couleurs subtile de chaque collection d'Ackermann.

PETER DE POTTER

PORTRAIT ALEX SALINAS. PHOTOGRAPHY ALEX SALINAS. STYLING TABASSOM CHARAF. MODEL DIANE M.

"Perfection is never achieved, so you need to go on working"
AZZEDINE ALAÏA

Azzedine Alaïa's place in the design hall of fame is guaranteed – his signature being the second skin that he creates when challenging the boundaries of flesh and fabric. Alaïa was born in Tunisia in the '40s to wheat-farming parents. A French friend of his mother's fed Alaïa's instinctive creativity with copies of 'Vogue' and lied about his age to get him into the local Ecole des Beaux-Arts to study sculpture – a discipline in which he didn't excel, but that he would put to good use in the future. After spotting an ad for a vacancy at a dressmaker's, Alaïa's sister taught him to sew and he started making copies of couture dresses for neighbours. Soon afterwards, he went to Paris to work for Christian Dior, but managed only five days of sewing labels before being fired. Alaïa moved to Guy Laroche, where for two seasons he learned his craft while earning his keep as housekeeper to the Marquise de Mazan. In 1960, the Blegiers family snapped up Alaïa, and for the next five years he was both housekeeper and dressmaker to the Countess and her friends, mixing with glamorous Paris society. His first ready-to-wear collection for Charles Jourdan in the '70s was not well received, but eventually fashion editors tuned in to Alaïa's modern elegance. Worldwide success followed with exhibitions, awards, supermodel disciples and the power to command an audience outside of the catwalk schedule: Alaïa shows when he wants, regardless of the round of timetabled international fashion weeks, and editors never miss it. In 1998, he published a book of photographs of his creations, entitled 'Alaïa'. In 2000, he was honoured with a solo exhibition at the New York Guggenheim. In October 2004, he opened his own hotel (5 rue de Moussy) adjoining the Alaïa headquarters in Paris. The headquarters also house an exhibition space that has been showing work by fashion and furniture designers such as Paul Poiret and Shiro Kuramata as well as several photo exhibitions since 2004. After a seven-year-long successful and positive partnership with the Prada group, Alaïa joined forces with the Richemont group in 2007. Azzedine Alaïa was named Chevalier de la Légion d'honneur by the French government in 2008.

Ein Platz in der Hall of Fame der Designer ist Azzedine Alaïa bereits sicher – dank seines Markenzeichens, der zweiten Haut, mit der er die Grenzen zwischen Körper und Stoff aufzuheben scheint. Geboren wurde der tunesische Bauernsohn in den 1940er-Jahren. Eine französische Freundin seiner Mutter förderte seine angeborene Kreativität mit Ausgaben der Vogue und mogelte bei seinem Alter, um ihn an der Kunstakademie von Tunis im Fach Bildhauerei unterzubringen. Er erwies sich zwar nicht als überragender Student, doch sollte ihm diese Ausbildung in der Zukunft noch von Nutzen sein. Weil ihn die Anzeige für eine freie Stelle in einer Schneiderei interessierte, ließ er sich von seiner Schwester das Nähen beibringen und kopierte schon bald Haute-Couture-Kleider für die Frauen der Nachbarschaft. Kurz darauf ging er nach Paris, um für Christian Dior zu arbeiten, dort nähte er allerdings gerade mal fünf Tage lang Etiketten ein, bevor man ihn feuerte. Daraufhin wechselte Alaïa zu Guy Laroche, wo er zwei Saisons lang sein Handwerk lernte und sich seinen Lebensunterhalt als Haushälter der Marquise de Mazan verdiente. 1960 engagierte ihn die Familie Blegiers, bei der er fünf Jahre lang Haushälter und Hausschneider für die Comtesse und ihre Freundinnen sein sollte und Zugang zur Glamour-Gesellschaft von Paris fand. Seine erste Prêt-à-porter-Kollektion für Charles Jourdan in den 1970er-Jahren kam nicht besonders gut an, doch irgendwann hatten sich die Modejournalisten an Alaïas moderne Eleganz gewöhnt. Der weltweite Erfolg wurde von Ausstellungen, Preisen und treu ergebenen Supermodels begleitet. Alaïa präsentiert seine Entwürfe, wann es ihm passt, und ignoriert einfach die exakt terminierten internationalen Modewochen. Die Journalisten sind trotzdem immer da. 1998 veröffentlichte der Designer einen Band mit Fotos seiner Kreationen unter dem Titel „Alaïa". Im Jahr 2000 begab er sich unter die Fittiche des Prada-Konzerns. Im selben Jahr ehrte das New Yorker Guggenheim Museum ihn mit einer Einzelausstellung. Sein Hotel in der Pariser Rue de Moussy Nummer 5, gleich neben der Alaïa-Zentrale, wurde im Oktober 2004 eröffnet. Der Firmensitz umfasst auch eine Austellungsfläche, wo seit 2004 Arbeiten von Mode- und Möbeldesignern wie Paul Poiret und Shiro Kuramata sowie einige Fotoschauen präsentiert wurden. Nach einer siebenjährigen erfolgreichen und einvernehmlichen Partnerschaft mit der Prada-Gruppe schloss Alaïa sich 2007 dem Richemont-Konzern an. Alaia wurde 2008 von der französischen Regierung zum Ritter der Ehrenlegion ernannt.

Défiant les frontières qui séparent la chair du tissu, les créations « seconde peau » qui distinguent le travail d'Azzedine Alaïa lui garantissent une place de choix dans l'Olympe de la mode. Alaïa est né dans les années 40 en Tunisie de parents cultivateurs de blé. Sa créativité instinctive se nourrit des exemplaires de Vogue d'une amie française de sa mère, qui mentira sur son âge pour le faire entrer à l'École des Beaux-Arts de Tunis. Il y étudie la sculpture, discipline dans laquelle il n'excelle pas particulièrement mais qu'il utilisera à bon escient par la suite. Après avoir repéré une offre d'emploi chez un couturier, la sœur d'Alaïa lui apprend à coudre et il commence à copier les robes haute couture pour ses voisines. Peu de temps après, il s'installe à Paris pour travailler chez Christian Dior, mais se fait mettre à la porte après cinq jours passés à coudre des étiquettes. Alaïa travaille ensuite pour Guy Laroche, chez qui il se forme au métier pendant deux saisons tout en gagnant sa vie en tant qu'intendant de la marquise de Mazan. En 1960, la famille Blegiers embauche Alaïa et pendant cinq ans, il est à la fois l'intendant et le couturier de la comtesse et de ses amis, se mêlant à la haute société parisienne. Dans les années 70, sa première collection de prêt-à-porter pour Charles Jourdan n'est pas bien accueillie, mais les journalistes de mode s'intéressent tout de même à l'élégance moderne d'Alaïa. Le succès mondial s'ensuit grâce à des expositions, des récompenses, le soutien des plus grands top models et le pouvoir de séduire le public même en dehors du calendrier officiel : Alaïa présente ses collections sans se soucier de l'agenda mondial des semaines de la mode, et la presse ne rate pas un seul de ses défilés. En 1998, il sort un livre de photos de ses créations intitulé Alaïa, puis en 2000, il s'associe au groupe Prada. La même année, le musée Guggenheim de New York lui consacre toute une exposition. En octobre 2004, il ouvre son propre hôtel (5, rue de Moussy), juste à côté du siège social parisien d'Alaïa. Son quartier général abrite aussi un espace d'exposition qui présente depuis 2004 les œuvres de couturiers et de designers tels que Paul Poiret et Shiro Kuramata, ainsi que plusieurs expositions de photographie. En 2007, après sept années d'un partenariat très réussi avec le groupe Prada, Alaïa s'associe au groupe Richemont. En 2008, Azzedine Alaïa a été décoré chevalier de la Légion d'honneur par le gouvernement français.

JAMIE HUCKBODY

PORTRAIT: KASIA WANDYCZ. PHOTOGRAPHY SIMON HARRIS. FASHION DIRECTOR EDWARD ENNINFUL. MODEL NAOMI CAMPBELL. JUNE 2008.

MCMILLAN · FASHION DIRECTOR EDWARD ENNINFUL MODE · JOURDAN DUNN · NOVEMBER 2018.

PHOTOGRAPHY HANS FEURER. STYLING ERIKA KURIHARA. MODEL CHANEL IMAN. MARCH 2008.

"I have realised over time that I have to take responsibility for my actions and beliefs"
GIORGIO ARMANI

Now in his fifth decade of working in fashion, Giorgio Armani is more than just a designer – he's an institution, an icon and a multinational, billion-dollar brand. Armani was born in 1934 in Piacenza, Northern Italy. He spent his formative years not in fashion but studying medicine at university and completing his national service. After working as a buyer for Milanese department store La Rinascente, he scored his first break in 1964, when he was hired by Nino Cerruti to design a menswear line, Hitman. Several years as a successful freelance designer followed, but it was in 1975 that the Giorgio Armani label was set up, with the help of his then business partner Sergio Galeotti. Armani's signature 'unstructured' jackets for both men and women (a womenswear line was established in 1976) knocked the stuffing out of traditional tailoring and, from the late '70s, his clothes became a uniform for the upwardly mobile. Men loved his relaxed suits and muted colour palette of neutral beiges and greys. His designs for women, meanwhile, were admired for an androgynous and modern elegance. Richard Gere's suits in 'American Gigolo' (1980) were a landmark for the designer, as was featuring on the cover of 'Time' magazine in 1982. The brand now encompasses six major fashion lines and has diversified into bedlinen, chocolates and even hotels. From 2000, his designs have been exhibited in a major retrospective show that has travelled worldwide. Armani has also picked up a dedicated Hollywood following, and January 2005 saw the launch in Paris of Giorgio Armani Privé, an haute-couture-like collection. In February 2009, Armani opened a flagship store on Fifth Avenue, New York, at the height of a global recession. With David Beckham sporting Armani undies on a billboard near you, it's a safe bet that the world of Armani, from bedroom to beyond, will continue to increase its global stature with quiet confidence, which in turn helps his personal projects for disadvantaged children in the global AIDS campaign.

Er arbeitet inzwischen seit fast 50 Jahren in der Modebranche und ist viel mehr als „nur" ein Designer. Giorgio Armani ist eine Institution, eine Ikone und ein internationales, milliardenschweres Markenzeichen. Geboren wurde er 1934 im norditalienischen Piacenza. Die ersten Jahre als Erwachsener verbrachte Armani jedoch nicht in der Modeszene, sondern beim Medizinstudium an der Universität und beim Militär. Nach einer Anstellung als Einkäufer für das Mailänder Kaufhaus La Rinascente landete er 1964 seinen ersten Coup, nachdem Nino Cerruti ihn mit dem Entwurf einer Herrenlinie namens Hitman beauftragt hatte. Es folgten einige Jahre als gefragter freischaffender Designer, bis 1975 mit der Gründung des Labels Giorgio Armani die Weichen für die Zukunft der Mode neu gestellt wurden. Daran beteiligt war damals auch Armanis Geschäftspartner Sergio Galeotti. Markenzeichen waren die „unstrukturierten" Jacketts für Männer wie Frauen (eine Damenlinie wurde 1976 gegründet), die im Unterschied zu traditionell geschneiderten Modellen ganz ohne Polster auskamen. Ab Ende der 1970er galt seine Mode als eine Art Uniform für Leute, die Karriere machten. Männer liebten seine legeren Anzüge und gedämpften Beige- und Grautöne. Dagegen fanden die Entwürfe für Frauen wegen ihrer Androgynität und modernen Eleganz großen Zuspruch. Richard Geres Anzüge in „American Gigolo" (1980) waren ein Meilenstein für den Modemacher, ebenso das Time-Cover

von 1982. Heute umfasst die Marke Armani sechs große Modelinien, aber auch Bereiche wie Bettwäsche, Schokolade und sogar Hotels. 2000 wurden seine Entwürfe im Rahmen einer großen Retrospektive weltweit gezeigt. Armani hat sich aber auch eine treue Anhängerschaft in Hollywood aufgebaut. Vielleicht eines seiner ambitioniertesten Projekte war die Präsentation von „Giorgio Armani Privé" im Januar 2005 in Paris, eine Kollektion im Stil der Haute Couture. Im Februar 2009, auf dem Höhepunkt der weltweiten Rezession, eröffnete Armani einen Flagship-Store an der New Yorker Fifth Avenue. Solange David Beckham auf einer Plakatwand in Armani-Slips posiert, kann man wohl ziemlich sicher davon ausgehen, dass Armani seinen Ruf in der Welt mit ruhiger Selbstverständlichkeit kontinuierlich steigern wird. Das nützt auf der anderen Seite auch den persönlichen Hilfsprojekten des Designers zugunsten unterprivilegierter Kinder in der weltweiten Kampagne gegen Aids.

Avec cinquante ans de métier, Giorgio Armani est bien plus qu'un couturier : c'est une véritable institution, une icône et une multinationale qui pèse plusieurs milliards de dollars. Armani est né en 1934 à Piacenza dans le nord de l'Italie. Il suit d'abord des études de médecine à l'université avant de faire son service militaire. Après avoir travaillé comme acheteur pour La Rinascente, le grand magasin milanais, il se lance dans la mode en 1964 quand Nino Cerruti le recrute pour dessiner une ligne pour homme, Hitman. Les années suivantes, il rencontre un grand succès en tant que styliste free-lance mais il faut attendre 1975 pour voir l'avenir de la mode se transformer grâce à la création de la griffe Giorgio Armani, qu'il fonde avec l'aide de Sergio Galeotti, son partenaire en affaires de l'époque. Les vestes « déstructurées » pour homme et pour femme devenues la signature d'Armani (une ligne pour femme sera lancée en 1976) bouleversent les codes et dès la fin des années 70, ses créations s'imposent comme l'uniforme des ambitieux aux dents longues. Les hommes adorent ses costumes décontractés et sa palette de beiges et de gris neutres, tandis que ses vêtements pour femme séduisent grâce à leur élégance androgyne et moderne. Les costumes dessinés pour le personnage de Richard Gere dans American Gigolo (1980) marquent un tournant dans la carrière du créateur, qui connaît la consécration en 1982 en faisant la couverture du Time. La marque, qui regroupe aujourd'hui six grandes lignes de mode, s'est aussi diversifiée dans des domaines tels que la literie, les chocolats et même les hôtels. En l'an 2000, son travail a fait l'objet d'une grande rétrospective présentée dans les musées du monde entier. Armani revendique aussi des fans parmi l'élite d'Hollywood. Son projet le plus ambitieux a été révélé en janvier 2005 à Paris, théâtre du lancement de « Giorgio Armani Privé », collection de haute couture de coupe traditionnelle. En février 2009, la marque a ouvert une immense boutique sur la 5ᵉ Avenue de New York en pleine crise mondiale. Impossible d'échapper aux affiches de David Beckham posant en sous-vêtements Armani, on peut être certain que l'univers Armani poursuivra son expansion internationale au-delà des chambres à coucher. En retour, ce succès profite aux initiatives personnelles de Giorgio Armani pour les enfants défavorisés dans le cadre de la campagne mondiale de lutte contre le sida.

LAUREN COCHRANE

PORTRAIT DAVID MCKNIGHT. PHOTOGRAPHY WILLY VANDERPERRE. STYLING OLIVIER RIZZO. MODEL ERIN WASSON. JULY 2004.

"The reward in seeing a garment being worn brings me endless pleasure"
KRIS VAN ASSCHE + DIOR HOMME

Born in Belgium in 1976, Kris Van Assche is a tall and gentle figure. His choice to have a hummingbird tattoo on his arm because the tiny bird has the biggest heart is symbolic of the man. Treading a considered path through menswear from the start, Van Assche followed in the footsteps of his Belgian fashion designer predecessors, studying at the Royal Academy in Antwerp, becoming the youngest graduate of the school. Moving to Paris in 1998, Van Assche soon took up an internship at Yves Saint Laurent under the direction of Hedi Slimane. In 2000, Van Assche followed Slimane to Dior, where, as first assistant, he helped the menswear maverick transform the French label into Dior Homme, reinventing the contemporary menswear silhouette. In September 2004, the Kris Van Assche label was established. The debut Autumn/Winter 2005/6 collection was met with instant critical and public success, as Van Assche presented a refined take on simple tailored classics. Collaborating with American photographer Jeff Burton on a set of distinctive campaigns, Van Assche soon established the label as one to watch. In 2007, Van Assche introduced womenswear, playing again with loose silhouettes and beautiful fabrics. In the same year, Van Assche also elected to return to Dior Homme as artistic director after Hedi Slimane's departure, bringing with him the relaxed contemporary tailoring and Latino casting that he had established so well with his own label. As well as designing for his own label and Dior Homme, Van Assche continues to collaborate with a wide artistic circle, including taking guest editorship of 'A Magazine' for issue 7, and working with Nan Goldin on a special backstage project for Dior Homme's Spring/Summer 2009 collection.

Der 1976 in Belgien geborene Kris Van Assche ist eine große, sanftmütige Erscheinung. Seine Entscheidung, sich einen Kolibri auf den Arm tätowieren zu lassen, weil der winzige Vogel das größte Herz besitzt, ist typisch für diesen Mann. Von Beginn an schlug er einen wohlüberlegten Weg durch die Herrenmode ein und trat dabei in die Fußstapfen seiner Vorgänger unter den belgischen Modedesignern, indem er an der Royal Academy of Fine Arts in Antwerpen studierte und dort als bislang jüngster Student seinen Abschluss machte. Nachdem er 1998 nach Paris gezogen war, begann er schon bald ein Praktikum bei Yves Saint Laurent unter dem damaligen Chef Hedi Slimane. Im Jahr 2000 folgte er Slimane zu Dior, wo er als erster Assistent den Rebell der Männermode half, das französische Label in Dior Homme zu verwandeln und dabei eine zeitgemäße Silhouette der Menswear zu erfinden. Im September 2004 wurde das Label Kris Van Assche gegründet. Die Debütkollektion für Herbst/Winter 2005/06 stieß auf unmittelbare Zustimmung bei Kritikern und Publikum, nachdem Van Assche eine verfeinerte Version schlicht geschneiderter Klassiker präsentierte. Durch seine Zusammenarbeit mit dem amerikanischen Fotografen Jeff Burton in einer Reihe außergewöhnlicher Kampagnen etablierte sich Van Assche rasch als ein Label, das es zu beachten galt. 2007 stellte Van Assche erstmals Damenmode vor und spielte dabei erneut mit lockeren Silhouetten und wunderbaren Stoffen. Im selben Jahr entschloss sich der Designer auch, zu Dior Homme zurückzukehren, wo er als Nachfolger von Hedi Slimane Artistic Director wurde. Er brachte dabei sein lässig modernes Verständnis von Schneiderei mit, das er bei seinem eigenen Label so erfolgreich etabliert hatte. Neben den Entwürfen für seine eigene Marke und Dior Homme arbeitet Van Assche weiterhin mit einem großen Kreis von Künstlern zusammen, etwa als Gast-Herausgeber der Ausgabe 7 von A Magazine oder mit Nan Goldin für ein besonderes Backstage-Projekt anlässlich der Kollektion Frühjahr/Sommer 2009 von Dior Homme.

Né en Belgique en 1976, Kris Van Assche est un homme grand et doux, comme le prouve le colibri qu'il a choisi de se faire tatouer sur le bras parce que ce minuscule volatile possède le plus gros cœur de tous les oiseaux. Évoluant de façon réfléchie dans la mode pour homme dès ses débuts, Van Assche marche sur les pas de ses prédécesseurs belges en suivant des études de mode à l'Académie Royale d'Anvers, dont il est d'ailleurs le plus jeune diplômé. Lorsqu'il s'installe à Paris en 1998, Van Assche décroche rapidement un stage chez Yves Saint Laurent sous la direction d'Hedi Slimane. En l'an 2000, il suit Slimane chez Dior où, en tant que premier assistant, il aide le dissident du menswear à transformer la griffe française en Dior Homme et à réinventer la silhouette masculine contemporaine. En septembre 2004, il fonde la marque Kris Van Assche. Sa première collection, pour la saison automne/hiver 2005 – 2006, séduit d'emblée la critique et le public, car Van Assche présente une vision raffinée des costumes simples et classiques. En travaillant avec le photographe américain Jeff Burton sur une série de campagnes de pub originales, Van Assche s'impose rapidement comme un créateur à suivre de près. En 2007, il se lance dans la mode pour femme en jouant à nouveau sur les silhouettes amples et les beaux tissus. La même année, il choisit aussi de revenir chez Dior Homme en tant que directeur artistique après le départ d'Hedi Slimane, apportant avec lui les coupes contemporaines décontractées et le style latino déjà bien établis par sa propre griffe. Outre sa collection éponyme et son travail chez Dior Homme, Van Assche poursuit ses collaborations dans des domaines artistiques très divers : il a notamment dirigé le n° 7 d'A Magazine et conçu un projet photo avec Nan Goldin pour les coulisses du défilé Dior Homme printemps/été 2009.

MAX PEARMAIN

PORTRAIT GAÉTAN BERNARD. PHOTOGRAPHY GILES PRICE. STYLING SIMON FOXTON. MODEL ARMANDO. FEBRUARY 2008.

PHOTOGRAPHY NAN GOLDIN. COURTESY DIOR HOMME. OCTOBER 2008.

"I love to meet someone who shows me his jacket and says: 'Look at it, it's all worn, I have been wearing it for six years!'"
AGNÈS B.

Believing that things do not have to be complicated to be beautiful, agnès b. designs clothes, simply, rather than high fashion. Shying away from global business practices, her outlook is alluringly fresh. Her style might be summed up as modern, crisp and definite. Born in Versailles (1941) as Agnès Trouble, she studied at Paris's Ecole Nationale Supérieure des Beaux-Arts before starting work as a junior editor for French 'Elle'. From here she assisted the designer Dorothée Bis as a stylist and worked as a freelance designer before opening her own Parisian boutique in 1975. A tonic for any wardrobe, agnès b.'s designs are intended to make one feel good in one's own skin. Her tailoring creates an air of unadulterated elegance, while her simple angular cuts ensure timelessness. A true lover of people rather than fashion, she neither shops nor attends catwalk shows, choosing instead to find inspiration in 'people watching', a trait she describes as very French. From her popular snap cardigan to her press-studded cotton jackets, there's something resolutely personal in agnès b.'s designs. She'll remake a piece from a past season if a customer requests it, reiterating her belief that people are more important than the clothes. She is also a photographer, film producer and avid art collector. With two art galleries, a modern-art magazine and a cinema production company of her own – having founded a joint film concern with Harmony Korine called O'Salvation – agnès b. has got her finger on the pulse of the creative world.

Gemäß der Überzeugung, dass etwas nicht kompliziert sein muss, um schön zu sein, entwirft agnès b. lieber schlichte Sachen als Haute Couture. Abseits internationaler Geschäftspraktiken, verfolgt sie einen verlockend unorthodoxen Ansatz. Man könnte ihren Stil als modern, frisch und zielstrebig charakterisieren. Unter dem Namen Agnès Trouble 1941 in Versailles geboren, studierte sie an der Pariser Ecole Nationale Supérieure des Beaux-Arts, bevor sie bei der französischen Elle als Jungredakteurin begann. Von dieser Position aus assistierte sie der Designerin Dorothée Bis als Stylistin und arbeitete als freie Designerin, bevor sie 1975 ihre eigene Boutique in Paris eröffnete. Ihre Kleider sind das reinste Tonikum für jede Garderobe, denn die Entwürfe sind so gestaltet, dass man sich in seiner eigenen Haut wohlfühlt. Sie erzeugen einen Flair unverfälschter Eleganz, die schlichten eckigen Schnitte garantieren Zeitlosigkeit. Die Designerin macht sich mehr aus Menschen als aus Mode und geht daher weder shoppen noch besucht sie Modenschauen. Ihre Inspirationen holt sie sich lieber beim „Menschen beobachten", einer Passion, die sie als typisch französisch empfindet. Angefangen bei ihrer beliebten Jacke mit Druckknöpfen (Cardigan pression) bis hin zu nietenbesetzten Baumwolljacken haben die Kreationen von agnès b. etwas absolut Persönliches. Und wenn ein Kunde es wünscht, fertigt sie auch ein Stück aus einer älteren Kollektion noch einmal. Die Modeschöpferin ist außerdem als Fotografin, Filmproduzentin und leidenschaftliche Kunstsammlerin tätig. Mit zwei Galerien, einer Zeitschrift für moderne Kunst und einer eigenen Filmproduktionsfirma – gemeinsam mit Harmony Korine gründete sie die Filmgesellschaft O'Salvation – hat agnès b. ihre Finger wahrlich am Puls der Kreativität.

Convaincue que les choses n'ont pas besoin d'être compliquées pour être belles, agnès b. dessine des vêtements, tout simplement, plutôt que des créations d'avant-garde. Elle fuit les grands groupes mondiaux et propose une vision qui séduit par sa fraîcheur. Son style peut être considéré comme moderne, précis et univoque. Née à Versailles (1941) sous le nom d'Agnès Trouble, elle étudie à l'École Nationale Supérieure des Beaux-Arts de Paris avant de travailler comme journaliste junior pour le Elle français. Ensuite, elle assiste Dorothée Bis en tant que styliste et travaille comme créatrice free-lance avant d'ouvrir sa propre boutique parisienne en 1975. Tel un tonique énergisant pour toute garde-robe, les créations agnès b. sont conçues pour que ceux qui les portent se sentent bien dans leur peau. Ses tailleurs dégagent une impression d'élégance pure, avec des coupes simples et angulaires qui ne sont pas près de se démoder. Aimant plus les gens que la mode, elle ne fait pas les boutiques et n'assiste à aucun défilé, préférant puiser son inspiration dans « l'observation des autres », une attitude qu'elle considère comme très française. De son célèbre cardigan à ses vestes de coton à boutons-pression, on distingue quelque chose de résolument personnel dans ses créations. Si un client le lui demande, elle n'hésitera pas à reproduire une pièce d'une saison passée, réitérant sa conviction selon laquelle les personnes comptent plus que les vêtements. La créatrice est également photographe, productrice de films et avide collectionneuse d'art. Avec deux galeries d'art, un magazine d'art moderne et sa propre société de production cinématographique O'Salvation – fondée en collaboration avec Harmony Korine –, agnès b. a toujours le doigt sur le pouls du monde créatif.

HOLLY SHACKLETON

PORTRAIT GASPAR NOE. PHOTOGRAPHY LARRY DUNSTAN. STYLING MARCIA TAYLOR. MODEL COMMON. JULY 2005.

"I'm a very down-to-earth designer"
CHRISTOPHER BAILEY · BURBERRY

Yorkshire-born Christopher Bailey has become something of a household name, thanks to his sterling work as creative director of Burberry, the British company he joined back in 2001. Yet Bailey (born 1971) is far from an overnight sensation, having previously notched up impressive fashion credentials. On completing a Master's degree at the Royal College of Art in London (1994), Bailey worked in New York for Donna Karan from 1994 to 1996, before being hired by Tom Ford as a senior designer of womenswear at Gucci in Milan, from 1996 to 2001. At Burberry, Bailey is responsible for the direction of all product lines, as well as the definition of the company's overall image and seasonal advertising concepts. His flagship collection contains the forward-thinking Prorsum lines for men and women that are presented in Milan to consistently rave reviews and from which he has banished almost all trace of the hallmark Burberry check. An unerring eye for clear, bright colour and subtle innovations in tailoring have emerged as key to both menswear and womenswear collections. Developing his codes gradually, Bailey is concerned with longevity, rather than resting on the corporate laurels. Nonetheless, the designs he has produced respectfully acknowledge the Burberry heritage (the company was founded in 1856). For example, he has made no secret of his admiration for their classic gabardine trenchcoat, which for Autumn/Winter 2004 he abbreviated into capes, for both men and women. Renowned for his hands-on approach to design and an enthusiasm for detail, he continues to propel the brand into the 21st century with his customary passion, enthusiasm and cheerful demeanour. In acknowledgement of his many successes, the Royal College of Art awarded Bailey an Honorary Fellowship in 2003. He was also twice awarded Menswear Designer of the Year by the British Fashion Awards (2007 and 2008). In 2008, Bailey, set up The Burberry Foundation, committed to dedicating global resources to help young people realise their dreams and achieve their goals and potential through their creativity.

Der aus Yorkshire stammende Christopher Bailey ist inzwischen selbst zu einer Art Markenzeichen avanciert. Zu verdanken hat er das seiner soliden Arbeit als Creative Director für das britische Modehaus Burberry, in das er 2001 eintrat. Bailey (Jahrgang 1971) wurde jedoch keineswegs über Nacht zum Star, sondern erwarb sich zunächst eindrucksvolle Referenzen. 1994 sein Studium am Londoner Royal College of Art mit dem Mastertitel abgeschlossen hatte, arbeitete er bis 1996 für Donna Karan in New York. Dann warb ihn Tom Ford als Senior Designer für die Damenmode bei Gucci ab, sodass er von 1996 bis 2001 in Mailand tätig war. Bei Burberry ist Bailey für die Leitung aller Produktlinien ebenso verantwortlich wie für das Image der Marke und die Werbekonzepte der jeweiligen Saison. Seine Flaggschiffkollektion ist die zukunftsorientierte Prorsum-Linie für Damen und Herren. Wenn diese in Mailand präsentiert wird, erntet er regelmäßig hymnische Kritiken. Das typische Burberry-Karo ist daraus übrigens fast vollständig verbannt. Sein unfehlbarer Blick für klare, leuchtende Farben und raffinierte handwerkliche Innovationen hat sich als Erfolgskriterium für die Herren- wie für die Damenkollektionen herauskristallisiert. Bailey, der seine Stile schrittweise entwickelt, hat eher die Langlebigkeit seiner Entwürfe im Sinn, anstatt

sich auf den Lorbeeren seines Hauses auszuruhen. Dennoch spricht aus seinen Kreationen die respektvolle Anerkennung des Vermächtnisses von Burberry (die Firma wurde bereits 1856 gegründet). So macht er kein Geheimnis aus seiner Bewunderung für den klassischen Trenchcoat aus Gabardine, den er für die Kollektion Herbst/Winter 2004 zu Capes für Damen und Herren abwandelte. Bailey ist bekannt für seine pragmatische Einstellung zum Thema Design und für seine Detailversessenheit. So führt er die Traditionsmarke weiter ins 21. Jahrhundert – mit gewohnter Leidenschaft, Enthusiasmus und einer optimistischen Grundhaltung. Als Anerkennung für seine diversen Leistungen wurde Bailey 2003 vom Royal College of Art ein Honorary Fellowship verliehen. Zweimal (2007 und 2008) wurde er bei den British Fashion Awards zum Menswear Designer of the Year gekürt. 2008 gründete er die Burberry-Foundation, die innovative Projekte zur Förderung des kreativen Talents junger Menschen in den Regionen unterstützt, in denen die Firma produziert.

Né en 1971 dans le Yorkshire, Christopher Bailey est aujourd'hui un nom connu de tous les Anglais grâce au travail remarquable qu'il a accompli à la direction de la création de Burberry, maison britannique qu'il a rejointe en 2001. Pourtant, Bailey n'a rien d'une star éphémère dans la mesure où son CV affichait déjà d'impressionnantes références dans le domaine de la mode. Après avoir décroché son master au Royal College of Art de Londres (1994), Bailey travaille à New York pour Donna Karan entre 1994 et 1996, avant d'être embauché par Tom Ford chez Gucci à Milan, où il occupera le poste de styliste senior des collections pour femme de 1996 à 2001. Chez Burberry, Bailey ne se contente pas de superviser toutes les lignes de produits, il développe également l'image de la maison et ses concepts publicitaires saisonniers. Sa collection phare inclut les lignes visionnaires Prorsum pour homme et femme qu'il a entièrement dépouillées des fameux carreaux Burberry, un travail salué par une critique unanime lors de chaque défilé milanais. Son œil aiguisé pour les couleurs claires et vives et ses innovations subtiles en matière de coupe distinguent aujourd'hui ses collections pour homme comme pour femme. Bien que Bailey impose progressivement ses propres codes, il cherche aussi à faire durer la marque Burberry sans se reposer sur ses lauriers. Ses créations rendent néanmoins un respectueux hommage à l'héritage de cette maison fondée en 1856. Par exemple, il n'a jamais caché son admiration pour le fameux trench-coat Burberry, un classique qu'il a raccourci sous forme de cape pour homme et pour femme lors de la saison automne/hiver 2004. Réputé pour son approche pratique de la création et pour sa passion du détail, il continue de propulser Burberry dans le 21e siècle, animé d'une passion et d'un enthousiasme qui sont aujourd'hui devenus sa marque de fabrique. En reconnaissance de ses nombreux succès, le Royal College of Art lui a décerné un doctorat honorifique en 2003. Il a également reçu deux fois le prix de Menswear Designer of the Year aux British Fashion Awards (en 2007 et en 2008). En 2008, il crée la Burberry Foundation qui apporte son soutien aux projets innovants et à la promotion des jeunes talents créateurs originaires des régions où l'entreprise a implanté ses sites de production.

JAMES ANDERSON

PHOTO: LARRY SOLVE SUSTISRO FASHION DIRECTOR EDWARD ENNINFUL MODEL JENNY HOWARTH MARCH 2009.

PHOTOGRAPHY HANS FEURER. STYLING ERIKA KURIHARA. MODEL CHANEL IMAN. MARCH 2008.

"It's good to listen, to discuss, but it has to be your own conviction that makes each decision"
NEIL BARRETT

With his own Milan-based label, a host of celebrity clients and a stint as an MTV presenter, Neil Barrett has come a long way from his Devonshire roots. Known for clothes that focus on detail and cut, Barrett's is an approach underpinned by an extensive knowledge of fabric production, which he employs to rejuvenate classic designs. With subdued colours and restrained tailoring, Barrett's menswear range is avowedly masculine – a factor that has contributed to its widespread appeal. Born in 1965, Barrett graduated in 1986 from Central Saint Martins, and received an MA from the Royal College of Art in 1989. Within a year, he was made senior menswear designer at Gucci in Florence, where he worked until 1994 – a period in which the brand underwent an important revival, both creatively and financially. Success at Gucci enabled Barrett to approach Prada with a proposal for a menswear line. Prada accepted his offer and he began work as the company's menswear design director. He remained at Prada until 1998, when he launched his first self-named menswear collection. This was an immediate success that was snapped up by over 100 designer stores across the world. The following year, Barrett set up White, his own Prada-produced label, which was invited to open the Pitti Immagine Uomo Fair in 2000, where he also introduced his first womenswear collection. The next few years saw Barrett sign a footwear deal with Puma and in 2004 he redesigned the Italian national football team's strip for the European Championship – an honour for a non-Italian and a testament to the worldwide success of his label. In 2006, the Italians won the world cup wearing the kit designed by Barrett, reinforcing his collaboration with Puma. This was the year he also launched his Indigo jean collection and showed his Autumn/Winter 2006, collection for the first time, in New York. His 'A-list' group of actors and musicians continues to grow with Zaha-Hadid-designed stores from Tokyo to West Coast Hollywood. Fans of Barrett love his sharp sartorial tailoring learnt from his great-grandfather and grandfather and fused with classic British street-style genres.

Ein eigenes Label mit Sitz in Mailand, eine Schar prominenter Kunden und ein Job als Moderator bei MTV – Neil Barrett, dessen Wurzeln in Devonshire liegen, hat es zweifellos weit gebracht. Er ist bekannt für den Detailreichtum und Schnitt seiner Kleider, dazu kommt noch sein umfangreiches Wissen über die Stoffproduktion, das er nutzt, um klassische Designs zu verjüngen. Mit gedämpften Farben und schlichten Schnitten ist Barretts Herrenlinie dezidiert maskulin – was zu seiner großen Beliebtheit sicher beigetragen hat. Der 1965 geborene Designer machte 1986 seinen Abschluss am Central Saint Martins und 1989 seinen Master am Royal College of Art. Innerhalb eines Jahres brachte er es dann zum Chefdesigner der Herrenmode bei Gucci in Florenz, wo er bis 1994 tätig war – in dieser Zeit erfuhr die Marke eine wichtige Renaissance, sowohl im kreativen wie in wirtschaftlichen Sinne. Der Erfolg bei Gucci versetzte Barrett in die Lage, Prada eine eigene Herrenlinie anzubieten. Dort ging man auf sein Angebot ein, und Barrett fing als Design Director der Herrenmode an. Bis 1998 blieb er bei Prada und präsentierte dann seine erste Herrenkollektion unter eigenem Namen. Der Erfolg stellte sich unmittelbar ein – über hundert Designläden in aller Welt sicherten sich seine Entwürfe. Ein Jahr später gründete Barrett White sein eigenes, bei Prada produziertes Label. 2000 wurde er eingeladen, die Messe Pitti Immagine Uomo zu eröffnen. Dort lancierte Barrett dann seine erste Damenkollektion. In den folgenden Jahren unterzeichnete Barrett u. a. einen Kooperationsvertrag mit Puma über eine Schuhkollektion und entwarf 2004 anlässlich der Europameisterschaft ein neues Dress für die italienische Fußballnationalmannschaft. Das war zum einen eine Auszeichnung für den Nicht-Italiener, zum anderen ein Beleg für den weltweiten Erfolg seines Labels. 2006 wurden die Italiener in dem Fußballdress Weltmeister, das Barrett entworfen hatte, was seine Zusammenarbeit mit Puma natürlich stärkte. Im selben Jahr präsentierte der Designer auch seine Jeanskollektion Indigo und zeigte seine Kreationen für Herbst/Winter 2006 erstmals in New York. Seine Kontakte zu den Stars der Schauspiel- und Musikszene von Tokio bis nach West Coast Hollywood wachsen mit den von Zaha Hadid gestalteten Stores. Seine Anhänger lieben Barretts messerscharfe Schnitte, die er von Großvater und Urgroßvater gelernt hat und mit den Genres des klassischen britischen Street-Style kombiniert.

Avec sa propre griffe à Milan, une profusion de clients célèbres et un job de présentateur sur MTV, on peut dire que Neil Barrett a fait du chemin depuis son Devon natal. Réputé pour des vêtements qui font la part belle aux détails et à la coupe, Barrett adopte une approche étayée par sa grande connaissance de la production de tissus, qu'il exploite pour rajeunir les classiques. Marquée par des couleurs sobres et des coupes maîtrisées, la mode pour homme de Barrett est, de son propre aveu, très masculine : un aspect qui contribuera à son immense succès. Né en 1965, Neil Barrett sort diplômé de Central Saint Martins en 1986 avant d'obtenir un MA du Royal College of Art en 1989. Un an plus tard, il devient styliste senior de la ligne masculine de Gucci à Florence, où il travaille jusqu'en 1994 : pendant cette période, la marque connaît un véritable renouveau, tant sur le plan créatif que financier. Son succès chez Gucci lui permet d'approcher Prada en proposant la création d'une ligne pour homme. Prada accepte son offre et le nomme directeur de la création pour homme. Il quittera Prada en 1998 pour lancer sa première collection éponyme de vêtements masculins. Il remporte un succès immédiat et ses créations sont achetées par plus de 100 boutiques de créateurs à travers le monde. L'année suivante, Barrett crée White, sa propre griffe produite par Prada, et il est invité à faire l'ouverture du salon professionnel Pitti Immagine Uomo en l'an 2000, à l'occasion duquel il lance également sa première collection pour femme. Les années suivantes, Puma lui commande une collection de chaussures, puis en 2004 il redessine la tenue officielle de l'équipe nationale de football d'Italie pour l'Euro 2004 : un véritable honneur pour un « étranger » et une reconnaissance du succès mondial de sa griffe. En 2006, les Italiens remportent la Coupe du Monde habillés en Barrett, ce qui consolide la collaboration du créateur avec Puma. La même année, il lance une collection de jeans baptisée Indigo et défile pour la première fois à New York lors de la saison automne/hiver 2006. Sa clientèle élitiste de stars de cinéma et de la musique ne cesse de s'agrandir, avec des magasins conçus par Zaha Hadid à Tokyo, Hollywood ou le reste de la Côte ouest. Les fans de Barrett raffolent des coupes précises que lui ont léguées son arrière-grand-père et son grand-père, et qu'il réinterprète dans des modèles typiques du « street style » britannique.

DAVID VASCOTT

PORTRAIT ANDREAS NEWMANN   PHOTOGRAPHY SIMON STYLING NEIL BARRETT MODELS MORGAN M. AND ARTHUR BAPTISTE, FEBRUARY 2008

"My goal is to change the boundaries of fashion"
WALTER VAN BEIRENDONCK

If Walter Van Beirendonck were in a band, it would play a fusion of punk, folk, trash, pop, techno and chamber music. One of Belgium's most prolific fashion designers, Van Beirendonck places his sense of humour to the fore of his creations in an approach that humanises the sexuality that is often woven into his garments as patterns and graphics. Safe sex is a common thematic thread, as are literary, cinematic and folkloric references. Knitwear also plays a large part in Van Beirendonck's repertoire, but no prim twinsets or crew necks for him – his jumpers are likely to come with matching balaclavas bearing garish cartoon faces, bold messages or sexual motifs. Born in Belgium in 1957, Van Beirendonck studied at Antwerp's Royal Academy. Part of the legendary 'Antwerp Six' who brought Belgian fashion to greater public consciousness with their 1987 London show, Van Beirendonck – along with Dirk Van Saene, Dries Van Noten, Dirk Bikkembergs, Marina Yee and Ann Demeulemeester – was responsible for moving fashion towards a new rationale. From 1993 to 1999, he created the cyberpunk label that was W&LT (Wild and Lethal Trash), after which he relaunched his eponymous line, Walter Van Beirendonck. A second line, Aestheticterrorists, was founded in 1999. He has taught at the Royal Academy since 1985 and has designed costumes for stage and film and for bands such as U2 and The Avalanches. He has curated exhibitions in the world's top galleries and has illustrated books, created his own comic and won numerous awards.
In March 1998, the book 'Mutilate' was dedicated to Van Beirendonck's first ten years in fashion, and in September 1998, he opened his own store, Walter, in Antwerp. Van Beirendonck could be described as the industry's blue-sky thinker, for both his visionary perspective, and his constantly optimistic outlook.

Wenn Walter van Beirendonck Mitglied einer Band wäre, würde die vermutlich eine Mischung aus Punk, Folk, Trash, Pop, Techno und Kammermusik spielen. Als einer der produktivsten Modedesigner Belgiens stellt er seinen Sinn für Humor in den Vordergrund seiner Kreationen. Das nimmt der Sexualität, die oft in Form von Mustern in seine Kleidung eingewoben ist, etwas von ihrer Schärfe. Safer Sex ist ein häufiges Thema, ebenso wie literarische, filmische und folkloristische Bezüge. Stricksachen spielen ebenfalls eine große Rolle in van Beirendoncks Repertoire, allerdings keine braven Twinsets oder Matrosenkragen: seine Pullis kommen eher mit passenden wollenen Kopfschützern daher, auf denen grelle Comicgrimassen, forsche Botschaften oder sexuelle Motive zu sehen sind. Der 1957 in Belgien geborene van Beirendonck studierte an der Königlichen Akademie von Antwerpen und war einer der legendären Antwerp Six, die 1987 mit ihrer Schau in London der belgischen Mode die Aufmerksamkeit eines breiteren Publikums sicherten. Zusammen mit Dirk van Saene, Dries van Noten, Dirk Bikkembergs, Marina Yee und Ann Demeulemeester brachte er eine neue Form von Rationalität in die Mode.

Zwischen 1993 und 1999 lancierte er das Cyberpunk-Label W&LT (Wild and Lethal Trash) und kümmerte sich anschließend um den Relaunch der nach ihm benannten Linie Walter van Beirendonck. Mit Aestheticterrorists wurde 1999 die zweite Linie gegründet. Seit 1985 lehrt der Designer an der Königlichen Akademie und entwirft außerdem Kostüme für Theater und Film sowie für Bands wie U2 und Avalanches. Er hat als Kurator Ausstellungen in den besten Museen der Welt konzipiert, Bücher illustriert, einen eigenen Comic kreiert und zahlreiche Auszeichnungen gewonnen. Im März 1998 erschien das Buch „Mutilate", das sich van Beirendoncks ersten zehn Jahren in der Modebranche widmet. Im September desselben Jahres eröffnete der Modemacher seinen ersten eigenen Laden namens ‚Walter' in Antwerpen. Man könnte van Beirendonck mit seinen visionären Perspektiven einen unverbesserlichen Optimisten der Branche nennen.

Si Walter Van Beirendonck était membre d'un groupe, il jouerait une fusion de punk, de folk, de trash, de pop, de techno et de musique de chambre. Créateur parmi les plus prolifiques de Belgique, Van Beirendonck place son sens de l'humour au cœur de ses créations en adoptant une approche qui humanise la sexualité, souvent intégrée à ses vêtements sous forme de motifs et de graphiques. Le « safe sex » apparaît comme le fil rouge de son travail, à côté des références littéraires, cinématographiques et folkloriques. La maille joue également un grand rôle dans le répertoire de Van Beirendonck, mais point de twin-sets guindés, ni de convenables pulls à col rond chez lui : ses pulls s'accompagnent plutôt de passe-montagnes ornés de messages osés, de motifs sexuels ou de visages criards de bande dessinée. Né en 1957 en Belgique, Van Beirendonck étudie à l'Académie Royale d'Anvers. Membre des légendaires « Six d'Anvers »qui ont fait connaître la mode belge lors de leur défilé londonien en 1987, Walter Van Beirendonck, aux côtés de Dirk Van Saene, Dries Van Noten, Dirk Bikkembergs, Marina Yee et Ann Demeulemeester, a contribué à faire avancer la mode vers une nouvelle logique. Entre 1993 et 1999, il crée une griffe cyberpunk baptisée W&LT (Wild and Lethal Trash) avant de relancer sa ligne éponyme, Walter Van Beirendonck, ainsi qu'une autre gamme, Aestheticterrorists, en 1999. Depuis 1985, il enseigne la mode à l'Académie Royale et dessine des costumes de théâtre, de cinéma et de scène, notamment pour les groupes U2 et les Avalanches. Walter van Beirendonck a illustré des livres et organisé des expositions dans les plus grands musées d'art du monde, créé sa propre bande dessinée et remporté de nombreux prix. En mars 1998, le livre Mutilate retrace les dix premières années de sa carrière et en septembre de la même année, il ouvre sa propre boutique, Walter, à Anvers. Van Beirendonck peut être considéré comme l'insouciant de la mode, tant pour sa perspective visionnaire que pour son indéfectible optimisme.

LIZ HANCOCK

PHOTOGRAPHY ALASDAIR MCLELLAN STYLING OLIVIER RIZZO MODEL RYAN NOVEMBER 2008

PHOTOGRAPHY ALASDAIR MCLELLAN·STYLING THOM MURPHY·OCTOBER 2009

"I like to provoke people to rethink about what can be done with menswear"
THOM BROWNE

There is no mistaking a Thom Browne suit. Narrow lapels, cropped jackets and, the cornerstones of a Browne design, Browne's ankle-skimming trousers revolutionised menswear and redefined the wardrobe of the modern man. Born in 1965, Browne was a one-time actor before landing himself a job as a salesman in Giorgio Armani's showroom in New York in 1997. At the Ralph-Lauren-owned Club Monaco, Lauren noticed Browne's creative flair and promptly installed Browne – who has no formal fashion training – in their design and merchandising departments. In 2001, Browne left to start work on his self-named fashion house. Way before launching his own label the designer would buy old Brooks Brothers' suits from thrift stores and cut them down to resemble the aesthetic he is known for today. Along with his precise approach, Browne was the perfect contender for Brooks Brothers' Black Fleece concept (a 50-piece men and women's high-end collection) in 2006. So successful was the collaboration that Brooks Brothers decided to carry on with Black Fleece until 2011. Launched in the UK in November 2007, Black Fleece is the first capsule collection for the 190-year-old brand by a guest designer. Browne received the 2006 CFDA Menswear Designer of the Year Award, was a finalist for the National Design Award from the Cooper-Hewitt National Design Museum for 2006 and 2008, and received the Rising Star Award for Menswear by Fashion Group International for 2005 and the runner-up prize of the 2005 CFDA Vogue Fund. In 2008, Browne teamed up with the Italian sportswear company and down apparel specialist Moncler to design their top men's line Moncler Gamme Bleu. In 2011, Browne showcased his first womenswear collection at New York Fashion Week, saying "There's no disconnect [between his womenswear and menswear] – and it all starts with a tailored point of view."

Ein Anzug von Thom Browne ist unverkennbar. Schmale Revers, kurze Jacken und Hosen bilden die Eckpfeiler des Browne-Designs. Seine die Knöchel zeigenden Hosen revolutionierten die Herrenmode und haben die Garderobe des modernen Mannes neu definiert. Der 1965 geborene Browne war ursprünglich Schauspieler, bevor er sich 1997 einen Job als Verkäufer in Giorgio Armanis Showroom in New York besorgte. Im Club Monaco, der Ralph Lauren gehört, fiel Lauren Brownes kreative Ausstrahlung auf und er holte ihn – obwohl er keinerlei reguläre Ausbildung im Bereich Mode hat – in seine Abteilungen für Design und Verkauf. 2001 ging Browne von dort weg, um ein Modehaus unter eigenem Namen zu starten. Lange bevor er sein eigenes Label präsentierte, kaufte der Designer in Second-Hand-Läden alte Anzüge von Brooks Brothers zusammen und schnitt sie nach den ästhetischen Vorstellungen zurecht, für die er heute bekannt ist. Mit seiner korrekten Art war Browne der perfekte Anwärter für das Konzept Black Fleece von Brooks Brothers (eine hochwertige 50-teilige Herren- und Damenkollektion) im Jahr 2006. Die Zusammenarbeit war sogar derart erfolgreich, sodass Brooks Brothers

entschied, Black Fleece bis 2011 fortzusetzen. Die im November 2007 in Großbritannien präsentierte Kollektion ist die erste Sonderkollektion eines Gastdesigners bei der 190 Jahre alten Marke. 2006 war Browne Menswear Designer of the Year der CFDA, Finalist beim National Design Award des Cooper-Hewitt National Design Museum (wie auch 2008). Den Rising Star Award for Menswear der Fashion Group International erhielt er 2005, im selben Jahr belegte er den zweiten Platz beim CFDA Vogue Fund. 2008 tat sich Browne mit dem italienischen Sportmodenhersteller und kultigem Spezialisten für Daunenjacken Moncler zusammen und entwarf dessen Männerlabel Moncler Gamme Bleu. 2011 präsentierte Browne seine erste Damenkollektion auf der New Yorker Fashion Week mit den Worten: „Es gibt keine Grenzen [zwischen Damen- und Herrenmode] – es ist alles eine Frage des Schnitts."

Impossible de confondre un costume Thom Browne avec un autre. Caractérisées par des revers étroits, des vestes courtes et des pantalons qui laissent voir les chevilles, les créations de Browne ont révolutionné la mode masculine et redéfini la garde-robe de l'homme moderne. Né en 1965, l'ex-acteur Thom Browne décroche un job de vendeur dans le showroom Giorgio Armani à New York en 1997, puis travaille pour la marque Club Monaco de Ralph Lauren. Ce dernier repère sa grande créativité et lui trouve rapidement une place de choix dans ses départements de création et de merchandising, alors que Browne ne possède aucune formation officielle dans ces domaines. En 2001, il quitte la maison Ralph Lauren pour travailler sur sa propre griffe. Bien avant de lancer sa collection, il achetait déjà de vieux costumes Brooks Brothers dans les boutiques d'occasion et les refaçonnait dans le style qui a depuis fait sa réputation. En ajoutant à cela son amour de la précision, Browne devient en 2006 le prétendant idéal au titre de styliste du concept Black Fleece de Brooks Brothers (une collection haut de gamme de 50 pièces pour homme et pour femme). Cette collaboration remporte un tel succès que Brooks Brothers décide de poursuivre la collection Black Fleece jusqu'en 2011. Lancée au Royaume-Uni en novembre 2007, Black Fleece est la première mini-collection que cette vénérable maison de 190 ans confie à un styliste invité. Lauréat du Menswear Designer of the Year du CFDA en 2006, Thom Browne était aussi finaliste pour le National Design Award du Cooper-Hewitt National Design Museum en 2006 et en 2008, le Rising Star Award for Menswear du Fashion Group International en 2005 et le CFDA Vogue Fund en 2005. En 2008, Browne s'associe à l'Italien Moncler, producteur de mode de sport et spécialiste culte de doudounes, et crée sa marque pour homme, Moncler Gamme Bleu. Et en 2011, il présente sa première collection pour femme à la New Yorker Fashion Week en l'introduisant avec les mots suivants : « Il n'y a aucune limite [entre la mode pour femme et la mode pour homme] – c'est juste une question de coupe. »

KAREN HODKINSON

PORTRAIT: CIRCE. PHOTOGRAPHY SEAN THOMAS. FEBRUARY 2008.

"In every collection there are pieces with which I literally fall in love"
CONSUELO CASTIGLIONI · MARNI

PORTRAIT SERGIO CALATRONI. PHOTOGRAPHY YELENA YEMCHUK. STYLING SORAYA DAYANI. MODEL JP. OCTOBER 2004.

In little more than fifteen years Consuelo Castiglioni's label Marni has become a byword for innovative Italian design, charming its way into fashion folklore with an eclectic vision of femininity. What began as a stint of fashion consulting for her husband's fur and leather company, Ciwi Furs, has developed into a business that has produced some of the most cultish items of the last few years – ponyskin clogs, corsages, charm-embellished bags, the cropped jacket – and a look that has helped define contemporary notions of prettiness. Marni was launched in 1994 with an experimental collection produced through Ciwi Furs (supplier to Prada and Moschino). Treating fur like a fabric, Castiglioni removed the lining, and with it the bulkiness, of the usual rich-bitch fur coat. With each collection she gradually introduced new fabrics, mixing fur with perfectly-cut leathers and suedes, and by 1999 Marni had become an established line independent from its furrier origins. The arts and crafts richness of the Marni look comes from a considered mismatching of print, cut and texture. The Marni girl wears a veritable haberdashery of luxurious and love-worn fabrics which are layered across the body and nipped in at the waist with a decorative belt. The Marni print – from faded florals and mattress ticking stripes to '50s retro and block prints – may have become an influential motif, but one that can distract from the slick couture finish that adds to the creatively haphazard look. Since 2000 Marni has undergone giddying retail expansion, opening 38 boutiques around the world, designed either by architecture firm Future Systems or Sybarite, and selling menswear, childrenswear and homeware alongside a successful line of accessories.

In wenig mehr als 15 Jahren ist Consuelo Castiglionis Label Marni zum Synonym für innovatives italienisches Design geworden. Mit einer eklektischen Vision von Weiblichkeit hat sich die Marke ihren Weg in die folkloristisch angehauchte Mode gebahnt. Begonnen hat es mit einem Job als Fashion Consultant für den Kürschnerbetrieb Ciwi Furs, der Castiglionis Mann gehört. Doch bald entwickelte sich das Ganze zu einem eigenständigen Geschäft, das einige der kultigsten Produkte der letzten Jahre hervorbrachte – Ponyfell-Clogs, Bandschleifen-Corsagen, mit Glücksbringern verzierte Taschen, Boleros. Der Marni-Look hat das gegenwärtige Verständnis von Schönheit mitbestimmt. Gegründet wurde Marni 1994 mit einer Versuchskollektion, die bei Ciwi Furs (u.a. Zulieferer von Prada und Moschino) produziert wurde. Castiglioni verarbeitete Pelz wie Stoff, verzichtete auf das Futter und reduzierte so das Volumen des traditionell protzigen Pelzmantels. Mit jeder Kollektion führte sie neue Materialien ein, mixte Pelz mit perfekt geschnittenem Leder und Wildleder, sodass Marni sich ab 1999 als eine von ihren pelzigen Ursprüngen unabhängige, eigenständige Marke etabliert hatte. Der bohemienhafte Marni-Look verdankt sich den absichtlichen Gegensätzen von Muster, Schnitt und Textur. So trägt das typische Marni-Girl einen veritablen

Mischmasch aus luxuriösen und abgetragenen Stoffen, die sich schichtweise um ihren Körper legen, in der Taille von einem dekorativen Gürtel zusammengehalten werden und eine organische Silhouette erzeugen. Das Marni-Muster – ob verblichen-floral, gestreift wie Matratzendrillich, 50er-Jahre-Retro oder Blockstreifen – mag ein wichtiges Motiv sein, kann jedoch nicht vom raffinierten Couture-Finish ablenken, das unverzichtbar für den bewusst kreierten, aber zufällig wirkenden Look ist. Seit dem Jahr 2000 hat Marni im Einzelhandel auf geradezu schwindelerregende Weise expandiert und 38 Boutiquen in aller Welt eröffnet, die von den Architekturbüros Future Systems oder Sybarite entworfen wurden. Dort verkauft man Herren- und Kindermode, Wohnbedarf sowie ein erfolgreiches Sortiment von Accessoires.

En un peu moins de 15 ans, la griffe Marni de Consuelo Castiglioni est devenue synonyme d'innovation à l'italienne, se frayant un chemin dans la mode aux accents folkloriques grâce à sa vision éclectique de la féminité. Ce qui a commencé par un job de consultante pour Ciwi Furs, fabricant de cuirs et de fourrures dirigé par son mari, s'est transformé en une grande entreprise qui produit certaines des pièces les plus cultes de ces dernières années : sabots en vachette, corsages, sacs ornés de grigris porte-bonheur, vestes tondues… pour un look qui a contribué à définir les canons contemporains de la beauté. Consuelo Castiglioni lance sa griffe Marni en 1994 avec une collection expérimentale produite par le biais de Ciwi Furs (fournisseur de Prada et Moschino). Travaillant la fourrure comme du tissu, elle en retire la doublure et, avec elle, la lourdeur généralement associée au manteau de fourrure tape-à-l'œil. Au fil des collections, elle introduit progressivement de nouvelles matières, coordonnant la fourrure à des cuirs et des daims parfaitement coupés ; en 1999, la griffe devient entièrement indépendante de ses origines de fourreur. La richesse artistique et artisanale du style Marni naît d'un assortiment d'imprimés, de coupes et de textures volontairement dépareillé. La fille Marni arbore donc avec amour tout un arsenal de tissus luxueux superposés sur le corps et pincés à la taille à l'aide d'une ceinture décorative pour produire une silhouette organique. Des floraux passés aux rayures matelas, des motifs rétro années 50 aux impressions à la planche, les imprimés Marni exercent certes beaucoup d'influence sur la mode, mais ils réussissent toujours à détourner l'attention du fini haute couture irréprochable qui caractérise ce look délibérément aléatoire. Depuis l'an 2000, les ventes de Marni connaissent une ascension vertigineuse: la marque a ouvert 38 boutiques à travers le monde, conçues par les cabinets d'architecture Future Systems ou Sybarite. Elles proposent des vêtements pour homme, une ligne pour enfant et des meubles, ainsi qu'une ligne d'accessoires à succès.

AIMEE FARRELL

"We're inspired by things that are normally not fashionable"
DEAN & DAN CATEN · DSQUARED

Dean and Dan Caten of Dsquared know a thing or two about mixing and matching. Not only did the now 40-year-old identical twins leave their native Canada in 1991 for Italy, the homeland of their paternal grandmother (Caten is short for Catenacci, while the maternal side is English), they've managed to turn the fashion world on its head with a ballsy blend of American pop culture and superior Italian tailoring. The Milan debut of their men's line in 1994 garnered fans such as Lenny Kravitz, Justin Timberlake and Ricky Martin for its cheeky, MTV-ready ebullience paired with precision craftsmanship. Soon afterwards, the duo further solidified their fashion credibility by creating the costumes for Madonna's 'Don't Tell Me' video and the cowboy segment of her 2002 Drowned World Tour, as well as the outfits for Christina Aguilera's 2003 Stripped Tour (the diminutive diva was later recruited to walk the catwalk for the Spring/Summer 2005 men's collection). The launch of a women's line in 2003 saw supermodels Naomi Campbell, Eva Herzigova, Karolina Kurkova and Fernanda Tavares saunter out of a pink private jet in unapologetically sex-charged regalia. For Autumn/Winter 2005, the brothers, who spent their childhoods as born-again Christians, looked to a higher power with skinny ties stitched with 'John 3:16', caps and T-shirts printed with the word 'Angel' and sweaters emblazoned with 'Jesus Loves Me' or, on one notable cardigan, 'Jesus Loves Even Me'. Apparently, even fashion designers know God is in the details, a well-worn principle that, along with backing from the Italian conglomerate Diesel, has shot scale the erstwhile party boys into the heavens. In 2007, their long-awaited 5400 sq ft Milan store was opened and they also launched their first fragrance.

Dean und Dan Caten von Dsquared verstehen einiges von Mixing und Matching. 1991 verließen die heute 40-jährigen eineiigen Zwillinge ihr kanadisches Zuhause, um nach Italien zu ziehen, in die Heimat ihrer Großmutter väterlicherseits (Caten ist die Abkürzung von Catenacci; die Familie mütterlicherseits hat englische Wurzeln). Mit einer gewagten Mixtur aus amerikanischer Popkultur und anspruchsvoller italienischer Schneiderkunst ist es ihnen gelungen, die Modewelt auf den Kopf zu stellen. Nach ihrem Mailänder Debüt der Herrenlinie 1994 zählten dank des frechen, mit handwerklicher Präzision gepaarten Überschwangs Lenny Kravitz, Justin Timberlake und Ricky Martin zu ihren Fans. Bald danach untermauerte das Duo seine modische Glaubwürdigkeit durch Madonnas Kostüme für das Video zu „Don't Tell Me" und die Cowboy-Outfits ihrer Drowned World Tour 2002. Es folgte die Ausstattung von Christina Aguilera bei ihrer Tour Stripped 2003 (die kleine Diva wurde später anlässlich der Herrenkollektion Frühjahr/Sommer 2005 für den Catwalk verpflichtet). Bei der Präsentation der Damenlinie im Jahr 2003 sah man die Supermodels Naomi Campbell, Eva Herzigova, Karolina Kur-

kova und Fernanda Tavares mit eindeutig zweideutigen Insignien einem pinkfarbenen Privatjet entsteigen. Für die Kollektion Herbst/Winter 2005 orientierten sich die Brüder, die ihre Kindheit in einer Gemeinde wiedergeborener Christen verbrachten, an einer höheren Macht und bestickten schmale Krawatten mit „Johannes 3.16", bedruckten Baseballcaps und T-Shirts mit dem Wort „Angel" und verzierten Pullover mit „Jesus Loves Me" sowie eine Strickjacke mit dem bemerkenswerten „Jesus Loves Even Me". Offenbar wissen selbst Modedesigner, dass Gott sich im Detail verbirgt. Dieses kluge Prinzip sorgte neben der Unterstützung durch den italienischen Diesel-Konzern dafür, dass die Verkaufszahlen der einstigen Partyboys in himmlische Höhen schossen. 2007 wurde schließlich der lang ersehnte 500 m² große Store in Mailand eröffnet. Außerdem kam der erste eigene Duft auf den Markt.

On peut dire que Dean et Dan Caten de Dsquared s'y connaissent en métissage des styles. Ces vrais jumeaux, aujourd'hui âgés de 40 ans, quittent leur Canada natal en 1991 pour l'Italie, patrie de leur grand-mère paternelle (Caten est une abréviation de Catenacci tandis qu'ils sont d'origine anglaise du côté de leur mère), et réussissent à bouleverser l'univers de la mode avec leur fusion osée entre pop culture américaine et coupe virtuose à l'italienne. En 1994, les débuts milanais de leur ligne pour homme ravissent des fans tels que Lenny Kravitz, Justin Timberlake et Ricky Martin grâce à leur exubérante insolence formatée pour MTV mais conjuguée à un savoir-faire de précision. Peu de temps après, le duo assoie sa crédibilité en créant les costumes du clip « Don't Tell Me » de Madonna et les tenues de cow-boy de sa Drowned World Tour en 2002, sans oublier les costumes de la tournée Stripped de Christina Aguilera en 2003 (la mini-diva sera plus tard recrutée pour défiler lors de leur collection pour homme printemps/été 2005). Le lancement d'une ligne pour femme en 2003 voit les top models Naomi Campbell, Eva Herzigova, Karolina Kurkova et Fernanda Tavares sortir d'un jet privé rose, vêtues d'insignes sexuellement explicites. Pour l'automne/hiver 2005, les frères jumeaux élevés dans la doctrine évangélique des Born-Again Christians semblent retrouver la foi avec des cravates étroites cousues de l'inscription « Jean 3.16 », des casquettes et des T-shirts imprimés du mot « Angel » et des pulls proclamant « Jesus Loves Me » ou, sur un certain cardigan, « Jesus Loves Even Me ». Apparemment, même les créateurs de mode savent que Dieu se cache dans les détails, un principe éprouvé qui, allié au soutien financier du conglomérat Diesel, propulse les ventes de ces anciens fêtards au firmament. En 2007, ils ont ouvert la boutique milanaise de 500 mètres carrés que tout le monde attendait et lancé leur tout premier parfum.

LEE CARTER

PORTRAIT ALEX GIACOMELLI PHOTOGRAPHY LAETITIA NEGRE STYLING ANNA BURNS MODEL ANDRÉ JULY 2004

PHOTOGRAPHY EILLEN VON UNWERTH. STYLING MARK MORRISON. MODEL OMAHYRA. AUGUST 2004.

"Nature is my main source of inspiration – I will never stop taking hints from what I call 'the greatest artist'"
ROBERTO CAVALLI

Roberto Cavalli (born 1940, Florence) designs some of the most glamorous clothes in fashion: baroque combinations of exotic feathers, overblown florals, animal prints and incredibly lightweight leathers comprise the signature Cavalli look for day or night, which is always shown on his Milan runway atop the highest heels and with the biggest blow-dried hair in the city. In winter collections, fur – the more extravagant the better – is dominant. And to think it all started on a ping-pong table. This is where, as a student at Florence's Academy of Art, Cavalli began to experiment with printing on leather, later patenting a similar technique. The son of a tailor and the grandson of a revered painter (of the Macchiaioli movement), Cavalli is an expert embellisher and decorator of textiles. After founding his own fashion company in the early '60s, Cavalli was one of the first to put leather on a catwalk, patchworking it together for his debut show in 1972, which was staged at the Palazzo Pitti in Florence. Cavalli was an outsider to high fashion during the '80s, but staged a remarkable comeback in the '90s. In this renaissance period, Cavalli has become the label of choice among the R&B aristocracy, not to mention any starlet with both the bravado and the body to carry off one of his attention-seeking frocks. Assisted by his second wife, Eva Düringer, a former Miss Universe, Cavalli brought his distinctive look – a unique combination of thrusting sex appeal, artisanal prints and frankly eccentric themes and catwalk shows – to the Milan collections, where press and clients alike received him with open arms. The collections bearing his name now include Just Cavalli, a menswear line, a childrenswear line and perfume licences, among others. In 2003, his company scored a turnover of €289 million and its collections are distributed in more than 50 countries. Cavalli also owns one of Italy's best racehorse stud farms.

Der 1940 in Florenz geborene Roberto Cavalli entwirft einige der glamourösesten Modekreationen überhaupt: Barocke Kombinationen aus exotischen Federn, schwülstigen Blumenmustern, Raubtier-Prints und unglaublich leichten Ledersorten ergeben zusammen den typischen Cavalli-Look für den Tag und den Abend. Präsentiert wird dieser ausschließlich auf dem Mailänder Catwalk des Designers, mit allerhöchsten Absätzen und den voluminösesten Fönfrisuren der ganzen Stadt. In den Winterkollektionen dominiert Pelz – je extravaganter desto besser. Kaum zu glauben, dass das alles auf einer Tischtennisplatte angefangen hat. Doch genau dort begann Cavalli als Student der florentinischen Kunstakademie mit dem Bedrucken von Leder zu experimentieren. Später ließ er sich diese Technik sogar patentieren. Als Sohn eines Schneiders und Enkel eines geachteten Malers (aus der Macchiaioli-Schule) ist Cavalli ein begnadeter Verschönerer und Dekorateur von Textilien. Nachdem er in den frühen 1960er-Jahren seine eigene Modefirma gegründet hatte, war er einer der Ersten, der Leder auf den Laufsteg brachte. Für seine Debütschau von 1972 im Palazzo Pitti in Florenz nähte er es im Patchworkstil zusammen. Die 1980er-Jahre erlebte er als Außenseiter der Haute Couture, in den 1990er-Jahren gelang ihm jedoch ein beachtliches Comeback. Im Zuge dieser Renaissance avancierte Cavalli zum Lieblingslabel der R&B-Stars, gar nicht zu reden von den zahlreichen Starlets, die die Courage und den Körper besaßen, eines von seinen Aufsehen erregenden Kleidern zu tragen. Unterstützt von seiner zweiten Frau, der ehemaligen Miss Universum Eva Düringer, brachte Cavalli seinen unverwechselbaren Look – eine Kombination aus offensivem Sexappeal, künstlerischen Mustern sowie exzentrischen Themen – in Mailand heraus, wo ihn Presse und Publikum mit offenen Armen empfingen. Zu den Labels unter seinem Namen zählen inzwischen u. a. Just Cavalli, eine Herrenlinie, eine Kinderkollektion und eine Parfümlizenz. 2003 machte das Unternehmen 289 Millionen Euro Umsatz mit dem Vertrieb der Kollektionen in mehr als 50 Ländern. Cavalli besitzt übrigens auch eines der besten italienischen Gestüte für Rennpferde.

Roberto Cavalli (né en 1940 à Florence) dessine certains des vêtements les plus glamour de la mode : combinaisons baroques de plumes exotiques, motifs de fleurs géantes, imprimés d'animaux et cuirs incroyablement légers composent son look signature pour le jour ou le soir, toujours présenté sur les podiums milanais par des mannequins haut perchées sur leurs talons et coiffées des brushings les plus flamboyants de la ville. Ses collections d'hiver font la part belle à la fourrure, toujours plus extravagante. Tout a commencé sur la table de ping-pong où l'étudiant de l'Académie des Beaux-Arts de Florence s'essayait à l'impression sur cuir, une technique qu'il finira par faire breveter. Fils de tailleur et petit-fils d'un illustre peintre (du mouvement Macchiaioli), Roberto Cavalli excelle dans l'embellissement et la décoration des textiles. Après la création de sa propre griffe au début des années 60, Cavalli fait figure de précurseur en proposant du cuir travaillé en patchworks pour son premier défilé donné au Palazzo Pitti de Florence en 1972. Pendant les années 80, Cavalli se marginalise un peu par rapport à la mode haut de gamme, mais fait un retour remarqué dans les années 90. Pendant cette période de renaissance, Cavalli devient la griffe de prédilection des stars du R&B, sans oublier toutes les starlettes assez courageuses et bien roulées pour oser porter ses robes scandaleuses. Épaulé par sa seconde épouse Eva Düringer, une ex-Miss Univers, Cavalli présente son look original (une combinaison unique entre sex-appeal explosif, imprimés artisanaux, thématiques et défilés franchement excentriques) aux collections milanaises, où la presse comme les acheteurs l'accueillent à bras ouverts. Les collections qu'il signe de son nom incluent désormais Just Cavalli, une ligne pour homme, une ligne pour enfant et des licences de parfums, entre autres. En 2003, son entreprise a réalisé un chiffre d'affaires de 289 millions d'euros, avec des collections distribuées dans plus de 50 pays à travers le monde. Cavalli possède également l'un des plus beaux haras de chevaux de course d'Italie.

SUSIE RUSHTON

ROBERTO CAVALLI

"My inspiration comes from anthropology, genetic anthropology, migration, history, social prejudice, politics, displacement, science fiction and, I guess, my own cultural background"
HUSSEIN CHALAYAN

Hussein Chalayan pushes clothing into sculpture, furniture, performance, art and beyond. Since his graduate collection at Central Saint Martins in 1993 he has confirmed his reputation as one of the most original designers working anywhere in the world today. Chalayan is famed for his spectacular shows in which anything could happen, from coffee tables turning into dresses to the use of confessional boxes and trampolines as catwalk props. At the same time, the designer's attention to technical detail, structure and stitching is exceptional. His collections have often focused on cultural displacement, something that Chalayan himself has experienced; his Spring/Summer 2003 collection Kinship Journey, for example, was inspired by Viking, Byzantine, Georgian and Armenian cultures following a DNA test taken by the designer. Aside from his eponymous label, Chalayan has during his career worked for cashmere brand TSE and was appointed creative director of Asprey in 2001, leaving the company in 2004. His creative touchstones are science and new technology. He is a twice-crowned British Designer of the Year, having picked up the prize in 1999 and 2000. 2004 saw Chalayan open his first store in Tokyo, to complement his existing womenswear and menswear collections; in 2005, he also launched a younger line, Chalayan. Chalayan's career has continued on the upward trajectory. He was awarded an MBE in the Queen's Birthday Honours List 2006 for his services to the fashion industry, and the prestigious Design Star Honoree by The Fashion Group International in 2007. In 2008, Chalayan was appointed Creative Director of German sportswear label Puma, where his passion for technology and forward-thinking design continues to breathe new life into the 80-year-old brand. Chalayan's retrospective at the Design Museum in London (2009) celebrated 15 years of ground-breaking experimental design and explored the inspirations and themes that continue to influence the designer, in particular issues of cultural identity, displacement and migration.

Hussein Chalayan überwindet mit seiner Kleidung die Grenzen zu Bildhauerei, Möbelherstellung, Performance und Kunst. Seit seiner Abschlusskollektion am Central Saint Martins im Jahr 1993 gelang es ihm, seinen Ruf als einer der originellsten Designer der Gegenwart weiter zu festigen. Chalayan ist berühmt für seine spektakulären Modenschauen, bei denen alles Mögliche passieren kann, von Kaffeetischen, die sich in Kleider verwandeln, bis zu Beichtstühlen und Trampolinen als Requisiten auf dem Laufsteg. Dazu kommt die außergewöhnliche Sorgfalt des Designers hinsichtlich technischer Details, Strukturen und Nähte. Oft stehen kulturelle Verschiebungen, die Chalayan auch selbst erfahren hat, im Mittelpunkt seiner Kollektionen. So war etwa seine Kollektion Frühjahr/Sommer 2003 von den Kulturen der Wikinger, Byzantiner, Georgier und Armenier inspiriert, nachdem der Designer sich einem DNA-Test unterzogen hatte. Außer für das nach ihm benannte Label hat er im Laufe seiner Karriere für die Kaschmirmarke TSE sowie von 2001 bis 2004 als Creative Director für Asprey entworfen. Seine kreativen Prüfsteine sind Wissenschaft und neue Technologien. Er wurde zweimal mit dem Titel British Designer of the

Year ausgezeichnet (1999 und 2000). 2004 eröffnete Chalayan seinen ersten Laden in Tokio. Und als Ergänzung der Damen- und Herrenkollektion lancierte er 2005 mit Chalayan noch eine jüngere Linie. Mit Chalayans Karriere geht es weiter bergauf. 2006 wurde er für seine Verdienste um die Modeindustrie anlässlich des Geburtstags der Queen als Member of the Order of the British Empire ausgezeichnet. 2007 erhielt er den angesehenen Design Star Honoree der Fashion Group International. 2008 wurde Chalayan Creative Director des Sportartikelherstellers Puma, wo sein Faible für Technologie und zukunftsorientiertes Design der 80 Jahre alten Marke neues Leben einhauchte. Die Chalayan-Retrospektive im Londoner Design Museum (2009) feierte 15 Jahre bahnbrechendes experimentelles Design und beleuchtete die Inspirationen und Themen, die den Designer nach wie vor beschäftigen, insbesondere die Bereiche kulturelle Identität, Heimatverlust und Migration.

Hussein Chalayan repousse la frontière de la mode aux confins de la sculpture, du mobilier, du théâtre et même au-delà. Depuis sa collection de fin d'études à Central Saint Martins en 1993, il a confirmé sa réputation de créateur parmi les plus originaux actuellement en exercice dans le monde. Chalayan est connu pour ses défilés spectaculaires où tout peut arriver, des tables basses transformées en robes aux confessionnaux et trampolines utilisés en guise de podiums. Parallèlement, le créateur fait preuve d'une attention exceptionnelle aux détails techniques, à la structure et aux coutures. Ses collections parlent souvent du « déplacement culturel », une expérience vécue par Chalayan en personne ; par exemple, pour sa collection printemps/été 2003 « Kinship Journey », il s'est inspiré des cultures viking, byzantine, géorgienne et arménienne après avoir obtenu les résultats de son test ADN. Outre sa griffe éponyme, Chalayan a travaillé pour la marque de cachemire TSE. En 2001, il a été nommé styliste d'Asprey, une maison qu'il quittera en 2004. Les pierres d'angle de sa démarche créative sont les sciences et les nouvelles technologies, et il a été couronné deux fois British Designer of the Year (1999 et 2000). En 2004, Chalayan a ouvert sa première boutique à Tokyo. Afin de compléter ses collections pour homme et pour femme, il a également lancé en 2005 une ligne plus jeune baptisée Chalayan. Depuis, la carrière de Chalayan reste sur une pente ascendante. En 2006, il a été nommé Membre de l'Ordre de l'Empire Britannique sur la « Birthday Honours List » de la Reine d'Angleterre pour services rendus à l'industrie de la mode, tandis qu'en 2007, Fashion Group International lui a décerné son prestigieux Design Star Honoree. En 2008, Chalayan est devenu directeur de la création de la griffe sportswear allemande Puma : grâce à sa passion de la technologie et sa créativité visionnaire, cette marque de 80 ans semble sans cesse se renouveler. La rétrospective Chalayan au Design Museum de Londres (2009) célèbre 15 années de création expérimentale révolutionnaire en revenant sur les sources d'inspiration et les thèmes qui continuent d'influencer le créateur, notamment les questions de l'identité, du « déplacement culturel » et de l'immigration.

SKYE SHERWIN

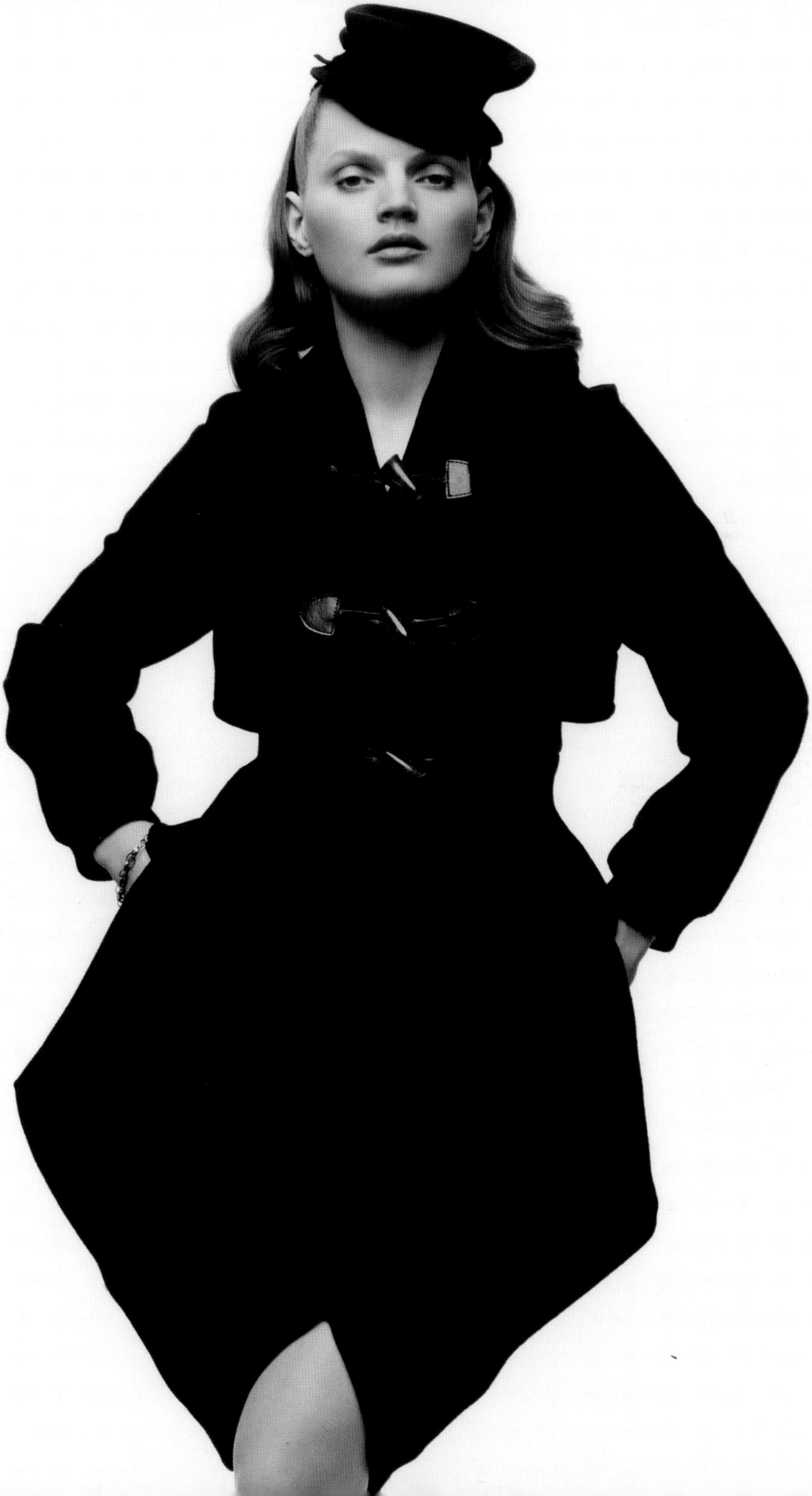

PHOTOGRAPHY TAKAY STYLING JO BARKER MODEL SONJA MARCH 2004

PHOTOGRAPHY PAOLO ROVERSI. FASHION DIRECTOR EDWARD ENNINFUL. MODEL: ANOUCK LEPERE. APRIL 2002.

"By questioning what you are doing, you evolve"
MARIA CORNEJO · ZERO

Chilean-born Maria Cornejo first arrived in the UK with her parents, having left their native country as political refugees. She later shot to prominence in the '80s, having graduated with flying colours with a fashion degree at Ravensbourne College. Her subsequent designs, produced in conjunction with John Richmond, under the label Richmond-Cornejo, were championed by the style press and garnered a strong cult following, helping to further establish her as a creative force – one able to see beyond mere seasonal modishness. From the outset of her career, Cornejo has been clear about her wish for longevity as a designer. By the late '80s, she had split from Richmond and was based in France, presenting her womenswear collections in Milan and Paris to much acclaim. She was also consulting and designing for British high street chain Jigsaw, in addition to over-hauling the French ready-to-wear label Tehen, as their creative director. Now based in New York under the label Zero, with her own store situated in the city's fashionable NoLita district, she continues to refine her design aesthetic, one that is wholly wearable yet ever-so-slightly unconventional. Her geometric constructions and pared-down approach to cutting attract a certain type of intelligent, open-minded woman. High-profile advocates of Cornejo's clothing include actress Sigourney Weaver and the artist Cindy Sherman. In 2006, Cornejo won the prestigious fashion prize from the Smithsonian Cooper-Hewitt National Design Award. Now she has moved the atelier and new Zero store to 33 Bleecker Street, New York. Together with her husband, the photographer Mark Borthwick, she has retained a truly personal vision, notably with her Autumn/Winter 2009 collection, returning to her punk/goth roots as a student in London. With global stockists currently ranging from stores such as Barneys in New York to Isetan in Japan, Cornejo clearly produces a style that can both cut though cultural difference and enhance the individuality of those who wear it. Cornejo has custom-made several pieces for First Lady Michelle Obama and counts Sofia Coppola and Tilda Swinton amongst her many fans.

Die in Chile geborene Maria Cornejo kam schon als Kind mit ihren Eltern nach Großbritannien, weil die Familie ihr Heimatland aus politischen Gründen verlassen musste. Anfang der 1980er-Jahre wurde sie auf einen Schlag prominent, nachdem sie ihr Modestudium am Ravensbourne College mit Bravour absolviert hatte. Ihre nächsten Entwürfe, die sie zusammen mit John Richmond unter dem Namen Richmond-Cornejo realisierte, brachten den beiden viel Lob von Modejournalisten und eine treue Fangemeinde ein. Cornejo half dieser Erfolg, sich als kreative Größe zu etablieren – und zwar als eine, die über die modischen Trends der aktuellen Saison hinaus Bestand hat. Denn in der Tat war der Designerin vom Beginn ihrer Karriere an Langlebigkeit ganz wichtig. Ende der 1980er-Jahre hatte Cornejo sich von Richmond getrennt und sich in Frankreich niedergelassen. Ihre Damenkollektionen präsentierte sie unter großem Beifall in Mailand und Paris. Außerdem war sie als Consultant und Designerin für die britische Nobel-Kaufhauskette Jigsaw tätig und hatte beim französischen Prêt-à-porter-Label Tehen die Funktion des Creative Director inne. Inzwischen arbeitet sie in New York für die Marke Zero und betreibt einen eigenen Laden im angesagten Viertel NoLita. Sie beschäftigt sich weiterhin mit der Verfeinerung ihrer Designästhetik, die absolut tragbare, aber sehr oft eine Spur unkonventionelle Stücke hervorbringt.

Ihre geometrischen Konstruktionen und betont schlichten Schnitte sprechen einen bestimmten Typ intelligenter, aufgeschlossener Frauen an. Zu den angesehensten Fürsprecherinnen von Cornejos Mode zählen die First Lady Michelle Obama, Schauspielerinnen wie Tilda Swinton und Sigourney Weaver, Sofia Coppola und die Künstlerin Cindy Sherman. 2006 gewann Cornejo den prestigeträchtigen Smithsonian Cooper-Hewitt National Design Award. Inzwischen ist sie mit ihrem Atelier und dem neuen Zero-Laden in die New Yorker Bleecker Street Nr. 33 umgezogen. Gemeinsam mit ihrem Ehemann, dem Fotografen Mark Borthwick, hat sie sich besonders in ihrer Herbst-/Winterkollektion 2009 eine wirklich persönliche Sicht der Dinge erhalten, indem sie zu den Punk/Goth-Wurzeln ihrer Studentenzeit in London zurückkehrte. Gegenwärtig findet man ihre Entwürfe in Nobelkaufhäusern rund um die Welt, etwa bei Barneys in New York oder bei Isetan in Japan. Ihre Mode besitzt die Fähigkeit, kulturelle Grenzen zu überwinden und gleichzeitig die Individualität der Trägerin zu unterstreichen.

La Chilienne Maria Cornejo est arrivée en Angleterre avec ses parents qui fuyaient la répression politique dans leur pays natal. Au début des années 80, elle se fait déjà remarquer en obtenant son diplôme de mode avec les félicitations du jury du Ravensbourne College. Elle s'associe ensuite avec John Richmond pour fonder la griffe Richmond-Cornejo. Encensées par la presse, les créations du duo remportent un énorme succès et deviennent rapidement culte, ce qui aide Maria à faire reconnaître son talent créatif : une force capable de voir au-delà des modes éphémères. Dès le début de sa carrière, Maria Cornejo déclarait déjà que son but était de durer dans le métier. À la fin des années 80, elle se sépare de John Richmond et s'installe en France, présentant ses grand succès ses collections pour femme à Milan et à Paris. Elle travaille également comme consultante et styliste pour la chaîne britannique des magasins Jigsaw, tout en assumant ses fonctions de directrice de la création du prêt-à-porter de Tehen. Aujourd'hui installée à New York sous la griffe Zero, avec sa propre boutique dans le quartier très tendance de NoLita (nord de Little Italy), elle continue de parfaire son esthétique de la mode à travers des créations très faciles à porter, mais toujours un peu surprenantes. Ses constructions géométriques et son approche épurée de la coupe attirent un certain type de femmes, intelligentes et ouvertes d'esprit. L'étendard du style Cornejo est donc porté par des femmes aussi admirées que la First Lady Michelle Obama, les actrices Tilda Swinton et Sigourney Weaver, ou encore Sofia Coppola et la comédienne Cindy Shermann. En 2006, Maria Cornejo remporte le prestigieux Smithsonian Cooper-Hewitt National Design Award. Son atelier et sa nouvelle boutique Zero sont désormais installés au 33 Bleecker Street à New York. Dans la collection automne/hiver 2009 notamment, Maria Cornejo et son mari, le photographe Mark Borthwick, présentent une vision toujours aussi personnelle en revenant aux influences punk goth qui ont marqué la créatrice pendant ses années d'étudiante à Londres. Distribuée dans le monde entier, de Barneys (à New York) à Isetan (au Japon), Maria Cornejo produit une mode qui fait clairement fi des différences culturelles tout en soulignant l'individualité de celles qui la portent.

JAMES ANDERSON

PHOTOGRAPHY ANETTE AURELL, STYLING ANNETT MONHEIM, MODEL ANNA VAN RAVENSTEIN, MARCH 2005

PHOTOGRAPHY MARK BORTHWICK. SUMMER 2009.

"I really enjoy translating an idea into a real product – it's energising"
FRANCISCO COSTA · CALVIN KLEIN

It's hard to imagine a young Francisco Costa growing up in the small Brazilian town where he was born, even to a family already rooted in fashion, and having even an inkling of the career he has now – a career that, in some ways, is only just starting. In the early '90s, the diminutive and cherubic immigrant arrived in New York as bright-eyed in the big city as any who had come before. He set about learning English and enrolled at the Fashion Institute of Technology, where he won the Idea Como/Young Designers of America award. After graduation, he was recruited to design dresses and knits for Bill Blass. But fate soon swept Costa towards his first big break when Oscar de la Renta asked him to oversee the signature and Pink Label collections of his own high-society house, plus Pierre Balmain haute couture and ready-to-wear. In 1998, at Tom Ford's bidding, Costa decamped for the red-hot Gucci studio, where he served as senior designer of eveningwear, a position in which he was charged with creating the custom designs for both high-rolling clients and high-profile celebrities. This is where Costa cut his teeth, acquiring the skills required to direct a major label, as he would soon do, returning to New York in 2002 to work for Calvin Klein. Here he assumed the role of creative director of the women's collections, where he remains today. Costa's first marquee Calvin Klein collection was shown in the autumn of 2003, following the departure of the namesake designer (and, as the man who invented designer denim and who in 1968 founded one of New York's mega-brands, Klein was hardly the easiest act to follow). Costa won the Council of Fashion Designers America (CFDA) award for Womenswear Designer of the Year in June 2006 as well as in June 2008. From his debut Calvin Klein collection he has garnered rave reviews across the board for his seamless integration of the label's signature minimalism with a deft vision of how fashion looks now.

Man kann sich den jungen Francisco Costa kaum vorstellen, wie er in seiner kleinen brasilianischen Heimatstadt (wenn auch als Kind einer Familie, die bereits mit Mode zu tun hat) aufwächst und noch keinen Schimmer von seiner späteren Karriere hat. Wobei diese Karriere genau genommen erst der Anfang ist. Zu Beginn der 1990er-Jahre kam er als kleiner, unschuldiger Immigrant so blauäugig wie viele andere in die Großstadt New York. Er machte sich daran, Englisch zu lernen, und schrieb sich am Fashion Institute of Technology ein, wo er später den Preis Idea Como/Young Designers of America gewann. Nach dem Studium bot sich ihm die Möglichkeit, bei Bill Blass Kleider und Strickwaren zu entwerfen. Das Schicksal bescherte Costa jedoch schon den ersten Durchbruch, als Oscar de la Renta ihm die nach ihm benannte Kollektion Oscar de la Renta und Pink Label seines High-Society-Modehauses sowie die Haute Couture und die Prêt-à-porter-Linie von Pierre Balmain anvertraute. 1998 folgte Costa dem Ruf von Tom Ford und wechselte in das damals absolut angesagte Atelier von Gucci, wo er als Chefdesigner der Abendmode fungierte. In dieser Position war er für die maßgefertigten Kreationen sowohl der betuchtesten Kunden als auch der Super-Promis

verantwortlich. Costa verdiente sich seine Sporen und eignete sich die Fähigkeiten an, die man braucht, um ein großes Label zu führen, was er auch bald tun sollte, denn 2002 kehrte er nach New York zurück, um für Calvin Klein zu arbeiten. Hier übernahm er den Posten des Creative Directors für alle Damenkollektionen, den er bis heute innehat. Costas erste unverkennbare Calvin-Klein-Kollektion wurde im Herbst 2003 gezeigt. Das war unmittelbar nach dem Ausscheiden des namengebenden Designers (der die Designerjeans erfunden und 1987 eines der New Yorker Mega-Labels gegründet hatte), in dessen Fußstapfen zu treten sicher keine leichte Aufgabe war. Costa wurde vom Council of Fashion Designers America (CFDA) im Juni 2006 und 2008 als Womenswear Designer of the Year ausgezeichnet. Seit seinem Debüt bei Calvin Klein erhielt er durchweg Bombenkritiken für die nahtlose Integration des für die Marke so typischen Minimalismus in eine überzeugende Vision dessen, was Mode heute ausmacht.

Élevé dans sa petite ville natale du Brésil (au sein d'une famille déjà établie dans la mode), le jeune Francisco Costa ne pouvait sans doute pas imaginer sa carrière actuelle qui, sous certains aspects, ne fait que commencer. Au début des années 90, ce minuscule immigrant au visage chérubin débarque à New York, les yeux pleins d'étoiles, à l'instar de tous ceux qui ont découvert la ville avant lui. Il apprend l'anglais et s'inscrit au Fashion Institute of Technology. Une fois diplômé, il dessine des robes et des pièces en maille pour Bill Blass. Mais le destin s'apprête à lui offrir sa première grande réussite : Oscar de la Renta lui demande de superviser sa collection signature et la griffe Pink Label de sa maison, si prisée par la haute société, ainsi que les lignes haute couture et prêt-à-porter de Pierre Balmain. En 1998, Tom Ford invite Costa à venir travailler dans l'atelier ultra-branché de Gucci en tant que styliste senior des tenues de soirée, où il est en charge des créations personnalisées sur mesure pour les clients les plus prestigieux et autres célébrités de premier plan. C'est là que Costa forge son style, acquérant les compétences requises pour diriger une grande marque, ce qu'il fera d'ailleurs rapidement en revenant à New York pour travailler chez Calvin Klein en 2002. Il y devient directeur de la création des collections pour femme, un poste qu'il occupe encore aujourd'hui. La première collection de Costa pour Calvin Klein est présentée à l'automne 2003, après le départ du fondateur de la maison (pas évident de reprendre le flambeau de l'homme qui a inventé le jean de créateur et fondé l'une des mégamarques new-yorkaises dès 1987). À deux reprises, en juin 2006 puis en juin 2008, Costa a reçu du Council of Fashion Designers America (CFDA) le titre de Womenswear Designer of the Year. Depuis ses débuts chez Calvin Klein, il suscite les éloges de la critique qui sait reconnaître son talent à fusionner le minimalisme, signature de la griffe, avec une vision habile de ce qu'est la mode aujourd'hui.

LEE CARTER

"I am always happy if people give my designs the time of day"
GILES DEACON

From one-time fashion illustrator to the 2004 British Fashion Awards Best New Designer, Giles Deacon bridges the gap between cutting-edge East London and high-end couture. Following an art foundation course in Harrogate, England, he graduated in fashion design from London's Central Saint Martins in 1992 – a course selected, he has said, purely for novelty value. From here, Yorkshire-born Deacon worked with Jean-Charles de Castelbajac in Paris for two years before being appointed in 1998 to a dream job: he was selected by Tom Ford, then of the Gucci Group, as head designer for the luxury accessories brand Bottega Veneta. As it turned out, the experience was a salutary one that eventually persuaded Deacon to go it alone. In 2004, he launched his first full solo collection, which he titled Disco Jacobean Fairytale. Sophisticated, feminine womenswear such as calf-length skirts, pussycat bow blouses, and '40s-style nipped-in jackets featured in his debut, which was shown during London Fashion Week, and modelled by world-famous supermodels. Deacon (born 1969) has been particularly quick to establish a glamorous signature look, one from which, he professes, there will be little deviation over the coming years. With his designs also showing an obvious leaning towards the handcrafted, Deacon is fast winning a reputation for working closely with many smaller British specialist companies – experts in their field of embroidery or beading, for instance. His prints are often inspired by Art Nouveau, which is perhaps a reflection of his ongoing interest in illustration. Deacon has also created a collection for the lingerie company Agent Provocateur. In 2006, Deacon collaborated with American Express on the Red project. Deacon introduced accessories in a two-season collaboration with Mulberry (Mulberry for Giles) and added an ongoing consultancy with high-street retailer New Look to design New Look Gold. Deacon continues to show in London, attracting the world's leading models to his catwalk.

Nachdem er es vom Modezeichner zum Best New Designer 2004 bei den British Fashion Awards gebracht hat, füllen Giles Deacons Entwürfe inzwischen genau die Lücke zwischen hippem East London und Haute Couture. Nach dem Grundstudium im englischen Harrogate machte er 1992 seinen Abschluss am Londoner Central Saint Martins. Laut eigener Aussage war für ihn allein der Reiz des Neuen ausschlaggebend für die Studienwahl. Später arbeitete der aus Yorkshire stammende Deacon zwei Jahre lang mit Jean-Charles de Castelbajac in Paris, bevor er 1998 das Angebot für einen Traumjob bekam: Tom Ford, damals noch bei Gucci, bestimmte ihn zum Chefdesigner der luxuriösen Accessoire-Marke Bottega Veneta. Diese Erfahrung war ein echter Segen, denn sie bewog Deacon, es schließlich allein zu versuchen. So lancierte er 2004 seine erste komplette Solokollektion unter dem Namen Disco Jacobean Fairytale. Raffiniert feminine Damenmode wie wadenlange Röcke, Blusen mit weichen Schleifen und Schlupfjacken im Stil der 1940er-Jahre prägten sein Debüt, das auf der Londoner Modewoche von weltberühmten Supermodels präsentiert wurde und für phänomenale Kritiken sorgte. Der 1969 gebo-

rene Deacon schaffte es in unglaublich kurzer Zeit, einen glamourösen eigenständigen Look zu entwickeln, von dem er in den nächsten Jahren auch nicht stark abzuweichen gedenkt. Seine Entwürfe zeigen ein Faible für handwerklich Anspruchsvolles. So erwarb er sich rasch den Ruf, jemand mit engen Kontakten zu vielen kleinen britischen Spezialbetrieben zu sein – Experten in den Bereichen Stickerei oder Pailletten etwa. Seine Muster sind oft vom Jugendstil inspiriert, was mit seinem nach wie vor regen Interesse an Illustrationen zusammenhängen mag. 2006 kooperierte Deacon bei dem Projekt Red mit American Express. Im Rahmen einer Kooperation über zwei Kollektionen (Mulberry for Giles) brachte Deacon Accessoires heraus. Darüber hinaus fungiert er als Berater der Nobel-Kette New Look, für die er New Look Gold designt. Deacon präsentiert weiterhin in London und schafft es, die weltweit gefragtesten Models für sich auf den Laufsteg zu bringen.

D'une expérience d'illustrateur de mode au prix de Best New Designer des British Fashion Awards 2004, les créations de Giles Deacon jettent un pont entre l'avant-garde d'East London et la haute couture de luxe. Après avoir suivi des cours à l'école d'art de Harrogate en Angleterre, il sort diplômé en mode de Central Saint Martins en 1992 : un cursus choisi, avoue-t-il, surtout pour l'attrait de la nouveauté. Ensuite, le jeune créateur du Yorkshire travaille pendant deux ans avec Jean-Charles de Castelbajac à Paris avant d'obtenir un job de rêve en 1998 : repéré par Tom Ford, qui travaille alors pour le Groupe Gucci, il est nommé styliste principal de la marque d'accessoires de luxe Bottega Veneta. Cette expérience s'avère salutaire pour Deacon, qui finit par trouver le courage de lancer sa propre griffe. En 2004, il présente une première collection complète baptisée « Disco Jacobean Fairytale » : les vêtements féminins et sophistiqués de ses débuts, tels que les jupes au mollet, les chemisiers à lavallière et les vestes cintrées très années 40, sont présentés lors de la London Fashion Week sur des top models mondialement célèbres et suscitent les louanges de la critique. Giles Deacon (né en 1969) a été particulièrement prompt à établir son glamour signature, dont il pense ne pas trop s'éloigner au cours de ces prochaines années. Avec des créations qui rendent un hommage évident au savoir-faire à l'ancienne, Deacon s'est aussi fait connaître pour ses étroites collaborations avec de petits artisans anglais, notamment des experts spécialisés dans la broderie ou les perles. Ses imprimés puisent souvent leur inspiration dans l'Art Nouveau, peut-être en référence à son intérêt de longue date pour l'illustration. En 2006, Deacon collabore avec American Express sur le projet Red. Dans le cadre d'une collaboration de deux saisons avec Mulberry, Deacon lance une ligne d'accessoires (Mulberry for Giles) et devient consultant permanent auprès du détaillant à succès New Look pour créer la ligne New Look Gold. Deacon continue de présenter ses collections à Londres avec des défilés qui attirent les plus grandes top-modèles du monde sur ses podiums.

JOSH SIMS

GILES DEACON | BORN 1969 IN DARLINGTON, ENGLAND | PHOTO BY MEL BLES, OFFENBACH MODEL MALGOSIA APRIL 2009

"I want my clothes to be exclusive, but not too exclusive"
CHRISTOPHE DECARNIN · BALMAIN

Born in the coastal town of Le Touquet in northern France, Balmain's creative director Christophe Decarnin dreamed of working in fashion from when he was a young boy. On graduating from the distinguished International Fashion University ESMOD in Paris, Decarnin consulted for various fashion houses, first as an illustrator and later as a designer, before working his way up to head designer of women's ready-to-wear at Paco Rabanne. Here he put his talents to work for ten years, before branching off to work as a consultant with several French contemporary brands in 2000. His hard work paid off and at the end of 2005, Decarnin was appointed Balmain's creative director, debuting his first collection for the heritage French fashion house in February 2006 to rapturous applause. He has since breathed new life into the label (founded in 1945 by Pierre Balmain and famed for its eveningwear), and today a heated buzz of excitement and anticipation greets every show. From the shortest, tightest Swarovski-spangled mini dress to sharp peak-shouldered military jackets (Decarnin's much copied signature shape for Balmain), again lathered in Swarovski crystals, stone-washed denim and studded high heels, Decarnin's clothes have become a byword for glamour, sophistication and after-dark cool. And, as a result, have earned their place as some of fashion's most highly coveted garments. The unremitting success meeting each of Balmain's womenswear collections provided Decarnin with the fuel he needed to relaunch Balmain Men in July 2008. The small but perfectly formed collection debuted in Paris to much critical acclaim. 2008 also saw Decarnin expand the brand to include fragrance, launching Balmain's first women's perfume, Ambre Gris, in partnership with Selective Beauty. After five years at the house, Balmain announced that Decarnin was to be succeeded by Olivier Rousteing.

Der in der nordfranzösischen Küstenstadt Le Touquet geborene Creative Director von Balmain, Christophe Decarnin, träumte schon als kleiner Junge davon, später einmal in der Modebranche zu arbeiten. Nach seinem Abschluss an der angesehenen internationalen Modeuniversität ESMOD in Paris arbeitete Decarnin für diverse Modehäuser, zunächst als Zeichner, später als Designer, bevor er sich zum Chefdesigner der Prêt-à-porter-Kollektion für Damen bei Paco Rabanne hochdiente. Dort ließ er seine Talente in den folgenden zehn Jahren wirken, bevor er ab 2000 als Berater für mehrere moderne französische Modemarken fungierte. Die harte Arbeit machte sich bezahlt, und Ende 2005 wurde Decarnin zum Creative Director bei Balmain ernannt. Seine Debütkollektion für das altehrwürdige französische Modehaus im Februar 2006 wurde mit stürmischem Applaus aufgenommen. Seither hat er dem 1945 von Pierre Balmain gegründeten Label, das berühmt für seine Abendmode ist, neues Leben eingehaucht, sodass heute vor jeder Schau größte Spannung und Vorfreude herrschen. Vom kürzesten, engsten, mit Swarovski-Steinen übersäten Minikleid bis hin zu Armeejacken mit scharf geschnittenen Schultern (Decarnins oft kopiertes Markenzeichen bei Balmain) und eben-

falls unzähligen Swarovski-Kristallen, stone-washed Jeans und High-Heels mit Glitzerbesatz – Decarnins Kleidung ist zum Synonym für Glamour, Raffinesse und After-Dark-Coolness geworden. In der Folge haben einige seiner Kreationen sich einen Platz unter den begehrtesten Stücken der Modegeschichte verdient. Der ungebrochene Erfolg jeder einzelnen von Balmains Damenkollektionen verlieh Decarnin den Antrieb, den er für den Relaunch von Balmain Men im Juli 2008 brauchte. Die kleine, aber perfekt gestaltete Kollektion stieß bei ihrem Pariser Debüt auf große Zustimmung der Kritik. 2008 kümmerte sich Decarnin außerdem um die Expansion der Marke im Bereich Duft. Mit Ambre Gris kam im Zuge einer Partnerschaft mit Selective Beauty Balmains erstes Damenparfüm auf den Markt. Bis heute gehören Decarnins Entwürfe für Balmain zu den Must-Haves in den Kleiderschränken jeder anspruchsvollen Fashionista. 2011 gab Balmain bekannt, dass Olivier Rousteing die Nachfolge Decarnins antreten wird.

Né au Touquet dans le nord de la France, Christophe Decarnin, l'actuel directeur de la création Balmain, rêvait de travailler dans la mode depuis sa plus tendre enfance. Diplômé de la prestigieuse école ESMOD à Paris, il se lance d'abord en tant que consultant auprès de plusieurs maisons, d'abord comme illustrateur puis comme créateur. Il devient ensuite styliste principal du prêt-à-porter pour femme chez Paco Rabanne, où il affûte son talent pendant dix ans. En 2000, il revient au consulting pour différentes marques françaises contemporaines. Fin 2005, il voit ses efforts récompensés quand il est nommé directeur de création chez Balmain : en février 2006, sa première collection pour la vénérable maison française soulève un tonnerre d'applaudissements. Depuis, il ne cesse de renouveler la marque (fondée en 1945 par Pierre Balmain et connue pour ses tenues de soirée), chacun de ses défilés étant désormais attendu avec beaucoup d'effervescence. Ultra-minirobe franchement moulante, brodée de cristaux Swarovski, veste militaire aux épaules pointues, également parée de galons en strass Swarovski (un modèle Balmain caractéristique de Decarnin et largement copié), denim délavé et talons aiguille cloutés, les créations de Decarnin sont devenues synonymes de glamour, de sophistication et de soirées branchées, s'octroyant une place de choix parmi les vêtements les plus convoités de la mode. Grâce à l'implacable succès de chaque collection Balmain pour femme, Christophe Decarnin trouve en juillet 2008 l'énergie nécessaire pour relancer Balmain Homme. Lors de sa présentation à Paris, une critique unanime encense cette collection courte mais savamment composée. La même année, Decarnin lance aussi Ambre Gris, le premier parfum Balmain pour femme, en partenariat avec Selective Beauty. Aujourd'hui, les créations Decarnin pour Balmain sont de véritables must-have pour les amateurs de mode les plus exigeants. En 2011, Balmain annonce qu'Olivier Rousteing prend la succession de Decarnin comme directeur artistique de la maison.

HOLLY SHACKLETON

"Fashion has a reason 'to be' because in fashion you can find new kinds of expressions about human beings"
ANN DEMEULEMEESTER

Ann Demeulemeester once told an interviewer that women are not like Barbie dolls, and that she finds a subtle femininity in men most pleasing. Inevitably, then, her own designs for both sexes are far removed from the types of clothing in which bimbos and himbos might typically attire themselves. Hers is a far more personal, subtle and emotional aesthetic, one frequently, and lazily, labelled as androgynous, but which could more accurately be termed as romantically modernist. Born in Belgium in 1959, Demeulemeester went on to study at Antwerp's Royal Academy, from which she graduated in 1981, as part of the now-legendary 'Antwerp Six' group of designers. In 1985, she launched her own label, along with her husband Patrick Robyn – a man she has cited as her biggest influence – and made her womenswear debut in Paris in 1992. By 1996, she would also be designing menswear collections. Given her long-entrenched fondness for the colour black (she has mainly clad herself in black since her Patti-Smith-loving teens) along with the severity of her earlier work, with its wilfully unfinished look, she became known as a key figure of the deconstruction era of fashion during the late '80s and early '90s. Avoiding the fickle whims and fads of the fashion industry, Demeulemeester has subsequently carved out her own unique niche, not to mention a loyal fan-base, which continues to grow. Not surprisingly, the designer now also creates extremely successful shoe and accessory lines, and her collections are sold in more than 30 countries around the world. She continues to champion clothing that favours high-quality, natural materials – leather, wool and flannels – over less covetable synthetic fabrics, and her poetic mix of edgy rebellion with sensuality, plus slick tailoring with softer layers, creates an ever-intriguing design proposition. In 2007, Demeulemeester launched her first jewellery collection, opened an Ann Demeulemeester shop in Seoul and, in 2008, reissued key pieces from the Ann Demeulemeester archives.

Ann Demeulemeester erklärte einmal in einem Interview, dass Frauen keine Barbiepuppen seien und sie eine Spur Weiblichkeit an Männern schätze. Folglich sind auch ihre Entwürfe für beide Geschlechter weit von der Art Kleidung entfernt, die Lieschen Müller und ihr männliches Pendant üblicherweise tragen. Sie besitzen eine sehr viel individuellere, raffiniertere und emotionalere Ästhetik, die oft aus Bequemlichkeit mit dem Etikett „androgyn" versehen wird. Dabei wäre romantisch-modernistisch viel treffender. Die 1959 in Belgien geborene Demeulemeester studierte an der Königlichen Akademie in Antwerpen, wo sie 1981 als Mitglied des heute legendären Designerteams Antwerp Six ihren Abschluss machte. Ihr eigenes Label präsentierte sie 1985 gemeinsam mit ihrem Ehemann Patrick Robyn den sie ihren wichtigsten Einfluss von außen nennt. Ihr Damenmoden-Debüt in Paris gab sie 1992. Ab 1996 entwarf sie auch Herrenkollektionen. Ihre lang gehegte Liebe zur Farbe Schwarz (seit ihrer Begeisterung für Patti Smith im Teenageralter kleidet sie sich hauptsächlich schwarz) sowie die Strenge der frühen Arbeiten mit ihrem absichtlich unfertigen Aussehen machten sie zu einer Schlüsselfigur der dekonstruktivistischen späten 1980er- und frühen 1990er-Jahre. Demeu-

lemeester mied die kurzlebigen Launen und Marotten der Modeindustrie und schuf sich stattdessen bald eine einzigartige Nische im Markt. Von ihrer treuen, ständig wachsenden Fangemeinde ganz zu schweigen. Deshalb überrascht es auch nicht, dass die Designerin inzwischen außerdem äußerst erfolgreich Schuhe und Accessoires entwirft und ihre Kollektionen in mehr als dreißig Ländern weltweit verkauft. Dabei gibt sie weiterhin einer Mode hoher Qualität den Vorzug, meist aus natürlichen Materialien Leder, Wolle und Flanell, kaum einmal aus synthetischen Stoffen. Mit ihrem poetischen Mix aus dezidierter Rebellion und Sinnlichkeit sowie eleganter Schneiderkunst und weichem Lagenlook gelingt ihr ein immer wieder ansprechendes designerisches Statement. 2007 brachte Demeulemeester ihre erste Schmuckkollektion heraus und eröffnete einen Laden in Seoul. Im Jahr 2008 wurden Basis-Teile aus den Ann-Demeulemeester-Archiven neu aufgelegt.

Un jour, Ann Demeulemeester a déclaré dans une interview que les femmes n'étaient pas des poupées Barbie et qu'elle adorait les hommes un peu féminins. Ses créations pour les deux sexes n'ont donc strictement rien à voir avec l'attirail dont se parent généralement les bimbos, hommes ou femmes. Son esthétique, qui se veut avant tout personnelle, subtile et émotionnelle, est souvent étiquetée d'androgyne par les journalistes paresseux, alors qu'elle relève davantage d'un certain romantisme moderne. Née en 1959 en Belgique, Ann Demeulemeester étudie la mode à l'Académie Royale d'Anvers dont elle sort diplômée en 1981, membre d'une promotion de créateurs désormais légendaires : les Six d'Anvers. Elle lance sa propre griffe en 1985 avec son mari Patrick Robyn, qu'elle considère comme sa principale influence, et présente son premier défilé pour femme en 1992 à Paris. En 1996, elle commence à dessiner des collections pour homme. Étant donné sa prédilection pour le noir (depuis sa passion adolescente pour Patti Smith, elle ne porte quasiment que du noir) et l'austérité de ses premières créations aux finitions délibérément brutes, elle émerge comme un personnage-clé de l'ère déconstructionniste de la fin des années 80 et du début des années 90. Fuyant le grand cirque des médias et de l'industrie de la mode, Ann Demeulemeester s'est imposée sur un marché de niche et revendique un nombre de fans sans cesse croissant. Rien d'étonnant à ce que les lignes de chaussures et d'accessoires qu'elle s'est mise à dessiner remportent un tel succès, ni à ce que ses collections soient vendues dans plus de 30 pays à travers le monde. Elle continue à défendre une mode privilégiant les matières naturelles de qualité supérieure (cuir, laine et flanelle) aux tissus synthétiques moins précieux. Son mélange poétique de rébellion décalée et de sensualité, conjugué à des coupes parfaites et des superpositions de tissus plus douces, produit une mode créative et toujours intrigante. En 2007, la créatrice lance sa première collection de bijoux et ouvre une boutique éponyme à Séoul. En 2008, elle réédite des pièces majeures issues des archives Ann Demeulemeester.

JAMES ANDERSON

PHOTOGRAPHY TESH. FASHION DIRECTOR EDWARD ENNINFUL. MODEL NATASHA VOJNOVIC. NOVEMBER 2001.

"We are both creative, both in a different way. We complete each other"
DOMENICO DOLCE & STEFANO GABBANA · DOLCE & GABBANA

Dolce & Gabbana are fashion's answer to Viagra: the full throbbing force of Italian style. The winning combination of Dolce's tailoring perfectionism and Gabbana's stylistic theatrics has made the label a powerhouse in today's celebrity-obsessed age and just as influential as the ambassadors of sport, music and film that they dress. Domenico Dolce was born in 1958 to a Sicilian family, his father a tailor from Palermo who taught him to make a jacket by the age of seven. Stefano Gabbana was born in 1962, the son of a Milanese print worker. But it was Sicily, Dolce's birthplace and Gabbana's favourite childhood holiday destination, that sealed a bond between them when they first met, and which has provided a reference for their aesthetic signatures ever since: the traditional Sicilian girl (opaque black stockings, black lace, peasant skirts, shawl fringing), the Latin sex temptress (corsetry, high heels, underwear as outerwear) and the Sicilian gangster (pinstripe suits, slick tailoring, fedoras). And it is the friction between these polar opposites – masculine/feminine, soft/hard and innocence/corruption – that makes Dolce & Gabbana so exciting. Established in 1985, the label continues to pay homage to such Italian film legends as Fellini, Visconti, Rossellini, Anna Magnani and Sophia Loren; in glossy art books, Dolce & Gabbana documents its own contribution to today's legends of film ('Hollywood'), music ('Music') and football ('Calcio'). They celebrated their 20th anniversary in 2005 and have now been designing for almost a quarter of a century. With an empire that includes the younger D&G line, childrenswear, swimwear, underwear, eyewear, fragrances, watches, accessories, the recently launched make-up line Dolce & Gabbana The Make-up and a global distribution through their own boutiques, Dolce & Gabbana are, quite simply, fashion's Italian stallions.

Dolce & Gabbana sind quasi die Antwort der Mode auf Viagra: die ganze pulsierende Kraft italienischer Eleganz. Die gewinnbringende Kombination aus Dolces Schneiderkunst in Perfektion und Gabbanas stilvoller Theatralik verliehen dem Label in unserer promibesessenen Zeit denselben Einfluss wie den Vertretern aus Sport, Musik und Film, die sich in D&G kleiden. Domenico Dolce wurde 1958 auf Sizilien geboren. Schon im Alter von sieben Jahren lehrte ihn sein Vater, ein Schneider aus Palermo, ein Jackett zu nähen. Der 1962 geborene Stefano Gabbana ist der Sohn eines Mailänder Setzers. Es war jedoch Sizilien, wo Dolce geboren wurde und Gabbana als Kind seine schönsten Ferien verbrachte, das die beiden von Anfang an verband. Ihre ästhetischen Markenzeichen haben seit jeher hier ihre Ursprünge: bei den traditionell streng erzogenen sizilianischen Mädchen (mit blickdichten schwarzen Strümpfen, schwarzer Spitze, Bauernröcken und Fransentüchern), beim Latino-Vamp (in Corsage, High Heels und gut sichtbar getragenen Dessous) und dem sizilianischen Gangster (in schick geschnittenem Nadelstreifenanzug und weichem Filzhut). Es sind die Brüche zwischen diesen extremen Gegensätzen – maskulin/feminin, weich/hart, unschuldig/korrupt –, die Dolce & Gab-

bana so aufregend machen. Das 1985 gegründete Label zollt zum einen italienischen Filmlegenden wie Fellini, Visconti, Rossellini, Anna Magnani und Sophia Loren Tribut und dokumentiert zum anderen in Hochglanz-Kunstbänden seinen eigenen Beitrag zu Legenden des Films („Hollywood"), der Musik („Music") und des Fußballs („Calcio"). 2005 feierten die beiden ihr 20-jähriges Jubiläum und kreieren nun schon seit einem knappen Vierteljahrhundert Mode. Mit ihrem Firmenimperium, das inzwischen die jugendlichere D&G-Linie, Kinder- und Bademode, Dessous, Brillen, Düfte, Uhren, Accessoires sowie die kürzlich auf den Markt gebrachte Make-up-Linie „Dolce & Gabbana The Make-up" umfasst, und dem weltweiten Vertrieb durch eigene Boutiquen sind Dolce & Gabbana schlichtweg die typischen italienischen Machos der Modebranche.

Cœur palpitant du style italien, Dolce & Gabbana sont la réponse de la mode au Viagra. La combinaison gagnante formée par le perfectionnisme de Dolce et le cabotinage de Gabbana a imposé la griffe comme un incontournable de notre époque obsédée par la célébrité, comme une marque aussi influente que les ambassadeurs du sport, de la musique et du cinéma qu'elle habille. Domenico Dolce est né en 1958 dans une famille sicilienne ; son père, tailleur à Palerme, lui apprend à faire une veste alors qu'il n'a que sept ans. Stefano Gabbana est né en 1962, fils d'un ouvrier d'imprimerie milanais. Patrie de Dolce et destination de vacances favorite de Gabbana lorsqu'il était enfant, c'est la Sicile qui scelle leur relation dès la première rencontre, une référence qui transparaît continuellement dans leur esthétique : la fille sicilienne traditionnelle (bas noirs opaques, dentelle noire, jupes de paysanne, franges « châle ») , la séductrice latine (corseterie, talons hauts, sous-vêtements portés en vêtements du dessus) et le gangster sicilien (costumes mille-raies, coupes élégantes, chapeaux mous). Ce sont ces oppositions de masculin et de féminin, de douceur et de dureté, d'innocence et de corruption qui rendent les créations de Dolce & Gabbana si fascinantes. Créée en 1985, la griffe continue de rendre hommage aux légendes du cinéma italien telles que Fellini, Visconti, Rossellini, Anna Magnani et Sophia Loren ; dans de superbes livres d'art, elle documente aussi sa propre contribution aux mondes du cinéma (Hollywood), de la musique (Music) et du football (Calcio). Aujourd'hui actifs depuis près d'un quart de siècle, les créateurs ont célébré les 20 ans de leur marque en 2005. Avec un empire incluant la ligne plus jeune D&G, une collection pour enfant, des maillots de bain, de la lingerie, des lunettes, des parfums (huit en tout), des montres, des accessoires, la toute nouvelle ligne de maquillage « Dolce & Gabbana The Make-up », mais aussi un réseau de distribution mondial composé de nombreuses boutiques indépendantes, Dolce & Gabbana restent, tout simplement, de vrais machos italiens.

JAMIE HUCKBODY

"I guess it's the search for perfection from season to season that moves me forward"
ALBER ELBAZ · LANVIN

Alber Elbaz is a modern romantic who found his perfect match in Lanvin, the Parisian house where he has been artistic director since 2001. His signature designs for the label – pleated silk dresses, satin ribbon details and costume jewellery – are now among the most sought-after in fashion, making his switchback route to success all the more surprising. Elbaz was born in Casablanca, Morocco, and raised in the suburbs of Tel Aviv by his mother, a Spanish artist. He studied at the Shenkar College of Textile Technology and Fashion, Tel Aviv, but received some of his most valuable training in New York, where for seven years he was right-hand man to the late Geoffrey Beene, couturier to East Coast high society. In 1996, Elbaz was appointed head of ready-to-wear for Guy Laroche in Paris, where he remained for almost three years. During November 1998, he was appointed artistic director for Yves Saint Laurent Rive Gauche, effectively taking over design duties from Saint Laurent himself. During his tenure at YSL, Elbaz attracted a younger clientele – Chloë Sevigny wore one of his dresses to the Oscars. However, at the start of 2000, the Gucci Group took control of YSL Rive Gauche and Tom Ford stepped into Elbaz's position. Following a short but successful spell at Milanese brand Krizia and time out travelling the world, in October 2001, Elbaz returned to French fashion via Lanvin, the couture house founded by Jeanne Lanvin in the 1880s. Under his creative direction, Lanvin has reestablished itself, and now includes a jewellery, shoe and handbag collection. Elbaz's own accolades reflect the brand's success and include an array of internationally recognised awards, including the CFDA International Fashion Award (2005 and 2006), the prestigious Couture Council Award for Artistry of Fashion (2007) and an award at The Fashion Group International's 24th Annual Night of Stars. For Lanvin, he continues to recommend an urban elegance of emotion and optimism.

Alber Elbaz ist ein moderner Romantiker, der bei Lanvin seine ideale Heimat gefunden hat. Seit 2001 ist er künstlerischer Direktor des Pariser Modehauses. Seine Markenzeichen bei diesem Label – plissierte Seidenkleider, Verzierungen aus Satinband und Modeschmuck – gehören inzwischen zum Gefragtesten in der Modewelt und lassen seinen Zickzackkurs zum Erfolg umso erstaunlicher erscheinen. Geboren wurde Elbaz im marokkanischen Casablanca. Seine Mutter, eine spanische Künstlerin, zog ihn in der Vorstadt von Tel Aviv groß. Am Shenkar College of Textile Technology and Fashion in Tel Aviv absolvierte Elbaz sein Studium, seine wertvollsten Erfahrungen erwarb er jedoch in den sieben Jahren in New York. Dort war er die rechte Hand des heute verstorbenen Geoffrey Beene, des legendären Couturiers der Ostküsten-High-Society. 1996 wurde Elbaz für knapp drei Jahre Chef des Prêt-à-porter-Bereichs bei Guy Laroche in Paris. Im November 1998 übernahm er praktisch von Monsieur Saint Laurent höchstpersönlich die Designerpflichten, als er zum Artistic Director von Yves Saint Laurent Rive Gauche berufen wurde. In seiner Zeit bei YSL zog er eine deutlich jüngere Klientel an – so trug etwa Chloë Sevigny bei einer Oscar-Verleihung eines seiner Kleider. Anfang 2000 machte ihm jedoch das Big Business zu schaffen, als der Gucci-Konzern

die Kontrolle über YSL Rive Gauche erwarb und Tom Ford seine Position einnahm. Es folgten ein kurzes, aber erfolgreiches Intermezzo beim Mailänder Label Krizia und eine Auszeit, in der er durch die Welt reiste. Im Oktober 2001 kehrte Elbaz über das in den 1880er-Jahren gegründete Modehaus Lanvin in die französische Couture zurück. Unter seiner Ägide hat sich Lanvin auf der internationalen Modebühne erneut als Marke etabliert, und inzwischen gehören auch eine Schmuck-, eine Schuh- sowie eine Handtaschenkollektion dazu. Elbaz' eigene Auszeichnungen spiegeln den Erfolg der Marke und umfassen international hochgeschätzte Preise wie den CFDA International Fashion Award (2005 und 2006), den angesehenen Couture Council Award for Artistry of Fashion (2007) und einen Preis bei The Fashion Group International's 24th Annual. Für Lanvin propagiert der Designer weiterhin urbane Eleganz, die auf Emotion und Optimismus baut.

Le romantique moderne Alber Elbaz a fini par trouver le job idéal chez Lanvin, maison parisienne dont il occupe la direction artistique depuis 2001. Ses créations signature pour la griffe (robes plissées en soie, détails en rubans de satin et bijoux fantaisie) comptent aujourd'hui parmi les pièces de mode les plus recherchées, ce qui rend son retour au succès d'autant plus surprenant. Né à Casablanca au Maroc, Alber Elbaz grandit auprès de sa mère, une artiste espagnole, dans la banlieue de Tel Aviv. Il étudie au Shenkar College of Textile Technology and Fashion de Tel Aviv, mais c'est New York qui lui offre sa formation la plus précieuse : pendant sept ans, Elbaz sera le bras droit de feu Geoffrey Beene, le couturier de l'élite de la côte est. En 1996, il est nommé directeur de la création du prêt-à-porter chez Guy Laroche à Paris, où il passe près de trois ans. En novembre 1998, il devient directeur artistique d'Yves Saint Laurent Rive Gauche, succédant avec efficacité à Monsieur Saint Laurent en personne. Pendant cette période, Elbaz réussit à attirer une clientèle plus jeune : Chloë Sevigny portera l'une de ses robes pour la nuit des Oscars. Mais au début de l'an 2000, le groupe Gucci prend le contrôle d'YSL Rive Gauche et remplace Elbaz par Tom Ford. Après avoir travaillé avec succès pour la maison milanaise Krizia pendant quelques mois et pris un congé sabbatique pour voyager à travers le monde, Elbaz fait son retour dans la mode parisienne en octobre 2001 via Lanvin, maison de haute couture fondée par Jeanne Lanvin dans les années 1880. Sous sa direction, celle-ci retrouve la place qui lui revient sur la scène mondiale de la mode. Lanvin propose désormais une collection de bijoux, de chaussures et de sacs à main. À travers tout un éventail de prix mondialement reconnus, dont l'International Fashion Award du CFDA (2005 et 2006), le prestigieux Couture Council Award for Artistry of Fashion (2007) et une récompense à la 24e édition annuelle des Fashion Group International Awards, les honneurs rendus à Alber Elbaz reflètent le succès de Lanvin. Aujourd'hui, il continue à prescrire une élégance urbaine empreinte d'émotion et d'optimisme.

SUSIE RUSHTON

"When I design, sometimes I have sensations which I could call 'visionary'"
SILVIA VENTURINI FENDI · FENDI

Fendi is a house of extremes: big furs and little handbags, a family business with a worldwide reputation, a chic past and a street-cool future. Established in 1925, the Fendi empire was founded by Adele Fendi from a small leather-goods shop and workroom in Rome, where she and her husband, Eduardo, worked with private clients. The family business expanded with the opening of a larger shop in 1946, but it wasn't until the death of Eduardo, eight years later, that the modern Fendi image emerged, when the family's five daughters injected the little company with some youthful glamour. After the death of Adele in 1978, each sister adopted a corner of the empire to look after. Paola (born 1931) worked with the furs, Anna (born 1933) the leather goods, Franca (born 1935) the customer relations, Carla (born 1937) the business co-ordination, and Alda (born 1940) the sales. By the end of the '80s, the name of Fendi had become shorthand for jet-set elitist luxury, thanks to its signature furs and instantly recognisable double-'F' logo (designed by Karl Lagerfeld). The politically correct '90s saw the company refocus on Adele Fendi's traditional leather goods, and so the Baguette bag was reborn and Fendi's star was in the ascendant yet again. Amid the late '90s' appetite for baroque excess, LVMH and Prada bought a 51 per cent stake in the label, with LVMH eventually becoming the sole partner in 2001. But Fendi is still very much a family business. The future lies with Silvia Venturini Fendi (born 1960, the daughter of Anna Fendi), who created the Fendissime line in 1987 and is now head designer of Fendi accessories. Karl Lagerfeld, as Creative Director, continues to work with the sisters – as he has done since 1965.

Fendi ist ein Modehaus der Extreme: mit opulenten Pelzen und winzigen Handtaschen, ein Familienbetrieb vom Weltruf, einer eleganten Vergangenheit und zeitgemäß cooler Zukunft. Das Fendi-Imperium wurde 1925 von Adele Fendi gegründet, in einem kleinen römischen Laden für Lederwaren mit angeschlossener Werkstatt. Dort arbeiteten sie und ihr Mann für einen kleinen Kreis von Privatkunden. 1946 expandierte das Familienunternehmen mit der Eröffnung eines größeren Geschäfts. Das moderne Image von Fendi begann sich jedoch erst acht Jahre später nach dem Tod von Eduardo Fendi herauszukristallisieren, als die fünf Töchter jugendlichen Charme in die Firma brachten. Nachdem 1978 auch Adele gestorben war, übernahm jede der Schwestern einen eigenen Bereich: die 1931 geborene Paola die Pelzabteilung, die 1933 geborene Anna die Lederwaren, die 1935 geborene Franca Werbung und PR, die 1937 geborene Carla die Finanzen und die 1940 geborene Alda den Verkauf. Ende der 1980er-Jahre war der Name Fendi dank der typischen Pelze und dem

unverwechselbaren Logo aus zwei Fs (eine Idee von Karl Lagerfeld) zum Synonym für elitären Luxus des Jet-Set avanciert. In den 1990er-Jahren mit ihrer Political Correctness besann man sich wieder verstärkt auf Adele Fendis traditionelle Lederwaren, entdeckte die Baguette-Tasche neu, und Fendis Stern stieg erneut. Angesichts der Lust an barocker Üppigkeit Ende der 1990er-Jahre kauften zunächst LVMH und Prada 51 Prozent des Unternehmens; seit 2001 ist LVMH einziger Partner. Trotzdem hat Fendi noch viel von einem Familienbetrieb. Die Zukunft liegt in den Händen von Silvia Venturini Fendi (der 1960 geborenen Tochter von Anna Fendi). Sie gründete 1987 die Linie Fendissime und ist heute Chefdesignerin der Fendi-Accessoires. Als Creative Director arbeitet Karl Lagerfeld weiterhin mit den Schwestern – seit nunmehr fast einem halben Jahrhundert.

Fendi est la marque des extrêmes : grosses fourrures et petits sacs à main, affaire familiale et réputation internationale, passé chic et avenir « street-cool ». L'empire Fendi a été fondé en 1925 par Adele Fendi à partir du petit atelier de maroquinerie de Rome où elle travaillait pour une clientèle privée avec son mari Eduardo. La petite affaire familiale se développe grâce à l'ouverture d'une plus grande boutique en 1946, mais ce n'est que huit ans plus tard, à la mort d'Eduardo, que naît l'image moderne de Fendi, lorsque leurs cinq filles commencent à insuffler tout leur glamour et leur jeunesse à l'entreprise. Quand Adele meurt en 1978, chaque sœur hérite d'un morceau de l'empire : Paola (née en 1931) s'occupe des fourrures, Anna (née en 1933) de la maroquinerie, Franca (née en 1935) des relations avec les clients, Carla (née en 1937) des finances et Alda (née en 1940) des ventes. À la fin des années 80, le nom Fendi est devenu synonyme de luxe élitiste et jet-set grâce à ses fourrures signature et à son logo en double F immédiatement identifiable (dessiné par Karl Lagerfeld). Pendant les années 90, ère du politiquement correct, l'entreprise ressort les sacs d'Adele Fendi : la Baguette est ressuscitée et l'étoile de Fendi remonte au firmament. L'appétit pour les excès baroques de la fin des années 90 voit LVMH et Prada racheter 51 % de la griffe, mais c'est LVMH qui finit par en devenir l'unique partenaire en 2001. Toutefois, Fendi reste encore une affaire très familiale : son avenir repose sur les épaules de Silvia Venturini Fendi (née en 1960, fille d'Anna Fendi), à l'origine de la ligne Fendissime en 1987 et qui occupe aujourd'hui la direction du département Accessoires de Fendi. Karl Lagerfeld, directeur de la création, continue à travailler pour les sœurs, comme il fait depuis 1965.

JAMIE HUCKBODY

"I try to transform a dream's magic into reality"
ALBERTA FERRETTI

As a woman famed for her fragile little dresses blown together from raw-edged chiffon, appliquéd ribbon and intricate rivulets of beading, Alberta Ferretti is an unlikely player in the boardroom wars of the world's luxury goods groups. Yet Aeffe SpA, the company she founded in 1980 with her brother Massimo as chairman, now owns the controlling stake in Moschino and brokered production and distribution deals with Jean Paul Gaultier (1994) and Narciso Rodriguez (1997). As well as Alberta Ferretti and her successful diffusion line, Philosophy di Alberta Ferretti, Aeffe owns swimwear/lingerie label Velmar and fashion label Pollini. Born in 1950 in Cattolica, Italy, Ferretti is the daughter of a dressmaker and was raised assisting in her mother's atelier. Not for her are the sharp, tight and angular silhouettes of the male Parisian couturiers. Ferretti was inspired instead by a lyrical femininity and fluidity as celebrated in the Fellini movies being made around Cattolica in the 1950s. At the age of 18, Ferretti opened a boutique in her hometown and in 1974 unveiled her own label. 1980 saw Alberta and Massimo go into business together. Alberta Ferretti's debut on the catwalk in Milan came in 1981 with sheer, ethereal chiffons and pin-tucked satin dresses. In 1994, Aeffe annexed the medieval village of Montegridolfo as its Italian headquarters. More than a decade later, her delicate, romantic but modern take on fashion is as relevant as it was when she started; with the label growing in size to include Alberta Ferretti Girls, a childrenswear line, a hugely successful diffusion line, Philosophy, a stylish eyewear range in conjunction with Elite Group SpA, and most recently an Alberta Ferretti fragrance with Elizabeth Arden.

Diese Frau, die für ihre zarten Kleidchen aus ungesäumtem Chiffon mit applizierten Bändern und raffinierten Perlenstickereien bekannt ist, kann man sich als Kämpferin auf dem Schlachtfeld der Luxuswarenkonzerne kaum vorstellen. Dabei besitzt Aeffe SpA, die 1980 mit Bruder Massimo als Geschäftsführer gegründete Firma, inzwischen die Mehrheit bei Moschino und blickt auf Produktions- und Vertriebskooperationen mit Jean Paul Gaultier (1994) und Narciso Rodriguez (1997) zurück. Neben dem Label Alberta Ferretti und der erfolgreichen Nebenlinie Philosophy di Alberta Ferretti gehört Aeffe auch noch das Bademoden- und Dessoushaus Velmar sowie das Modelabel Pollini. Ferretti kam 1950 im italienischen Cattolica als Tochter einer Schneiderin zur Welt und half schon in ihrer Kindheit im mütterlichen Atelier. Die scharfen, harten und geometrischen Silhouetten der Pariser Couturiers waren noch nie ihre Sache. Ferretti ließ sich stattdessen von einer lyrischen Weiblichkeit und den weichen Konturen inspirieren, wie sie in den Fellini-Filmen gefeiert wurden, die in den 1950er-Jahren in der Gegend um Cattolica

gedreht wurden. Mit 18 eröffnete Ferretti in ihrer Heimatstadt einen Laden, 1974 präsentierte sie ihr eigenes Label. 1980 schließlich taten sich die Geschwister Alberta und Massimo geschäftlich zusammen. Ihr Debüt auf dem Laufsteg gab Alberta 1981 in Mailand mit hauchdünnen ätherischen Chiffonkleidchen und mit Stecknadeln gerafften Satinroben. 1994 erkor Aeffe das mittelalterliche Städtchen Montegridolfo zu seinem Firmensitz in Italien. Fünfzehn Jahre danach besitzt Ferrettis zarte, romantische, aber dennoch moderne Mode nach wie vor dasselbe Gewicht wie zu Beginn ihrer Karriere. Das beständig wachsende Label umfasst inzwischen auch die Kindermarke Alberta Ferretti Girls, eine ungeheuer erfolgreiche Nebenlinie namens Philosophy, elegante Brillen in Kooperation mit Elite Group SpA sowie das erst kürzlich bei Elizabeth Arden auf den Markt gekommene Parfüm Alberta Ferretti.

Réputée pour ses délicates petites robes en mousseline de soie aux finitions brutes, applications de rubans et rivières de perles très élaborées, Alberta Ferretti fait figure de personnage improbable au sein des guerres que se livrent les conseils d'administration des grands groupes de luxe mondiaux. Pourtant, Aeffe SpA, l'entreprise qu'elle fonde en 1980 avec son frère Massimo au poste de président, possède aujourd'hui une part majoritaire dans la société Moschino et a conclu des accords de production et de distribution avec Jean Paul Gaultier (1994) et Narciso Rodriguez (1997). Aux côtés de la griffe Alberta Ferretti et de sa ligne à succès Philosophy di Alberta Ferretti, Aeffe possède la marque de maillots de bain et de lingerie Velmar, ainsi que le label de mode Pollini. Fille de couturière, Alberta Ferretti est née en 1950 à Cattolica en Italie et grandit dans l'atelier de sa mère dont elle est aussi l'assistante. Les silhouettes acérées, angulaires et restreintes des couturiers parisiens ne la séduisent pas. Elle s'inspire au contraire de la féminité lyrique et de la fluidité célébrées dans les films que Fellini tourne dans la région de Cattolica dans les années 1950. À 18 ans, Alberta Ferretti ouvre une boutique dans sa ville natale avant de lancer sa propre griffe en 1974. En 1980, Alberta et Massimo s'associent en affaires. Pour son premier défilé à Milan en 1981, Alberta Ferretti présente des robes transparentes et aériennes en mousseline de soie et en satin nervuré. En 1994, Aeffe installe son siège italien dans le village médiéval de Montegridolfo. Quinze ans plus tard, sa mode délicate et romantique mais néanmoins moderne n'a rien perdu de sa pertinence. Sa griffe s'est née en 1950 à Cattolica en Italie, une collection pour enfant, la ligne à succès Philosophy plus accessible, une gamme de lunettes très stylées conçue en collaboration avec Elite Group SpA, et tout récemment, le parfum Alberta Ferretti avec Elizabeth Arden.

JAMES SHERWOOD

PHOTOGRAPHY KAYT JONES. STYLING BELÉN CASADEVALL. MODEL LIBERTY ROSS. APRIL, 2001.

ALBERTA FERRETTI

"I'm more of a patternmaker than a designer"
LIMI FEU

Limi Feu, born Limi Yamamoto to the acclaimed Japanese fashion designer Yohji Yamamoto, grew up with fashion in her DNA. Born in Fukuoka in southern Japan, Limi moved to Tokyo in 1994 to enrol at the acclaimed Bunka Fashion College. Two years later, she began her official training as a patternmaker for Yohji's diffusion line, Y's. Here she perfected her skills, before branching out on her own as a designer in 1999 with Y's bis LIMI, presenting her first collection for Autumn/Winter 2000–2001 at the Garden Hall in Ebisu, Tokyo. With Yohji as her mentor, the collection was naturally a success and, in 2002, Limi changed the label's name from Y's bis LIMI to Limi Feu, 'feu' meaning 'fire' in French. The change in name not only mirrored her passion but marked a new direction for the young Japanese designer, with Limi establishing Limi Yamamoto Inc. soon after, in 2006. After several successful shows in Tokyo, Limi moved the collection to Paris to show her debut collection for Spring/Summer 2008 at the Garage Turenne. Highly anticipated by the international press, the collection did not disappoint, firmly establishing Limi's position at the forefront of a new wave of Japanese designers. From Yohji she inherited her conceptual use of layering, asymmetry and a predominantly monochromatic palette. But that is where the similarities end. Limi's love of oversized proportions, and masculine/feminine interplay, place her firmly in a league of her own – a position that was cemented in 2008, when she received the prestigious Designer of the Year award from The 51st Fashion Editor's Club of Japan. Based in Nishi-Azabu in Tokyo, Limi Feu has since expanded her business to include three flagship stores around the city.

Limi Feu, geborene Yamamoto, ist die Tochter des gefeierten japanischen Designers Yohji Yamamoto und wuchs bereits mit Mode in ihrer DNA auf. Von ihrem Geburtsort Fukuoka im Süden Japans zog sie 1994 nach Tokio, um sich am berühmten Bunka Fashion College einzuschreiben. Zwei Jahre später begann sie ihre offizielle Ausbildung in der Schnittabteilung von Yamamotos Nebenlinie Y's. Dort perfektionierte sie ihre Fähigkeiten, bevor sie sich 1999 mit Y's bis LIMI als eigenständige Designerin versuchte und ihre erste Kollektion, Herbst/Winter 2000/2001, in der Ebisu Garden Hall in Tokio präsentierte. Mit ihrem Vater als Mentor war die Kollektion selbstverständlich ein Erfolg, und 2002 änderte Limi den Namen des Labels von Y's bis LIMI in Limi Feu, nach dem französischen Wort für „Feuer". Diese Änderung sollte nicht nur ihre Leidenschaft zum Ausdruck bringen, sondern auch die Neuausrichtung der jungen japanischen Designerin kennzeichnen, die im Jahr 2006 die Limi Yamamoto Inc. gründete. Nach einigen erfolgreichen Schauen in Tokio

zog Limi mit ihrer Kollektion nach Paris, wo sie mit ihrer Frühjahr-/Sommerkollektion 2008 ihr Debüt in der Garage Turenne gab. Von der internationalen Presse mit reichlich Vorschusslorbeeren bedacht, enttäuschte sie nicht, sondern festigte ihre Position an der Spitze einer neuen Generation japanischer Designer. Von ihrem Vater Yohji Yamamoto hat sie die konzeptionelle Vorliebe für Lagen, Asymmetrie und eine vornehmlich monochrome Farbpalette geerbt. Doch damit endet die Ähnlichkeit auch schon. Limis Faible für überdimensionale Proportionen und das Wechselspiel zwischen maskulin und feminin hat ihr eine solide Eigenständigkeit eingebracht. Gefestigt wurde diese Position nicht zuletzt 2008, als sie vom 51st Fashion Editor's Club of Japan mit dem angesehenen Preis Designer of the Year ausgezeichnet wurde. Der Firmensitz liegt im Tokioter Viertel Nishi-Azabu, allerdings hat Limi Feu ihre Geschäfte inzwischen auf drei Flagship-Stores an verschiedenen Stellen der Stadt ausgedehnt.

Fille du brillant créateur japonais Yohji Yamamoto, Limi Feu est née avec le gène de la mode dans son ADN. Originaire de Fukuoka au sud du Japon, elle s'installe à Tokyo en 1994 pour suivre des études au prestigieux Bunka Fashion College. Deux ans plus tard, elle entame sa formation pratique et se perfectionne dans l'art du traçage de patrons pour Y's, la ligne de diffusion de Yohji Yamamoto. En 1999, elle se lance en tant que styliste avec la griffe Y's bis LIMI et présente sa première collection automne/hiver 2000 – 2001 au Garden Hall d'Ebisu à Tokyo. Avec un mentor tel que Yohji, Limi remporte évidemment un grand succès et rebaptise sa griffe Limi Feu en 2002. Référence littérale au terme français, ce changement de nom reflète sa passion tout en ouvrant un nouveau chapitre dans la carrière de la jeune créatrice japonaise, qui fonde Limi Yamamoto Inc. en 2006. Après plusieurs défilés acclamés à Tokyo, Limi fait son « baptême du feu » à Paris en présentant sa collection printemps/été 2008 au Garage Turenne. Loin de décevoir la presse internationale, cette collection très attendue installe fermement Limi à l'avant-garde de la nouvelle vague de créateurs nippons. De son père, elle a hérité un usage conceptuel des superpositions, l'asymétrie et une palette principalement monochrome, mais ce sont bien là leurs seules similitudes. Le penchant de Limi pour les proportions exagérées et les interactions masculin/féminin la classe dans une catégorie à part entière, une originalité distinguée en 2008 par le prestigieux prix de Designer of the Year remis lors de la 51ᵉ édition du Fashion Editor's Club of Japan. Depuis son Q.G. de Nishi-Azabu à Tokyo, Limi Feu a développé son activité en ouvrant trois boutiques à travers la ville.

HOLLY SHACKLETON

PHOTOGRAPHY TERRY JONES. AUTUMN/WINTER 2009.

"I like to think that I brought a certain hedonism back to fashion"
TOM FORD

Tom Ford has redefined the role of fashion designer. Born in Austin, Texas, in 1961, he spent his teenage years in Santa Fe, New Mexico, before enrolling in an art history course at New York University. In Manhattan, Ford's extracurricular activities included acting in TV advertisements and hanging out at both Studio 54 and Warhol's Factory. He eventually transferred to Parsons School of Design in New York and Paris, studying architecture, but by the end of the course, Ford had realised that he wanted to work in fashion. In 1986, back in New York, he joined the design studio of Cathy Hardwick, moving to Perry Ellis two years later as design director. In 1990, Ford became womenswear designer at Gucci. In 1994, he was made creative director at Gucci and the following March showed a landmark collection. His velvet hipster trousers and jewel-coloured satin shirts – unbuttoned to the navel and impossibly lean – were part of a slick, alluring package of unapologetic flash and sex appeal. Almost overnight, Gucci became a byword for desirability, offering the most aspirational and hedonistic kind of fashion. When the Gucci Group purchased Yves Saint Laurent in January 2000, Ford began designing menswear and womenswear for Yves Saint Laurent Rive Gauche. In 2002, he was awarded Accessory Designer of the Year for his work, and soon earned the titles of both creative director of the Gucci Group, and vice-chairman of the management board of Gucci Group. In 2004, Ford left the company and exactly one year later announced the creation of the Tom Ford brand, which today includes luxury men's ready-to-wear and made-to-measure clothing, footwear and accessories, in addition to an award-winning eyewear label in conjunction with the Marcolin Group, and a glossy men's fragrance and beauty range with Estée Lauder. Ford opened his flagship store in New York in 2007. His success as a designer and a personality increases with every passing year. He has received dozens of industry awards, including four from the prestigious CFDA and five from the VH1/Vogue Fashion Awards. Meticulous in his own personal appearance, Ford has also been recognised for his personal style, winning 'Elle' magazine's Style Icon Award and GQ's International Man of the Year Award. In 2009, Ford made his film directorial debut with the highly acclaimed A Single Man, which was nominated for an Academy Award and Golden Globe, subsequently winning a BAFTA. Is there no end to this man's talents!

Tom Ford hat die Rolle des Modeschöpfers neu definiert. Er wurde 1961 in Austin, Texas, geboren und studierte Architektur an der Parsons School of Design in New York und in Paris, doch gegen Ende der Ausbildung erkannte Ford, dass er eigentlich in der Modebranche arbeiten wollte. 1986 schloss er sich, nach New York zurückgekehrt, dem Designatelier von Cathy Hardwick an. Zwei Jahre später ging er als Design Director zu Perry Ellis. 1990 wurde er Designer für Damenmode bei Gucci. Dort wurde Ford 1994 zum Creative Director befördert und zeigte im darauf folgenden März eine Kollektion, die den Wendepunkt darstellen sollte. Seine Hüfthosen aus Samt und Satinblusen in Edelsteintönen – bis zum Nabel aufgeknöpft und unglaublich schmal geschnitten – waren Teil eines raffinierten, verführerischen, keineswegs zurückhaltenden sexy Looks. Fast über Nacht wurde Gucci zum Synonym für Begehrlichkeit, zu einem Label, das die ambitionierteste und hedonistischste Mode von allen bot. Als der Gucci-Konzern im Januar 2000 Yves Saint Laurent kaufte, begann Ford, Herren- und Damenmode für Yves Saint Laurent Rive Gauche zu entwerfen. Im Jahr 2002 wurde er für seine Arbeit als Accessory Designer of the Year ausgezeichnet und avancierte bald zum Creative Director sowie zum stellvertretenden Vorstandsvorsitzenden des Gucci-Konzerns. 2004 verließ Ford das Unternehmen und gab genau ein Jahr später die Gründung der Marke Tom Ford bekannt, die heute luxuriöse Prêt-à-porter sowie Maß-Mode für Herren umfasst, dazu Schuhwerk, Accessoires, inklusive eines preisgekrönten Brillenlabels in Zusammenarbeit mit der Marcolin Group sowie ein glanzvolles Duft- und Beauty-Sortiment für Herren unter dem Dach von Estée Lauder. Den eigenen Flagship-Store in New York eröffnete Ford 2007. Sein Erfolg als Designer und als Persönlichkeit wächst mit jedem Jahr. Ford hat Dutzende Branchenpreise gewonnen, darunter vier der angesehenen CFDA und fünf VH1/Vogue Fashion Awards. Sorgsam auf seine persönliche Erscheinung bedacht, wurde Ford auch für seinen eigenen Stil schon ausgezeichnet, mit dem Style Icon Award der Zeitschrift Elle und mit GQ's International Man of the Year Award. 2009 gab er sein Debüt als Regisseur des hochgelobten Films „A Single Man", der eine Oscar-Nominierung erhielt und für den Golden Globe vorgeschlagen war, bevor er schließlich von der BAFTA ausgezeichnet wurde. Was kann dieser Mann eigentlich nicht!

Tom Ford a redéfini le rôle du créateur de mode. Né en 1961, Tom Ford étudie l'architecture à la Parsons School of Design de New York puis à Paris. Ce n'est qu'à la fin de ses études que Ford prend enfin conscience de sa vocation. En 1986, il rejoint à New York le studio de création de Cathy Hardwick puis part travailler deux ans plus tard chez Perry Ellis comme directeur de la création. En 1990, il devient styliste pour femme chez Gucci, puis est nommé directeur de la création en 1994 et présente en mars une collection séduisante et maline, au sex-appeal sans complexe, qui fait date : pantalons taille basse en velours et chemises en satin aux couleurs de pierres précieuses, déboutonnées jusqu'au nombril et très près du corps. Quasiment du jour au lendemain, Gucci devient une marque indispensable en proposant la mode la plus désirable et la plus hédoniste du moment. Quand le groupe Gucci rachète Yves Saint Laurent en janvier 2000, Ford commence à concevoir les collections pour homme et pour femme Yves Saint Laurent Rive Gauche. En 2002, son travail sur les accessoires lui vaut le titre d'Accessory Designer of the Year. Il devient rapidement directeur de la création et vice-président du conseil d'administration du groupe Gucci qu'il quitte en 2004. Exactement un an plus tard, il annonce la création de la marque Tom Ford – prêt-à-porter de luxe et sur mesure pour homme, chaussures, accessoires, un parfum et une gamme de produits cosmétiques pour homme avec Estée Lauder.

En 2007, Tom Ford ouvre sa boutique phare à New York. Son succès de créateur de mode star. augmente chaque année. Il reçoit des dizaines de prix, dont quatre du prestigieux CFDA et cinq des VH-1/Vogue Fashion Awards. Très soigneux de sa propre apparence, Ford a aussi été distingué pour son style personnel par un Style Icon Award du magazine Elle et par le titre d'International Man of the Year de GQ. En 2009, il fait ses débuts en tant que réalisateur avec le film A single Man, encensé par la critique, nominé aux Oscars, proposé au Golden Globe et récompensé par la BAFTA. Y a-t-il un domaine où cet homme ne sait pas faire ?

"Creations from a fresh and innovative vision, which are free from the existing theories of making clothes"
DAI FUJIWARA · ISSEY MIYAKE

Dai Fujiwara joined the Issey Miyake Design Studio in 1994, after graduating from Tokyo's Tama Art University in textile design. As part of Miyake's collection staff, he collaborated with Miyake on the A-POC (A Piece of Cloth) project, which wowed editors, journalists and buyers alike when 23 models appeared on the Paris catwalk in 1998 connected by one tube of fabric. For his work on A-POC, Fujiwara was awarded the Good Design Grand Prize in 2000 and was nominated for the Mainichi Design Award in 2003. Three years later, his continued dedication to fabric research and development culminated in his appointment as creative director of the Issey Miyake collections, with Fujiwara unleashing his debut collection 'Rondo' for Autumn/Winter 2007. Just like Miyake, Fujiwara enjoys collaborating with artists and product designers across the globe. Spring/Summer 2008 saw him join forces with James Dyson – inventor of the dual cyclone vacuum cleaner – on an atmospheric wind stage set. For his Autumn/Winter 2008 collection, Apocalyptic Lovers, the maverick designer took part in Finland's 5th International Alvar Aalto Design Seminar 'It's a Beautiful Day', working closely with some of the world's most renowned design companies to visualise and kit out the wedding of an ordinary Finnish couple. Always one to think outside the box, Fujiwara goes to great lengths to research the theme of his collection, flying a part of his design team to the Amazon rainforest to research 'real colour' for his Spring/Summer 2009 collection Colour Hunting. Autumn/Winter 2009 saw the Japanese designer recruit Karate Kata masters as models to accurately demonstrate the high-performance quality of his clothing. The Issey Miyake men's collections continue to be shown in the Paris showroom in Place des Vosges twice yearly. August 2009 marked the much-awaited launch of Issey Miyake's new fragrance, A Scent. Housed in a slick glass bottle designed by Paris-based designer Arik Levy, the fragrance arrived 17 years after the huge success of L'Eau D'Issey. Yoshiyuki Miyamae was appointed as head womenswear designer, following the departure of Fujiwara in February 2011.

Dai Fujiwara fing 1994 im Issey Miyake Design Studio an, nachdem er seinen Abschluss in Textildesign an der Tokioter Tama Art University gemacht hatte. Als Mitglied von Miyakes Kollektionsteam war er an dessen Projekt A-POC (A Piece of Cloth) beteiligt, das Journalisten und Einkäufer gleichermaßen begeisterte, als 1998 auf einem Pariser Catwalk 23 Models auftraten, die alle durch einen Stoffschlauch miteinander verbunden waren. Für seine Arbeit an A-POC wurde Fujiwara 2000 mit dem Good Design Grand Prize ausgezeichnet und 2003 für den Mainichi Design Award nominiert. Drei Jahre später fand seine anhaltende Hingabe zur Materialforschung und -entwicklung ihren Höhepunkt in der Ernennung zum Creative Director der Kollektionen von Issey Miyake. Seine Debütkollektion in dieser Position war „Rondo" für Herbst/Winter 2007. Ganz wie Miyake hat auch Fujiwara seine Freude an der Zusammenarbeit mit Künstlern und Produktdesignern aus aller Welt. Für Frühjahr/Sommer 2008 tat er sich etwa mit James Dyson – dem Erfinder des Dual-Zyklon-Staubsaugers – zusammen, um eine atmosphärereiche Bühne mit viel Wind zu kreieren. Für „Apocalyptic Lovers", seine Kollektion für Herbst/Winter

2008, nahm der rebellische Designer an Finnlands 5. Internationalem Alvar-Aalto-Design-Seminar „It's a Beautiful Day" teil und arbeitete eng mit einigen der bekanntesten Designfirmen der Welt zusammen, um die Hochzeit eines ganz normalen finnischen Paares zu visualisieren und auszustatten. Als passionierter Querdenker scheut Fujiwara keine Mühen, um das Thema einer Kollektion zu erforschen. So ließ er etwa einen Teil seines Designteams in den Regenwald am Amazonas fliegen, um dort „echte Farben" für seine Kollektion „Colour Hunting" für Frühjahr/Sommer 2009 zu studieren. Für Herbst/Winter 2009 rekrutierte der japanische Designer dagegen Karate-Kämpferinnen als Models, um die Strapazierfähigkeit seiner Kleidung anschaulich zu demonstrieren. Die Herrenkollektionen von Issey Miyake werden weiterhin zweimal jährlich im Pariser Showroom an der Place des Vosges gezeigt. Im August 2009 kam A Scent, der neue Duft von Issey Miyake auf den Markt: in einer Glasflasche, die der Designer Arik Levy entworfen hat. Er soll an den Riesenerfolg von L'Eau d'Issey vor 17 Jahren anknüpfen. Yoshiyuki Miyamae wurde als Nachfolger von Fujiwara im Februar 2011 zum Chefdesigner für Damenmode ernannt.

Dai Fujiwara rejoint le studio de création Issey Miyake en 1994, après avoir obtenu son diplôme en design textile de la Tama Art University de Tokyo. Membre de l'équipe en charge des collections, il collabore avec Miyake sur le projet A-POC (A Piece of Cloth) qui laisse rédacteurs et acheteurs sans voix devant 23 mannequins défilant reliées par un tube de tissu en 1998 à Paris. Son travail sur A-POC lui vaut le Good Design Grand Prize en 2000 et une nomination au Mainichi Design Award en 2003. Trois ans plus tard, son dévouement à la recherche et au développement de tissus est récompensé par son accession au poste de directeur de la création des collections Issey Miyake : Fujiwara présente sa première collection baptisée « Rondo » pour l'automne/hiver 2007. Tout comme Miyake, Fujiwara aime collaborer avec des artistes et designers du monde entier. Pour le printemps/été 2008, il travaille avec James Dyson – inventeur de l'aspirateur cyclonique sans sac – sur la création d'un podium balayé par le vent. Pour « Apocalyptic Lovers », en automne/hiver 2008, le créateur dissident participe à « It's a Beautiful Day », le 5e Séminaire international Alvar Aalto en Finlande, où il imagine et crée des objets de mariage d'un couple finnois ordinaire. Privilégiant systématiquement le décalage, Fujiwara est prêt à tout pour trouver le thème de ses collections : pour « Colour Hunting », au printemps/été 2009, il emmène son équipe dans la forêt amazonienne en quête de « vraies couleurs ». Pour la collection automne/hiver 2009, le créateur japonais recrute des maîtres de karaté comme mannequins et démontre ainsi la qualité et les hautes performances de ses vêtements. Les collections pour homme Issey Miyake sont présentées deux fois par an dans le showroom parisien de la griffe place des Vosges. Au mois d'août est lancé A Scent, le nouveau parfum très attendu d'Issey Miyake : dans un flacon en verre épuré conçu par le designer parisien Arik Levy, il fait suite à L'Eau D'Issey, immense succès depuis 17 ans. En février 2011, Yoshiyuki Miyamae succède à Fujiwara comme styliste principal de la collection pour femme.

JAMES SHERWOOD

"I am here to make people dream, to seduce them into buying beautiful clothes and to strive to make amazing clothing to the best of my ability. That is my duty"
JOHN GALLIANO

John Galliano is one of Britain's fashion heroes. Born in 1960 to a working-class Gibraltan family, Galliano lived on the island until he left at the age of six for south London. But it was the young Juan Carlos Antonio's early life, with its religious ceremonies and sun-drenched culture, which has proved a constant inspiration for Galliano; stylistic eclecticism wedded to the Latin tradition of 'dressing-up' has become his signature. Having attended Wilson's Grammar School for boys, Galliano won a place at Central Saint Martins, graduating in 1984. And it was that graduation collection – inspired by the French Revolution and titled 'Les Incroyables' – that was bought by Joan Burstein of Browns, catapulting the young designer into the spotlight. In 1990 – after suffering a period notorious for problems with backers and collections deemed 'uncommercial' because they dared to dream beyond the conventional – Galliano started to show in Paris, moving to the city in 1992. A champion of the romantic bias-cut dress and the dramatic tailoring of '50s couture at a time when minimalism and grunge dominated fashion, it was announced in 1995 that Galliano would succeed Hubert de Givenchy at the dusty maison de couture. Two seasons later, and with an unprecedented four British Designer of the Year awards under his belt, Galliano became creative director at Christian Dior, presenting his first collection for the Spring/Summer 1997 haute couture show. Since then, Galliano has financially and creatively revitalised the house, while continuing to design his own collections for men and women in Paris, a city where he is accorded the status of fashion royalty, who celebrated a decade at Christian Dior in 2007. Despite firmly cementing his place amongst Fashion Royalty, he regrettably hit the headlines for the wrong reasons in February 2011, when Dior announced that they had suspended Galliano over alleged anti-Semitic remarks in a Parisian bar. In July 2011 his close friend Kate Moss asked him to design her wedding dress for her marriage to Jamie Hince.

John Galliano ist eine Ikone der britischen Mode. Er wurde 1960 als Arbeiterkind auf Gibraltar geboren und verbrachte die ersten sechs Lebensjahre auf der Insel. Dann zog er mit seiner Familie in den Süden Londons. Es waren jedoch die frühen Jahre des Juan Carlos Antonio mit ihren religiösen Zeremonien und der sonnendurchfluteten Umgebung, die Galliano bis heute inspirieren. Eklektizismus in Verbindung mit der südländisch-katholischen Tradition des „Sich-schön-Anziehens" wurde zu seinem Markenzeichen. Nach dem Besuch der Wilson's Grammar School for Boys ergatterte Galliano einen Studienplatz am Central Saint Martins, das er 1984 abschloss. Seine von der Französischen Revolution inspirierte Schlusskollektion mit dem Namen „Les Incroyables", die Joan Burstein für Browns aufkaufte, katapultierte den Jungdesigner ins Rampenlicht. Nach einer schwierigen Phase – geprägt von Problemen mit Geldgebern und Kollektionen, die als nicht kommerziell genug abgeschmettert wurden, weil er darin Unkonventionelles wagte – begann Galliano 1990, seine Kreationen in Paris zu präsentieren. Zwei Jahre später verlegte er auch seinen Wohnsitz hierher. Als Verfechter des romantischen Diagonalschnitts und der dramatischen Effekte der Couture der 1950er-Jahre in einer Zeit, als Minimalismus und Grunge die Mode dominierten, wurde Galliano 1995 als Nachfolger von Hubert de Givenchy in dessen leicht verstaubtes Couture-Haus gerufen. Zwei Saisons später und mit noch nie da gewesenen vier Titeln als British Designer of the Year in der Tasche wurde Galliano schließlich Creative Director bei Christian Dior, wo er als erste Kollektion die Haute Couture für Frühjahr/Sommer 1997 präsentierte. Seit damals ist es dem Designer gelungen, das Haus sowohl in finanzieller wie in kreativer Hinsicht zu revitalisieren. 2007 feierte er sein zehnjähriges Jubiläum bei Christian Dior. Trotz seines unangefochtenen Platzes unter der Besten seines Fachs geriet er in negative Schlagzeilen, als Dior im Februar 2011 bekannt gab, sich wegen angeblicher antisemitischer Äußerungen in einer Pariser Bar von Galliano zu trennen. Im Juli 2011 bat ihn seine enge Freundin Kate Moss, das Hochzeitskleid für ihre Heirat mit Jamie Hince zu entwerfen.

John Galliano est un héros de la mode britannique. Né en 1960 à Gibraltar dans une famille d'ouvriers, il quitte son île natale pour le sud de Londres à l'âge de six ans. La tendre enfance du jeune Juan Carlos Antonio, avec ses cérémonies religieuses et sa culture du soleil, représente une source d'inspiration constante pour Galliano ; l'éclectisme stylistique et la tradition du chic latin sont devenus sa signature. En sortant du lycée pour garçons Wilson's Grammar School, Galliano réussit à entrer à Central Saint Martins, dont il sort diplômé en 1984. Inspirée par la Révolution française et baptisée « Les Incroyables », sa collection de fin d'études est achetée par Joan Burstein de chez Browns, ce qui le catapulte directement sur le devant de la scène. En 1990, après de célèbres déboires avec ses financiers et des collections vouées à l'échec commercial parce qu'elles osaient défier les conventions, Galliano commence à présenter ses défilés à Paris, où il s'installe en 1992. Fervent défenseur des coupes asymétriques romantiques et de la haute couture théâtrale des années 50 au sein d'une mode alors dominée par le minimalisme et le grunge, sa nomination à la succession d'Hubert de Givenchy dans l'antique maison éponyme est annoncée en 1995. Deux saisons plus tard et couronné de quatre British Designer of the Year Awards, un exploit sans précédent, Galliano devient directeur de la création chez Christian Dior et présente sa première collection aux défilés haute couture printemps/été 1997. Galliano redonne vie à la maison Dior, tant sur le plan financier que créatif, et fête ses dix ans chez Christian Dior en 2007. En dépit de sa position incontestée parmi les meilleurs designers de mode, il fait, bien malgré lui, la une des journaux lorsque Dior annonce en février 2011 que l'entreprise se sépare de Galliano après ses propos soi-disant racistes dans un bar parisien. En juillet 2011, son amie proche, Kate Moss, lui demande de dessiner sa robe pour son mariage avec Jamie Hince.

JAMIE HUCKBODY

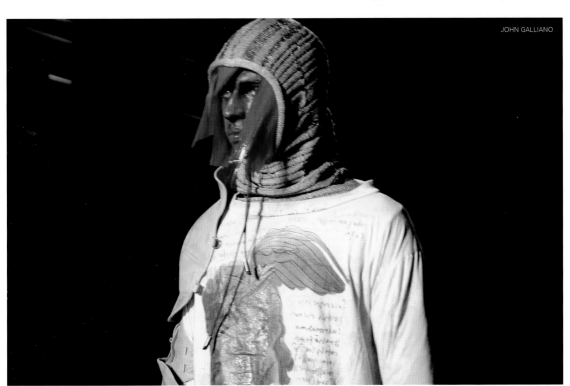

"I love fashion and I love making fashion"
JEAN PAUL GAULTIER

The former 'enfant terrible' of French fashion is one of the most significant designers working today, his appeal bridging the elite and mass markets. On one hand, Jean Paul Gaultier is hailed as the saviour of haute couture (Gaultier Paris was launched 1997) and, from 2004 to 2010, designed and refined womenswear for Hermès, alongside his own well-established ready-to-wear label. On the other, he is one of the world's most famous living Frenchmen, partly due to a presenting job on the TV show Eurotrash in the early '90s (not to mention his personal fondness for striped Breton shirts and other Gallic clichés). Born in 1952, he was beguiled by fashion from a young age and would sketch showgirls from the Folies Bergère to impress his classmates. In the early '70s, he trained under Pierre Cardin and Jean Patou, eventually launching his own ready-to-wear collection in 1976. He soon became known for iconoclastic designs such as the male skirt, corsetry worn as outerwear and tattoo-printed body stockings. The classics of Parisian fashion are also central to his repertoire, particularly the trench coat and 'le smoking'. In 1998, he launched a diffusion line, Junior Gaultier (since replaced by JPG), followed by excursions into perfumes (1993) and film costume (notably for Luc Besson's 'The Fifth Element' and Peter Greenaway's 'The Cook, The Thief, His Wife and Her Lover'). But it was his wardrobe for Madonna's Blonde Ambition tour of 1990 that made him world-famous, in particular for a certain salmon-pink corset with conical bra cups. A celebrity and a genius possessed of both a piquant sense of humour and a deadly serious talent, in 2004 Gaultier staged a unique exhibition at the Fondation Cartier in Paris, entitled Pain Couture, which showcased clothing constructed entirely from bread. Gaultier celebrated his 30th anniversary as a fashion designer in 2006 with a fashion show in Paris recapping his greatest hits followed by a magic show and party. Grace Coddington, Suzy Menkes, Hillary Alexander, Audrey Marnay, Lily Cole and Lucinda Chambers participated in magic tricks entertaining an audience of celebrities and journalists.

Das frühere Enfant terrible der französischen Mode ist einer der bedeutendsten Designer der Gegenwart, dem es gelingt, Eliteklientel und breite Masse gleichermaßen anzusprechen. Einerseits wurde Jean Paul Gaultier als Retter der Haute Couture gepriesen (Gaultier Paris existiert seit 1997) und entwarf neben der Arbeit für sein eigenes bestens eingeführtes Prêt-à-porter-Label von 2004 bis 2010 elegante Damenmode für Hermès. Andererseits ist er einer der berühmtesten Franzosen weltweit, nicht zuletzt dank seiner Moderation der Fernsehshow Eurotrash Anfang der 1990er-Jahre (von seiner Vorliebe für gestreifte bretonische Fischerhemden und andere gallische Klischees ganz zu schweigen). 1952 geboren, war er schon früh von Mode fasziniert und beeindruckte seine Klassenkameraden mit Zeichnungen der Tänzerinnen der Folies Bergère. In den frühen 1970er-Jahren lernte er bei Pierre Cardin und Jean Patou, bis er schließlich 1976 seine eigene Prêt-à-porter-Kollektion herausbrachte. Er erlangte bald Berühmtheit für ikonoklastische Entwürfe wie Männerröcke, Korsetts als Oberbekleidung und Bodystockings mit Tatoo-Muster. Aber auch die Klassiker der Pariser Mode sind aus seinem Repertoire nicht wegzudenken, insbesondere der Trenchcoat und der Smoking. 1998 gründete er die Nebenlinie Junior Gaultier (inzwischen ersetzt durch JPG), unternahm Ausflüge zu den Parfümeuren (1993) und in die Kostümbildnerei beim Film (für Luc Bessons „Das Fünfte Element" und für Peter Greenaways „Der Koch, der Dieb, seine Frau und ihr Liebhaber"). Weltberühmt machten ihn jedoch erst die Kostüme für Madonnas „Blonde Ambition"-Tour 1990, insbesondere das lachsrosa Korsett mit den konischen Körbchen. Inzwischen ist er selbst Promi und Genie, besessen von einem pikanten Sinn für Humor und todernstem Talent. 2004 präsentierte er in der Pariser Fondation Cartier eine einzigartige Ausstellung unter dem Titel „Pain Couture" mit Kleidungsstücken, die ausschließlich aus Brot gefertigt waren. Sein 30-jähriges Jubiläum als Modedesigner feierte Gaultier 2006 mit einer Modenschau in Paris, auf der man seine größten Erfolge rekapitulierte und anschließend eine Zauberschau und Party erlebte. Grace Coddington, Suzy Menkes, Hillary Alexander, Audrey Marnay, Lily Cole und Lucinda Chambers beteiligten sich an Zaubertricks, die ein Publikum von Prominenten und Journalisten unterhielten.

L'ancien « enfant terrible » de la mode française reste l'un des plus importants couturiers actuellement en exercice, capable de bâtir un pont entre le marché du luxe et celui de la grande consommation. D'une part, Jean Paul Gaultier est acclamé comme le sauveur de la haute couture (la collection Gaultier Paris a été lancée en 1997) et, de 2004 à 2010, il dessine également une ligne pour femme très raffinée chez Hermès, en plus de sa propre griffe de prêt-à-porter déjà bien établie. D'autre part, c'est aussi l'un des Français vivants les plus connus au monde, en grande partie grâce à son job de présentateur dans l'émission de télé « Eurotrash » au début des années 90 (sans parler de sa passion pour les pulls rayés bretons et autres clichés gaulois). Né en 1952, il s'intéresse très tôt à la mode et dessine des danseuses des Folies Bergère pour impressionner ses petits camarades de classe. Au début des années 70, il entame sa formation auprès de Pierre Cardin et de Jean Patou, avant de lancer sa propre collection de prêt-à-porter en 1976. Il se fait rapidement remarquer par ses créations iconoclastes comme la jupe pour homme, le corset porté en vêtement de dessus et les collants de corps imprimés de tatouages. Les classiques de la mode parisienne occupent aussi un rôle central dans son répertoire, en particulier le trench-coat et le smoking. En 1998, il crée Junior Gaultier, une ligne de diffusion (remplacée depuis par JPG) suivie par le lancement de plusieurs parfums (1993), puis par la création de costumes pour le cinéma (pour Le Cinquième Élément de Luc Besson et Le Cuisinier, le Voleur, sa Femme et son Amant de Peter Greenaway, entre autres). Mais ce sont les costumes dessinés en 1990 pour la tournée Blonde Ambition de Madonna qui lui valent sa notoriété mondiale, notamment un certain corset rose saumon à bonnets coniques. Star et génie doté d'un sens de l'humour piquant et d'un talent incontestable, Gaultier a organisé en 2004 une exposition exclusive à la Fondation Cartier de Paris : baptisée « Pain Couture », elle présentait des vêtements entièrement faits de pain. En 2006, il a célébré ses 30 ans de carrière lors d'un défilé parisien qui présentait ses plus grandes créations, suivi d'un kitschissime spectacle de magie et d'une grande fête. Grace Coddington, Suzy Menkes, Hillary Alexander, Audrey Marnay, Lily Cole et Lucinda Chambers ont toutes participé aux tours de magie pour divertir un public composé de célébrités et de journalistes.

SUSIE RUSHTON

JEAN PAUL GAULTIER

JEAN PAUL GAULTIER

PHOTOGRAPHY SØLVE SUNDSBØ. FASHION DIRECTOR EDWARD ENNINFUL. MODEL NAOMI CAMPBELL. MARCH 200

"The history of the house is incredible, which means I can work with a lot of freedom"
NICOLAS GHESQUIÈRE · BALENCIAGA

When the great Cristobal Balenciaga closed the doors of his couture house in 1968, he lamented, "There is no one left worth dressing". For decades, the house lay dormant, until 26-year-old Frenchman Nicolas Ghesquière was appointed creative director of Balenciaga in 1997 after the departure of Josephus Thimister. Since 1995, Ghesquière had quietly freelanced for Balenciaga's licences. Three years later, Ghesquière won the Vogue/VH1 Avant Garde Designer of the Year Award. Suzy Menkes of the 'International Herald Tribune' called him "the most intriguing and original designer of his generation". Though relatively unknown when he was appointed to Balenciaga, Ghesquière's is a life in fashion. He won work placements at agnès b. and Corinne Cobson while still at school in Loudon, central France. At 19, he became an assistant designer to Gaultier and then Mugler, before a brief tenure as head designer at Trussardi. But his great achievement has been his revival of Balenciaga. His green silk crop combat pants for Spring/Summer 2002 were the most copied garment of the season and Neoprene miniskirts and dresses for Spring/Summer 2003 kept Balenciaga on the edge, creatively and commercially. In 2002, a menswear line was launched, a year after the house of Balenciaga was bought by the Gucci Group. For Autumn/Winter 2005, he showed A-line leather dresses trimmed with pale ostrich feathers and sleek tailoring fitted with chrome fastenings. He was elected as one of the 100 Most Influential People in the World by 'Time' magazine in 2006, and awarded the prestigious Insigne de Chevalier des Arts et des Lettres for his continued creativity in 2008. Under Ghesquière's influence, Balenciaga today includes seven extremely lusted-after diffusion lines: Balenciaga Edition, a collection of items inspired by Cristobal Balenciaga's haute couture archives Balenciaga Leather, Balenciaga Pants, Balenciaga Knits, Balenciaga Denim, Balenciaga Black Dress and Balenciaga Silk. Former Gucci CEO Domenico De Sole has said: "Balenciaga has one fantastic asset. He's called Nicolas Ghesquière".

Als der große Cristobal Balenciaga 1968 die Tore seines Couture-Hauses schloss, klagte er: „Es gibt niemanden mehr, der es wert wäre, eingekleidet zu werden." Danach lag das Modehaus jahrzehntelang in einer Art Dornröschenschlaf, bis der Franzose Nicolas Ghesquière 1997 nach dem Weggang von Josephus Thimister Chefdesigner von Balenciaga wurde. Bereits ab 1995 hatte Ghesquière im Stillen als freier Mitarbeiter für Balenciagas Lizenzmarken entworfen. Drei Jahre später gewann er den Avant Garde Designer of the Year Award von Vogue und VH1. Suzy Menkes von der International Herald Tribune nannte ihn „den faszinierendsten und originellsten Designer seiner Generation". Auch wenn er bei seiner Verpflichtung für Balenciaga noch relativ unbekannt war, drehte sich doch bis dahin schon sein ganzes Leben um Mode. Bereits während seiner Schulzeit im französischen Loudon ergatterte er Praktikumsplätze bei agnès b. und Corinne Cobson. Mit 19 assistierte er Gaultier, anschließend Thierry Mugler, dann folgte ein kurzes Intermezzo als Chefdesigner bei Trussardi. Seine größte Leistung bis dato ist jedoch die Wiederbelebung von Balenciaga. Die abgeschnittenen Army-Hosen aus grüner Seide für Frühjahr/Sommer 2002 gehörten zu den meistkopierten Kleidungsstücken der Saison. Die Miniröcke und -kleider aus Neopren

für Frühjahr/Sommer 2003 sorgten dafür, dass Balenciaga führend blieb – kreativ wie kommerziell. 2002 wurde erstmals eine Herrenkollektion präsentiert, ein Jahr später kaufte der Gucci-Konzern Balenciaga. Im Herbst/Winter 2005 zeigte Ghesquière Lederkleider in A-Form mit hellem Straußenfederbesatz, schmaler Silhouette und Verschlüssen aus Chrom. So wählte das Time Magazine ihn 2006 unter die 100 einflussreichsten Menschen der Welt. 2008 wurde er für seine unerschöpfliche Kreativität mit dem angesehenen Insigne de Chevalier des Arts et des Lettres ausgezeichnet. Ghesquières Einfluss verdankt Balenciaga heute sieben ausgesprochen gefragte Nebenlinien: Balenciaga Edition, eine von Cristobal Balenciagas Haute-Couture-Klassikern inspirierte Kollektion, Balenciaga Leather, Balenciaga Pants, Balenciaga Knits, Balenciaga Denim, Balenciaga Black Dress und Balenciaga Silk. Der ehemalige CEO von Gucci, Domenico De Sole, sagte einmal: „Balenciaga besitzt einen fantastischen Aktivposten. Er heißt Nicolas Ghesquière."

Quand le grand Cristobal Balenciaga ferme sa maison en 1968, il déplore que « plus personne ne mérite d'être habillé ». Plusieurs décennies durant, la griffe semble plongée dans un sommeil de Belle au bois dormant jusqu'à ce que Nicolas Ghesquière, un jeune Français de 26 ans, succède à Josephus Thimister comme directeur de la création de Balenciaga en 1997. Depuis 1995, Ghesquière travaillait comme styliste free-lance pour les collections sous licence de Balenciaga. En 1998, il remporte le prix d'Avant Garde Designer of the Year décerné par Vogue et la chaîne VH1. Suzy Menkes de l'International Herald Tribune le considère comme « le créateur le plus fascinant et le plus original de sa génération ». Presque inconnu à ses débuts chez Balenciaga, Ghesquière revendiquait pourtant un beau parcours dans la mode : stages chez agnès b. et Corinne Cobson alors qu'il était lycéen à Loudon, puis à 19 ans, assistant-styliste chez Gaultier et chez Mugler, avant de travailler brièvement comme styliste principal chez Trussardi. Mais la renaissance de Balenciaga reste sa plus grande réalisation. Le treillis-pantacourt en soie verte de sa collection printemps/été 2002 est le vêtement le plus copié de la saison ; quant aux minijupes et robes en néoprène du printemps/été 2003, elles placent Balenciaga au pinacle de la mode, tant sur le plan créatif que commercial. En 2002, Balenciaga lance une ligne pour homme, un an après le rachat de la maison par le groupe Gucci. Pour l'automne/hiver 2005, il présente des robes trapèze en cuir, ornées de plumes d'autruche aux couleurs pâles, et des tailleurs épurés dotés d'attaches en chrome. Élu parmi les « 100 personnes les plus influentes du monde » par le magazine Time en 2006, il est fait Chevalier des Arts et des Lettres en 2008 pour son inépuisable créativité. Grâce à sa contribution, Balenciaga commercialise désormais sept lignes de diffusion extrêmement convoitées : Balenciaga Edition, une collection de pièces inspirées par les archives haute couture de Cristobal Balenciaga, Balenciaga Leather, Balenciaga Pants, Balenciaga Knits, Balenciaga Denim, Balenciaga Black Dress et Balenciaga Silk. Domenico De Sole, ancien PDG de Gucci, a un jour déclaré : « Balenciaga possède un atout fantastique. Il s'appelle Nicolas Ghesquière. »

JAMES SHERWOOD

"I think of a mood, a way of living, of certain needs"
FRIDA GIANNINI · GUCCI

In March 2005, Frida Giannini was charged with pushing Gucci, one of the most recognisable status labels of the late 20th century, into a new era. She is responsible for its high-profile accessories and womenswear collections, which have become synonymous with figure-hugging pencil skirts, glamorous sportswear and vixenish eveningwear, a look established by Gucci's former designer, Tom Ford, during the '90s. Established in 1921 by Guccio Gucci as a saddlery shop in Florence, the company had been a traditional family-run Italian business until Guccio's grandson Maurizio sold his final share of the brand in 1993. It was Guccio who first intertwined his initials to create the iconic logo. Yet until Tom Ford came along in the mid-'90s, the brand's image was lacklustre. In 2004, Ford exited Gucci, and new management filled his position not with a single designer but with a team of three, all of whom were promoted internally: John Ray for menswear, Alessandra Facchinetti for womenswear and Frida Giannini for accessories. In March 2005, Facchinetti also left Gucci, and Giannini was then also made responsible for women's clothing collections. Born in Rome in 1972, Giannini studied at the city's Fashion Academy; in 1997, she landed a job as ready-to-wear designer at Fendi, before first joining Gucci in 2002. Her Flora collection of flowery-printed accessories was the commercial hit of 2004. By 2005, she was named creative director of Gucci women's ready-to-wear. In 2006, she took over menswear. Frida has since put her distinctive stamp on the label, celebrating the house's inimitable past and expertise in luxury craftsmanship, while adding youth, colour and a playful extravagance. Giannini has also been integral in bringing celebrities to the brand – Drew Barrymore and Claire Danes for the jewellery campaigns, and James Franco for fragrance, while working closely with Madonna and Rihanna on charitable initiatives.

Im März 2005 erhielt Frida Giannini den Auftrag, eines der bekanntesten Statuslabels des ausgehenden 20. Jahrhunderts in eine neue Ära zu führen. Sie ist zuständig für Guccis viel beachtete Accessoires sowie für die Damenkollektionen, die für ihre figurbetonten Bleistiftröcke, glamouröse Sportswear und aggressive Abendmode bekannt ist. Diesen Look hatte der frühere Gucci-Designer Tom Ford etabliert. 1921 hatte Guccio Gucci die Firma in Florenz als Sattlerei gegründet. Und sie blieb auch ein traditioneller italienischer Familienbetrieb, bis Guccios Enkel Maurizio seine letzten Anteile an der Marke 1993 verkaufte. Doch war es bereits Guccio gewesen, der seine Initialen zum berühmten Logo zusammenfügte. Bis Tom Ford Mitte der Neunziger auf den Plan trat, war das Markenimage jedoch ziemlich glanzlos. 2004 verließ Ford Gucci. Das neue Management entschied sich bei der Nachfolge nicht für einen einzigen Designer, sondern für ein Dreierteam, dessen Mitglieder alle aus dem eigenen Haus stammten: John Ray für die Herrenmode, Alessandra Facchinetti für die Damenmode und Frida Giannini für die Accessoires. Als Facchinetti im März 2005 das Unternehmen verließ, übernahm Giannini die Damenmode noch mit. Giannini wurde 1971 in Rom geboren

und studierte an der dortigen Modeakademie. 1997 erhielt sie bei Fendi den Job der Designerin für Prêt-à-porter. 2002 fing sie dann bei Gucci an. Dort landete sie mit ihrer blumenbedruckten Kollektion Flora den kommerziellen Hit des Jahres 2004. 2005 wurde sie Creative Director von Guccis Prêt-à-porter für Damen. 2006 übernahm sie auch die Menswear. Seither hat Frida Giannini das Label auf unübersehbare Weise geprägt, indem sie die unnachahmliche Vergangenheit und Erfahrung in luxuriöser Handwerkskunst feiert und zugleich Jugendlichkeit, Farbe und eine ausgelassene Extravaganz ins Spiel bringt. Giannini war auch dafür verantwortlich, Prominente an die Marke zu binden – Drew Barrymore und Claire Danes für die Schmuck-Kampagnen oder James Franco für den Duft. Gleichzeitig arbeitet sie eng mit Madonna und Rihanna an Wohltätigkeitsprojekten zusammen.

En mars 2005, Frida Giannini se voit confier la mission de faire entrer Gucci, l'une des griffes les plus incontournables de la fin du 20e siècle, dans une nouvelle ère. Elle y est responsable des lignes d'accessoires de luxe et des collections pour femme, qui sont surtout connues pour les jupes droites moulantes, le sportswear glamour et les tenues de soirée archi-sexy, un look établi par Tom Ford, anciennement styliste de Gucci. La petite boutique de sellier fondée en 1921 à Florence par Guccio Gucci reste une affaire familiale traditionnelle à l'italienne jusqu'à ce que Maurizio, petit-fils de Guccio, revende sa dernière part de l'entreprise en 1993. C'est Guccio le premier qui a entrecroisé ses initiales pour produire le logo signature. Mais jusqu'à l'arrivée de Tom Ford au milieu des années 90, l'image de la marque manquait sérieusement de lustre. En 2004, Tom Ford quitte Gucci. La nouvelle équipe de direction le remplace non pas par un nouveau créateur, mais par une écurie de trois stylistes, tous promus en interne : John Ray à la mode masculine, Alessandra Facchinetti à la collection pour femme et Frida Giannini aux accessoires. En mars 2005, Alessandra Facchinetti quitte également Gucci et c'est désormais Frida Giannini, qui dirige les collections pour femme. Née en 1972 à Rome, Frida Giannini étudie à l'Académie de mode de la ville ; en 1997, elle décroche un poste de styliste en prêt-à-porter chez Fendi, puis rejoint Gucci en 2002. Sa collection « Flora » aux imprimés floraux s'impose comme le grand succès de l'année 2004, et en 2005, elle est nommée directrice de la création du prêt-à-porter Gucci pour femme, puis pour homme en 2006. Depuis, Frida Giannini imprime son style bien particulier à la griffe en célébrant le passé inimitable de la maison et son expertise du luxe artisanal tout en lui insufflant plus de jeunesse, de couleur et une extravagance ludique. Frida Giannini a aussi joué un rôle crucial pour attirer les célébrités vers la marque : Drew Barrymore et Claire Danes ont prêté leurs visages aux campagnes publicitaires pour les bijoux, et James Franco aux parfums. De plus, elle travaille étroitement avec Madonna et Rihanna sur des projets caritatifs.

SUSIE RUSHTON

"Every experience permanently alters the way you perceive beauty"
KATHARINE HAMNETT

For many fans, Katharine Hamnett defines '80s style. Her trademark use of functional fabrics such as parachute silk and cotton jersey has continued to inspire many in the industry ever since. She spearheaded a number of style directions, including the military look, utility fashion and casual day-to-evening sportswear, all of which still resonate today. And 21 years after her logo T-shirts first became front-page news (in 1984, she famously met Mrs Thatcher and wore one that read: '58% Don't Want Pershing'), Hamnett can still make the fashion world sit up and pay attention to her ideas. Born in 1948, she graduated from Central Saint Martins in 1969 and freelanced for ten years before setting up her own label, Katharine Hamnett London. This was followed in 1981 by menswear and a denim diffusion range in 1982. She became the BFC's Designer of the Year in 1984 and her ad campaigns helped to launch the careers of photographers including Juergen Teller, Terry Richardson and Ellen von Unwerth. Projects such as her flagship stores in London's Brompton Cross and Sloane Street, designed by Norman Foster, Nigel Coates and David Chipperfield, were famous for their forward-thinking retail design. A political conscience has always been key to the Katharine Hamnett ethos. She created antiwar T-shirts ('Life is Sacred') in 2003 that were widely worn by peace protesters marching in London; Naomi Campbell modelled a 'Use a Condom' design for Hamnett's Spring/Summer 2004 catwalk show in order to highlight the designer's concern over the AIDS epidemic in Africa. She decided to relaunch as Katharine E. Hamnett for Autumn/Winter 2005 and often continues to voice her concerns about unethical and non-environmental manufacturing processes. In 2007, she was appointed professor at the University of the Arts London and launched a line of ethically and environmentally mined gold and diamond jewellery with Cred Jewellery. Hamnett was appointed Commander of the Order of the British Empire (CBE) in the 2011 New Year Honours for services to the fashion industry

Für viele Fans verkörpert Katharine Hamnett den Stil der 1980er-Jahre. Ihr Markenzeichen ist die Verwendung funktionaler Materialien wie Fallschirmseide und Baumwolljersey, womit sie seither viele in der Modeindustrie inspiriert hat. Sie war Vorkämpferin für verschiedene Stilrichtungen wie etwa den Military Look, Utility Fashion und lässige Sportswear für tagsüber und abends. All diese Trends wirken bis heute fort. Und selbst 21 Jahre, nachdem sie mit ihren „Slogan"-T-Shirts erstmals Schlagzeilen machte (unvergessen, wie sie 1984 bei einem Treffen mit Margaret Thatcher ein T-Shirt mit dem Aufdruck „58 % Don't Want Pershing" trug), gelingt es Hamnett immer noch, in der Modewelt für Aufmerksamkeit zu sorgen. Die 1948 geborene Designerin machte 1969 ihren Abschluss am Central Saint Martins. Danach war sie zehn Jahre lang freischaffend tätig, bevor sie ihr eigenes Label – Katharine Hamnett London – gründete. 1981 kam Herrenmode dazu, 1982 eine Nebenlinie für Jeans. Den Titel BFC's Designer of The Year erhielt Hamnett 1984. Nebenbei beflügelten ihre Werbekampagnen auch die Karrieren von Fotografen wie Jürgen Teller, Terry Richardson und Ellen von Unwerth. Projekte wie ihre Londoner Flagship-Stores in Brompton Cross und der Sloane Street nach Entwürfen von Norman Foster, Nigel Coates und David Chipperfield erregten durch ihr innovatives Ladenkonzept Aufsehen. Katharine Hamnetts Ethos war schon immer von

politischem Bewusstsein geprägt. So kreierte sie T-Shirts gegen den Krieg („Life is Sacred"), die 2003 unter den Londoner Friedensdemonstranten sehr verbreitet waren. In Hamnetts Catwalk Show für Frühjahr/Sommer 2004 präsentierte Naomi Campbell den Schriftzug „Use a Condom", um die Betroffenheit der Designerin angesichts der Ausmaße der Aids-Epidemie in Afrika zum Ausdruck zu bringen. Für die Kollektion Herbst/Winter 2005 entschloss sie sich zu einem Relaunch ihres Labels unter dem Namen Katharine E Hamnett und kritisiert nach wie vor unmoralische und umweltschädliche Produktionsbedingungen. 2007 wurde sie als Professorin an die University of the Arts in London berufen und brachte zusammen mit Cred Jewellery eine Linie für Gold- und Diamantschmuck auf den Markt, deren Ausgangsprodukte nach ethischen und ökologischen Gesichtspunkten einwandfrei sind. In der New Year Honours List wurde Hamnett 2011 aufgrund ihrer Verdienste um die Modeindustrie für die Ernennung zum Commander des Order of the British Empire (CBE) vorgeschlagen.

Aux yeux de ses nombreux fans, Katharine Hamnett est « la » créatrice des années 80. Son utilisation caractéristique de tissus utilitaires tels que les soies de parachute et le jersey de coton continue depuis à inspirer bon nombre de stylistes. Elle a lancé de nombreuses tendances, notamment le look militaire, la mode utilitaire et un sportswear décontracté à porter le jour comme le soir, autant d'innovations qui résonnent encore de nos jours. 21 ans après que ses T-shirts à slogan aient fait la une des journaux (en 1984, elle a rencontré Margaret Thatcher vêtue d'un T-shirt proclamant « 58 % Don't Want Pershing »), Katharine Hamnett peut encore étonner l'univers de la mode et attirer l'attention sur ses idées. Née en 1948, elle sort diplômée de Central Saint Martins en 1969 et travaille en freelance pendant 10 ans avant de fonder sa propre griffe, Katharine Hamnett London, qui sera suivie d'une ligne pour homme en 1981 et d'une autre collection en denim en 1982. Elle est nommée British Designer of the Year en 1984, et ses campagnes publicitaires donnent un coup de pouce aux carrières des photographes Juergen Teller, Terry Richardson et Ellen von Unwerth. Des projets tels que ses boutiques de Brompton Cross et Sloane Street à Londres, conçues par Norman Foster, Nigel Coates et David Chipperfield, deviennent célèbres pour leur conception visionnaire en matière d'espace de vente. Une certaine conscience politique occupe toujours une place centrale dans la démarche de Katharine Hamnett. En 2003, elle a créé des T-shirts anti-guerre (« La vie est sacrée ») largement portés par les défenseurs de la paix qui manifestaient à Londres ; lors de son défilé printemps/été 2004, Naomi Campbell arborait un T-shirt proclamant « Use a Condom » afin d'exprimer les inquiétudes de la créatrice quant à l'épidémie du sida en Afrique. Pour la saison automne/hiver 2005, elle décide de relancer sa griffe sous le nom de « Katharine E Hamnett » et continue à clamer son inquiétude face aux procédés de fabrication non équitables et nuisibles à l'environnement. En 2007, elle devient professeur à l'University of the Arts de Londres et lance avec Cred Jewellery une collection de bijoux fabriqués à partir d'or et de diamants extraits dans le respect des règles éthiques et environnementales. Enfin, dans le cadre de la New Year Honours List 2011, Hamnett est faite membre de l'Ordre de l'Empire Britannique (CDB) pour services rendus à l'industrie de la mode.

TERRY NEWMAN

"I work on the cut"
ANNE VALÉRIE HASH

Anne Valérie Hash is a thoroughly modern couturière. Known for her virtuoso cutting skills, Hash transforms pieces of classic men's tailoring into elegant and unusual womenswear. For example, a man's white shirt is upended to become a sculpted blouse, or pleated pinstriped trousers are deconstructed to become a strapless dress. Hash, who was born in Paris in 1971, was one of the first of a younger generation of designers to be invited to show during haute couture week, despite being unable to fulfil all the traditional requirements for qualification as an haute couture house. She made her debut in July 2001. Before this, Hash had studied at both the Ecole des Arts Appliqués Duperré (1992) and the prestigious Ecole de la Chambre Syndicale de la Couture Parisienne (1995). She also completed internships at Nina Ricci, Chloé, Christian Lacroix and Chanel – the latter a particular high point for Hash, who has been constantly rereading the biography of Coco Chanel since the age of 18. From her first collection, Hash has demonstrated how the refined handcraft techniques of haute couture can be applied to an aesthetic that has more in common with Martin Margiela than Valentino. In recent seasons, Hash has softened her androgynous look to allow for the inclusion of more obviously romantic pieces such as layered tulle dresses – an aesthetic also seen in her handbags line (launched in 2007) and Anne Valérie Hash Mademoiselle collection for girls aged 4 to 14 (2008). However, the skeleton of her garments – their bindings, linings and seams – remain deliberately exposed, the result of her investigations into tailoring. Hash has further expanded into shoes (2006) and a capsule collection called Dress Me (2007). In January 2009, Hash was honoured with the L'Ordre des Arts et des Lettres from France's Ministry of Culture.

Anne Valérie Hash ist eine durch und durch moderne Couturière. Berühmt für ihre virtuosen Schnitte, transformiert sie Kleidungsstücke aus der klassischen Herrenschneiderei zu eleganter und außergewöhnlicher Damenmode. Da wird beispielsweise ein weißes Herrenhemd zur skulpturalen Bluse umgestülpt oder eine Nadelstreifenhose mit Bügelfalte zum schulterfreien Kleid umgeschneidert. Die 1971 in Paris geborene Hash war eine der Ersten einer jüngeren Designergeneration, die man einlud, bei der Haute-Couture-Woche zu präsentieren, auch wenn sie nicht alle traditionellen Anforderungen erfüllte, um als echtes Haute-Couture-Haus zu gelten. Ihr Debüt gab sie im Juli 2001. Zuvor hatte Hash sowohl an der Ecole des Arts Appliqués Duperré (1992) als auch an der angesehenen Ecole de la Chambre Syndicale de la Couture Parisienne (1995) studiert. Sie absolvierte auch Praktika bei Nina Ricci, Chloé, Christian Lacroix und Chanel. Wobei Chanel einen besonderen Höhepunkt für Hash darstellte, weil sie sich schon seit ihrem 18. Lebensjahr intensiv mit Coco Chanels Biografie auseinandergesetzt hatte. Bereits mit ihrer ersten Kollektion bewies die Designerin, dass die raffinierten handwerklichen Techniken

der Haute Couture sich auf eine Ästhetik anwenden lassen, die mehr mit Martin Margiela als mit Valentino verbindet. In den letzten Saisons hat Hash ihren androgynen Look etwas abgemildert und sich auch eindeutig romantische Kreationen wie mehrlagige Tüllkleider gestattet. Diese Ästhetik findet man übrigens auch in ihren Handtaschenkollektionen (seit 2007) sowie bei Anne Valérie Hash Mademoiselle für Mädchen von 4 bis 14 Jahren (2008). Das Gerüst ihrer Kleidung – Einfassungen, Futter und Säume – bleibt jedoch bewusst sichtbar, sozusagen als Ergebnis ihrer Recherchen in der hohen Schneiderkunst. Hash hat ihre Produktpalette seit 2006 um Schuhe erweitert und entwirft zudem eine Extra-Kollektion namens Dress Me (2007). Im Januar 2009 ehrte sie das französische Kultusministerium sie mit dem Ordre des Arts et des Lettres.

Anne Valérie Hash est une couturière résolument moderne. Réputée pour ses coupes virtuoses, elle transforme les pièces du costume classique pour homme en vêtements pour femme élégants et insolites. Par exemple, elle renverse une chemise blanche masculine pour la transformer en un sculptural chemisier, ou déconstruit un pantalon mille-raies à pinces pour en faire une robe bustier. Née en 1971 à Paris, Anne Valérie Hash figure parmi la nouvelle génération de créateurs invités à défiler pendant la semaine de la haute couture, bien qu'elle ne soit pas en mesure de satisfaire à tous les critères traditionnels requis pour être officiellement qualifiée de styliste de haute couture. Elle fait ses débuts en juillet 2001, après avoir étudié à l'École des Arts Appliqués Duperré (1992) et dans la prestigieuse École de la Chambre Syndicale de la Couture Parisienne (1995). Elle effectue également des stages chez Nina Ricci, Chloé, Christian Lacroix et surtout Chanel, grande source d'inspiration pour elle qui, depuis l'âge de 18 ans, ne cesse de relire la biographie de Coco Chanel. Depuis sa première collection, Anne Valérie Hash démontre comment les techniques artisanales raffinées de la haute couture peuvent être appliquées à une esthétique plus proche de Martin Margiela que de Valentino. Ces dernières saisons, elle a atténué son look androgyne pour permettre l'introduction de pièces franchement plus romantiques, telles que ses robes composées de plusieurs couches de tulle, une approche esthétique que l'on retrouve dans sa ligne de sacs à main (lancée en 2007) et la collection Anne Valérie Hash Mademoiselle destinées aux filles de 4 à 14 ans (2008). Toutefois, l'ossature de ses vêtements (leurs points de liage, leurs doublures et leurs coutures) reste délibérément exposée, conséquence de ses recherches à travers la coupe. Anne Valérie Hash a poursuivi sa diversification à travers une ligne de chaussures (2006) et une mini-collection baptisée « Dress Me » (2007). En janvier 2009, le ministère français de la Culture l'a décorée de l'Ordre des Arts et des Lettres.

SUSIE RUSHTON

"We don't design things we would not need if we were the client"
DESIRÉE HEISS & INES KAAG · BLESS

Whether Bless counts as a fashion label at all is a moot point. Preferring to describe their venture as "a project that presents ideal and artistic values to the public via products", Desirée Heiss (born 1971) and Ines Kaag (born 1970) formed Bless in 1995, positioning themselves as a collaborative experiment in fashion. The business is split between two European capitals: Heiss, who graduated from the University of Applied Arts in Vienna in 1994, is based in Paris, while Kaag, who graduated from the University of Arts and Design in Hanover in 1995, is based in Berlin. The two met by chance when their work was shown adjacently at a Paris design competition. The Bless modus operandi is in reinventing existing objects to produce new garments and accessories that are released in quarterly limited editions and are available through subscription. Their work has included fur wigs for Martin Margiela's Autumn/Winter 1997 collection, customisable trainers for Jean Colonna and the creation of 'Human-Interior-Wear' for Levi's. While these all function as wearable garments, many of their products cross entirely into the realm of art. 'Embroidered Flowers', for instance, is a series of photographic prints, while their 'Hairbrush Beauty-Product' (a brush with human hair for bristles) is closer to the work of Joseph Beuys or Marcel Duchamp than that of any fashion designer. Consequently, when the 'Bless Shop' goes on tour, it visits Europe's alternative galleries, rather than department stores. In 2004, Heiss and Kaag's abstractive style has earned them the ANDAM Fashion Foundation prize. Heiss and Kaag's success is in providing a unique comment on fashion that can also (usually) be worn.

Ob man Bless überhaupt zu den Modelabels zählen kann, ist umstritten. Desirée Heiss (Jahrgang 1971) und Ines Kaag (Jahrgang 1970) bezeichnen ihr Unternehmen lieber als „ein Projekt, das der Öffentlichkeit mittels Produkten ideelle und künstlerische Werte präsentiert". Sie gründeten Bless 1995 und positionierten sich selbst als kollaboratives Modeexperiment. Das Unternehmen ist auf zwei europäische Hauptstädte aufgeteilt: Heiss, die 1994 ihren Abschluss an der Wiener Universität für angewandte Kunst machte, ist in Paris stationiert, während Kaag, die an der Fachhochschule für Kunst und Design in Hannover studiert hat, von Berlin aus arbeitet. Kennengelernt haben sich die beiden per Zufall, als ihre Arbeiten bei einem Pariser Designwettbewerb nebeneinander ausgestellt waren. Das Konzept von Bless besteht darin, bereits existierende Objekte neu zu erfinden. Diese Kleidungsstücke oder Accessoires werden vierteljährlich in limitierten Auflagen an Abonnenten verkauft. Zu ihren bisherigen Arbeiten gehören Pelzperücken für Martin Margielas Kollektion Herbst/Winter 1997, „verstellbare" Turnschuhe für Jean Colonna und eine Kreation namens „Human Interior Wear" für Levi's. Die

genannten Produkte lassen sich alle tragen, während viele andere reine Kunstobjekte sind. So etwa die Fotoserie „Embroidered Flowers". Mit ihrem „Hairbrush Beauty-Product" (einer Art Bürste mit „Borsten" aus Menschenhaar) nähern sich Heiss und Kaag mehr als jeder andere Modedesigner den Arbeiten von Joseph Beuys oder Marcel Duchamp an. Da ist es nur folgerichtig, dass man den „Bless Shop" auf Tour eher in Europas alternativen Galerien als in Kaufhäusern antrifft. 2004 erhielten Heiss und Kaag für ihren außergewöhnlichen Stil den ANDAM Fashion Foundation Preis. Der Erfolg des Labels liegt wohl darin begründet, dass es einzigartige Kommentare zur Mode abgibt, die man (meistens) sogar anziehen kann.

Peut-on vraiment considérer Bless comme une marque de mode ? Desirée Heiss (née en 1971) et Ines Kaag (née en 1970) décrivent plutôt leur association comme « un projet présentant au public des valeurs idéales et artistiques par le biais de produits ». Elles créent Bless en 1995 dans l'optique d'une collaboration expérimentale autour de la mode. Leur activité se divise entre deux capitales européennes : Desirée Heiss, diplômée de l'Université des Arts appliqués de Vienne en 1994, travaille à Paris, tandis qu'Ines Kaag, diplômée de l'Université des Arts et du Design de Hanovre en 1995, est installée à Berlin. Elles se sont rencontrées par hasard à Paris lors d'un concours de design où leurs travaux respectifs étaient présentés côte à côte. Le modus operandi de Bless consiste à réinventer des objets existants pour produire de nouveaux vêtements et accessoires, commercialisés chaque trimestre en édition limitée et uniquement sur abonnement. Entre autres, elles ont créé des perruques en fourrure pour la collection automne/hiver 1997 de Martin Margiela, des tennis personnalisables pour Jean Colonna et travaillé sur un concept de « Human-Interior-Wear » pour Levi's. Bien que toutes ces pièces soient portables, la plupart de leurs produits s'apparentent entièrement au domaine de l'art. Par exemple, « Embroidered Flowers » est une série d'impressions photographiques, tandis que leur « Hairbrush Beauty-Product » (une brosse en cheveux humains) relève davantage du travail de Joseph Beuys ou de Marcel Duchamp que de la pure création de mode. Quand le « Bless Shop » part en tournée, il préfère donc faire étape dans les galeries d'art alternatives d'Europe plutôt que dans les grands magasins. En 2004, Heiss et Kaag se voient attribuer le prix de la ANDAM Fashion Foundation pour leur style hors du commun. Le succès de Desirée Heiss et d'Ines Kaag repose avant tout sur leur approche unique d'une mode que l'on peut aussi porter, la plupart du temps.

MARK HOOPER

"The collection has so many different components. But that's how we design and how people dress – with intellect, with spirit and an eye for the mix"
LAZARO HERNANDEZ & JACK MCCOLLOUGH · PROENZA SCHOULER

Lazaro Hernandez and Jack McCollough are the American duo behind Proenza Schouler. The label has secured accounts with the world's most exclusive stores, won a Council of Fashion Designers of America (CFDA) award for new talent and, for many, has put the New York collections back on the must-see fashion map. Its fans include American 'Vogue''s editor Anna Wintour and her super-chic French counterpart Carine Roitfeld. All this has been achieved within the space of a few seasons. Both born in 1978, Hernandez, who was born in Miami of Spanish Cuban heritage, and McCollough, who was born in Tokyo and raised in New Jersey, first met at Parsons College in New York City. After Hernandez completed an internship at Michael Kors (on Anna Wintour's recommendation), and McCollough at Marc Jacobs, they made the unusual decision of working together on their senior collection. Winning the Designer of the Year award at Parsons' student show and with their whole graduation collection snapped up by Barneys, Hernandez and McCollough quickly had to find a name. They came up with the nom de plume Proenza Schouler, combining their mothers' maiden names. Since then, Proenza Schouler have become part of a new breed of American designers who are choosing polish and sincere sophistication over grunge and thrift-store irony, quickly perfecting a style that is particular to New York: a blend of tailored uptown glamour with sporty downtown nonchalance. Inspired by '50s couture – Christian Dior, Cristobal Balenciaga and Coco Chanel – and pictures by Avedon and Penn, Proenza Schouler's signatures include their play with proportion, bolero jackets, bustiers and heavily worked detailing – a fusion of old-world luxury and new-world lifestyle. In 2004, the duo scooped the first-ever Vogue/CFDA Fashion Fund award, winning a $200,000 cash prize and business mentoring. In 2007, the duo received the esteemed CFDA Womenswear Designer of the Year Award. Only a few months later, Proenza Schouler partnered with Valentino Fashion Group SpA. Proenza Schouler is sold in over 100 of the most exclusive retail outlets worldwide, including Barneys New York, Bergdorf Goodman, Harvey Nichols, Colette, and Joyce.

Lazaro Hernandez und Jack McCollough sind das amerikanische Duo hinter Proenza Schouler. Das Label hat sich seinen Platz in über 100 der exklusivsten Läden der Welt gesichert – es wird u. a. bei Barneys, New York, Bergdorf Goodman, Harvey Nichols, Colette und Joyce angeboten –, einen Preis des Council of Fashion Designers of America (CFDA) für neue Talente gewonnen und in den Augen vieler den New Yorker Kollektionen zu neuem Ansehen in der Modebranche verholfen. Zu den Fans gehören die Herausgeberin der amerikanischen Vogue, Anna Wintour, und deren französischer Widerpart Carine Roitfeld. Hernandez, 1978 als Kind spanisch-kubanischer Eltern in Miami geboren, und der im selben Jahr in Tokio geborene, in New Jersey aufgewachsene McCollough lernten sich am Parson's College in New York kennen. Nachdem Hernandez (auf Empfehlung von Anna Wintour) ein Praktikum bei Michael Kors und McCollough eines bei Marc Jacobs absolviert hatte, fällten die beiden die ungewöhnliche Entscheidung, sich für ihre Abschlusskollektion zusammenzutun. Nachdem sie damit den Preis Designer of the Year bei der Studentenschau am Parson's gewonnen hatten und Barneys sich ihre komplette Kollektion gesichert hatte, mussten sich Hernandez und McCollough rasch einen Namen einfallen lassen. Sie kamen auf den Kunstnamen Proenza Schouler, für den sie die Mädchennamen ihrer Mütter kombinierten. Seit damals ist Proenza Schouler Teil einer neuen Generation amerikanischer Designer, die strahlender echter Eleganz den Vorzug vor Grunge und Second-Hand-Ironie geben. Daraus entwickelte sich rasch ein Stil, der eng mit New York verbunden ist: ein Mix aus maßgeschneidertem Uptown-Glamour und sportlichem Downtown-Lässigkeit. Inspiriert von den Couturiers der 1950er-Jahre – Christian Dior, Cristobal Balenciaga und Coco Chanel – sowie den Bildern von Avedon und Penn, gehört das Spiel mit Proportionen, Bolerojäckchen, Bustiers und arbeitsaufwendige Details zu den Markenzeichen von Proenza Schouler. Kurz gesagt: eine Melange aus dem Luxus der Alten und dem Lifestyle der Neuen Welt. Im Jahr 2004 sicherte sich das Designerduo den erstmals ausgelobten Vogue/CFDA Fashion Fund, der 200.000 Dollar in bar und Business Mentoring umfasste. Im Jahr 2007 verlieh die CFDA dem Designerduo den angesehenen Preis Womenswear Designer of the Year. Nur ein paar Monate später ging Proenza Schouler eine Partnerschaft mit der Valentino Fashion Group SpA ein.

Proenza Schouler est l'œuvre du duo américain formé par Lazaro Hernandez et Jack McCollough. Cette griffe vendue dans les boutiques les plus sélectives du monde, dont Barneys New York, Bergdorf Goodmann, Harvey Nichols et Colette and Joyce, leur a valu le prix du CFDA décerné aux nouveaux talents et beaucoup estiment qu'elle a contribué à remettre les collections new-yorkaises sur le devant de la scène. Proenza Schouler compte des fans tels que la rédactrice du Vogue américain Anna Wintour et son homologue française ultra-chic Carine Roitfeld. Tous deux sont nés en 1978 ; Hernandez grandit à Miami dans une famille d'origine hispano-cubaine tandis que McCollough, né à Tokyo, grandit dans le New Jersey. Ils se rencontrent au Parson's College de New York et effectuent des stages pendant leurs études, Hernandez chez Michael Kors (sur les recommandations d'Anna Wintour) et McCollough chez Marc Jacobs. Contrairement aux habitudes, ils décident de travailler ensemble sur leur collection de fin d'études, avec un défilé couronné par le prix de Parson's Designer of the Year et une collection complète achetée par Barneys. Hernandez et McCollough doivent alors rapidement se trouver un nom de plume et optent pour Proenza Schouler, une combinaison des noms de jeune fille de leurs mères. Depuis, Proenza Schouler fait partie de la nouvelle génération de griffes américaines qui préfèrent la sophistication classe et sincère à l'ironie du grunge et du vintage, perfectionnant rapidement un style typiquement new-yorkais : coupes sophistiquées et glamour alliées à une nonchalance sport. Inspirées par la haute couture des années 50 (Dior, Balenciaga et Chanel) comme par les photos d'Avedon et de Penn, les signatures de Proenza Schouler se distinguent par un jeu sur les proportions qui se décline dans des boléros, des bustiers et des détails très travaillés : une fusion entre luxe à l'ancienne et lifestyle du nouveau monde. En 2007, le duo a gagné le prix très convoité de Womenswear Designer of the Year remis par le CFDA. Quelques mois plus tard, Proenza Schouler s'associait avec Valentino Fashion Group SpA.

JAMIE HUCKBODY

"People always want something unexpected and exciting. That's what drives me"
TOMMY HILFIGER

Born one of nine children in 1951 in Elmira, New York, Tommy Hilfiger's eponymous brand is often viewed as epitomising the American Dream. His career famously began in 1969 with $150 and 20 pairs of jeans. When customers to his People's Palace store in upstate New York failed to find what they were after, he took to designing clothes himself, with no previous training. In 1984, having moved to New York City, Hilfiger launched his first collection under his own name. With his distinctive red, white and blue logo and collegiate/Ivy League influences, Hilfiger presented a preppy vision of Americana, which, coupled with his looser sportswear aesthetic, found a surprising new audience in the burgeoning hip-hop scene of the early '90s. Hilfiger, a dedicated music fan himself, welcomed this re-interpretation of his work, but rumours that he was less than enamoured of his new audience led him to make an admirable response, lending his support to the Anti-Defamation League and the Washington DC Martin Luther King Jr National Memorial Project Foundation. By 1992, his company had gone public and Hilfiger was named the CFDA's Menswear Designer of the Year in 1995. A new 'semi-luxe' line of tailored separates, entitled simply H, was launched in 2004 as a higher-priced, more upmarket addition to the global brand, which now incorporates everything from denim and eyewear to fragrances, homeware, sporting apparel and children's lines. In keeping with his music and fashion influences, Hilfiger chose to market his new 'grown-up' range by asking David Bowie and Iman to appear in ad campaigns for H. In December 2004, Hilfiger looked set on further expansion when he announced an agreement made with Karl Lagerfeld to globally distribute the latter's own-label collections. Hilfiger, in 2005, hosted and sponsored a CBS TV reality show called 'The Cut' in which contestants competed for a design job with Hilfiger. In 2006, Hilfiger sold his company for $1.6 billion to a private investment company, Apax Partners. In March 2010, Phillips-Van Heusen, owner of Calvin Klein, bought the Tommy Hilfiger Corporation for $3 billion.

Die Marke des 1951 als eines von neun Kindern in Elmira, New York, geborenen Tommy Hilfiger gilt vielen als der Inbegriff des amerikanischen Traums. Seine Karriere begann, wie inzwischen allgemein bekannt ist, 1969 mit 150 Dollar und 20 Paar Jeans. Wenn die Kundschaft in seinem Laden People's Palace nicht fand, wonach sie suchte, stellte er die Stücke – ohne jegliche Vorkenntnisse – eben selbst her. Nach seinem Umzug nach New York City präsentierte Hilfiger 1984 seine erste Kollektion unter eigenem Namen. Mit seinem auffälligen Logo in Rot, Weiß und Blau sowie den Einflüssen des Ivy-League-Stils präsentierte Hilfiger eine Vision von Amerikana im Preppy-Look, die, gepaart mit lässiger Sportswear-Ästhetik überraschenderweise eine neue Klientel in der gerade erblühenden Hip-Hop-Szene der frühen Neunziger fand. Als leidenschaftlicher Musikfan begrüßte Hilfiger diese Neuinterpretation seiner Arbeit. Dennoch brachten ihn Gerüchte, er sei von seiner neuen Anhängerschaft wenig angetan, zu dezidierten Reaktionen, etwa der Unterstützung der Anti-Defamation League und der Washington DC Martin Luther King Jr. National Memorial Project Foundation. 1992 ging das Unternehmen an die Börse, 1995 wurde Hilfiger von der CFDA zum Menswear Designer

of the Year gekürt. Unter dem schlichten Kürzel H kam 2004 eine neue, halb-luxuriöse Linie von aufwendiger geschneiderten Einzelstücken auf den Markt, quasi die höherpreisige, elitäre Ergänzung der internationalen Marke, die inzwischen von Jeans und Brillen über Düfte, Heimtextilien, Sportartikel bis hin zu Kinderkleidung praktisch alles umfasst. Passend zu seinen musikalischen und modischen Einflüssen entschloss sich Hilfiger, für seine neue „erwachsene" Linie bei David Bowie und Iman anzufragen, die anschließend in der Werbekampagne für H posierten. 2005 moderierte und sponserte Hilfiger eine Reality-Show namens ‚The Cut' beim TV-Sender CBS. Dort kämpften die Kandidaten um einen Job als Designer für Hilfiger. Im Jahr 2006 verkaufte Hilfiger sein Unternehmen für 1,6 Milliarden Dollar an die private Investmentfirma Apax Partners. Im März 2010 erwarb der amerikanische Modekonzern Phillips-Van Heusen, dem auch die Marke Calvin Klein gehört, die Tommy Hilfiger Corporation für 3 Milliarden Dollar.

Né en 1951 dans une famille de neuf enfants à Elmira dans les environs de New York, Tommy Hilfiger et sa marque éponyme sont souvent considérés comme l'incarnation du rêve américain. La légende dit qu'il a entamé sa carrière en 1969 avec 150 dollars en poche et 20 paires de jeans. Comme les clients de sa boutique People's Palace au nord de l'État de New York n'arrivent pas à trouver ce qu'ils cherchent, il décide de dessiner lui-même des vêtements, sans formation préalable. En 1984, une fois installé à New York, Hilfiger lance une première collection baptisée de son propre nom. Avec son célèbre logo rouge, blanc et bleu et influencé par le style des universités de l'Ivy League, Hilfiger présente une vision BCBG du style américain qui, associée à une esthétique sportswear plus décontractée, séduit une clientèle inattendue au sein de la jeune scène hip-hop du début des années 90. Lui-même passionné de musique, Hilfiger accepte cette interprétation de son travail, mais les rumeurs qui courent sur le fait qu'il ne soit pas particulièrement fan de son nouveau public le conduisent à réagir admirablement en offrant son soutien à la ligue anti-raciste américaine (Anti-Defamation League) et à la Fondation du projet de mémorial national de Martin Luther King Junior. En 1992, son entreprise est introduite en bourse et le CFDA le couronne Menswear Designer of the Year en 1995. Une nouvelle ligne « semi-luxe » de séparés baptisée tout simplement « H » est lancée en 2004 en guise de complément plus haut de gamme et plus onéreux pour cette marque mondiale qui intègre aujourd'hui toutes sortes de lignes, du denim aux lunettes en passant par les parfums, le mobilier, les articles de sport et la mode pour enfant. Fidèle à ses influences vestimentaires et musicales, Hilfiger décide de commercialiser sa nouvelle gamme « adulte » en demandant à David Bowie et Iman d'apparaître dans les campagnes publicitaires de « H ». En 2005, il anime et sponsorise « The Cut », une émission de télé-réalité diffusée sur CBS où les candidats se disputent une place de styliste chez Hilfiger. En 2006, il vend son entreprise au fonds d'investissement Apax Partners pour un montant de 1,6 milliard de dollars. En mars 2010, le groupe américain Phillips-Van Heusen, qui détient également la marque Calvin Klein, rachète la Tommy Hilfiger Corporation pour trois milliards de dollars.

MARK HOOPER

PHOTOGRAPHY MATT JONES. STYLING CATHY DIXON. JANUARY/FEBRUARY 2000.

"The illusion that next time it might be perfect keeps us going"
VIKTOR HORSTING & ROLF SNOEREN · VIKTOR & ROLF

Inseparable since they met whilst studying at Arnhem's Fashion Academy, Dutch duo Viktor Horsting and Rolf Snoeren (both born 1969) decided to join forces after graduating in 1992. Their first feat was winning three awards at the 1993 Hyères Festival with a collection that already betrayed their preferences for sculptural, experimental clothes. Soon afterwards, they joined the ranks of Le Cri Néerlandais, a loose collective of like-minded young designers from the Netherlands who organised two shows in Paris. However, once Le Cri disbanded, Viktor & Rolf continued to produce collections, including one in 1996 called Viktor & Rolf On Strike that decried the lack of interest in their work from press and buyers. Refusing to give up, the duo created a toy-like miniature fashion show and a fake perfume bottle with an accompanying ad campaign. These artefacts, presented in the Amsterdam art gallery Torch in 1996, established them as upstart designers with an unconventional agenda. But what really launched their careers was their introduction to Paris couture in 1998, where Viktor & Rolf stunned ever-growing audiences with their highly innovative creations based on exaggerated volumes and shapes. To everyone's surprise and delight, the duo have managed to translate their earlier spectacular couture designs into wearable yet groundbreaking prêt-à-porter pieces, showing their first ready-to-wear collection for Autumn/Winter 2000. Clinging to a love of ribbons and perfectly cut smoking suits, Viktor & Rolf shows have become a must-see on the Paris prêt-à-porter schedule, and in 2004 they launched their first fragrance, Flowerbomb. The next few years saw the pair reach new heights: the opening of the Viktor & Rolf Boutique on Milan's Via Sant'Andrea (2005), a collaboration with H&M (2006) and their first ever UK exhibition, at The Barbican (2008). In 2008 Viktor & Rolf entered into a partnership with Italian clothing magnate Renzo Rosso, allowing the company to develop new product ranges and open further boutiques. They continue to live and work in Amsterdam.

Seit sie sich als Studenten an der Modeakademie von Arnheim kennenlernten, sind die beiden Holländer Viktor Horsting und Rolf Snoeren (beide Jahrgang 1969) unzertrennlich. Nach ihrem Studienabschluss 1992 beschlossen sie folglich, ihre Kräfte zu bündeln. Ihre erste Meisterleistung waren drei Preise beim Hyères-Festival 1993, und zwar mit einer Kollektion, die ihre Vorliebe für skulpturale, experimentelle Kleidung zum Ausdruck brachte. Bald danach reihten sie sich bei Le Cri Néerlandais ein, einem losen Kollektiv von gleichgesinnten Jungdesignern aus Holland, die zwei Schauen in Paris organisierten. Nachdem Le Cri sich aufgelöst hatte, machten Viktor & Rolf mit der Produktion von Kollektionen weiter, darunter eine von 1996 mit dem Titel ‚Viktor & Rolf On Strike', die das geringe Interesse von Journalisten und Käufern beklagte. Das Designerduo schuf eine spielzeugartige Modenschau en miniature und einen falschen Parfümflakon mit dazugehöriger Werbekampagne. Diese Artefakte wurden 1996 in der Amsterdamer Kunstgalerie Torch präsentiert und etablierten die beiden als Newcomer mit unkonventionellem Programm. Was ihrer Karriere jedoch den entscheidenden Schub gab, war ihre Einführung in die Pariser Couture 1998, wo Viktor & Rolf ein stän-

dig wachsendes Publikum mit höchst innovativen Kreationen erstaunte, die auf extremem Volumen und überzeichneten Formen basierten. Es gelang dem Duo, seine frühere spektakuläre Couture in tragbare, aber dennoch völlig neuartige Prêt-à-porter zu transponieren, wovon man sich bei ihrer ersten Kollektion für Herbst/Winter 2000 überzeugen konnte. Mit ihrer Vorliebe für Bänder und perfekt geschnittene Smokings sind die Schauen von Viktor & Rolf Pflichtprogramm im Pariser Prêt-à-porter-Kalender. 2004 wurde mit Flowerbomb der erste Duft des Designerteams vorgestellt. In den darauffolgenden Jahren erzielte das Kreativ-Duo weitere Erfolge: die Eröffnung der Viktor & Rolf Boutique an der Mailänder Via Sant'Andrea (2005), die Zusammenarbeit mit H&M (2006) sowie ihre allererste Ausstellung in Großbritannien, im Londoner Barbican (2008). 2008 taten sich Viktor & Rolf mit dem italienischen Modezaren Renzo Rosso zusammen, was das Unternehmen weiter expandieren ließ. Die beiden Designer leben und arbeiten nach wie vor in Amsterdam.

Inséparables depuis leur rencontre sur les bancs de l'académie de mode d'Arnhem, les Hollandais Viktor Horsting et Rolf Snoeren (tous deux nés en 1969) décident de travailler ensemble après l'obtention de leurs diplômes en 1992. Ils réalisent un premier exploit en remportant trois prix au Festival de Hyères en 1993 grâce à une collection qui trahit déjà leur prédilection pour une mode sculpturale et expérimentale. Peu de temps après, ils rejoignent les rangs du Cri Néerlandais, collectif libre de jeunes designers hollandais partageant le même état d'esprit et qui a présenté deux défilés à Paris. Après la dissolution du Cri, Viktor & Rolf continuent de travailler ensemble. En 1996, ils baptisent l'une de leurs collections « Viktor & Rolf On Strike » pour dénoncer le manque d'intérêt de la presse et des acheteurs à leur égard. Refusant d'abandonner, ils créent un mini-défilé jouet, un faux flacon de parfum et une campagne publicitaire pour l'accompagner : ces artefacts, présentés dans la galerie d'art Torch à Amsterdam en 1996, les imposent comme de nouveaux rebelles à suivre de très près. Mais c'est lorsqu'ils débarquent dans la haute couture parisienne que leur carrière décolle enfin : depuis 1998, Viktor & Rolf éblouissent un public sans cesse croissant grâce à des créations très innovantes qui jouent sur l'exagération des volumes et des formes. À la surprise générale et pour le plus grand bonheur de tous, le duo parvient à traduire les créations haute couture de ses débuts spectaculaires en vêtements prêt-à-porter à la fois novateurs et portables, qu'ils présentent pour la première fois aux collections automne/hiver 2000. Revendiquant leur amour des rubans et smokings aux coupes irréprochables, chaque défilé est un événement absolument incontournable de la semaine du prêt-à-porter de Paris. En 2004, ils lancent leur premier parfum, Flowerbomb. Les années suivantes voient le duo atteindre de nouveaux sommets : ouverture de la boutique Viktor & Rolf sur la Via Sant'Andrea de Milan (2005), collaboration avec H&M (2006) et toute première exposition britannique au Barbican (2008). Avec son association en 2008 au roi italien de la mode, Renzo Rosso, l'entreprise continue de se développer. Les créateurs vivent et travaillent aujourd'hui encore à Amsterdam.

JAMIE HUCKBODY

"I design for men and women who value quality over quantity, and simplicity over decoration"
MARGARET HOWELL

Margaret Howell creates beautiful, understated clothes for everyday life. Taught to sew and knit by their mother, the Howells were a practical and creative tour de force, with mum making the kids' clothes, and the kids, indeed, following suit. They would while away many an hour rummaging through jumble sales, where Howell would find a shirt and be instantly attracted to the way it was made. Around this time, Howell was buying and adapting dressmaking patterns by Yves Saint Laurent into her own masculine style. Joseph had arrived in this country as a hairdresser, wanted to sell clothes in his shop and formed an easy alliance with Howell and stocked her burgeoning shirting collection in his store. Browns were next to place an order, as did Ralph Lauren and Paul Smith. Howell's take on the classic shirt shape was to remake it in a gentler, more casual fabric, instantly making it easier to wear. Joseph witnessed the business potential within Howell's easy aesthetic and offered her the chance to open a boutique to house her first complete range of menswear (1977). Howell realised the potential was there to cater for both sexes and downscaled the sizing, added some skirting and the women's range was launched (1980). There has been succession of notable and carefully controlled photographic campaigns, shot on location in black and white by sympathetic spirits such as Bruce Weber, Alasdair McLellan, and Venetia Scott. Howell later parted company with Joseph, and the company went independent and continued to grow. Now based in London's Wigmore Street, the store showcases her collection of fabulous knick-knacks – like chopping boards and stationery – alongside the clothing collections, which often feature polka dots, shirting, double- or single-breasted tuxedos, tweeds and cotton as the recurring themes. Echoing the peaceful time of 'Miss Marple', 'The Darling Buds of May' and a quintessential English summertime in full bloom, these clothes are for a modern world and perfect for times in which frivolity and lewd design features, such as logos and labelling, seem rather unnecessary.

Margaret Howell entwirft wunderbar schlichte Kleidung für den Alltag. Nähen und Stricken lernten die Kinder der Familie von ihrer Mutter, was eine praktische und zugleich kreative Herausforderung darstellte, denn die Mama fertigte die Kinderkleidung selbst an, und die Kids folgten postwendend ihrem Beispiel. Sie verbrachten Stunden mit dem Stöbern in Trödelläden, wo Howell ein Hemd entdeckte und sofort von seiner Machart begeistert war. Etwa um diese Zeit kaufte Howell auch Schnittmuster von Yves Saint Laurent und adaptierte sie gemäß ihrem eigenen maskulinen Stil. Joseph, der als Friseur ins Land gekommen war, wollte in seinem Laden auch Klamotten anbieten und ging bereitwillig eine Verbindung mit Howell ein, deren aufblühende Hemdenkollektion er fortan bei sich verkaufte. Browns gaben als erste eine Bestellung auf, gefolgt von Ralph Lauren und Paul Smith. Howells Version des klassischen Herrenhemds ist ein Remake aus weicherem, lässigerem Material, was den Tragekomfort ungemein steigert. Joseph erkannte das geschäftliche Potenzial in Howells unbeschwerter Ästhetik und bot ihr die Chance, eine Boutique zu eröffnen, in der ihre erste komplette Herrenkollektion Platz fand (1977). Howell wiederum realisierte die Möglichkeit, für beide Geschlechter zu designen, verkleinerte die Größen, fügte ein paar Röcke

hinzu, und fertig war die Damenkollektion (1980). Es folgten eindrucksvolle, an Originalschauplätzen in Schwarz-Weiß aufgenommene Kampagnen einfühlsamer Fotografen wie Bruce Weber, Alasdair McLellan und Venetia Scott. Als die geschäftliche Verbindung zu Joseph endete, wurde Howells Firma unabhängig und expandierte weiter. Der Laden in der Londoner Wigmore Street präsentiert auch ihre Kollektion aus fabelhaftem Krimskrams – wie Schneidbrettern und Briefpapier – und dazu die Kleiderkollektionen, häufig mit Tupfenmuster, aus Hemden, Ein- und Zweireihern, Smokings, Tweed und Baumwolle. Das Ganze erinnert an die friedvollen Zeiten von ‚Miss Marple' und ‚Darling Buds of May' und an den typisch englischen Hochsommer. Trotzdem sind diese Kleider für eine moderne Welt gemacht und perfekt für Momente, in denen Oberflächlichkeit und anstößige Design-Features wie Logos und Etiketten eher überflüssig scheinen.

Margaret Howell crée des vêtements à la fois sobres et magnifiques pour le quotidien. La famille Howell représente un exploit pratique et créatif en soi, avec une mère qui confectionnait elle-même les habits de ses enfants et leur a appris à coudre et à tricoter, une tradition qu'ils ont d'ailleurs perpétuée. Alors qu'ils passent leur temps à chiner dans les ventes de charité, Margaret reste fascinée devant une chemise, instantanément attirée par son mode de construction. À cette époque, elle achète des patrons de couture Yves Saint Laurent et les interprète à sa façon dans un style masculin. Nouvellement immigré en Angleterre en tant que coiffeur, Joseph désire vendre des vêtements dans son salon et conclut un accord avec Margaret Howell pour distribuer sa jeune collection de chemises. Browns lui passe commande ainsi que Ralph Lauren et Paul Smith. Sa vision de la chemise classique consiste alors à la refaçonner dans un tissu plus doux, plus décontracté et donc tout de suite plus facile à porter. Joseph, qui a flairé le potentiel commercial de cette esthétique, propose à Margaret d'ouvrir une boutique pour y vendre toutes ses créations pour homme (1977). Prenant conscience qu'elle peut créer pour les deux sexes, elle réduit ses proportions, ajoute quelques jupes et lance sa collection pour femme (1980). S'en suivent d'impressionnantes campagnes de photographies d'une extrême sensibilité, prises en noir et blanc sur les lieux d'origine, comme Bruce Weber, Alasdair McLellan et Venetia Scott. Après la fin de la relation d'affaires avec Joseph, l'entreprise d'Howell continue de se développer en toute indépendance. Désormais installée dans Wigmore Street à Londres, la boutique de Margaret Howell présente sa fabuleuse collection de gadgets – entre planches à découper et articles de papeterie – aux côtés de lignes de vêtements qui affichent souvent des pois, des tissus de chemise, des vestes droites ou croisées, des smokings, des tweeds et du coton comme thèmes récurrents. Faisant écho à l'époque paisible de « Miss Marple », de « The Darling Buds of May » et à la quintessence de l'été anglais en pleine floraison, ces vêtements conçus pour le monde d'aujourd'hui s'avèrent parfaitement adaptés en cette ère où la frivolité, les logos et les étiquettes sont autant d'inventions lubriques devenues plutôt inutiles.

BEN REARDON

"It's important for me that my clothes are not just an exercise in runway high jinks"
MARC JACOBS

Season after season, Marc Jacobs (born 1963), manages to predict exactly what women all over the world want to wear, whether that be his super-flat 'mouse' pumps, Sergeant-Pepper-style denim jackets or 'Venetia' handbags fitted with outsized silver buckles. Born in New York's Upper West Side to parents who both worked for the William Morris Agency, Jacobs was raised by his fashion-conscious grandmother. As a teenager, Jacobs immersed himself in club culture, observing the beautiful people at the Mudd Club, Studio 54 and Hurrah. Today, Jacobs' most fruitful source of inspiration is still the crowd of cool girls that surround him (including the stylist Venetia Scott, director Sofia Coppola and numerous art-house actresses). After high school, Jacobs completed a fashion degree at Parsons School of Design; his graduation collection (1984), which featured brightly coloured knits, caught the eye of Robert Duffy, an executive who remains Jacobs' business partner to this day. Together they launched the first Marc Jacobs collection (1986), winning a CFDA award the following year. In 1989, Jacobs was named head designer at Perry Ellis. His experience there was tempestuous and his infamous 'grunge' collection of 1992 – featuring satin Birkenstocks and silk plaid shirts – marked his exit from the company. By 1997, Jacobs' star was in the ascendant once again, when LVMH appointed him artistic director at Louis Vuitton. Jacobs has enhanced the luggage company's image – not least through his collaborations with artists Takashi Murakami and Stephen Sprouse on seasonal handbag designs – and repositioned it as a ready-to-wear fashion brand. Meanwhile LVMH have supported Jacobs' own company, which has now expanded to more than 100 stores worldwide. The company's impressive portfolio includes Marc Jacobs Collection ready-to-wear, Marc by Marc Jacobs womenswear, Men's Collection ready-to-wear, Marc by Marc Jacobs menswear, two shoe collections, two optical collections, two sunglasses collections, one collection of watches, nine fragrances, the children's collection and the much-loved collection of special items.

Saison für Saison gelingt es dem 1963 geborenen Marc Jacobs, exakt vorherzusagen, was die Frauen überall auf der Welt tragen wollen – seien es superflache Mouse-Pumps, Jeansjacken im Sergeant-Pepper-Stil oder Venetia-Handtaschen mit überdimensionalen Silberschnallen. Der an der New Yorker Upper West Side als Kind von Eltern, die beide für die William Morris Agency tätig waren, geborene Jacobs wurde von einer modebewussten Großmutter aufgezogen. Als Teenager vertiefte er sich in die Clubkultur und studierte die Beautiful People der 1970er-Jahre im Mudd Club, im Studio 54 sowie im Hurrah. Noch heute ist Jacobs' fruchtbarste Inspirationsquelle die Truppe von coolen Girls, die ihn umgeben (darunter die Stylistin und Fotografin Venetia Scott, die Regisseurin Sofia Coppola und zahlreiche Art-House-Schauspielerinnen). Nach der Highschool machte Jacobs sein Modeexamen an der Parsons School of Design. 1984 erregte seine Abschlusskollektion mit leuchtend bunten Stricksachen die Aufmerksamkeit des Managers Robert Duffy, der bis heute sein Geschäftspartner ist. Gemeinsam brachten sie 1986 die erste Marc-Jacobs-Kollektion heraus und gewannen damit ein Jahr später ihren ersten CFDA-Preis. 1989 wurde Jacobs Chefdesigner bei Perry Ellis. Dort erlebte er ziemlich stürmische Zeiten und verabschiedete sich mit

seiner berüchtigten Grunge-Kollektion von 1992, zu der Birkenstocks aus Satin und Karohemden aus Seide gehörten. Ab 1997 war Jacobs' Stern wieder im Steigen begriffen, als ihn der LVMH-Konzern zum künstlerischen Direktor von Louis Vuitton ernannte. Jacobs verbesserte das Image des traditionellen Reisegepäck-Labels, nicht zuletzt durch seine Zusammenarbeit mit den Künstlern Takashi Murakami und Stephen Sprouse im saisonalen Handtaschendesign. Außerdem hat er die Prêt-à-porter-Mode des Hauses neu positioniert. Inzwischen unterstützt LVMH auch Jacobs' eigenes Unternehmen, das auf über 100 Läden weltweit expandiert ist. Das eindrucksvolle Portfolio des Unternehmens umfasst die Prêt-à-porter Marc Jacobs Collection, die Damenlinie Marc by Marc Jacobs, die Prêt-à-porter Men's Collection, die Herrenlinie Marc by Marc Jacobs, zwei Schuhkollektionen, zwei Brillenkollektionen, zwei Sonnenbrillenkollektionen, eine Uhrenkollektion, neun Düfte, die Kinderkollektion und die überaus beliebte Kollektion besonderer Dinge.

Saison après saison, Marc Jacobs (né en 1963) réussit à prédire exactement ce que les femmes du monde entier auront envie de porter, qu'il s'agisse de ses ballerines « souris » ultraplates, de ses vestes en denim à la Sergeant Pepper ou des sacs à main Venetia ornés d'énormes boucles en argent. Né à New York dans l'Upper West Side de parents travaillant tous deux pour la William Morris Agency, Jacobs est élevé par sa grand-mère passionnée de mode. Adolescent, il s'immerge dans la culture club du milieu des années 70 et aime à observer les beautiful people qui se retrouvent au Mudd Club, au Studio 54 et au Hurrah. Aujourd'hui, la source d'inspiration la plus fructueuse de Jacobs réside dans la foule de filles branchées qui l'entoure (incluant la styliste Venetia Scott, la réalisatrice Sofia Coppola et nombreuses actrices du cinéma indépendant). Après le lycée, Jacobs obtient un diplôme en mode de la Parsons School of Design ; sa collection de fin d'études (1984), avec sa maille aux couleurs vives, attire l'attention de l'homme d'affaires Robert Duffy, qui reste son partenaire commercial à ce jour. Ensemble, ils lancent la première collection Marc Jacobs (1986), couronnée l'année suivante par un prix du CFDA. En 1989, Jacobs est nommé styliste principal de Perry Ellis. Son expérience est orageuse et sa scandaleuse collection « grunge » de 1992, avec ses Birkenstocks en satin et ses chemises en soie à carreaux écossais, signe ses adieux à la maison. En 1997, l'étoile de Marc Jacobs remonte au firmament quand LVMH le nomme directeur artistique de Louis Vuitton. Jacobs révolutionne l'image du fabricant de bagages, notamment grâce à des collaborations artistiques avec Takashi Murakami et Stephen Sprouse sur la création de sacs à main de saison, et repositionne Vuitton comme une marque de prêt-à-porter. Parallèlement, LVMH finance la griffe éponyme de Jacobs, qui compte désormais plus de 100 boutiques à travers le monde. L'impressionnant portefeuille de l'entreprise inclut Marc Jacobs Collection prêt-à-porter, Marc by Marc Jacobs pour femme, Men's Collection prêt-à-porter, Marc by Marc Jacobs pour homme, deux collections de chaussures, deux collections optiques, deux collections de lunettes de soleil, une collection de montres, neuf parfums, une collection pour enfant et une gamme d'articles spéciaux très appréciée.

SUSIE RUSHTON

"My ultimate goal is always to improve on the last collection"
ROSSELLA JARDINI · MOSCHINO

The Italian fashion house Moschino owes much to Rossella Jardini who, since the untimely death of its founder Franco Moschino in 1994, has successfully held the reins of a brand which today still puts the kook into kooky. Moschino, having burst onto the scene in 1983, has grown up since its logo-mania '80s heyday (remember phrases like 'Ready To Where?' or 'This Is A Very Expensive Shirt' splashed onto garments?). But Jardini, as creative director of all Moschino product lines (sold through 22 shops worldwide), has steered this label in a contemporary direction while retaining its traditional wit. Since the millennium, we have seen Jardini and her team continue to tease the market through parody and stereotype, both of which are central to the original philosophy of the house. Rompish catwalk parades featuring housewives in curlers and sleeping masks, demure '50s ladies à la Chanel (one of Jardini's most important personal influences), over-the-top prints, trompe l'œil and swishy petticoats have all provided gleeful style moments. Born in Bergamo, Italy, in 1952, Jardini began her career selling clothes rather than designing them. Then, in 1976, she met Nicola Trussardi and began assisting with the development of that company's clothing and leather goods. Creating her own line in 1978 with two model friends, she soon made the acquaintance of Franco Moschino and in 1981 began assisting him. A stint designing accessories for Bottega Veneta followed, but by 1984 she had settled into a permanent role at Moschino. Ten years later, before his tragically early death, Franco Moschino made it quite clear he wished Jardini to take over the helm. She has been there ever since.

Das italienische Modehaus Moschino verdankt Rossella Jardini viel. Seit dem frühen Tod des Firmengründers Franco Moschino im Jahr 1994 steuert sie eine Marke, die man bis heute als verrückt im besten Sinne des Wortes bezeichnen kann. Moschino hatte 1983 sein Debüt in der Modeszene und ist erwachsen geworden, wenn man an die Logo-Manie im Boom der 1980er-Jahre denkt (wer erinnert sich nicht an auf Kleidungsstücken prangende Sätze wie „Ready To Where?" oder „This Is A Very Expensive Shirt"?). Als Chefdesignerin aller Produktlinien des Hauses (die weltweit in 22 Läden verkauft werden) hat Jardini das Label in eine moderne Richtung gesteuert und dabei seinen traditionellen Witz bewahrt. Seit der Jahrtausendwende kann man wieder verstärkt beobachten, wie Jardini und ihr Team den Markt mit Parodien und Klischees necken, die beide von zentraler Bedeutung für die ursprüngliche Unternehmensphilosophie sind. So präsentierte man auf dem Catwalk schon Paraden von Hausfrauen mit Lockenwicklern und Schlafmasken, prüden Damen im 50er-Jahre-Stil von Chanel (einer der wichtigsten Einflüsse für Jardini), völlig verrückten Mustern, Trompe l'œil und raschelnden

Petticoats – was für jede Menge Ausgelassenheit sorgte. Die 1952 in Bergamo geborene Jardini begann ihre Karriere übrigens nicht mit dem Design, sondern mit dem Verkauf von Textilien. 1976 lernte sie Nicola Trussardi kennen und begann, ihm bei der Entwicklung des Textil- und Lederwarengeschäfts seiner Firma zu assistieren. Gemeinsam mit zwei befreundeten Models kreierte sie 1978 ihr eigenes Label und lernte bald darauf Franco Moschino kennen, dessen Assistentin sie ab 1981 war. Es gab noch ein kurzes Intermezzo als Designerin für Accessoires bei Bottega Veneta, bis sie 1984 ihre Dauerstellung bei Moschino einnahm. Zehn Jahre danach und kurz vor seinem tragischen frühen Tod ließ Franco Moschino keinen Zweifel an seinem Wunsch, Jardini das Ruder zu überlassen. Seither hat sie es nicht mehr aus der Hand gegeben.

La maison italienne Moschino doit beaucoup à Rossella Jardini, car depuis le décès prématuré de son fondateur Franco Moschino en 1994, elle tient avec succès les rênes d'une marque qui reste aujourd'hui fidèle à son côté fou et décalé. Apparue sur la scène de la mode en 1983, la griffe Moschino s'est depuis départie de la logomania qui a marqué son âge d'or dans les années 80 (qui aurait pu oublier les slogans « Ready To Where ? » ou « This Is A Very Expensive Shirt » ?). Mais Rossella Jardini, directrice de la création de toutes les lignes de produits Moschino (vendues dans 22 boutiques à travers le monde), a orienté la griffe vers un style plus contemporain tout en respectant l'état d'esprit qui a fait son succès. Depuis l'an 2000, Rossella Jardini et son équipe continuent à séduire le marché à travers la parodie et le stéréotype, deux piliers de la philosophie originelle de la maison. Défilés tapageurs où paradent des ménagères portant bigoudis et masques de nuit, discrètes dames années 50 à la Chanel (l'une des plus importantes contributions personnelles de Rossella Jardini), imprimés surchargés, effets trompe-l'œil et jupons précieux nous ont tous offert des moments de mode jubilatoires. Née en 1952 à Bergame, Rossella Jardini débute dans le métier par la vente et non par la création. En 1976, elle rencontre Nicola Trussardi et commence à l'assister dans le développement des vêtements et des articles de maroquinerie de sa marque. Elle crée sa propre ligne en 1978 avec deux amis mannequins, mais peu de temps après, elle fait la connaissance de Franco Moschino, dont elle devient l'assistante en 1981. Après un bref détour par Bottega Veneta, pour qui elle crée des accessoires, elle revient définitivement chez Moschino en 1984. Dix ans plus tard, avant sa mort tragique et précoce, Franco Moschino exprimera clairement son désir de voir Rossella Jardini reprendre le flambeau. Elle n'a plus jamais quitté la maison.

SIMON CHILVERS

"I can find inspiration anywhere"
CHRISTOPHER KANE

Born in 1982 in Glasgow, Christopher Kane's first taste of the fashion world was through Fashion TV, hosted by Jenny Baker. Growing up on a council estate until his father's business took off, Fashion TV introduced Kane to the world of Karl Lagerfeld, Gianni Versace, Thierry Mugler, Christian Lacroix and Helmut Lang. Straight after his 18th birthday, Kane applied to Central Saint Martins; going to London for the interview was the first time he came to the city. Winning a Lancôme Colour Award (2005) while at college proved a turning point; through the acquaintance of fashion journalist Sarah Mower, Kane went on to meet Anna Wintour and Donatella Versace. In September 2006 Kane was awarded the New Generation sponsorship from the British Fashion Council and held his first solo catwalk show. Kane's neon-coloured bandage dresses took the fashion press by storm, instantly sealing his name as the one to look forward to at every London catwalk season. Each and every one of the collections produced together with his sister, Tammy, who is his collaborator and business partner, has continued to surprise, impress and seduce. In November 2007 he was awarded the New Designer of the Year award at the British Fashion Awards. In addition, Kane has been instrumental in the relaunch of Versus and showcased his first full collection for the brand in Milan in September 2009.

Der 1982 in Glasgow geborene Christopher Kane kam erstmals durch die von Jenny Baker moderierte Sendung ‚Fashion TV' auf den Geschmack in Sachen Mode. Kane, der in einer Sozialwohnung aufwuchs, bis das Geschäft seines Vaters florierte, schenkte ‚Fashion TV' Einblick in die Welt von Karl Lagerfeld, Gianni Versace, Thierry Mugler, Christian Lacroix und Helmut Lang. Gleich nach seinem 18. Geburtstag bewarb Kane sich am Central Saint Martins – und die Reise zum Aufnahmegespräch war sein erster Ausflug in die Hauptstadt. Als er noch als Student einen Lancôme Colour Award (2005) gewann, war das der Wendepunkt für ihn. Über die Bekanntschaft mit der Modejournalistin Sarah Mower lernte Kane Anna Wintour und Donatella Versace kennen. Im September 2006 gewann er das New-Generation-Stipendium des British Fashion Council und veranstaltete seine erste Solo-Schau auf dem Catwalk. Kanes

neonfarbene Bandagenkleider eroberten die Modepresse im Sturm und sorgten unverzüglich dafür, dass man sich seither in jeder Londoner Catwalk-Saison auf seinen Namen freut. Gemeinsam mit seiner Schwester Tammy, die als Mitarbeiterin und Geschäftspartnerin zugleich fungiert, ist es ihm gelungen, wirklich all seine Kollektionen überraschend, eindrucksvoll und verführerisch zu gestalten. Im November 2007 wurde er bei den British Fashion Awards als New Designer of the Year ausgezeichnet. Außerdem hat der Designer entscheidend zum Relaunch von Versus beigetragen und zeigte seine erste vollständige Kollektion für diese Linie im September 2009 in Mailand.

Né à Glasgow en 1982, Christopher Kane a découvert la mode sur Fashion TV grâce à l'animatrice Jenny Baker. Jusqu'à ce que l'entreprise de son père décolle, il grandit dans des logements sociaux et regarde cette chaîne de télévision qui l'introduit au monde de Karl Lagerfeld, Gianni Versace, Thierry Mugler, Christian Lacroix et Helmut Lang. Juste après son dix-huitième anniversaire, Kane postule à Central Saint Martins : son entretien de candidature lui donne l'opportunité de venir à Londres pour la première fois. Le Lancôme Colour Award (2005) qu'il remporte pendant ses études s'avère décisif ; ami avec la journaliste de mode Sarah Mower, Kane finit par rencontrer Anna Wintour et Donatella Versace. En septembre 2006, il décroche la bourse New Generation du British Fashion Council et donne son tout premier défilé en solo. Ses robes «bandage» fluorescentes prennent la presse spécialisée par surprise et font immédiatement de lui le nouveau talent à suivre à chaque édition de la London Fashion Week. Avec sa sœur Tammy, à la fois sa collaboratrice et son associée, il présente des collections qui ne se lassent pas de surprendre, d'impressionner et de séduire. En novembre 2007, les British Fashion Awards le consacrent New Designer of the Year. Par ailleurs, la contribution du créateur dans la transformation et le relancement de Versus est décisive et Christofer Kane présente sa première collection complète pour cette marque en septembre 2009 à Milan.

KAREN HODKINSON

HAMBURGER 1/6
EGG ROLL 1/-   BACON ROLL 1/3

TEA
COFFEE   6d
OXO   9d
HOT DRINKS   10d
HOT CHOCOLATE   10d
HORLICKS (CHOC. or PLAIN) 1/-
MINERALS   1/3
                          9d
CAKES 6d   SANDWICHES 9d
CHOCOLATE BISCUITS   5d

"I never see one woman when I design, it's always a universe of women"
DONNA KARAN

While she was still a student at the Parsons School of Design in New York, Long Island native Donna Karan was offered a summer job assisting Anne Klein. After three years as associate designer, Karan was named as Klein's successor and, following her mentor's death in 1974, Karan became head of the company. After a decade at Anne Klein, where she established a reputation for practical luxury sportswear separates, typically in stretch fabrics and dark hues, Karan founded her own company in 1984 with her late husband, Stephan Weiss. A year later, her highly acclaimed Donna Karan New York Collection, based on the concept of 'seven easy pieces', unveiled the bodysuit that was to become her trademark. Karan's emphasis on simple yet sophisticated designs, including everything from wrap skirts to corseted eveningwear, captured the popular mood of 'body consciousness' that swept Hollywood in the '80s. By 1989, she had expanded this philosophy to the street-smart diffusion line DKNY. In 1992, inspired by the desire to dress her husband, a menswear line was launched, with a DKNY Men emerging a year later. Since then, Donna Karan International has continued to diversify and expand to cover every age and lifestyle, including a children's range, eyewear, fragrances and home furnishings. She has been honoured with an unprecedented seven CFDA awards, including 2004's Lifetime Achievement Award to coincide with her 20th anniversary. The company became a publicly traded enterprise in 1996 and was acquired by French luxury conglomerate LVMH in 2001 for a reported $643 million. Karan remains the chief designer. Today Donna Karan International boasts over 100 company-owned, licensed, free-standing Donna Karan Collection, DKNY and DKNY Jeans stores worldwide. In 2007, she launched The Urban Zen Foundation, a non-profit organisation inspired by her global travels. The Foundation includes The Urban Zen store and Urban Zen fashion line, proceeds of which go towards raising awareness in areas of well-being, empowering children and preserving cultures.

Noch während ihres Studiums an der New Yorker Parsons School of Design bekam die aus Long Island stammenden Donna Karan einen Ferienjob als Assistentin von Anne Klein angeboten. Nach drei Jahren als Associate Designer wurde sie schließlich Kleins Nachfolgerin und übernahm nach dem Tod ihrer Mentorin 1974 die Firmenleitung. Nach einem Jahrzehnt bei Anne Klein, in dem sie den Ruf des Modehauses als erste Adresse für praktische, aber zugleich luxuriöse Sportswear-Separates – üblicherweise aus Stretchmaterialien und in dunklen Farbtönen – etabliert hatte, erfolgte 1984 die Gründung der eigenen Firma, zusammen mit Stephan Weiss, ihrem späteren Ehemann. Ein Jahr später wurde die viel gelobte Donna Karan New York Collection präsentiert, die auf dem Konzept von „sieben einfachen Teilen" basierte. Dazu zählte auch der schwarze Body, der ihr Markenzeichen werden sollte. Karans Faible für schlichte und doch raffinierte Entwürfe, egal ob Wickelröcke oder Abendkleider mit Corsage, entsprach ganz dem Trend zu mehr Körperbewusstsein, der im Hollywood der 1980er-Jahre so verbreitet war. 1989 wandte Karan diese Philosophie auch auf die street-smarte Nebenlinie DKNY an. Inspiriert von dem Wunsch, den eigenen Mann einzukleiden, entstand 1992 eine Linie für Herrenmode. Seit damals diversifiziert und expandiert Donna Karan International weiter und bedient inzwischen jedes Alter und diverse Lebensstile, u. a. mit Kindermode, Brillen, Düften und Wohnaccessoires. Bislang unerreicht sind ihre sieben Auszeichnungen durch die CFDA, darunter 2004 ein Lifetime Achievement Award, der mit ihrem 20-jährigen Berufsjubiläum zusammenfiel. Zum börsennotierten Unternehmen wurde die Firma 1996. Im Jahr 2001 kaufte sie schließlich der französische Luxuswarenkonzern LVMH für angeblich 643 Millionen Dollar auf. Heute hat Donna Karan International über 100 firmeneigene, lizenzierte, aber selbstständige Filialen von Donna Karan Collection, DKNY und DKNY Jeans weltweit vorzuweisen. 2007 rief Karan The Urban Zen Foundation ins Leben, eine Non-Profit-Organisation, zu der ihre Reisen in alle Welt sie inspiriert haben. Die Foundation umfasst auch einen Laden namens The Urban Zen und eine gleichnamige Modelinie. Ziele dieses Projekts sind ein verbessertes Gesundheitsbewusstsein, Stärkung von Kinderrechten sowie der Schutz bedrohter Völker.

Alors qu'elle est encore étudiante à la Parsons School of Design de New York, la jeune Donna Karan, originaire de Long Island, se voit proposer un job d'été comme assistante d'Anne Klein. Après trois années au poste de styliste associée, elle est nommée à la succession d'Anne Klein et, à la mort de son mentor en 1974, elle reprend la direction de l'entreprise. Après une décennie passée chez Anne Klein, où elle se forge une solide réputation en créant des séparés sportswear luxueux et faciles à porter généralement coupés dans des tissus stretch aux couleurs sombres, Donna Karan fonde sa propre griffe en 1984 avec son mari Stephan Weiss, aujourd'hui décédé. Un an plus tard, sa collection à succès Donna Karan New York articulée autour du concept des « seven easy pieces » dévoile le bodysuit qui devait devenir sa signature. Sa prédilection pour les pièces simples mais sophistiquées, de la jupe portefeuille aux tenues de soirée corsetées, capture tout l'esprit de la tendance au « body consciousness » qui déferle sur Hollywood dans les années 80. En 1989, elle étend cette philosophie à sa ligne de diffusion DKNY. Inspirée par l'envie d'habiller son mari, elle lance une ligne pour homme en 1992. Depuis, la société Donna Karan International ne cesse de se diversifier et se développer pour couvrir toutes les tranches d'âge et styles de vie, notamment avec une gamme pour enfant, des lunettes, des parfums et des meubles. Elle a reçu sept prix du CFDA, un record sans précédent, notamment un Lifetime Achievement Award couronnant sa carrière en 2004, une année où elle célèbre également le 20e anniversaire de sa société. Introduite en bourse en 1996, son entreprise a été rachetée par le groupe de luxe français LVMH en 2001 pour un montant estimé à 643 millions de dollars. Aujourd'hui, Donna Karan International possède plus de 100 boutiques indépendantes distribuant les collections Donna Karan, DKNY et DKNY Jeans dans le monde entier. En 2007, Donna Karan crée The Urban Zen Foundation, une association à but non lucratif inspirée par ses voyages autour du monde. Au sein même de la fondation, la boutique The Urban Zen vend, entre autres, la collection de vêtements du même nom et réinvestit ses bénéfices dans la sensibilisation du public aux questions du bien-être, de l'émancipation des enfants et de la sauvegarde des cultures.

MARK HOOPER

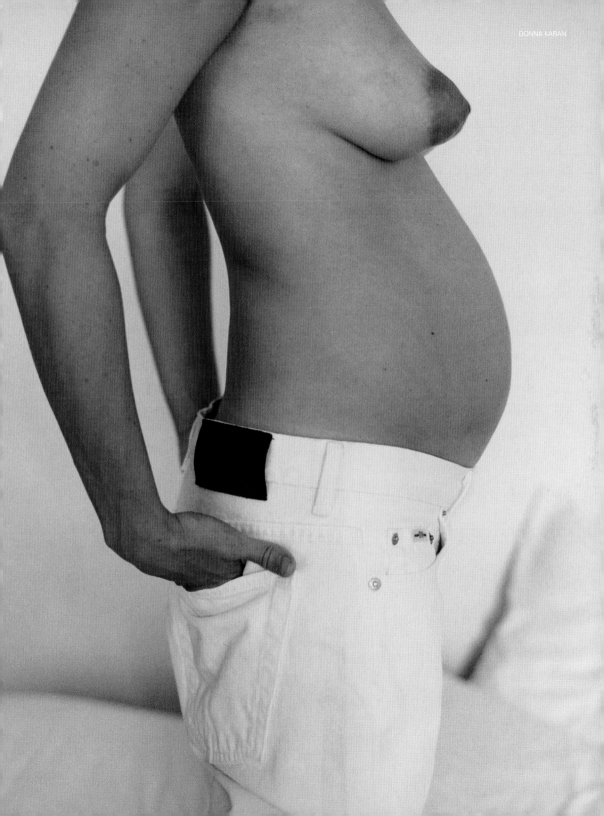

"The same spirit runs through everything I do"
REI KAWAKUBO · COMME DES GARÇONS

Rei Kawakubo established Comme des Garçons in Tokyo in 1973. A designer who has dispensed with the rule book, who cuts and constructs in such a way that her clothes have skirted art, Kawakubo's readiness to challenge conventions – to produce uniform-like clothes that are neither obviously for men nor for women, that distort rather than enhance the female form, that use unusual fabrics and deconstruct them sometimes to the point of destruction – has nevertheless created a global concern. She launched Comme des Garçons to the West in 1981, when she showed her first collection in Paris and was among the avant-garde Japanese to introduce black as an everyday fashion staple – unthinkingly dubbed 'Hiroshima Chic' by some critics. Then as now, it bewildered as much as it excited. The self-taught, multiple-award-winning Kawakubo (born in Tokyo in 1942) did not, however, follow the standard route into the fashion industry. She began her career by reading literature at Tokyo's Keio University and, on graduation in 1964, joined the Ashai Kasei chemical and textiles company, working in its advertising department. Unable to find the garments she wanted for herself, she started to design them. She launched menswear in 1978, and a furniture line in 1982. Comme remains progressive: the label's fragrances, for instance, have played with tar, rubber and nail polish odours. Retail projects have included short-term 'guerrilla' stores in the backwater areas of what are, for the fashion world, unexpected cities, through to London's monolithic Dover Street Market, in which the company, which she co-runs with British husband Adrian Joffe, also rents space to like-minded designers. Recent collaborations include a capsule collection for H&M and a bag collaboration with Louis Vuitton to celebrate 30 years of Louis Vuitton in Japan. Kawakubo created a highly successful 2008 Autumn collection for high-street retailer H&M, designing men's and women's clothing along with some children's and a unisex perfume. It sold out within hours.

Rei Kawakubo gründete Comme des Garçons 1973 in Tokio. Sie ist eine Designerin, die alle Regeln bricht und so zuschneidet und konstruiert, dass ihre Kleider geschneiderte Kunstwerke sind. Kawakubo war bereit, Konventionen infrage zu stellen, indem sie uniformähnliche Teile produzierte, die weder eindeutig als Herren- noch als Damenmode identifizierbar waren, die weibliche Formen eher verzerrten als unterstrichen und die aus ungewöhnlichen, oft bis zur Zerstörung dekonstruierten Materialien gefertigt waren – und schuf trotzdem einen weltweit agierenden Konzern. Im Westen wurde Comme des Garçons erstmals 1981 lanciert, als Kawakubo ihre erste Kollektion in Paris zeigte. Damals gehörte sie zu den avantgardistischen Japanern, die Schwarz in der Alltagsmode etablierten – was einige Kritiker gedankenlos als „Hiroshima Chic" geißelten. Damals wie heute ruft diese Mode ebenso viel Verwirrung wie Interesse hervor. Die 1942 in Tokio geborene und mit zahlreichen Auszeichnungen überhäufte Autodidaktin war übrigens nicht auf dem klassischen Pfad in die Modeindustrie. Vielmehr begann sie ihre Berufslaufbahn mit einem Literaturstudium an der Keio Universität von Tokio. Nach ihrem Abschluss 1964 trat sie in die Werbeabteilung des Chemie- und Textilunternehmens Ashai Kasei ein. Weil sie keine Kleidung fand, die ihr gefiel, begann sie, diese selbst zu entwerfen. Ihre erste Herrenkollektion präsentierte sie dann 1978, eine Möbellinie kam 1982 hinzu. Das Label bleibt progressiv: So experimentierte man etwa bei Comme-des-Garçons-Düften mit Teer, Gummi und dem Geruch von Nagellack. Alternative Vertriebsprojekte waren u. a. die zeitlich begrenzten Guerilla Stores in rückständigen Gegenden von – zumindest für die Modewelt – unbedeutenden Städten. Nicht zu vergessen der gigantische Dover Street Market in London, wo das Unternehmen, das Kawakubo gemeinsam mit ihrem britischen Ehemann Adrian Joffe führt, auch anderen gleichgesinnten Designern Raum bietet. Jüngste Kooperationen waren eine einmalige Kollektion für H&M im Herbst 2008, für die sie neben Herren-, Damen- und Kindermode auch ein Unisexparfum entwarf, das binnen weniger Stunden ausverkauft war, und eine Taschenkollektion bei Louis Vuitton anlässlich des 30-jährigen Jubiläums von Louis Vuitton in Japan.

Rei Kawakubo a créée Comme des Garçons à Tokyo en 1973. Tournant le dos aux règles établies, Rei Kawakubo taille et construit des vêtements qui ressemblent plus à des œuvres d'art qu'à des créations de mode. Son enthousiasme à défier les conventions attire l'attention du monde entier avec des vêtements confinant à l'uniforme – dont on n'arrive pas vraiment à savoir s'ils ont été conçus pour les hommes ou les femmes, qui déplacent la forme du corps féminin plutôt que de la souligner, qui utilisent des tissus atypiques et les déconstruisent parfois jusqu'au point de non retour. En 1981, elle lance Comme des Garçons en Occident lors de son premier défilé parisien et s'impose alors à l'avant-garde de la mode japonaise, qui introduit le noir comme un basique de la mode : un style que certains critiques peu inspirés surnommeront le « Hiroshima Chic ». À l'époque comme aujourd'hui, sa mode déroute autant qu'elle ravit. Autodidacte maintes fois primée, Rei Kawakubo (née en 1942 à Tokyo) est arrivée dans l'univers de la mode par des chemins détournés. Elle étudie d'abord la littérature à l'université Keio de Tokyo. En 1964, après l'obtention de son diplôme, elle travaille pour le département publicité d'Ashai Kasei, un fabricant de produits chimiques et textiles. Comme elle n'arrive pas à trouver dans le commerce les vêtements qu'elle a envie de porter, elle apprend à les confectionner elle-même. Elle lance une ligne pour homme en 1978, puis une collection de meubles en 1982. Comme des Garçons reste une griffe progressiste : par exemple, les parfums Comme des Garçons jouent sur d'étonnantes notes de goudron, de caoutchouc ou de vernis à ongles. Parmi ses projets les plus récents, elle a installé des boutiques-concepts éphémères dans des quartiers peu fréquentés de villes inattendues dans l'univers de la mode. Et dans le monolithique Dover Street Market de Londres, l'entreprise qu'elle dirige avec son mari anglais Adrian Joffe, loue également des ateliers à d'autres créateurs partageant le même état d'esprit. Ses dernières collaborations incluent une collection unique pour H&M en 2008, pour qui elle crée une ligne de mode et un parfum unisexe, vendus en quelques heures, et la création de sacs Louis Vuitton pour célébrer les 30 ans de présence de la marque au Japon.

JOSH SIMS

"I tell a story every season"
ADAM KIMMEL

Adam Kimmel began his career studying architecture at New York University, all the while sketching clothes on the side. In August 2003, he met a former president of Calvin Klein Menswear, and with his help began learning the business and craft, establishing relations with top production mills, and studying cut and design from Italian tailors and pattern makers. Upon returning to New York, Kimmel created his first full collection – a line of conservative outerwear, suits and what would become his signature jumpsuit, cut from utilitarian twills and cotton jersey, juxtaposed with heavy wools and cashmere. The collection was previewed for Autumn 2004, with a truthful, homecooked presentation – a look book, shot by his brother, photographer Alexei Hay, and styled, modelled and produced by his close friends. Colette immediately picked up his collection; and fashion editors, stylists and photographers began requesting made-to-measure pieces, leading Kimmel to set up an atelier in Manhattan's West Chelsea district. For Kimmel, men's clothes are about pushing towards a new sensibility while maintaining wearability. For him, it is about finding uncommon fabrics and unique proportions while keeping a simple, masculine silhouette. In Kimmel's collections, there also emerges an overall feeling of New York City, the atmosphere that he knows and loves best. It's that New York sense of versatility and attitude, worn by some of the key members of the downtown scene like Dan Colen, Ryan McGinley, Jack Pierson and Rita Ackerman. Kimmel's collection is sold in over 50 outlets throughout the world, including Colette in Paris, Bergdorf Goodman in New York, Comme des Garçons in Tokyo, 10 Corso Como in Milan and Dover Street Market in London. In summer 2008, Kimmel was invited to Florence Pitti L'Uomo, where he set up a studio and flew the artists in for a digital photo-shoot that was presented in hours on big screens. In 2009, he took over a gallery in Paris to show portraits by Gerard Malanga, reminding us of his groundbreaking black-and-white moving portraits in the '60s with Andy Warhol.

Adam Kimmel begann seine berufliche Laufbahn als Architekturstudent an der New York University, wobei er bereits damals nebenher Kleider zeichnete. Im August 2003 lernte er einen ehemaligen Chef der Calvin Klein Menswear kennen und ließ sich von ihm in das Modegeschäft und -handwerk einführen. Er baute sich Kontakte zu den besten Produktions-firmen auf und studierte Schnitt und Design bei italienischen Schneidern und Zuschneidern. Nach seiner Rückkehr entwarf Kimmel in New York seine erste komplette Kollektion – eine Linie mit konservativer Oberbeklei-dung, Anzügen und einem Hosenanzug, der zu seinem Markenzeichen werden sollte. Letzterer bestand aus praktischem Twill und Baumwoll-jersey sowie kontrastierender schwerer Wolle und Kaschmir. Man ver-anstaltete eine Preview der Kollektion für Herbst 2004, die wirklich eine ehrliche, hausgemachte Präsentation war – mit einem Lookbook, das sein Bruder, der Fotograf Alexei Hay, gemacht hatte, und von seinen engsten Freunden organisiert, gestylt und gemodelt. Colette griff seine Kollektion sofort auf, während Modejournalisten, Stylisten und Fotografen began-nen, Maßanfertigungen zu bestellen, sodass Kimmel bald ein Atelier in Manhattan, genauer gesagt in West Chelsea, eröffnete. In der Herrenmode geht es ihm um eine neue Sensibilität, die aber immer noch tragbar sein soll. In seinen Augen drückt sich das durch ungewöhnliche Stoffe und einzigartige Proportionen aus, während die Silhouette schlicht maskulin bleibt. In Kimmels Kollektionen spürt man auch allenthalben New York City, eine Atmosphäre, die der Designer selbst am besten kennt und am meisten liebt. Dieses New Yorker Gespür für Vielseitigkeit und innere Hal-tung merkt man auch einigen Schlüsselfiguren der Szene von Downtown an, etwa Dan Colen, Ryan McGinley, Jack Pierson und Rita Ackerman. Kimmels Kollektion wird in über 50 Läden in aller Welt verkauft, u. a. bei Colette in Paris, Bergdorf Goodman in New York, bei Comme des Garçons in Tokio, 10 Corso Como in Mailand und im Dover Street Market in Lon-don. Im Sommer 2008 lud man Kimmel zur Pitti L'Uomo nach Florenz, wo er ein Atelier aufbaute und die Künstler für ein digitales Fotoshooting einfliegen ließ, das innerhalb weniger Stunden auf großen Leinwänden zu sehen war. 2009 übernahm er eine Galerie in Paris, um dort Porträts von Gerard Malanga auszustellen, die an dessen bahnbrechende Filmporträts mit Andy Warhol in den Sechzigern erinnern.

Pendant ses études d'architecture à l'Université de New York, Adam Kimmel passe son temps libre à dessiner des vêtements. En août 2003, il rencontre un ancien dirigeant de Calvin Klein Menswear qui l'initie aux ficelles commerciales et créatives du métier : il noue des relations avec de grands fabricants et étudie l'art de la coupe et de la création auprès de tailleurs et de traceurs de patrons italiens. De retour à New York, Kimmel conçoit sa première collection complète : des vêtements d'extérieur classiques, des costumes et ce qui deviendra son « jumpsuit » signature, où les toiles utilitaires et le jersey de coton côtoient la grosse laine et le cachemire. Sa collection est présentée en avant-première pour la saison automne 2004 avec les moyens du bord : un look book réalisé par son frère, le photographe Alexei Hay, et ses amis proches dans les rôles de D.A., mannequins et producteurs. Colette se jette d'emblée sur sa collection, les journalistes, les stylistes de magazines et les photographes de mode commencent à lui commander des vêtements sur mesure, ce qui conduit Kimmel à ouvrir un atelier dans West Chelsea à Manhattan. Selon lui, les vêtements pour homme doivent afficher une nouvelle sensibilité tout en restant portables. Il explore des tissus insolites et des proportions uniques tout en préservant la simplicité de la silhouette masculine. En général, les créations de Kimmel laissent transparaître une sensibilité purement new-yorkaise, celle qu'il connaît le mieux et qu'il aime le plus. Elle correspond à l'esprit de polyvalence et à l'attitude adoptés par certains des membres les plus éminents de la scène de New York, comme Dan Colen, Ryan McGinley, Jack Pierson et Rita Ackerman. Les collections de Kimmel sont distribuées dans plus de 50 points de vente à travers le monde, notamment chez Colette à Paris, Bergdorf Goodman à New York, Comme des Garçons à Tokyo, 10 Corso Como à Milan et au Dover Street Market de Londres. Quand Kimmel est invité au salon Pitti Uomo de Florence en été 2008, il y crée un atelier et fait venir plusieurs artistes pour une séance photo numérique présentée à peine quelques heures plus tard sur des écrans géants. En 2009, il reprend la direction d'une galerie parisienne pour promouvoir les portraits du photographe Gerard Malanga qui rappellent les films révolutionnaires en noir et blanc que ce dernier a réalisés avec Andy Warhol dans les années 60.

TERRY JONES

"My aim is always to hit a chord"
SOPHIA KOKOSALAKI

Sophia Kokosalaki has never gone about things the usual way. Instead, she relies on single-minded individualism. Born in Athens in 1972, Kokosalaki's first love was literature, studying Greek and English at the University of Athens. She went to London in 1996 and completed a womenswear MA at Central Saint Martins. For her graduation show, she worked with Abigail Lane to produce the video installation 'Never Never Mind' and her graduate collection was snapped up by the (now defunct) London boutique Pellicano. Kokosalaki set up her own label in 1999 and quickly established a trademark style, dipping into the rich heritage of ancient Greek drapery, a '70s folk aesthetic and complex leatherwork. It wasn't long before others wanted a piece of the action. In June 1999, Kokosalaki worked on a knitwear line for Joseph. By 2000, after just three solo collections, she was invited to work as a guest designer for Italian leather goods label Ruffo Research. She also entertained the more accessible end of the fashion market, producing two capsule collections for Topshop's TS label. In 2004, she was chosen to design the costumes for the Athens Olympic Games, the highlight of which was a vast marine-blue dress worn by Björk. Despite such demanding extracurricular activities, her day job has flourished. A menswear line was set up in 2000 and a shoe collection was added in 2003. The recipient of many awards, Kokosalaki's notable gongs include the first ever Art Foundation Award given to a fashion designer. Kokosalaki constantly develops her themes, and dedicated fans return every season as she evolves – rather than rethinks – her signatures. Both cerebral and fun-loving, Kokosalaki is never complacent.

Sophia Kokosalaki ist die Dinge noch nie auf herkömmliche Weise angegangen. Stattdessen setzt sie auf zielstrebigen Individualismus. Die erste Liebe der 1972 in Athen geborenen Designerin galt der Literatur, weshalb sie zunächst Griechisch und Englisch an der Universität ihrer Heimatstadt studierte. 1996 ging sie nach London, wo sie einen Master in Damenmode am Central Saint Martins erwarb. Für ihre Abschlusskollektion tat sie sich mit Abigail Lane zusammen und produzierte die Videoinstallation „Never Never Mind". Die Kollektion selbst sicherte sich die inzwischen nicht mehr existierende Londoner Boutique Pellicano. 1999 gründete Kokosalaki ihr eigenes Label und etablierte schnell einen unverwechselbaren Stil. Dazu nahm sie Anleihen bei den im antiken Griechenland üblichen Drapierungen sowie der Folk-Ästhetik der 1970er-Jahre und kombinierte beides mit aufwendigen Lederarbeiten. Schon bald waren ihre Entwürfe extrem begehrt. Kokosalaki kreierte im Juni 1999 eine Strickkollektion für Joseph. Und bereits im Mai 2000, nach nur drei Solokollektionen, wurde sie als Gastdesignerin vom italienischen Lederwarenhersteller Ruffo Research eingeladen. Sie bediente aber auch das

erschwinglichere Ende des Modemarktes mit zwei Minikollektionen für das Label TS bei Topshop. 2004 bekam sie den Auftrag für die Kostüme zu den Olympischen Spielen von Athen. Das Highlight dieser Kollektion war das aufwendige marineblaue Kleid für die Sängerin Björk. Trotz solch anspruchsvoller Nebentätigkeiten ist die Designerin auch in ihrem Hauptberuf produktiv. Im Jahr 2000 wurde eine Herrenlinie ins Leben gerufen, eine Schuhkollektion kam 2003 hinzu. Unter ihren zahlreichen Auszeichnungen verdient der erste je für Modedesign verliehene Art Foundation Award besondere Beachtung. Kokosalaki entwickelt ihre Themen ständig weiter, und so kehren pflichtbewusste Fans in jeder Saison zu ihr zurück, um zu sehen, wie sie ihre Charakteristika mehr aus- als umarbeitet. Kokosalaki ist nachdenklich und lebenslustig zugleich, aber niemals selbstgefällig.

Privilégiant son farouche individualisme, Sophia Kokosalaki ne fait jamais rien comme tout le monde. Née en 1972 à Athènes, elle se passionne d'abord pour la littérature et étudie le grec et l'anglais à l'université d'Athènes. Elle s'installe à Londres en 1996, où elle décroche un master en mode féminine à Central Saint Martins. Pour sa présentation de fin d'études, elle collabore avec Abigail Lane sur l'installation vidéo « Never Never Mind », une collection sur laquelle se jette la boutique londonienne Pellicano (fermée depuis). Sophia Kokosalaki crée sa propre griffe en 1999 et impose rapidement son style caractéristique, inspiré par le riche héritage des drapés grecs antiques, une esthétique folk très années 70 et un travail élaboré du cuir. Son travail ne tarde pas à attirer l'attention d'autres créateurs. En juin 1999, Sophia Kokosalaki conçoit une ligne en maille pour Joseph. En l'an 2000, après seulement trois collections en solo, le maroquinier italien Ruffo Research lui commande également des collections. Elle a aussi travaillé pour le marché plus accessible de la grande consommation en produisant deux mini-collections pour la griffe TS de Topshop. En 2004, on lui confie la création des costumes des Jeux olympiques d'Athènes, dont personne n'oubliera jamais la volumineuse robe bleu marine portée par Björk. En dépit de ses nombreuses activités annexes, sa propre griffe prospère. Elle a lancé une ligne pour homme en l'an 2000 et une collection de chaussures en 2003. Couronnée de nombreux prix, elle a notamment reçu le premier Art Foundation Award jamais remis à un couturier. Sophia Kokosalaki n'a de cesse de développer ses propres thématiques et ses fans lui restent fidèles chaque saison, quand elle propose une évolution plutôt qu'une réinterprétation de ses looks signature. À la fois cérébrale et insouciante, Sophia Kokosalaki ne fait jamais dans la complaisance.

LAUREN COCHRANE

"There's no point in design for design's sake. Everything I believe in is about getting women dressed"
MICHAEL KORS

Michael Kors designs pure American opulence: luxurious perfectly tailored sportswear in contrasting textures of leather and cashmere with a cheeky flash of pelt. Growing up in deepest suburbia, Kors (born Long Island) always had a healthy focus on fashion and the city of New York. After studying design at the Fashion Institute of Technology, New York, by the age of 19 he was designing and merchandising for Lothar's boutique. The attention this received by the fashion press led him to launch the Michael Kors label in 1981. The Kors Michael Kors bridge line followed in 1995. After launching a capsule menswear collection in 1997, Kors was named the first women's ready-to-wear designer for the house of Céline. By February 1999, he had become creative director of the luxury label, overseeing all women's products. 1999 marked the beginning of a remarkable period for Kors: he received the CFDA Award for Womenswear Designer of the Year, followed by the Menswear Designer of the Year Award in 2003. His contribution to the world of accessories was also recognised, with Kors being nominated five years in a row (2001–06) for the prestigious Accessories Designer of the Year award. He has also had success in the fragrance world, launching his signature scent in 2000, a cologne Michael for Men in 2001, and the FiFi-award-winning Island scent in 2005. While 2004 saw Kors make his TV debut as one of the judges on the Emmy-nominated reality TV show 'Project Runway', a role that he continues to hold for the programme's five series. With celebrity fans including Jennifer Lopez, Charlize Theron, Liv Tyler, Gwyneth Paltrow, Anjelica Huston and Madonna, Kors continues to design to a sophisticated ethic, a sexy American Dream.

Michael Kors entwirft amerikanische Opulenz in Reinkultur: luxuriöse, perfekt geschnittene Freizeitmode aus Leder und Kaschmir als Materialien mit kontrastierender Textur, dazu frech aufblitzender Pelz. Aufgewachsen ist der auf Long Island geborene Kors in der Vorstadt, doch hatte er bereits dort die Mode und New York City genau im Blick. Nach dem Studium am New Yorker Fashion Institute of Technology entwarf er schon mit 19 erfolgreich für Lothar's Boutique. Nachdem er damit bereits die Aufmerksamkeit der Modepresse auf sich gezogen hatte, wagte er sich 1981 an die Gründung eines eigenen Labels mit seinem Namen. Die preiswertere Nebenlinie Kors Michael Kors folgte 1995. Nach der Präsentation einer kleinen Herrenkollektion im Jahr 1997 wurde Kors erster Designer für die Prêt-à-porter-Damenmode im Hause Céline. Bis Februar 1999 war er zum Creative Director des Luxuslabels aufgestiegen und fortan für alle Damenprodukte zuständig. 1999 war aber auch in anderer Hinsicht ein bemerkenswertes Jahr für Kors: Das CFDA ernannte ihn

zum Womenswear Designer of the Year. 2003 folgte die Auszeichnung als Menswear Designer of the Year. Seine Leistungen im Bereich Accessoires wurden ebenfalls honoriert, denn Kors war von 2001 bis 2005 fünfmal in Folge für den renommierten Titel Accessories Designer of the Year nominiert. Auch in der Welt der Düfte kann Kors Erfolge verzeichnen: Im Jahr 2000 brachte er ein Parfüm mit seinem Namen heraus, 2001 Michael for Men, 2005 folgte der mit dem Fifi ausgezeichnete Duft Island Michael Kors. 2004 gab Kors sein TV-Debüt als einer der Juroren in der für die Emmys nominierten Reality-Show „Project Runway". Diese Rolle übernimmt er seit nunmehr fünf Staffeln der Sendung. Mit prominenten Fans wie Jennifer Lopez, Charlize Theron, Liv Tyler, Gwyneth Paltrow, Anjelica Huston und Madonna setzt Kors seine Arbeit am Design eines sexy American Dream fort.

Michael Kors crée dans la plus pure tradition de l'opulence américaine : sportswear luxueux aux coupes impeccables, taillé dans des matières contrastées de cuir et de cachemire, avec quelques touches audacieuses de peau ça et là. Né à Long Island et élevé en banlieue, Kors a toujours eu une vision plutôt saine de la mode et de la ville de New York. Après des études de design au Fashion Institute of Technology, dès l'âge de 19 ans il commence à dessiner pour la boutique Lothar's. Encouragé par l'intérêt de la presse spécialisée, il crée la griffe Michael Kors en 1981, suivie en 1995 par la ligne de vêtements plus abordables Kors Michael Kors. Après le lancement d'une collection capsule pour homme en 1997, Kors est nommé styliste principal du prêt-à-porter féminin de la maison Céline. En février 1999, il devient directeur de la création de la griffe de luxe et supervise tous les produits pour femme. 1999 est une année en or pour Kors : le CFDA le consacre Womenswear Designer of the Year, puis Menswear Designer of the Year en 2003. Sa contribution dans le domaine des accessoires est également distinguée par cinq nominations consécutives (2001 – 2005) au prestigieux Accessories Designer of the Year Award. Il remporte tout autant de succès côté parfums : il lance sa fragrance éponyme en l'an 2000, le parfum masculin Michael for Men en 2001 et Island Michael Kors en 2005, couronné d'un Fifi Award. En 2004, Kors fait ses débuts à la télévision dans le jury de l'émission de télé-réalité « Project Runway », nommée aux Emmy Awards, un rôle qu'il continue d'assumer pour la cinquième saison du programme. Avec des fans aussi célèbres que Jennifer Lopez, Charlize Theron, Liv Tyler, Gwyneth Paltrow, Anjelica Huston et Madonna, Kors conserve toutefois une éthique sophistiquée, à l'image d'un sexy American Dream.

"Creation never ends, once you start you can't stop"
TAO KURIHARA

Comme des Garçons protégée Tao Kurihara is one of the most exciting young Japanese designers working today. Born in Tokyo in 1973, Kurihara moved to London when she finished school to study fashion at Central Saint Martins. In 1998, one year after graduating, she began work at Comme des Garçons, and in 2002 was appointed designer of the Tricot Comme des Garçons line. She spent the next eight years working closely with Junya Watanabe, before launching her own label under the Comme umbrella in 2005. Kurihara rose to the challenge, presenting her debut collection Tao for Spring/Summer 2006 to instant critical acclaim. Working with knitwear, lace and lingerie, the small, concentrated collection of coquettish corsets, shorts and baby-doll dresses notched up more editorial than other new designers could hope to achieve in a lifetime. Always true to her own vision, Kurihara fiercely pursues her own path, claiming she doesn't make clothes she thinks people will like, but rather clothes she likes herself. In just a short number of years, she has risen up the ranks from showing off-schedule to being one of the most hyped and talked about shows on the catwalk schedule, with journalists and buyers falling over themselves to gain attendance. From her wedding dress collection to her vast twisting and voluminous silhouettes, Kurihara's clothes continue to challenge the imagination as much as she challenges the zeitgeist.

Tao Kurihara, Protegé von Comme des Garçons, ist wohl eine der aufregendsten japanischen Designerinnen der Gegenwart. 1973 in Tokio geboren, zog sie am Ende ihrer Schulzeit nach London, um am Central Saint Martins Mode zu studieren. Ein Jahr nach ihrem Studienabschluss (1998), begann sie bei Comme des Garçons, wo man sie 2002 zur Designerin der Tricot-Linie ernannte. In den folgenden acht Jahren arbeitete sie eng mit Junya Watanabe zusammen, bevor sie 2005 ihr eigenes Label unter dem Schirm von Comme gründete. Kurihara stellte sich der Herausforderung und präsentierte ihre Debütkollektion „Tao" für Frühjahr/ Sommer 2006, die bei den Kritikern auf Anhieb Zustimmung fand. Ihre Arbeiten aus Strick, Spitze und Dessous im Rahmen dieser kleinen, konzentrierten Kollektion aus koketten Corsagen, Shorts und Baby-Doll-Kleidern erzielte mehr Medienecho, als andere Jungdesigner in ihrem ganzen Leben bekommen. Kurihara bleibt stets ihrer eigenen Vision treu, verfolgt ihren Weg konsequent und behauptet von sich, keine Kleider zu machen, von denen sie glaubt, sie könnten den Leuten gefallen, sondern vielmehr Kleidung, die ihr selbst gefällt. In nur wenigen Jahren hat sie den Sprung von den Off-Präsentationen zu einem der meist gehypten und besprochenen Events im offiziellen Catwalk-Kalender vollbracht. Journalisten wie Einkäufer überschlagen sich fast, um daran teilnehmen zu können. Ob mit ihren Hochzeitskleidern oder den riesigen verwundenen und voluminösen Silhouetten – Kuriharas Kleider fordern nach wie vor die Fatansie ebenso heraus wie sie selbst den Zeitgeist.

Petite protégée de Comme des Garçons, Tao Kurihara est l'une des jeunes créatrices japonaises les plus prometteuses du moment. Née à Tokyo en 1973, Tao s'installe à Londres après ses études secondaires pour suivre le cursus en mode du Central Saint Martins. En 1998, un an après l'obtention de son diplôme, elle commence à travailler chez Comme des Garçons, où elle est nommée styliste de la ligne Tricot Comme des Garçons en 2002. Elle collabore étroitement avec Junya Watanabe pendant huit ans avant de lancer sa propre griffe sous la houlette de Comme des Garçons en 2005, un défi que Tao Kurihara relève sans problème : la première collection baptisée « Tao » qu'elle présente pour le printemps/été 2006 est immédiatement plébiscitée par la critique. Marquée par la maille, la dentelle et la lingerie, cette petite collection concentrée sur les corsets aguichants, les shorts et les robes baby-doll fait l'objet de plus d'articles de presse que tout autre jeune créateur n'espère en obtenir dans sa vie. Toujours fidèle à son approche personnelle, Tao Kurihara poursuit son chemin avec acharnement, affirmant qu'elle ne crée pas des vêtements pour qu'ils plaisent aux gens, mais pour qu'ils lui plaisent à elle. En quelques années seulement, elle a quitté le calendrier « off » pour s'imposer parmi les noms dont on parle le plus dans l'agenda des défilés officiels, les journalistes et les acheteurs faisant des pieds et des mains pour y assister. De sa collection de robes de mariée à ses nombreux modèles tordus et volumineux, les collections de Tao Kurihara ne cessent de défier l'imagination tout comme la créatrice défie l'esprit du temps.

HOLLY SHACKLETON

"I love fashion and the evolution of time"
KARL LAGERFELD + CHANEL

Karl Lagerfeld is perhaps the ultimate fashion designer. Lagerfeld's ever-present ponytail, fan and sunglasses are iconic; his personal preference for bespoke white shirts by Hilditch & Key, Chrome Hearts jewellery and Dior Homme suits is well documented. In addition to his work for both Chanel and Fendi, since 1998 Lagerfeld has designed his own label, Lagerfeld Gallery. Born in Hamburg in 1938, Lagerfeld moved to Paris at the age of 14. At just 17, he landed his first job, at Pierre Balmain, moving to Jean Patou three years later. Despite this traditional start, Lagerfeld chose not to establish his own house but instead to pursue a career as a freelance designer. From 1963 to 1983 and 1992 to 1997 Lagerfeld designed Chloé. In 1965, he also began to design for Fendi, a role that he retains to this day; in 1983, he was appointed artistic director of Chanel. 1984 saw the first incarnation of his own label, Karl Lagerfeld, which was later superseded by Lagerfeld Gallery, an art/retail venture. It is the latter that expresses the remarkable range of this genuine polymath. In addition to ready-to-wear collections, Lagerfeld Gallery is a platform for his myriad passions, including photography (he often shoots his own ad campaigns, along with editorial for numerous magazines), books (he has his own imprint, 7L, and a personal library of 230,000 volumes), perfume, art and magazines. In December 2004, it was announced that Tommy Hilfiger had purchased Lagerfeld Gallery. This followed a phenomenally successful link-up with mass-market retailer H&M in autumn 2004, when shoppers clamoured for a garment designed by an acknowledged maestro of fashion. Lagerfeld's artistic direction continues to build on Chanel's empire in the 21st century: epic commercials for Chanel No.5 starring Nicole Kidman (2005) and a Mobile Art project designed by Zaha Hadid that travelled from Tokyo to New York (2008). In 2011, Karl still designs for Fendi and Chanel, and for his own line, but has recently decided to take a less central role, instead focusing his attentions on a new collection based on mass elitism, entitled 'Masstige'. Between creating new labels, sketching, filming and reading books (and producing them), it's hard to believe Karl still finds time to catch his precious eight hours' sleep a night.

Man könnte Karl Lagerfeld als den Inbegriff des Modedesigners bezeichnen. Sein Pferdeschwanz, sein Fächer und seine Sonnenbrille sind legendär, seine persönliche Vorliebe für weiße Maßhemden von Hilditch & Key, Schmuck von Chrome Hearts und Anzüge von Dior Homme bestens dokumentiert. Neben seiner Tätigkeit für Chanel und Fendi entwirft Lagerfeld seit 1988 auch für sein eigenes Label Lagerfeld Gallery. Geboren wurde der Modeschöpfer 1938 in Hamburg. Mit 14 Jahren kam er nach Paris, und mit 17 Jahren hatte er bereits seinen ersten Job. Drei Jahre später wechselte er zu Jean Patou. Trotz dieses traditionellen Karrierestarts entschied Lagerfeld sich gegen die Gründung eines eigenen Modehauses und für die Laufbahn eines unabhängigen Designers. Von 1963 bis 1983 sowie von 1992 bis 1997 entwarf er für Chloé. 1965 begann er außerdem mit seiner Tätigkeit für Fendi, die bis heute andauert. 1983 berief man ihn zum künstlerischen Leiter von Chanel. 1984 machte er dann erstmals mit einem eigenen Label, Karl Lagerfeld, von sich reden, das später von dem Kunst- und Einzelhandelsprojekt Lagerfeld Gallery abgelöst wurde. Dieses Unternehmen wird der Bandbreite des Universalgenies am besten gerecht. Neben den Prêt-à-porter-Kollektionen ist Lagerfeld Gallery auch

Bühne für die unzähligen Passionen des Designers, darunter Fotografie (oft fotografiert er außer Fotostrecken für zahlreiche Magazine auch seine Kampagnen selbst), Bücher (sein eigenes Imprint heißt 7L, die Privatbibliothek umfasst 230.000 Bände), Parfüm, Kunst und Zeitschriften. Im Dezember 2004 wurde bekannt, dass Tommy Hilfiger Lagerfeld Gallery gekauft hatte. Dem war eine erfolgreiche Kooperation mit der Kette H&M im Herbst desselben Jahres vorausgegangen. Damals rissen sich die Kunden um die Entwürfe des berühmten Modezaren. Lagerfelds künstlerische Ziele liegen nach wie vor in der Weiterentwicklung des Chanel-Imperiums: etwa durch epische Spots für Chanel No.5 mit Nicole Kidman (2005) oder mittels eines von Zaha Hadid kreierten Kunstprojekts namens Mobile Art, das von Tokio bis nach New York tourte (2008). Vor Kurzem hat Karl beschlossen, sich ein wenig aus dem Rampenlicht zurückzuziehen und sich stattdessen mit einer neuen Kollektion zu beschäftigen: eine bezahlbare Modelinie im Niedrigpreissegment, die unter dem Namen „Masstige" auf den Markt kommt. Schläft er wirklich jede Nacht acht Stunden?

Karl Lagerfeld est peut-être l'incarnation même du créateur de mode. La queue de cheval, l'éventail et les lunettes noires qu'il porte en permanence sont devenus cultes ; son goût personnel pour les chemises blanches taillées sur mesure par Hilditch & Key, les bijoux Chrome Hearts et les costumes Dior Homme a été largement commenté. Outre son travail chez Chanel et Fendi, Lagerfeld dessine sa propre griffe depuis 1998 sous le nom de Lagerfeld Gallery. Né en 1938 à Hambourg, Lagerfeld s'installe à Paris dès 14 ans. À 17 ans, il décroche son premier emploi chez Pierre Balmain puis part chez Jean Patou trois ans plus tard. En dépit de ces débuts classiques, Lagerfeld n'ouvre pas sa propre maison préférant poursuivre sa carrière de créateur free-lance. De 1963 à 1983 et de 1992 à 1997, il dessine les collections de Chloé. En 1965, il commence aussi à travailler pour Fendi, poste qu'il occupe encore aujourd'hui ; en 1983, il est nommé directeur artistique de Chanel. 1984 voit la naissance de sa propre griffe, Karl Lagerfeld, plus tard remplacée par Lagerfeld Gallery, mêlant art et mode. Lagerfeld Gallery, avec sa boutique rue de Seine à Paris et une autre à Monaco, exprime toute la palette des talents de ce grand érudit. Outre le prêt-à-porter, Lagerfeld Gallery représente une belle plate-forme d'expression pour sa myriade de passions, comme la photographie (il réalise souvent ses propres campagnes publicitaires ainsi que des shootings photo pour de nombreux magazines), les livres (sa propre maison d'édition 7L et sa bibliothèque personnelle de 230 000 volumes), le parfum, l'art et les magazines. En décembre 2004, Tommy Hilfiger annonce le rachat de Lagerfeld Gallery, peu après une collaboration couronnée de succès avec la chaîne de boutiques H&M : la vente de la petite collection dessinée par Lagerfeld provoque de véritables scènes d'empoigne chez les clients impatients de s'offrir des vêtements signés par un maestro de la mode. Au 21e siècle, la direction artistique de Lagerfeld continue à développer l'empire Chanel, des films publicitaires épiques pour Chanel N° 5 avec Nicole Kidman (2005) au pavillon d'exposition itinérant conçu avec l'architecte Zaha Hadid, un projet qui a voyagé de Tokyo à New York (2008). Récemment, Karl s'est éloigné de la scène pour se dédier à une nouvelle collection, abordable en termes de prix, et baptisé « Masstige ». Dort-il vraiment huit heures chaque nuit ?

SUSIE RUSHTON

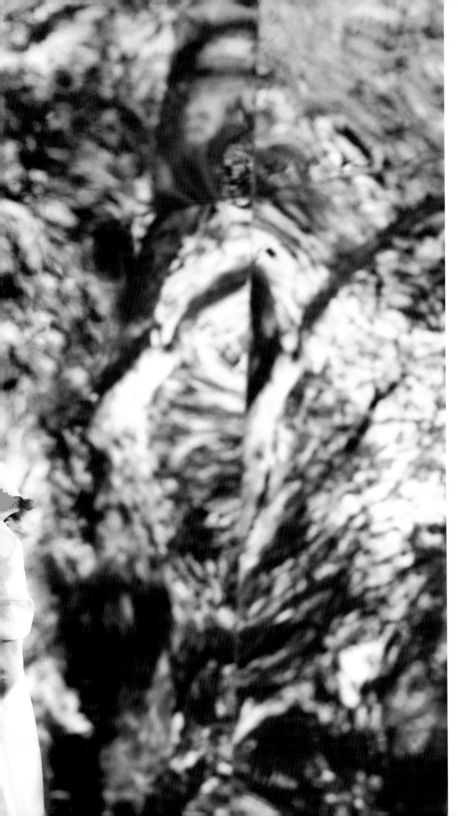

PHOTOGRAPHY KAYT JONES. STYLING PIPPA VOSPER. MODEL CHANEL IMAN. MAY 2009.

"I believe in style, not fashion"
RALPH LAUREN

Ralph Lauren (born 1939) is a household name. Jamaica has even issued a commemorative stamp (in 2004) featuring Lauren. The man and his brand's logo of a polo player riding a horse is recognised by all. From a $50,000 loan in 1968, Polo Ralph Lauren's grew from humble beginnings into the internationally famous lifestyle brand that everyone knows today. Lauren was one of the first designers to extend his production of clothing lines to houseware and furniture. He was also the first of the megabrand American designers to set up shop in Europe, in 1981; the Polo Ralph Lauren Corporation now has over 300 stores in operation globally and its collections are divided into myriad different labels. In October 2004 in Boston the company opened its first Rugby store, a lifestyle collection for 18-to-25-year-old men and women. The Rugby line joins Lauren's other collections, Purple Label (1994), Blue Label (2002) and Black Label (2005). Underpinning Lauren's designs is an unmistakable preference for old-world gentility. In fact, he has made the Ivy League, preppy style his own. "I don't want to be in fashion – I want to be a fashion," he once told 'Vogue' magazine. And indeed, the Ralph Lauren look is distinctive, nowhere more purely expressed than in his advertising campaigns that always feature a cast of thoroughbred models, often posed as if holidaying in the Hamptons. Lauren's entrance into fashion can be traced back to 1964 with Brooks Brothers, and then Beau Brummell Neckwear in 1967, where he designed wide ties. In the following year, the beginnings of what was to become a billion-dollar brand took root. The Polo menswear line was launched and in 1970 he won the Coty Menswear Award; Lauren added womenswear to the brand in 1971. He has been awarded the CFDA's Lifetime Achievement Award (1992) along with its Menswear designer (1995) and Womenswear designer (1996) prizes. Lauren is also involved in philanthropic activities. The Polo Ralph Lauren Foundation organises campaigns such as Pink Pony (2000), which supports cancer care and medically underserved communities. In 2006, Lauren became the official outfitter of Wimbledon and in 2008 an official outfitter of the 2008 US Olympic and Paralympic teams.

Ralph Lauren (Jahrgang 1939) ist ein allgemein bekannter Name. Jamaika brachte 2004 sogar eine Lauren-Gedenkbriefmarke heraus. Polo Ralph Laurens bescheidene Anfänge mit einem Kredit über 50.000 Dollar im Jahr 1968 haben sich zu einem international berühmten Lifestylelabel, das heute jeder kennt, entwickelt. Lauren dehnte als einer der ersten Modedesigner seine Produktpalette auf Wohnaccessoires und Möbel aus. Er war auch einer der ersten Designer amerikanischer Megamarken, die Läden in Europa eröffneten (1981). Heute betreibt die Polo Ralph Lauren Corporation über 300 Läden rund um den Globus und hat ihre Kollektionen auf unzählige verschiedene Labels verteilt. Im Oktober 2004 eröffnete das Unternehmen in Boston den ersten Laden namens Rugby, der eine Lifestylekollektion für 18- bis 25-jährige Männer und Frauen führt. Rugby ergänzt die Linien Purple Label (1994), Blue Label (2002) und Black Label (2005). Allen Entwürfen Laurens liegt eine unzweifelhafte Vorliebe für das Elitedenken der Alten Welt zugrunde. Genau genommen hat sich der Designer den Ivy-League- und Preppy-Stil zu eigen gemacht. „Ich möchte nicht in Mode sein – ich möchte eine Mode sein", hat er der Vogue einmal gesagt. Und tatsächlich ist sein Look unverwechselbar und springt nirgendwo klarer ins Auge als in seinen Werbekampagnen, die immer eine

rassige Schar von Models zeigen, die wirken, als machten sie gerade Ferien in den Hamptons. Laurens Anfänge in der Modebranche lassen sich bis ins Jahr 1964 und zu Brooks Brothers zurückverfolgen. 1967 entwarf er bei Beau Brummell Neckwear breite Krawatten, und bereits im folgenden Jahr nahm das, was einmal eine Milliarden-Dollar-Marke werden sollte, seinen Anfang. Alles begann mit der Herrenlinie Polo, für die Lauren 1970 den Coty Menswear Award erhielt. 1971 kam Damenmode ins Sortiment des Labels. Von der CFDA wurde er mit dem Lifetime Achievement Award (1992) ausgezeichnet, bevor er den Designerpreis sowohl für Menswear (1995) als auch für Womenswear (1996) erhielt. Lauren ist aber auch gemeinnützig tätig. Die Polo Ralph Lauren Foundation organisiert Kampagnen wie Pink Pony (2000), die Krebspatienten und medizinisch unterversorgten Gemeinden in den USA zugute kommen. 2006 wurde Lauren offizieller Ausstatter von Wimbledon und 2008 offizieller Ausstatter der amerikanischen Olympia- und Paralympics-Mannschaft.

Ralph Lauren (né en 1939) est célèbre dans le monde entier. En 2004, la Jamaïque a même édité un timbre commémoratif à son effigie. Tout le monde connaît l'homme, comme son logo de joueur de polo. À partir d'un prêt de 50 000 dollars obtenu en 1968, les débuts modestes de Polo Ralph Lauren se sont transformés en une marque de lifestyle incontournable. Ralph Lauren est l'un des premiers créateurs de mode à s'être diversifié dans le meuble et les articles pour la maison. Sa mégamarque américaine est également la première à ouvrir une boutique en Europe dès 1981 ; Polo Ralph Lauren Corporation possède aujourd'hui plus de 300 boutiques à travers le monde et ses collections sont divisées en une myriade de griffes différentes. En octobre 2004, l'entreprise ouvre sa première boutique Rugby à Boston, une collection complète destinée aux 18 – 25 ans, hommes et femmes. La ligne Rugby vient s'ajouter à Purple Label (1994), Blue Label (2002) et Black Label (2005). Une indubitable prédilection pour la distinction à l'ancienne étaye les créations de Lauren, qui s'est en fait approprié le chic BCBG de l'Ivy League. « Je ne veux pas être à la mode : je veux être une mode », déclare-t-il un jour au magazine Vogue. En effet, le look distingué de Ralph Lauren s'exprime de façon plus qu'évidente dans ses campagnes publicitaires qui présentent toujours un casting de mannequins racés, souvent mis en situation dans un décor de vacances rappelant les Hamptons. Les débuts de Lauren dans la mode remontent à 1964 chez Brooks Brothers, puis chez Beau Brummell Neckwear en 1967, où il commence à dessiner des cravates larges. L'année suivante voit la naissance de ce qui devait devenir un énorme groupe évalué à un milliard de dollars. Après avoir lancé la ligne masculine Polo, Ralph Lauren remporte le Coty Menswear Award en 1970, puis crée une collection pour femme en 1971. Le créateur a été couronné du Lifetime Achievement Award du CFDA (1992), avant d'obtenir des prix dans les catégories masculines (1995) et féminines (1996). Ralph Lauren s'implique également dans des activités caritatives : la fondation Polo Ralph organise des campagnes telles que Pink Pony (2000) en faveur du traitement contre le cancer et des communautés mal desservies sur le plan médical. En 2006, il devient le styliste officiel de Wimbledon et en 2008 des équipes olympiques et paralympiques américaines.

KAREN HODKINSON

PHOTOGRAPHY MITCHELL SAMS. AUTUMN/WINTER 2009.

"I find designing actually quite natural and exciting"
CHRISTOPHE LEMAIRE · LACOSTE

Recognised for his fresh, flawless cuts and elegant tailoring, Christophe Lemaire of Lacoste is concerned more with the quality of his lines than with slavishly following trends. With a style he describes as "graphic, pure, relaxed and precise", he captures the balance between fashion and function, creating classic, wearable clothing season after season. Born in Besançon, France, in April 1965, Lemaire initially assisted at the Yves Saint Laurent design studio before going on to work for Thierry Mugler and Jean Patou. Through the Jean Patou house, he met Christian Lacroix, who was so impressed with the young designer that he appointed him head of his own women's ready-to-wear line in 1987. Lemaire went solo with his eponymous womenswear label in 1990. His functional designs, with their understated elegance, ensured the label's success and a menswear label followed in 1994. In May 2001, Lemaire became creative director of heritage sportswear brand Lacoste, where he has re-established the company's position on the fashion map. Infusing his own contemporary, sharp style into classics such as the tennis skirt, polo shirt or preppy college jumper, he has attracted new customers while retaining enough of the brand's 70-year-old tradition so as not to lose the old. In June 2001, under his direction, Lacoste staged its first catwalk show. A true fashion DJ, for his own collections Lemaire mixes Western classics with one-of-a-kind ethnic pieces. The result is resolutely modern yet always wearable. "I don't create in a rush," he explains. "I always take time so I can distance myself from things that are too fashionable. As a designer, I aim for an accessible balance between beauty and function to create a vision of contemporary 'easy wearing'." The synergy between Lemaire and Lacoste has been a classic win-win that has allowed Lemaire to retail his own label while reinventing Lacoste as a cool, savvy brand for a global market. For his Autumn/Winter 2009 collection, Lemaire introduced a more upmarket tailoring and streamlined silhouettes with the crocodile subtly camouflaged tone on tone. Felipe Oliveira Baptista succeeded Lemaire in 2010 following Lemaire's appointment as Creative Director at Hermes. Oliveira's much anticipated first collection will debut Spring/Summer 2012.

Der für seine frischen, tadellosen Schnitte und die elegante Verarbeitung bekannte Christophe Lemaire kümmert sich mehr um die Qualität seiner Linien als um die sklavische Befolgung von Trends. Sein Stil, den er selbst „grafisch, puristisch, entspannt und präzise" nennt, trifft exakt den richtigen Ton zwischen Fashion und Function und bringt Saison für Saison klassische, tragbare Kreationen hervor. Lemaire wurde im April 1965 im französischen Besançon geboren. Bevor er für Thierry Mugler und Jean Patou arbeitete, war er bei Yves Saint Laurent. Über Jean Patou lernte er Christian Lacroix kennen, der von dem jungen Designer so begeistert war, dass er ihn 1987 zum Chef seiner Prêt-à-porter-Linie für Damen machte. Sein eigenes Damenmodelabel brachte Lemaire 1990 auf den Markt. Die zurückhaltende Eleganz der Entwürfe sorgte für unmittelbaren Erfolg. Ein entsprechendes Männerlabel folgte 1994. Im Mai 2001 wurde Lemaire Creative Director der traditionellen Sportswear-Marke Lacoste und brachte das Unternehmen zurück in die Erste Liga der Mode. Er ließ seinen zeitgemäß klaren Stil in Klassiker wie Tennisröcke, Polohemden und Collegepullover einfließen und sprach damit eine neue Klientel an, bewahrte aber genug von der 70-jährigen Tradition der Marke, um

die Stammkundschaft nicht zu verprellen. Im Juni 2001 veranstaltete Lacoste unter Lemaires Leitung seine erste Catwalk-Show. Als wahrer Fashion-DJ mixt Lemaire für seine eigenen Kollektionen abendländische Klassiker mit Ethno-Unikaten. „Meine Entwürfe folgen nie einem spontanen Impuls", erläutert er seine Arbeitsweise. „Ich lasse mir immer Zeit, um Abstand zu Dingen zu gewinnen, die mir zu modisch sind. Als Designer suche ich einen gangbaren Weg zwischen Schönheit und Funktionalität, um eine Vision von zeitgemäßem ‚Easy Wearing' zu kreieren." Die Synergie von Lemaire und Lacoste ist eine klassische Win-win-Situation, die Lemaire erlaubte, sein eigenes Label zu vertreiben, während er Lacoste als eine coole, abgeklärte Marke für den Weltmarkt neu erfand. Für seine Kollektion Herbst/Winter 2009 setzte Lemaire auf exklusivere Schnitte, stromlinienförmige Silhouetten und tarnte das Krokodil dezent Ton in Ton. 2010 übernahm Felipe Oliveira Baptista Lemaires Posten, der als Creative Director zu Hermès wechselte. Oliveiras wird mit der Kollektion Frühjahr/Sommer 2012 sein mit Spannung erwartetes Debüt geben.

Reconnaissable à ses coupes inédites parfaites comme à ses tailleurs élégants, Christophe Lemaire s'intéresse plus à la qualité de ses lignes qu'aux tendances servilement suivies. Dans un style « graphique, pur, décontracté et précis », il saisit l'équilibre entre mode et fonction en créant saison après saison des classiques faciles à porter. Né en avril 1965 à Besançon, Lemaire commence sa carrière comme assistant dans l'atelier d'Yves Saint Laurent avant de travailler pour Thierry Mugler et Jean Patou. Par l'intermédiaire de la maison Jean Patou, il rencontre Christian Lacroix qu'il impressionne à tel point que ce dernier le nomme directeur de sa propre ligne de prêt-à-porter en 1987. Lemaire lance sa griffe éponyme pour femme en 1990. Ses créations fonctionnelles douées d'une élégance discrète assurent le succès de la griffe et une collection pour homme suit en 1994. En mai 2001, Lemaire devient directeur de la création de la respectable marque de sportswear Lacoste dont il redore le blason. Insufflant son style contemporain et précis à des classiques tels que la jupe tennis, le polo ou le pull BCBG à l'américaine, il attire une nouvelle clientèle tout en respectant suffisamment les 70 ans d'histoire de Lacoste pour ne pas perdre ses clients d'origine. Sous son impulsion, Lacoste donne son tout premier défilé en juin 2001. Véritable DJ de la mode, pour ses propres collections, Lemaire mélange les classiques occidentaux à des pièces ethniques uniques en leur genre. Le résultat est résolument moderne mais toujours portable. « Je n'aime pas créer dans l'urgence », explique-t-il. « J'ai toujours pris mon temps afin d'avoir suffisamment de recul par rapport aux choses trop à la mode. En tant que créateur, je cherche à trouver un équilibre accessible entre beauté et fonction pour proposer une vision contemporaine de l'easy wearing ». La synergie mutuellement profitable entre Lemaire et Lacoste a permis au créateur de commercialiser sa propre griffe tout en imposant Lacoste comme une marque cool et branchée sur le marché mondial. Dans sa collection automne/hiver 2009, Christophe Lemaire a introduit des coupes plus haut de gamme et des silhouettes épurées où le crocodile apparaît subtilement camouflé en ton sur ton. En 2010, Felipe Oliveira Baptista a repris la succession de Lemaire qui est désormais directeur de la création de la maison Hermès.

HOLLY SHACKLETON

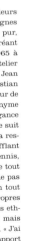

"Ultra-sexy, ultra-glamourous, sparkly and short: that sums up what I do"
JULIEN MACDONALD

"I don't want to be avant-garde," says Julien Macdonald of his upfront brand of showgirl glamour: "I like beautiful clothes. I don't care what people think about me." Macdonald's love for fashion was inspired by the knitting circles his mother held at home in the Welsh village of Merthyr Tydfil. Studying fashion textiles at Brighton University, his sophisticated knitwear went on to win him a scholarship at London's Royal College of Art. By the time he graduated in 1996, with a spectacular collection styled by Isabella Blow, he had already designed for Koji Tatsuno, Alexander McQueen and Karl Lagerfeld. Lagerfeld spotted Macdonald's knits in the pages of 'i-D' and appointed him head knitwear designer for Chanel collections in 1997. Utterly devoted to the female form, Macdonald reinvigorated knitwear with his glitzy red-carpet creations. His barely-there crochet slips of cobwebs and crystals, shocking frocks and furs guarantee headlines for a devoted throng of starlets and celebrities. Macdonald's catwalk antics – including appearances from the Spice Girls and a Michael Jackson lookalike, plus an Autumn / Winter 2001 presentation held at the Millennium Dome and directed by hip-hop video supremo Hype Williams – have earned him a reputation as a showmaster. After being crowned the British Glamour Designer of the year for the first time in 2001 (an award he picked up again in 2003), Macdonald went on to take his high-octane street style to couture house Givenchy, where he succeeded Alexander McQueen as creative director. Under his direction, sales for the luxury label increased despite some mixed reviews from fash-ion critics, and with three years under his belt, he produced an acclaimed farewell show for Autumn/ Winter 2004. For now, Macdonald continues to present his flamboyant collections in London, where he also oversees his homeware, fragrance and high-street lines. In 2006, he was awarded an OBE for services to fashion. Julien Macdonald's career has since extended beyond the catwalk and into broadcast media, including the top-rated show 'Britain's Next Top Model'.

„Ich möchte nicht Avantgarde sein", sagt Julien Macdonald über seine freizügige Revuegirl-Mode. „Ich mag schöne Kleider. Und es ist mir egal, was die Leute von mir denken." Macdonalds Interesse an Mode wurde von den Strickkränzchen seiner Mutter zu Hause in dem walisischen Dorf Merthyr Tydfil geweckt. Nach dem Modestudium an der Universität Brighton brachten ihm seine raffinierten Stricksachen ein Stipendium am Londoner Royal College of Art ein. Als er 1996 mit einer spektakulären, von Isabella Blow gestylten Kollektion seinen Abschluss machte, hatte er bereits für Koji Tatsuno, Alexander McQueen und Karl Lagerfeld entworfen. Lagerfeld entdeckte Macdonalds Strickkreationen in i-D und machte ihn 1997 zum Chefdesigner der Strickwaren für die Chanel-Kollektion. Als absolutem Verehrer weiblicher Formen gelang es Macdonald mit seinen schillern den Kreationen, die für den roten Teppich prädestiniert sind, die Strickmode neu zu beleben. Seine klitzekleinen Häkelslips aus Spinnwebmustern und Kristallen, die schockie renden Kleider und Pelze garantieren dem treuen Anhängerschaft aus Starlets und Prominenten Schlagzeilen. Macdonalds Mätzchen auf dem Laufsteg, wie Auftritte der Spice Girls und eines Michael-Jackson-Doubles oder die Präsentation der Kollektion Herbst/Winter 2001 im Millennium Dome unter der Regie des Hip-Hop-Videostars Hype Williams, haben ihm den Ruf eines Showmas-

ters eingebracht und seinen Status als König der Londoner Glitzerwelt gefestigt. Nach der ersten Auszeichnung als British Glamour Designer of the year 2001 (ein Preis, der ihm erneut 2003 verliehen wurde) machte Macdonald sich daran, seinen hochklassigen Street Style auf die Couture bei Givenchy zu übertragen, wo er als Creative Director die Nachfolge von Alexander McQueen antrat. Unter seiner Leitung stiegen die Verkaufs-zahlen des Luxuslabels, auch wenn einige Journalisten ihn kritisierten. Nach drei Jahren lieferte er mit der Kollektion für Herbst/Winter 2004 eine hochgelobte Abschiedsshow. Gegenwärtig präsentiert Macdonald seine extravaganten Kollektionen weiterhin in London, wo er auch über seine Wohnkollektion, seine Düfte und hochwertigen Street-Labels wacht. 2006 wurde er für seine Verdienste um die Mode als Officer of the British Empire ausgezeichnet. Julien Macdonald machte darüber hinaus auch als Juror in der erstklassig beurteilten Fernsehshow „Britains Next Top Model" Karriere.

« Je ne cherche pas à être d'avant-garde », dit Julien Macdonald de son glamour sans détour digne des showgirls de Las Vegas : « J'aime les beaux vêtements. Je me fiche pas mal de ce que les gens pensent de moi. » La passion de Macdonald pour la mode est née dans les cercles de tricot que sa mère organisait chez eux dans le village gallois de Merthyr Tydfil. Après avoir étudié le textile à l'Université de Brighton, sa maille sophisti-quée lui vaut une bourse d'études pour le Royal College of Art de Londres. Lorsqu'il en sort diplômé en 1996 avec une collection spectaculaire mise en style par Isabella Blow, il a déjà collaboré avec Koji Tatsuno, Alexander McQueen et Karl Lagerfeld. Ce dernier, qui avait repéré les créations de Macdonald dans les pages du magazine i-D, l'embauche comme respon-sable de la maille des collections Chanel en 1997. Entièrement dévoué aux formes du corps féminin, Macdonald a ressuscité la maille à travers ses créations brillantes et ultra-glamour. Ses combinaisons très osées réalisées au crochet en toile d'araignée et ornées de cristaux, ses robes choquantes et ses fourrures garantissent la une des journaux à une foule dévouée de starlettes et autres célébrités. Grâce à l'extravagance de ses défilés, avec des apparitions des Spice Girls et d'un sosie de Michael Jackson, sans oublier la présentation de sa collection automne/hiver 2001 au Millennium Dome sous la direction du parrain de la vidéo hip-hop Hype Williams, Macdonald s'est forgé une réputation de maître du spectacle. Couronné British Glamour Designer of the year pour la pre-mière fois en 2001 (un prix qu'il raflera de nouveau en 2003), Macdonald traduit son streetwear explosif pour la maison Givenchy, où il succède à Alexander McQueen en tant que directeur de la création. Sous son impulsion, la griffe de luxe voit ses ventes décoller en dépit de critiques mitigées, mais après trois années à ce poste, Macdonald fait ses adieux à Givenchy avec une collection automne/hiver 2004 cette fois largement plébiscitée. Aujourd'hui, il continue de présenter ses flamboyantes col-lections à Londres, d'où il supervise également ses lignes de mobilier, de parfums et de grande diffusion. En 2006, il a été fait membre de l'Ordre de l'Empire Britannique pour services rendus à la mode. Julien Macdonald a, en outre, fait carrière comme membre du jury dans le show télévisé, considéré de grande qualité, « Britains Next Top Model ».

JAMIE HUCKBODY

"I find the women around me always a great inspiration"
HANNAH MACGIBBON · CHLOÉ

Born in 1970 in Camden Town, London, Hannah MacGibbon is raising the heat at the house of Chloé. After Phoebe Philo's departure in 2005, the company lost its magic touch in igniting the flames of desire amongst fashion critics and Chloé fans. Her Autumn/Winter 2009 collection of luxurious blanket coats and relaxed evening glamour showed that MacGibbon had her finger firmly on the pulse of Chloé. After graduating from Central Saint Martins, MacGibbon cut her teeth at Valentino (she was Mr Valentino's first assistant) before joining Chloé in 2001. Working closely with Philo, MacGibbon was integral to the ascendancy of Chloé in the early noughties. When Philo left Chloé, MacGibbon was offered the top job but she turned it down – she went on to art-direct special projects including the Eau de Parfum launch. On 10 March 2008, MacGibbon was named creative director, taking over from Paolo Melim Andersson. In May 2011 MacGibbon announced that she was leaving Chloé to pursue "new projects". Clare Waight Keller, previously head designer of Pringle of Scotland for five years, was announced as her successor in June 2011.

Die 1970 im Londoner Viertel Camden Town geborene Hannah MacGibbon sorgt gegenwärtig im Hause Chloé für steigende Temperaturen. Seit dem Weggang von Phoebe Philo 2005 hatte das Unternehmen seine zauberische Gabe verloren, flammende Begierde bei Modekritikern und Chloé-Fans zu entzünden. Ihre Kollektion für Herbst/Winter 2009 mit luxuriösen Blanket Coats und lässig glamouröser Abendmode bewies, dass MacGibbon den Finger exakt am Puls von Chloé hat. Nach ihrem Abschluss an der Central Saint Martins sammelte MacGibbon ihre ersten eigenen Erfahrungen bei Valentino (als Signor Valentinos erste Assistentin), bevor sie 2001 bei Chloé anfing. Als enge Mitarbeiterin von Phoebe Philo war sie wesentlich am Aufstieg Chloés zu Beginn des 21. Jahrhunderts beteiligt. Als Philo Chloé verließ, bot man MacGibbon den Job an der Spitze an, doch sie lehnte ab – und blieb zunächst als Art Director für Spezialprojekte wie die Markteinführung des Eau de Parfum zuständig. Am 10. März 2008 wurde Hannah MacGibbon schließlich als Nachfolgerin von Paolo Melim Andersson zum Creative Director ernannt. Im Mai 2011 gab MacGibbon bekannt, dass sie Chloé verlassen würde, um sich neuen Herausforderungen zu stellen. Clare Waight Keller, vormals Chefdesignerin beim Traditionslabel Pringle of Scotland, wurde im Juni 2011 zu ihrer Nachfolge bestimmt.

Née en 1970 dans le quartier londonien de Camden Town, Hannah MacGibbon fait monter la température chez Chloé. Depuis le départ de Phoebe Philo en 2005, la maison avait perdu cette magie qui attisait le désir des critiques de mode et des fans de Chloé. Entre de luxueux manteaux-capes et des tenues de soirée aussi glamour que décontractées, sa collection automne/hiver 2009 a démontré qu'elle avait vraiment le doigt sur le pouls de Chloé. Après l'obtention de son diplôme à Central Saint Martins, la créatrice s'est fait les dents chez Valentino (elle était la première assistante de M. Valentino) avant de rejoindre Chloé en 2001. Travaillant en étroite collaboration avec Phoebe Philo, elle a joué un rôle essentiel dans l'ascension de la maison au début des années 2000. Après le départ de Phoebe Philo, son poste a été proposé à Hannah MacGibbon, qui a préféré décliner l'offre pour s'occuper de la direction artistique de projets spéciaux comme le lancement de l'Eau de Parfum. Le 10 mars 2008, elle a repris la direction de la création à la suite de Paolo Melim Andersson. En mai 2011, MacGibbon annonce qu'elle quitte Chloé pour relever de nouveaux défis. Clare Waight Keller, anciennement styliste principale de la marque de tradition Pringle of Scotland, lui succède en juin 2011.

KAREN HODKINSON

"At the end of every cycle there is a desire to move on"
TOMAS MAIER • BOTTEGA VENETA

Bottega Veneta's pedigree in fine leather goods makes it a world leader in its field. Founded in Vicenza, Italy, in 1966, the house quickly became the choice of the Studio 54 crowd; Andy Warhol bought his Christmas presents at the New York store. At that time, Bottega was a family company designed and run by husband-and-wife team Vittorio and Laura Moltedo, and it was famed for its handmade, super-soft bags created from signature 'intrecciato' woven leather. Following this heyday, Bottega looked like being consigned to fashion history until the intervention of two forces. One was the Gucci Group, which in 2001 spent $60 million on acquiring two thirds of the company, giving it the financial clout to undergo an extensive relaunch. The other was the appointment of Tomas Maier as creative director; previously in the company's recent history, British designer Giles Deacon had been head designer. Maier's revamp has included BV's Milan headquarters, its stationery, staff and uniforms. Collections, too, have returned to a more sophisticated aesthetic and have been extended to cover laptop cases, shoes in exotic leathers, cashmere knits and homeware ranges. The focus, Maier has stated, is to stick with accessories and niche products. Miami-based, German-born (1958) Maier trained at the Chambre Syndicale de la Haute Couture in Paris and has a long history as a luxury-goods designer – including nine years as designer of womenswear for Hermès and, in 1998, the launch of his own collection – being tipped as a man to watch. The collection is now sold at over 100 stores in more than 30 countries around the world.

Bottega Venetas langjähriger Ruf als Hersteller feinster Lederwaren machte die 1966 im italienischen Vicenza gegründete Firma zu einer der internationalen Marktführerinnen. Bald kauften die Leute vom Studio 54 dort. Andy Warhol erledigte seine Weihnachtseinkäufe im New Yorker Laden. Das vom Ehepaar Vittorio und Laura Moltedo erdachte und geführte Familienunternehmen war berühmt für seine handgefertigten, superweichen Taschen aus dem typisch eingeflochtenen (intrecciato) Leder. Nach dieser Blütezeit schien es zunächst, als wäre Bottega bald nur noch Modegeschichte, doch dann traten zwei Kräfte auf den Plan: zum einen die Gucci-Gruppe, die 2001 für 60 Millionen Dollar zwei Drittel des Unternehmens erwarb und diesem damit einen umfassenden Relaunch ermöglichte; zum anderen die Ernennung von Tomas Maier zum Creative Director. Maiers Großreinemachen umfasste einfach alles – auch den Firmensitz in Mailand, Briefpapier, Personal und dessen Outfits. Bei den Kollektionen kehrte man zu einer edleren Ästhetik zurück und erweiterte

die Produktpalette um Laptophüllen, Schuhe aus exotischen Ledersorten, Kaschmirschals und Heimtextilien. Dabei ist es allerdings Maiers erklärtes Ziel, bei Accessoires und Nischenprodukten zu bleiben. Der in Miami lebende, 1958 in Deutschland geborene Maier hat an der Chambre Syndicale de la Haute Couture in Paris gelernt und besitzt langjährige Erfahrung als Designer von Luxusartikeln. Dazu gehören u. a. neun Jahre als Designer für Damenmode bei Hermès und die erste eigene Kollektion 1998. In der Branche gilt er als ein Mann, den man unbedingt im Auge behalten sollte. Heute werden seine Kollektionen in über 100 Läden in mehr als 30 Ländern angeboten.

Grâce à son immense savoir-faire, le maroquinier de luxe Bottega Veneta est devenu l'un des leaders mondiaux dans son domaine. Fondée en 1966 à Vicence en Italie, la maison s'impose rapidement comme le choix de prédilection des habitués du Studio 54 : Andy Warhol avait l'habitude d'acheter ses cadeaux de Noël dans la boutique de New York. L'entreprise est alors une affaire familiale créée et dirigée par les époux, Vittorio et Laura Moltedo, qui proposent des sacs ultra-souples faits à la main et coupés dans le cuir tressé « intrecciato » qui a fait la gloire de la maison. Après cet âge d'or, Bottega Veneta semble voué à sombrer dans les oubliettes de la mode jusqu'à l'intervention de deux puissantes forces : d'abord le groupe Gucci, qui en 2001 investit 60 millions de dollars pour acquérir les deux tiers de l'entreprise et lui offrir ainsi le poids financier nécessaire pour être relancée sur le marché, et ensuite le recrutement de Tomas Maier à la direction de la création, en remplacement du styliste anglais Giles Deacon. Maier ira même jusqu'à transformer le siège milanais de l'entreprise, son papier à lettres et l'uniforme de ses employés. Les collections reviennent alors à une esthétique plus sophistiquée et s'enrichissent de housses d'ordinateurs portables, de chaussures taillées dans des cuirs exotiques, de pulls en cachemire et de gammes d'articles pour la maison, l'intention déclarée de Maier consistant à rester spécialisé sur les accessoires et les produits de niche. Né en 1958, le styliste allemand Tomas Maier vit aujourd'hui à Miami. Il a suivi une formation à la Chambre Syndicale de la Haute Couture de Paris et revendique une longue expérience de création dans l'industrie du luxe : il a notamment travaillé pendant neuf ans comme styliste pour femme chez Hermès et lancé sa propre collection en 1998, considéré comme un talent à suivre de très près. Aujourd'hui, ses collections sont vendues dans plus de 100 magasins présents dans plus de 30 pays.

JOSH SIMS

"To evolve is to continue to breathe creatively"
MARTIN MARGIELA · MAISON MARTIN MARGIELA

Martin Margiela is the fashion designer's fashion designer. Normally this comment could be read as a casual cliché, but in the case of Margiela, it is justified. For unlike any other designer, he produces work that could be seen as a distinct form of 'metafashion': his clothes are essentially about clothes. With his own peculiar yet precise vision, he is one of the most influential and iconoclastic designers to have emerged over the past 15 years. Born in 1959 in Limbourg, Belgium, he studied at Antwerp's Royal Academy and was part of the first wave of talent that would emerge from the city. Between 1984 and 1987, he assisted Jean Paul Gaultier; in 1988, Maison Martin Margiela was founded in Paris and his first womenswear collection, for Spring/Summer 1989, was shown the same year. Struggling to come to terms with a definition of Margiela's fashion, with its exposure of and mania for the process and craft of making clothes, the press labelled this new mood 'deconstruction'. Eschewing the cult of personality that attends many designers, Martin Margiela has instead fostered a cult of impersonality. Never photographed, never interviewed in person or as an individual ('Maison Margiela' answers faxed questions), even the label in his clothing remains blank (as in the main womenswear line) or simply has a circled number ('6' for women's basics and '10' for menswear). In 2000, the first Margiela shop opened, in Tokyo, followed by stores in Brussels, Paris and London, and three further shops in Japan. From 1997 to 2003, in addition to his own collections, Margiela designed womenswear for Hermès, and in July 2002, Renzo Rosso, owner and president of the Diesel Group, became the major shareholder in Margiela's operating group, Neuf SA, allowing the company further expansion. Margiela has also participated in numerous exhibitions and in 2004 curated 'A Magazine'.

Martin Margiela ist der Modedesigner der Modedesigner. Diese Aussage könnte wie ein unbedachtes Klischee klingen, doch im Fall von Margiela hat sie tatsächlich ihre Berechtigung. Im Unterschied zu allen anderen Modeschöpfern erschafft er etwas, das man als besondere Form von „Meta-Mode" bezeichnen könnte: Seine Kleider sind die Quintessenz ihrer selbst. Dank seiner eigenwilligen, aber präzisen Vorstellungen ist er einer der einflussreichsten und umstürzlerischsten Designer, die in den vergangenen 15 Jahren von sich reden gemacht haben. Geboren wurde Margiela 1959 im belgischen Limbourg. Nach seinem Studium an der Königlichen Akademie in Antwerpen gehörte er zur ersten Welle neuer Talente aus dieser Stadt. Von 1984 bis 1987 arbeitete Margiela als Assistent für Jean Paul Gaultier, 1988 gründete er dann in Paris sein Label Maison Martin Margiela und präsentierte noch im selben Jahr seine erste Damenkollektion für Frühjahr/Sommer 1989. Die Presse taufte diese neue Strömung „Dekonstruktion", weil es ihr schwerfiel, den Stil des Designers mit seiner Passion für die Entstehung von Mode und die Offenlegung dieses Prozesses genau zu umreißen. Margiela lehnte den Personenkult ab, den so viele Designer pflegen, und machte stattdessen eher

Unpersönlichkeit zum Kult. Der Designer lässt sich weder fotografieren noch als Person oder als Individuum interviewen – Maison Margiela beantwortet lediglich gefaxte Anfragen. Und selbst die Etiketten in den Kleidern bleiben leer (wie in der Hauptkollektion für Damen) oder tragen nur einen Kreis mit einer Ziffer darin (eine 6 für Damen-Basics, eine 10 für Herrenmode). Im Jahr 2000 wurde der erste Margiela-Laden in Tokio eröffnet, gefolgt von Filialen in Brüssel, Paris und London sowie drei weiteren Dependancen in Japan. Zwischen 1997 und 2003 entwarf Margiela zusätzlich zu seinen eigenen Kollektionen auch Damenmode für Hermès. Im Juli 2002 wurde der Eigentümer und Präsident der Diesel-Gruppe, Renzo Rosso, Mehrheitsaktionär von Margielas Betreibergesellschaft Neuf SA, was dem Unternehmen die weitere Expansion ermöglichte. Margiela hat bereits an zahlreichen Ausstellungen teilgenommen und kuratierte 2004 eine Ausgabe des A-Magazins.

Martin Margiela est le créateur de mode des créateurs de mode et en l'occurrence, ce banal cliché est tout à fait justifié. Contrairement à tout autre créateur, il produit un travail qui s'apparente à une forme distincte de « métamode » : en effet, ses vêtements parlent avant tout de vêtements. Sa vision particulière et bien définie l'a imposé comme l'un des stylistes les plus influents et les plus iconoclastes qui ont émergé ces 15 dernières années. Né en 1959 à Limbourg en Belgique, Martin Margiela étudie à l'Académie Royale d'Anvers et fait partie de la première vague de nouveaux talents de la ville. Entre 1984 et 1987, il est assistant de Jean Paul Gaultier ; en 1988, il fonde Maison Martin Margiela à Paris et présente sa première collection pour femme printemps/été 1989 la même année. Cherchant désespérément à définir la mode de Margiela, avec sa franchise et sa manie du procédé artisanal, la presse baptise ce nouveau style « déconstruction ». Évitant le culte de la personnalité qui guette de nombreux designers, Martin Margiela cherche au contraire à développer un culte de l'impersonnalité. Jamais pris en photo, jamais interviewé en personne (c'est Maison Margiela qui répond aux questions envoyées par fax), même la griffe de ses vêtements reste vierge (comme c'est le cas de la ligne principale pour femme) ou comporte simplement un numéro dans un cercle (« 6 » pour les basiques féminins et « 10 » pour les hommes). En l'an 2000, la première boutique Margiela ouvre ses portes à Tokyo, suivie par Bruxelles, Paris et Londres, puis par trois autres boutiques au Japon. Entre 1997 et 2003, outre ses propres collections, Margiela travaille comme styliste des lignes pour femme chez Hermès. En juillet 2002, Renzo Rosso, propriétaire et président du groupe Diesel, devient actionnaire majoritaire de Neuf SA, le groupe d'exploitation de Margiela, ce qui permet à l'entreprise de poursuivre son expansion. Margiela a également participé à de nombreuses expositions et présidé le comité de rédaction du magazine A en 2004.

JO-ANN FURNISS

"Every single piece is a piece of my heart"
ANTONIO MARRAS + KENZO

Since 2003, Antonio Marras has been in the limelight as artistic director of womenswear for Kenzo – an appointment, perhaps, that reflects the sense of tradition that was so important to Kenzo Takada when designing his eponymous line. With his first collection under his own name launched in 1999 and his first menswear ready-to-wear collection in 2002, Marras was already established as an international designer in his own right. He remains firmly based in his native Sardinia, working with his extended family in Alghero, where the locality and culture have a strong influence on his design. It is here that Marras (born 1961) pulls together his cut-and-paste aesthetic. This is characterised by his high standard of craftsmanship (laborious and highly detailed embroidery), random destruction (holes burned in fine fabrics), extravagant brocades sitting cheek by jowl with an unfinished hem, deconstructed shapes with vintage fabrics and a wide repertoire of what Marras calls 'mistreatments': tearing, matting, staining, encrusting with salt and so on. Marras creates off-the-peg one-offs made from material scraps from his main line, the kind of scraps he grew up surrounded by in his father's fabrics shop. As Marras lacks any formal training, it took a Rome-based entrepreneur to spot his potential, allowing him to launch a career as a designer in 1988. That same year, he won the Contemporary Linen Prize for a wedding dress. In 2006, the Fondazione Pitti Discovery published the monograph 'Antonio Marras' and, to mark the decade anniversary of the brand, the Fondazione Sandretto Re Rebaudengo of Turin hosted the photography exhibition Antonio Marras. Dieci anni dopo (Antonio Marras. Ten Years Later). In May 2007, Marras was once again owner of the brand that bears his name and at the same time he signed an agreement with Interfashion for the licensed production and marketing of a second line beginning with the Autumn/Winter 2008–2009 season. In September 2007, he licensed the prestigious Florentine company Gibò to produce and distribute his top men's and women's lines. Following his huge success at the house, Marras showed his final collection for Kenzo at Paris Men's Fashion Week in June 2011. He was succeeded by Humberto Leon and Carol Lim, the duo behind cult US clothing store Opening Ceremony, taking over as creative director.

Seit 2003 steht Antonio Marras als Artistic Director der Damenmode bei Kenzo im Rampenlicht – eine Besetzung, die das Traditionsbewusstsein Kenzo Takadas widerspiegelt. Mit seiner ersten Kollektion unter eigenem Namen, die er 1999 präsentierte, und seiner ersten Pret-à-porter-Linie für Herren im Jahr 2002 etablierte Marras sich sofort als eigenständiger internationaler Designer. Seiner Heimat Sardinien bleibt er eng verbunden. Diese Region und ihre Kultur üben einen starken Einfluss auf seine Entwürfe aus. Der 1961 geborene Marras bezieht von dort seine Cut & Paste-Ästhetik. Diese ist wiederum geprägt von hohem handwerklichem Niveau (wie arbeitsintensive und äußerst detailreiche Stickereien), zufälliger Dekonstruktion (wie in kostbare Stoffe gebrannte Löcher), extravaganten Brokaten neben unfertigen Säumen, dekonstruierten Formen aus Vintage-Stoffen und einem großen Repertoire von „Mistreatments": reißen, mattieren, verflecken, mit Salz verkrusten usw. Marras führt seinen Ansatz zu einer logischen Konsequenz und kreiert eine Reihe von Prêt-à-porter-Unikaten aus Materialresten, die beim Designen seiner

Hauptlinie übrig bleiben. Das sind Reste, wie sie ihn im Stoffgeschäft seines Vaters umgaben. Obwohl er keine traditionelle Ausbildung hat, erkannte ein römischer Unternehmer sein Potenzial und ermöglichte ihm 1988 den Beginn seiner Designerkarriere. Im selben Jahr gewann er den Contemporary Linen Prize für ein Hochzeitskleid. 2006 publizierte die Fondazione Pitti Discovery die Monografie „Antonio Marras". Die Fondazione Sandretto Re Rebaudengo in Turin präsentierte anlässlich des zehnjährigen Jubiläums der Marke die Fotoausstellung „Antonio Marras. Dieci anni dopo". Im Mai 2007 war Marras erneut Eigentümer des Labels, das seinen Namen trägt. Gleichzeitig unterschrieb er eine Vereinbarung mit Interfashion über die Produktion und Vermarktung einer Zweitlinie, beginnend mit der Herbst-/Winterkollektion 2008/2009. Im September 2007 erteilte er Gibò in Florenz die Lizenz zur Produktion und zum Vertrieb seiner Premiumlinien für Herren und Damen. Auf der Pariser Men's Fashion Week im Juni 2011 präsentierte er seine letzte Kenzo-Kollektion. Humberto Leon und Carol Lim, das Duo hinter dem amerikanischen Label Opening Ceremony, bildet nun die neue Design-Spitze des Hauses.

Depuis 2003, Antonio Marras occupe les feux de la rampe comme directeur artistique des lignes pour femme de Kenzo : ce poste reflète sans doute le sens de la tradition auquel Kenzo Takada accordait tant d'importance quand il concevait lui-même sa ligne éponyme. Après avoir lancé sa propre griffe en 1999 et sa première collection de prêt-à-porter pour homme en 2002, Marras est déjà un styliste international à part entière. Refusant de quitter sa Sardaigne natale, il travaille avec sa famille à Alghero, village dont la culture influence ses créations. C'est là que Marras (1961) élabore son esthétique du « couper/coller », caractérisée par un immense savoir-faire artisanal (broderies méticuleuses fourmillant de détails), une destruction aléatoire (trous brûlés dans des tissus de luxe), des brocarts extravagants côtoyant des ourlets non finis, des formes déconstruites coupées dans des tissus vintage et un vaste répertoire de ce qu'il appelle des « maltraitances » : déchirures, feutrage, taches, incrustations au sel, etc. Marras adopte cette approche jusqu'à sa conclusion logique, créant une palette de pièces uniques mais prêtes à porter, taillées dans les coupons de tissu qu'il récupère en créant sa ligne principale : le genre de chutes au milieu desquelles il a grandi dans le magasin de tissus de son père. En 1988, un entrepreneur romain détecte le potentiel de Marras et l'aide à se lancer comme styliste sans formation préalable. La même année, sa robe de mariée remporte le prix Contemporary Linen. En 2006, la Fondazione Pitti Discovery publie la monographie Antonio Marras et, pour célébrer les dix ans de la marque, la Fondazione Sandretto Re Rebaudengo de Turin accueille l'exposition de photos « Antonio Marras. Dieci anni dopo ». En mai 2007, Marras redevient propriétaire de la marque éponyme et signe un contrat avec Interfashion pour la production et commercialisation d'une seconde ligne dès la saison automne/hiver 2008 – 2009. En septembre 2007, il octroie une licence à la prestigieuse entreprise florentine Gibò pour produire et distribuer sa collection de luxe homme/femme. En juin 2011, il présente à la Men's Fashion Week de Paris sa nouvelle collection Kenzo. Humberto Leon et Carol Limdu label américain Opening Ceremony sont désormais les créateurs vedettes de la maison.

JOSH SIMS

"I represent something for women. I've built up trust with them and that's important"
STELLA MCCARTNEY

Stella McCartney's stratospheric success story has only a little to do with her fabulous connections. Born in 1971, she graduated from Central Saint Martins in 1995. Her final-year collection was snapped up by the biggest names in retail (including Browns and Bergdorf Goodman) and a mere two years later she got the top job as creative director at Chloé. In 2001, McCartney left Chloé and relaunched her own eponymous line, this time backed by the Gucci Group. The first Stella McCartney store opened in New York's Meatpacking District in 2002, followed a year later by additional shops in London and Los Angeles. In 2004 she got a Designer of the Year award in London. Like her late mother, Linda, she is serious about animal rights and refuses to use leather or fur in any of her designs. She also received a Women of Courage Award for her work with cancer charities. Whether working on experimental projects (such as the collaboration with artist Gary Hume in 2002 to produce handmade T-shirts and dresses), designing costumes for Gwyneth Paltrow's action movie 'Sky Captain' (2004) or enjoying the mainstream success of her two perfumes, McCartney is forever working a new angle. Summer 2005 saw her latest project unveiled, a collection of keep-fit-wear designed in conjunction with Adidas, with a special collection for H&M launched later the same year that has successfully grown to incorporate running, gym, yoga, tennis, swimming, dance, golf and winter sports. In November 2005, Stella worked on a special one-off collection for H&M that sold out worldwide in record time, and for Spring/Summer 2006 collaborated with the artist Jeff Koons on printed dresses and miniature chrome bunny accessories. Today the Stella McCartney label includes a luxury organic skincare line, a stunning lingerie range and a limited-edition travel collection with LeSportsac. In 2007, Stella won the Elle Style Award for Best Designer of the Year and The British Style Award for Best Designer of the Year. The appreciation continued worldwide, with Stella receiving the Green Designer of the Year at the ACE Awards in New York. She is designing the Adidas sportswear for the British Olympic and Paralympic teams for the London 2012 Summer Olympics and Paralympics.

Stella McCartneys kometenhafter Aufstieg hat nur wenig mit ihren fabelhaften Connections zu tun. Die 1971 geborene Designerin machte 1995 ihren Abschluss am Central Saint Martins. Bereits die Kollektion ihres letzten Studienjahres wurde von einigen der größten Einzelhändler (unter anderem Browns und Bergdorf Goodman) ins Sortiment genommen. Nur zwei Jahre später erhielt sie den Spitzenjob Creative Director bei Chloé. 2001 verließ McCartney Chloé und unternahm einen Relaunch des nach ihr benannten Labels, diesmal mit Unterstützung des Gucci-Konzerns. Ihren ersten Laden eröffnete sie 2002 im New Yorker Meatpacking District, ein Jahr später folgten Geschäfte in London und Los Angeles. 2004 wurde McCartney in London mit einem Designer of the Year Award ausgezeichnet. Wie ihre Mutter Linda engagiert sie sich für den Tierschutz und verwendet weder Leder noch Pelz in Entwürfen. Für die Unterstützung von Initiativen zum Schutz vor Krebs erhielt sie einen Women of Courage Award. Ob es sich um eher experimentelle Projekte handelt (wie 2002 die Zusammenarbeit mit dem Künstler Gary Hume, wo es um die Produktion handgefertigter T-shirts und Kleider ging), um Gwyneth Paltrows Kostüme in dem Actionfilm „Sky Captain" (2004) oder um die

Freude am Erfolg ihres Parfüms – McCartney tut immer alles aus einer neuen Perspektive. Im Sommer 2005 präsentierte sie gemeinsam mit Adidas eine Kollektion Fitnesskleidung, die inzwischen die Sportarten Laufen, Yoga, Tennis, Schwimmen, Tanzen, Golf sowie Wintersport umfasst. Im November 2005 legte Stella McCartney eine Sonderkollektion bei H&M vor, die weltweit in Rekordzeit ausverkauft war. Für Frühjahr/Sommer 2006 tat sie sich für bedruckte Kleider und Miniaccessoires aus Chrom in Häschengestalt mit Jeff Koons zusammen. Heute umfasst das Label Stella McCartney eine Naturkosmetik-Linie, eine Lingerie-Kollektion sowie eine Sonderkollektion Reisegepäck bei LeSportsac. 2007 erhielt die Designerin den Elle Style Award und den British Style Award als Best Designer of the Year. Anerkennung findet sie auch weltweit, etwa mit der Auszeichnung als Green Designer of the Year im Rahmen der ACE Awards in New York. McCartney hat im Auftrag von Adidas die Ausstattung der britischen Teams bei den Olympischen Sommerspielen und den Paralympics 2012 in London übernommen.

La success story planétaire de Stella McCartney a peu à voir avec son fabuleux réseau de relations. Née en 1971, elle sort diplômée de Central Saint Martins en 1995. Sa collection de fin d'études est immédiatement raflée par les plus grands noms de la vente et à peine deux ans plus tard, elle devient directrice de la création chez Chloé. En 2001, Stella McCartney quitte Chloé pour relancer sa ligne éponyme, cette fois avec le soutien du groupe Gucci. En 2002, la première boutique Stella McCartney ouvre ses portes à New York dans le Meatpacking District, suivie un an plus tard par d'autres boutiques à Londres et Los Angeles. En 2004, elle remporte le Designer of the Year Award à Londres. Comme feue sa mère Linda, elle s'engage résolument dans la défense des droits des animaux et se refuse à utiliser du cuir ou de la fourrure. Son travail auprès des associations de lutte contre le cancer lui a également valu un Women of Courage Award. Qu'elle travaille sur des projets expérimentaux (comme sa collaboration en 2002 avec l'artiste Gary Hume pour produire des T-shirts et robes cousus main), qu'elle dessine les costumes du film d'action de Gwyneth Paltrow Capitaine Sky et le monde de demain (2004) ou qu'elle profite de l'immense succès de son parfum, Stella McCartney ne se lasse jamais d'explorer de nouvelles approches. Elle dévoile son nouveau projet à l'été 2005, une collection de sportswear conçue pour Adidas avec des tenues de course à pied, de fitness, de yoga, de tennis, de natation, de danse, de golf et de sports d'hiver. En novembre 2005, Stella McCartney crée une collection éphémère pour H&M qui s'écoule partout en un temps record, tandis que pour la saison printemps/été 2006, elle collabore avec l'artiste Jeff Koons sur des robes imprimées et de minuscules accessoires chromés en forme de lapin. Aujourd'hui, la marque Stella McCartney comprend une gamme de cosmétiques biologiques, une ligne de lingerie et une collection d'articles de voyage en édition limitée avec LeSportsac. Stella remporte en 2007 l'Elle Style Award de Best Designer of the Year et le British Style Award dans la même catégorie. Elle est internationalement reconnue avec notamment le prix de Green Designer of the Year aux ACE Awards à New York et dessine les tenues des équipes britanniques aux Jeux olympiques et paralympiques d'été 2012.

TERRY NEWMAN

PHOTOGRAPHY ALASDAIR MCLELLAN. STYLING JANE HOW. MODEL MAGDALENA FRACKOWIAK. SEPTEMBER 2008.

"There is still a lot I want to achieve. There isn't any room for complacency in this head!"
ALEXANDER MCQUEEN

The Gothic sensibility of a Brothers Grimm fairytale is closer in spirit to Alexander McQueen's clothing than the fetish, gore and misogyny he was often accused of promoting. However dark McQueen's design, it still achieved a femininity that seduced everyone from Björk to the Duchess of Westminster. The East End taxi driver's son, born in 1969, was apprenticed to the Prince of Wales' tailor Anderson & Sheppard on Savile Row, where he infamously scrawled obscenities into the linings of HRH's suits. He worked with Romeo Gigli, theatrical costumiers Angels & Bermans and Koji Tatsuno before Central Saint Martins MA course director Bobby Hilson suggested he enrol. His 1992 Jack the Ripper graduation collection thrilled members of the British fashion press, none more so than Isabella Blow who bought the entire collection and adopted McQueen as one of her protégés. McQueen's bloodline of angular, aggressive tailoring inherited from MGM costume designer Adrian, Christian Dior and Thierry Mugler. His 'Highland Rape' and 'The Birds' collections used Mr Pearl corsetry to draw in the waist and exaggerate square shoulders and sharp pencil skirts. By 1996, he was named British Designer of the Year. 1996 also saw McQueen replace John Galliano as head of Givenchy haute couture. But by 2001 the Gucci Group had acquired a controlling stake in McQueen's own label and the designer left both Givenchy and LVMH. McQueen's eponymous label dazzled Paris with bittersweet theatrical presentations. 2003 saw the launch of his first perfume, Kingdom, and a bespoke menswear collection produced by Savile Row tailor Huntsman; in 2004, his men's ready-to-wear was shown in Milan for the first time followed by 'McQueen' in 2005. By 2006 he launched McQ – Alexander McQueen, which is a denim-based ready-to-wear collection for women and men. His Autumn/Winter 2009 womenswear show celebrated his ten-year anniversary and was dedicated to his mum. Tragically, the designer committed suicide in February 2010. The Alexander McQueen label continues under Creative Director Sarah Burton, who worked alongside McQueen for more than 14 years.

Die Kleidung von Alexander McQueen entspricht in ihrem Geist eher dem schauerlichen Reiz eines Märchens der Gebrüder Grimm als dem Fetischcharakter, der Blutrünstigkeit und der Frauenfeindlichkeit, die man ihm oft vorgeworfen hat. Wie düster die Entwürfe McQueens auch sein mögen, er erzielte damit dennoch eine Weiblichkeit, die Frauen angefangen bei Björk und bis hin zur Herzogin von Westminster ansprach. Der Sohn eines Taxifahrers aus dem Londoner East End wurde 1969 geboren und absolvierte seine Lehre beim Schneider des Prince of Wales, Anderson & Sheppard, in der Savile Row. Dort kritzelte er heimlich Obszönitäten in das Futter der Anzüge Seiner Königlichen Hoheit. Anschließend arbeitete er mit Romeo Gigli sowie den Kostümbildnern Angels & Berman und Koji Tatsuno, bevor ihm der Leiter des Magisterstudienganges Bobby Hilson vorschlug, sich am Central Saint Martins zu immatrikulieren. Mit seiner Abschlusskollektion „Jack the Ripper" entzückte er 1992 die britische Modepresse wie auch Isabella Blow, die die gesamte Kollektion kaufte und McQueen als Protegé unter ihre Fittiche nahm. McQueens kantige, geradezu aggressive Form der Schneiderei hat ihre Wurzeln beim MGM-Kostümdesigner Adrian, bei Christian Dior und Thierry Mugler. Für seine Kollektionen „Highland Rape" und „The Birds" benutzte er Korsetts von Mr Pearl, um die Taillen zu verschmälern und so die eckigen Schultern

wie auch die scharf geschnittenen Bleistiftröcke zu betonen. 1996 wurde er British Designer of the Year und trat die Nachfolge von John Galliano als Chef der Haute Couture bei Givenchy an. 2001 hatte der Gucci-Konzern allerdings schon die Kontrollmehrheit an McQueens eigenem Label erworben, und so verließ der Designer Givenchy und LVMH. McQueen verwirrte Paris mit dem nach ihm benannten Label mehrfach mit bittersüßen, theatralischen Präsentationen. 2003 wurde mit Kingdom sein erstes Parfüm lanciert. Seine erste Prêt-à-porter-Kollektion für Herren war 2004 in Mailand zu sehen. 2005 folgte „McQueen", und 2006 präsentierte der Designer McQ – Alexander McQueen, eine Prêt-à-porter-Linie für Damen und Herren mit Schwerpunkt Denim. Mit der seiner Mutter gewidmeten Show anlässlich der Damenkollektion für Herbst/Winter 2009 feierte McQueen sein Zehnjähriges. Im Februar 2010 setzte er seinem Leben auf tragische Weise ein Ende. Das Label Alexander McQueen wird von Sarah Burton, die mehr als 14 Jahre mit Lee zusammengearbeitet hat, fortgeführt.

Il a souvent été accusé de faire la promotion du fétichisme, d'un certain côté gore et de la misogynie, pourtant la mode d'Alexander McQueen est plus proche de la sensibilité gothique d'un conte de Grimm. Quelle qu'était l'importance du côté obscur de McQueen dans son travail, il a toujours proposé une féminité qui a séduit le plus grand nombre, de Björk à la Duchesse de Westminster. Né en 1969 d'un père chauffeur de taxi dans l'East End, il a commencé son apprentissage à Savile Row chez Anderson & Sheppard, tailleurs du Prince de Galles, où l'on raconte qu'il gribouillait des obscénités dans les doublures des costumes de Son Altesse Royale. Il a travaillé ensuite avec Romeo Gigli, les costumiers de théâtre Angels & Bermans ainsi que pour Koji Tatsuno, avant de suivre un cursus à Central Saint Martins sur les conseils de Bobby Hilson, son directeur d'études. En 1992, sa collection de fin d'études « Jack the Ripper » ravit les journalistes de mode britanniques et en particulier Isabella Blow qui, en achetant l'intégralité de sa collection, fit entrer McQueen dans le cercle de ses protégés. Les coupes signature de McQueen, viscéralement angulaires et brutales, lui ont été inspirées par Adrian, costumier de la MGM, par Christian Dior et Thierry Mugler. Ses collections « Highland Rape » et « The Birds » utilisaient des corsets de Mr Pearl pour cintrer la taille et exagérer les épaules carrées et les jupes droites aux lignes sévères. En 1996, il remporte le prix de British Designer of the Year. La même année, il est nommé directeur de la création haute couture chez Givenchy, où il succède à John Galliano. Mais en 2001, le Groupe Gucci acquiert une part majoritaire dans la propre griffe du créateur, qui décide de quitter Givenchy et LVMH. La griffe éponyme de McQueen éblouit alors le tout-Paris à travers des présentations grandiloquentes au style doux-amer. En 2003, le créateur lance son premier parfum, Kingdom, sa ligne de prêt-à-porter pour homme à Milan en 2004, suivie par la collection « McQueen » en 2005. L'année suivante, il présente McQ-Alexander McQueen, du prêt-à-porter féminin et masculin tournant autour du denim. Dédiée à sa mère, sa collection pour femme automne/hiver 2009 célèbre les dix ans de sa griffe. En février 2010, il met tragiquement fin à ses jours. Sa collaboratrice de longue date, Sarah Burton, assure désormais la continuation de la griffe Alexander McQueen.

JAMES SHERWOOD

PHOTOGRAPHY DAVID LACHAPELLE. STYLING PATTI WILSON. MODEL JAMIE BOCHERT. SEPTEMBER 2002.

"I grew up with my parents' work"
ANGELA MISSONI · MISSONI

With a history that spans over 50 years, the house of Missoni is that rare phenomenon in fashion, an enduring force to be reckoned with. Established in 1953 by Rosita and Ottavio Missoni, what began as a small knitwear factory following the traditional Italian handicraft techniques has evolved into a world-famous luxury label whose technical innovation and freethinking approach have redefined notions of knitwear. A fateful meeting with Emmanuelle Khanh in Paris resulted in an important early collaboration and the first Missoni catwalk show took place in Florence, in 1967. By 1970, the Missoni fusion of organic fabrics, a mastery of colour and instantly recognisable motifs – stripes, zigzags, Greek keys and space-dyed weaves – saw the house become the last word in laid-back luxury. The layered mismatching of pattern and colour, mainly in the form of slinky knits, has become synonymous with Missoni, inspiring the American press to describe the look as "put-together". Since taking over design duties in 1997, Angela Missoni has imaginatively updated the brand, introducing florals and even denim without losing the essence of classic Missoni. After working alongside her mother, Rosita, for 20 years, in 1993, Angela Missoni produced her own collection, becoming Missoni's overall creative director when her parents retired a few years later. Angela has subtly transformed the beguiling feminine looks of the Missoni archive with tailored lines and sassy slimline silhouettes. Working with world-class photographers such as Mario Testino, Mario Sorrenti and Mert Alas & Marcus Piggott, today Missoni attracts a new generation of devotees whilst maintaining the kudos of cool it established during its '70s heyday. The brand also boasts a Missoni fragrance in conjunction with Estée Lauder, two hotels (Hotel Missoni), in Edinburgh and Kuwait, a children's collection, a furniture line and flagship stores in New York, Paris and Tokyo. In October 2006, Rosita, Angela and Margherita received 'Glamour' magazine's Women of the Year Award, celebrating their joint contribution to the fashion industry and their own timeless style.

Mit seiner über 50-jährigen Geschichte ist das Modehaus Missoni eines der seltenen Phänomene der Branche: eine beständige Kraft, mit der man rechnen muss. Aus der 1953 von Rosita und Ottavio Missoni gemäß der italienischen Handwerkstradition gegründeten kleinen Strickwarenfabrik entwickelte sich ein weltberühmtes Luxuslabel, dessen technische Innovationen und freimütiger Ansatz die Wahrnehmung von Strickwaren neu definierte. Ein schicksalhaftes Treffen mit Emmanuelle Khanh in Paris führte zu einer wichtigen frühen Zusammenarbeit. Die erste Missoni-Kollektion wurde dann 1966 präsentiert. 1970 war Missoni dank der Verbindung von Naturmaterialien, dem meisterhaften Umgang mit Farbe und unverwechselbaren Motiven – Streifen, Zickzack, griechische Mäander – zum Inbegriff des legeren Luxus avanciert. Die Lagen aus eigentlich nicht zusammenpassenden Mustern und Farben, vornehmlich aus hautengem Strick, wurden zum Synonym für Missoni und von der amerikanischen Presse als „put-together" tituliert. Seit sie das Familienunternehmen 1997 von ihren Eltern übernahm, hat Angela Missoni die Marke fantasievoll aktualisiert, etwa durch die Einführung von floralen Mustern und sogar Denim, ohne darüber den klassischen Missoni-Stil zu vernachlässigen. Nachdem sie 20 Jahre lang an der Seite ihrer Mutter Rosita gearbeitet hatte, produzierte Angela Missoni 1993 ihre erste

eigene Kollektion. Damit war der Weg zum Creative Director der Firma vorgezeichnet, als ihre Eltern sich einige Jahre später aus dem Geschäft zurückzogen. Angela Missoni transformiert auf subtile Weise die betörend femininen Looks aus dem Missoni-Archiv durch tadellos gearbeitete Linien und schicke, schmale Silhouetten. Dank der Zusammenarbeit mit Weltklassefotografen wie Mario Testino, Mario Sorrenti und Mert Alas & Marcus Piggott spricht Missoni heute eine neue Generation von Fans an, während man sich zugleich den in den 70ern erworbenen Ruhm bewahrt hat. Sehr erfolgreich ist die Marke auch mit einem Missoni-Duft bei Estée Lauder, zwei Hotels unter eigenem Namen in Edinburgh und Kuwait, einer Kinderkollektion, einer Möbellinie sowie Flagship-Stores in New York, Paris und Tokio. Im Oktober 2006 wurden Rosita, Angela and Margherita Missoni mit dem Preis Women of the Year der Zeitschrift Glamour für ihre gemeinsamen Verdienste um die Modebranche und für ihren persönlichen zeitlosen Stil geehrt.

Avec plus d'un demi-siècle d'histoire, la maison Missoni est un phénomène rare dans la mode, une force endurante absolument incontournable. Créée en 1953 par Rosita et Ottavio Missoni, ce qui a commencé avec une petite manufacture de tricot respectant les techniques artisanales italiennes traditionnelles s'est transformée en une griffe de luxe mondialement connue et dont l'innovation technique et la libre pensée ont redéfini la notion même de maille. Le destin de la petite maison est scellé lors d'une réunion fatidique avec Emmanuelle Khanh à Paris, première collaboration importante qui voit naître la première collection Missoni en 1966. En 1970, la fusion typique de Missoni entre tissus naturels, maîtrise de la couleur et motifs immédiatement identifiables (rayures, zigzags, motifs grecs et tissus à fils teints par zone) voit la griffe occuper l'avant-garde du luxe décontracté. À travers l'utilisation de tricots moulants, les superpositions de motifs et de couleurs dépareillés sont devenues synonymes de Missoni, incitant la presse américaine à qualifier ce look de « put-together ». Depuis qu'elle a repris l'affaire familiale de ses parents en 1997, Angela Missoni modernise la marque avec imagination, introduisant les motifs floraux et même le denim sans pourtant perdre de vue le style Missoni des origines. Après avoir travaillé pendant 20 ans aux côtés de sa mère Rosita, Angela Missoni produit en 1993 sa propre collection, une expérience bienvenue pour devenir directrice de la création de Missoni lorsque ses parents prendront leur retraite quelques années plus tard. Angela Missoni transforme avec subtilité les looks étonnamment féminins des archives Missoni à travers de nouvelles coupes et des silhouettes élancées plutôt branchées. Avec des photographes mondialement célèbres comme Mario Testino, Mario Sorrenti et Mert Alas & Marcus Piggott, Missoni attire aujourd'hui une nouvelle génération de fans tout en préservant le côté cool qui a fait l'âge d'or de la marque dans les années 70. La marque a aussi lancé un parfum Missoni conçu en collaboration avec Estée Lauder, une collection pour enfant et une gamme de mobilier. Elle a aussi ouvert deux hôtels (Hotel Missoni) à Édimbourg et au Koweït, et possède des boutiques à New York, Paris et Tokyo. En octobre 2006, Rosita, Angela et Margherita ont reçu le prix de Women of the Year du magazine Glamour récompensant leur contribution à la mode et leur propre style intemporel.

AIMEE FARRELL

"My ultimate goal is to build a fashion house that outlives me"
ROLAND MOURET

When Roland Mouret (born 1961) set up his label in 1998, he was no newcomer to fashion. Then aged 36, the butcher's son from Lourdes had previous experience as a model, art director and stylist in Paris and London, though, while Jean Paul Gaultier, Paris 'Glamour' and 'i-D' are namechecked on his stylist CV, he had little experience of making clothes, with only two years at fledgling label People Corporation under his belt. His first collection of 15 one-off pieces obviated the need for patterns. Instead, the critically acclaimed garments were put together using skilful draping and strategically placed hatpins. While his method may have become more refined with subsequent collections, Mouret's motto remains the same: "It all starts from a square of fabric." Inspired by folds, Mouret makes staggeringly beautiful clothes with the minimum of fuss. This formula has been hugely successful. His label is stocked all over the world in high-profile stores, including Harrods and Bergdorf Goodman. As well as the clothing line, it now includes rough diamond jewellery line RM Rough and the recently introduced Cruise collection. Since 2003, the London-based designer has chosen to show in New York and this move has seen more Mouret on the red carpet. The fashion world is just as devoted as his celebrity clientele. Mouret's work has been acknowledged with a Vidal Sassoon Cutting Edge award and the Elle Style Awards named him British Designer of the Year in 2002. At the beginning of 2006, Roland Mouret left his company Roland Mouret Designs Ltd. and entered a new partnership later in the year with Simon Fuller's 19 Entertainment. His newly launched RM satellite collection was presented off-schedule during haute couture in July 2007. A new collection – RM Bespoke Limited Edition – was next introduced in October 2008. In March 2009, Mouret, through his RM line, made a triumphant return to the ready-to-wear market. He presented a menswear collection in January 2010, for the first time. In September 2010, Roland Mouret announced that he had secured the rights to market his designs under his name, becoming one of only a few fashion designers in the world ever to have achieved this.

Als der 1961 geborene Roland Mouret 1998 sein Label gründete, war er in der Mode längst kein Newcomer mehr. Der damals 36-jährige Metzgerssohn aus Lourdes hatte bereits Erfahrungen als Model, Art Director und Stylist in Paris und London gesammelt. Während Jean Paul Gaultier, Paris Glamour und i-D in seiner Stylisten-Vita auftauchten, hatte er mit lediglich zwei Jahren beim Anfänger-Label People Corporation wenig Erfahrung in der Produktion von Kleidern. Bei seiner ersten Kollektion, die aus 15 Unikaten bestand, scherte er sich überhaupt nicht um Schnittmuster. Stattdessen wurden die von der Kritik hochgelobten Kleider durch kunstvolle Drapierungen und strategisch platzierte Hutnadeln zusammengehalten. Und auch wenn sich seine Methoden in den folgenden Kollektionen etwas verfeinert haben, bleibt Mourets Motto doch unverändert: „Alles beginnt mit einem quadratischen Stück Stoff." Von der Faltkunst animiert, erzeugt der Designer mit minimalem Aufwand umwerfend schöne Kleider. Diese Formel erwies sich als überaus erfolgreich. Die Modewelt verehrt ihn ebenso wie seine prominente Klientel. Seine Arbeit wurde bereits mit dem Vidal Sassoon Cutting Edge Award ausgezeichnet. Bei den Elle Style Awards war er 2002 British Designer of the Year. 2006 verließ Mouret sein Unternehmen Roland Mouret Designs Ltd. und ging eine Partnerschaft mit Simon Fullers 19 Entertainment ein. Seine neu dazugekommene Nebenkollektion RM wurde außerhalb des offiziellen Kalenders im Rahmen der Haute Couture im Juli 2007 vorgestellt. Im Oktober 2008 folgte mit RM Bespoke Limited Edition die nächste neue Kollektion. Im März 2009 gelang Mouret der erfolgreiche Einstieg in die Konfektionsmode, im Januar 2010 präsentierte er zum ersten Mal eine Männerkollektion. Im September desselben Jahres gab er bekannt, dass er sich die Rechte an der Vermarktung seiner Designs gesichert habe. Er ist damit einer von wenigen Designern weltweit, denen das gelungen ist.

Quand Roland Mouret (né en 1961) lance sa griffe en 1998, ce n'est déjà plus un débutant. Alors âgé de 36 ans, ce fils de boucher venu de Lourdes a déjà travaillé comme mannequin, directeur artistique et styliste à Paris et à Londres. Bien que Jean Paul Gaultier, le Glamour français et le magazine i-D figurent sur son CV de styliste, il ne possède à son actif pratiquement aucune expérience de la création de mode, avec seulement deux années de travail pour la bébé griffe People Corporation. Composée de 15 pièces uniques, sa première collection prouve que l'on peut créer des vêtements sans utiliser de patrons. En fait, ces pièces saluées par la critique sont assemblées à l'aide de drapés experts et d'épingles à chapeau stratégiquement placées. Bien qu'il ait affiné sa méthode au fil des collections, la devise de Mouret reste la même : « Tout commence à partir d'un carré de tissu. » Inspiré par les plis, Mouret propose des vêtements d'une beauté renversante et pourtant extrêmement simples, une formule qui s'avère largement gagnante. Et l'univers de la mode lui est tout aussi dévoué que ses célèbres clientes : son travail a été honoré d'un prix Vidal Sassoon Cutting Edge et les Elle Style Awards l'ont couronné British Designer of the Year en 2002. Début 2006, il ferme son entreprise Roland Mouret Designs Ltd. et conclut la même année un nouveau partenariat avec la société de production 19 Entertainment de Simon Fuller. Son tout dernier projet satellite, RM, a été présenté en marge des défilés haute couture en juillet 2007, avant le lancement de la nouvelle collection RM Bespoke Limited Edition en octobre 2008. En mars 2009, Mouret fait une entrée remarquée dans le monde de la mode et en janvier 2010, il présente pour la première fois une collection pour homme. En septembre de la même année, il annonce qu'il s'est assuré les droits commerciaux pour toute sa création sous son propre nom. Il devient ainsi l'un des rares créateurs au monde à avoir réussi ce coup de maître.

LAUREN COCHRANE

"The process and the product are completely intertwined in terms of our collections"
KATE & LAURA MULLEAVY · RODARTE

"And the winners are: Rodarte." In Zurich, November 2008, Kate and Laura Mulleavy won the prestigious Swiss Textile Award and a much-needed injection of cash. Kate and Laura have been familiar names on the fashion awards nominations roster in the last few years: Ecco Domani Fashion Foundation Award (2005), nominated for CFDA Swarovski Emerging Womenswear Designer award (2006 and 2007), runner-up in the CFDA/Vogue Fashion Fund (2006) and winner of CFDA Swarovski Emerging Womenswear Designer award (2008); and, more recently, they were awarded the Star Honoree Award from Fashion Group International (2011). The two sisters, born in 1979 (Kate) and 1980 (Laura), grew up with unconventional parents in the post-hippie paradise of Santa Cruz, California, before studying liberal arts at the University of California, Berkeley. After graduation, the sisters moved back to their parents' home in Pasadena, where they founded Rodarte – named after their mother's Mexican maiden name. When American 'Vogue' editor Anna Wintour spotted their special talents in a 'Women's Wear Daily' feature, the girls were airlifted to New York and presented their first runway collection in 2005, which was an instant success. Buyers from Barneys in New York to Colette in Paris were among the first support team. Their special mix of theatrical and cinematic fabrics, colours and artisan techniques combined with a naïve, almost amateur enthusiasm has created their own personal fan club. Somewhere between sci-fi, salvage and culture, each collection launches a wave of copycats, which may amount to some idea of flattery. Rodarte created costumes for the film 'Black Swan', directed by Darren Aronofsky. Nominated for Best Costume Design for the 2011 Critics' Choice Movie Awards, Kate and Laura designed the costumes for the Swan Lake ballet in 'Black Swan', as well as other iconic pieces worn by Natalie Portman and Mila Kunis in the film. The sisters' confidence is growing with every accolade, opening up their shyness and opportunities to expand their international clientele. Their collection is currently available at over 40 of the world's premier fashion outlets.

„Und die Gewinner sind: Rodarte." In Zürich gewannen im November 2008 Kate und Laura Mulleavy den angesehenen Swiss Textile Award und die damit verbundene, dringend benötigte Finanzspritze. Die beiden waren in den letzten Jahren aber auch schon auf zahlreichen Nominierungslisten für Modepreise vertreten: Ecco Domani Fashion Foundation Award (2005), CFDA Swarovski Emerging Womenswear Designer Award (2006 und 2007), Zweitplatzierte beim CFDA/Vogue Fashion Fund (2006), Gewinner des CFDA Swarovski Emerging Womenswear Designer Award (2008), und kürzlich erhielten sie den Star Honoree Award der Fashion Group International (2011). Die beiden 1979 (Kate) and 1980 (Laura) geborenen Schwestern wuchsen im kalifornischen Post-Hippie-Paradies Santa Cruz auf, bevor sie an der University of California, Berkeley, Kunst studierten. Nach ihrem Abschluss zogen die beiden zurück in das Haus ihrer Eltern in Pasadena, wo sie Rodarte gründeten, das nach dem Mädchennamen ihrer mexikanischen Mutter benannt ist. Als die Herausgeberin der amerikanischen Vogue, Anna Wintour, durch ein Feature in ‚Woman Wear Daily' auf ihre herausragenden Talente aufmerksam wurde, ließ sie die Mädchen postwendend nach New York einfliegen. Ihre erste Catwalk-Kollektion 2005 war auf Anhieb ein Erfolg. Einkäufer von Barneys in New York und Colette in Paris zählten zu ihren ersten Förderern. Die besondere Mischung aus Materialien, Farben und handwerklicher Technik, die man üblicherweise für Theater- und Filmkostüme verwendet, kombiniert mit einer naiven, geradezu amateurhaften Begeisterung, hat den beiden Designerinnen einen ganz eigenen Fanclub beschert. Irgendwo zwischen Science-Fiction-Zweitverwertung und Hochkultur angesiedelt, sorgt jede Kollektion für eine Welle von Nachahmungen, die man ja durchaus als Kompliment verstehen kann. Von den Critics' Choice Movie Awards wurden sie für das beste Kostümdesign 2011 („Black Swan", Regie: Darren Aronofsky) nominiert. Mit jeder Auszeichnung wächst das Selbstvertrauen der Schwestern, die ihre Schüchternheit ablegen und zunehmend Gelegenheit zur Expansion auf dem internationalen Markt finden. Gegenwärtig ist ihre Kollektion in über 40 der besten Fashion Outlets überall auf der Welt zu finden.

« Et le gagnant est: Rodarte ! » En novembre 2008 à Zurich, Kate et Laura Mulleavy ont remporté le prestigieux Swiss Textile Award, assorti d'une injection de cash dont elles avaient grand besoin. Ces dernières années, on a souvent entendu leurs noms dans les annonces de nominations aux prix de mode : Ecco Domani Fashion Foundation Award (2005), Swarovski Emerging Womenswear Designer Award du CFDA (en 2006 et 2007), finalistes du CFDA/Vogue Fashion Fund (2006) et lauréates du Swarovski Emerging Womenswear Designer du CFDA (2008) et, en 2011, le Star Honoree Award de Fashion Group International. Nées en 1979 (Kate) et 1980 (Laura), les deux sœurs sont élevées par des parents anticonformistes dans le paradis californien post-hippie de Santa Cruz, puis suivent des études d'art à l'Université de Californie, Berkeley. Une fois diplômées, elles rentrent chez leurs parents à Pasadena, où elles créent leur griffe, baptisée Rodarte d'après le nom de jeune fille mexicain de leur mère. Quand Anna Wintour, rédactrice en chef du Vogue américain, repère leurs talents si particuliers dans un dossier de Woman Wear Daily, les filles gagnent leurs billets d'avion pour New York et présentent en 2005 une collection qui remporte un succès immédiat. Leurs supporters de la première heure incluent les acheteurs de Barneys à New York comme ceux de Colette à Paris. Leur mélange étonnant entre tissus de théâtre et de cinéma, couleurs et techniques artisanales, conjugué à leur enthousiasme naïf, voire amateur, leur vaut un véritable fan-club. À mi-chemin entre la récup' et la culture sci-fi, chaque collection déclenche une vague de copies ce qui, dans une certaine mesure, est assez flatteur. Elles sont nominées par les Critics' Choice Movie Awards pour le prix du meilleur costume 2011 (Black Swan, réalisation : Darren Aronofsky). À chaque témoignage de reconnaissance, les sœurs prennent davantage confiance en elles, sortent de leur coquille et saisissent toutes les chances d'étendre leur clientèle internationale. Leurs créations sont actuellement distribuées par plus de 40 enseignes de prestige dans le monde entier.

TERRY JONES

"Both the process and the product are important.
In a way, the process forms the product's soul"
RICHARD NICOLL

Richard Nicoll was born in London in 1977 to New Zealander parents. From the age of three, Nicoll grew up in the Australian city of Perth, where his ophthalmologist father raised him and his older sister. On leaving school, Nicoll returned to London and enrolled at Central Saint Martins, where he completed a BA in menswear. A brief period of hectic creativity ensued with Nicoll selling his own T-shirts through Paris store Colette and assisting the stylist Camille Bidault-Waddington. It was at this time that he first began collaborating on projects with 'i-D' photographer Jason Evans, a partnership that remains intact to this day. (Evans produced a photographic slide show for Nicoll's Spring/Summer 2005 collection as part of London Fashion Week's Fashion East group show for new talent). In 2002, he completed and gained an MA in womenswear, back at Central Saint Martins; Italian design duo Dolce & Gabbana bought Nicoll's final collection and, following graduation, the young designer was awarded a bursary that enabled him to establish his own label. To date, Nicoll has shown twice as part of Fashion East (October 2004 and February 2005) and also during Osaka Fashion Week in Japan. Nicoll seems equally adept at fine drapery – as in his Madame Grès-inspired Spring/Summer 2005 collection – as he is at sophisticated tailoring, using perspex and wood for unusual details. Print, too, is emerging as a bold design signature for this promising designer, lending his work an energetic pop art slant. Nicoll has progressively developed his personal style, winning the Fashion Forward award for the second time in 2007. His graphic simplicity combined with overt sexuality has increased his stockists worldwide.

Richard Nicoll wurde 1977 als Kind neuseeländischer Eltern in London geboren. Ab seinem dritten Lebensjahr wuchs er mit seiner älteren Schwester bei seinem Vater, einem Augenarzt, im australischen Perth auf. Nachdem er die Schule beendet hatte, zog Nicoll zurück nach London und immatrikulierte sich am Central Saint Martins, wo er einen Bachelor im Fach Herrenmode erwarb. Darauf folgte eine kurze Phase hektischer Kreativität, in der Nicoll seine eigenen T-Shirts über das Pariser Kaufhaus Colette vertrieb und der Stylistin Camille Bidault-Waddington assistierte. Zu jener Zeit begann auch die projektbezogene Zusammenarbeit mit dem i-D-Fotografen Jason Evans, die bis heute andauert. (Evans produzierte eine Diaschau für Nicolls Kollektion Frühjahr/Sommer 2005, die bei der London Fashion Week im Rahmen von Fashion East, der Gruppenschau für neue Talente, gezeigt wurde.) 2002 machte Nicoll – wiederum am Central Saint Martins – noch seinen Master in Damenmode. Das italienische Designerduo Dolce & Gabbana kaufte seine Abschlusskollektion. Nach bestandenem Studium erhielt der Jungdesigner ein Stipendium, das

ihm ermöglichte, sein eigenes Label zu gründen. Nicoll hat bereits zweimal im Rahmen von Fashion East präsentiert (im Oktober 2004 und im Februar 2005) sowie bei der Osaka Fashion Week in Japan. Er scheint in der feinen Draperie – zu sehen in seiner von Madame Grès inspirierten Kollektion Frühjahr/Sommer 2005 – ebenso bewandert wie in der raffinierten Maßschneiderei, wo er Perspex und Holz für außergewöhnliche Details benutzt. Ein weiteres Markenzeichen dieses vielversprechenden Designers sind kräftige Muster, die seinen Arbeiten einen deutlichen Touch Pop-Art verleihen. Nicoll hat schrittweise seinen ganz eigenen Stil entwickelt und damit 2007 zum zweiten Mal den Fashion Forward Award gewonnen. Grafisch schlicht in Kombination mit explizit sexy – damit hat er sich Vertriebswege in alle Welt eröffnet.

Richard Nicoll est né en 1977 à Londres de parents néo-zélandais. Dès l'âge de trois ans, il grandit dans la ville australienne de Perth auprès de son père ophtalmologiste et de sa grande sœur. Après le lycée, Nicoll revient à Londres pour étudier à Central Saint Martins, où il obtient un BA en mode masculine. S'ensuit une brève période de créativité mouvementée pendant laquelle Nicoll vend ses propres T-shirts à la boutique parisienne Colette et assiste la styliste Camille Bidault-Waddington. C'est à cette époque qu'il commence à collaborer avec le photographe d'i-D Jason Evans, un partenariat toujours d'actualité (Evans a produit un diaporama photographique pour la collection printemps/été 2005 de Nicoll dans le cadre de l'exposition de groupe Fashion East dédiée aux nouveaux talents au cours de la London Fashion Week). En 2002, il décroche un MA en mode féminine de Central Saint Martins avec une collection de fin d'études achetée par le duo italien Dolce & Gabbana. Après l'obtention de son diplôme, le jeune créateur se voit remettre une bourse qui lui permet de fonder sa propre griffe. Richard Nicoll a effectué deux présentations dans le cadre de Fashion East (octobre 2004 et février 2005) et participé à la Semaine de la Mode d'Osaka au Japon. Il semble tout aussi adepte des beaux drapés, comme en témoigne sa collection printemps/été 2005 inspirée par Madame Grès, que des coupes sophistiquées, utilisant du Perspex et du bois pour créer des détails insolites. Les imprimés émergent également comme l'une des signatures audacieuses de ce couturier prometteur et confèrent à son travail un côté Pop Art plein d'énergie. Richard Nicoll a progressivement développé son propre style, couronné du Fashion Forward Award pour la seconde fois en 2007. Sa simplicité graphique et son sex-appeal assumé n'ont fait qu'augmenter le nombre de ses distributeurs à travers le monde.

DAVID LAMB

"Ape shall never kill Ape"
NIGO® · A BATHING APE

NIGO® is the independent entrepreneur, businessman, graphic designer, figurehead, president and creative director of Tokyo-based clothing brand A Bathing Ape. The name 'BAPE' is short for 'A Bathing Ape In Lukewarm Water'. BAPE is a modern lifestyle brand with two kids' stores, a café and wrestling franchise BAPESTA in Japan. By producing high-end, well-designed luxurious apparel (all in extremely limited quantities), NIGO® single-handedly revolutionised streetwear. NIGO® moved to Tokyo to study fashion journalism at the world-renowned Bunka Fukuso Gakuin fashion college and he and his best friend Jonio (Jun Takahashi from Undercover) became two prominent 'cool hunters' on the scene and soon launched their own store named Nowhere, which sold their Undercover and A Bathing Ape brands and which has since been relaunched as a pop-up shop in Rei Kawakubo's Dover Street Market in London. Items were so exclusive that people were soon queuing up round the block to secure their chosen piece. Standalone BAPE stores followed, with neon signing, moving conveyor belts, BAPE camo, and plastic and chrome fittings being their futuristic retail experience. Soon BAPE expanded into Nagoya and Osaka before launching overseas with the Busy Workshop opening in London in 2001. Bape now has 22 stores worldwide including Japan, Hong Kong, London, New York, Taipei and Los Angeles. Believing in moving forward by building on the past, NIGO® has recently created HUMANMADE with each piece in the line a direct reference to an iconic item from his vintage collection. Mr BATHING APE, now in its second season, combines the sophistication of Savile Row and the attitude of BAPE. This is a wardrobe of formal wear with distinctively BAPE features and twists. His continued re-appropriation of classic items and Americana, from jackets to jeans, hoodies to tees, is considered with the highest care and the utmost love and attention. By keeping their taste levels at the highest, most impeccable standards, by never advertising the brand, and by shying away from paid celebrity endorsement, NIGO® has kept interest in his brand ever in the ascendant whilst being championed by leading musical talents.

NIGO® ist der unabhängige Entrepreneur, Geschäftsmann, Grafikdesigner, Aushängeschild, Präsident und Creative Director des Textillabels A Bathing Ape mit Sitz in Tokio. Der Name BAPE ist eigentlich die Abkürzung für ‚A Bathing Ape In Lukewarm Water'. BAPE ist eine moderne Lifestyle-Marke mit zwei Kinderboutiquen, Café und der Wrestling-Lizenz BAPESTA in Japan. Mit der Produktion von gut designter Luxuskleidung (stets in extrem begrenzter Stückzahl) hat NIGO® im Alleingang die Streetwear revolutioniert. NIGO® war ursprünglich nach Tokio gekommen, um an der weltberühmten Mode-Uni Bunka Fukuso Gakuin Modejournalismus zu studieren und wurde gemeinsam mit seinem besten Freund Jonio (Jun Takahashi von Undercover) zum prominenten „Cool Hunter" der Szene. Bald machten die beiden ihren eigenen Laden unter dem Namen Nowhere auf und verkauften dort ihre Marken Undercover und A Bathing Ape. Inzwischen wurde der Laden als ein ‚Pop Up Shop' in Rei Kawakubos Dover Street Market in London relaunched. Die dort angebotenen Artikel waren so exklusiv, dass die Leute bald bis auf die Straße anstanden, um sich die begehrten Stücke zu sichern. Also folgten eigenständige BAPE-Stores mit Neonschildern, Fließband, BAPE-Camouflage-Muster und Umkleiden aus Plastik und Chrom für ein futuristisches Einkaufserleb-

nis. Bald expandierte BAPE nach Nagoya und Osaka, bevor man mit der Eröffnung von Busy Workshop 2001 in London auch in Europa auftrat. Heute betreibt BAPE weltweit 22 Läden, unter anderem in Japan, Hongkong, London, New York, Taipeh und Los Angeles. Mit HUMANMADE hat NIGO® eine Linie geschaffen, in der jedes einzelne Stück auf eines seiner vorausgegangenen Kollektionen verweist. Mr. BATHING APE kombinierte in seiner zweiten Saison die Raffinesse von Saville Row mit der Philosophie von BAPE. Es ist formelle Kleidung mit unverwechselbaren BAPE-Merkmalen und witzigen Zitaten. Seine fortgesetzte Aneignung von klassischen Kleidungsstücken und Americana, von Jacken bis Jeans, von Kapuzensweatern bis zu T-Shirts, erfolgt mit höchster Sorgfalt, größter Liebe und Aufmerksamkeit. Weil sein Geschmacksniveau immer höchsten, tadellosen Ansprüchen genügen musste, er das Label nie beworben hat und gleichzeitig vor bezahlter Unterstützung durch Prominente zurückschreckte, hat NIGO® dafür gesorgt, dass das Interesse an seiner Marke stetig wächst. Inzwischen wird sie von Stars der Musikbranche favorisiert.

NIGO® est à la fois le fondateur, l'homme d'affaires, le graphiste, la figure de proue et le directeur de la création de la marque tokyoïte A Bathing Ape. Le nom « BAPE » est une forme abrégée de « A Bathing Ape In Lukewarm Water ». BAPE est une marque de lifestyle moderne avec deux boutiques pour enfant, un café et même sa propre licence de catch, BAPESTA, au Japon. En produisant des vêtements haut de gamme, luxueux et bien coupés (toujours en quantités extrêmement limitées), NIGO® a révolutionné à lui seul le streetwear. NIGO® s'installe à Tokyo pour étudier le journalisme de mode dans la célèbre école Bunka Fukuso Gakuin, où il rencontre son meilleur ami Jonio (Jun Takahashi d'Undercover). Ces deux éminents « chasseurs de cool » ouvrent vite leur propre boutique, Nowhere, pour présenter leurs marques Undercover et A Bathing Ape, un projet d'ailleurs récemment relancé sous forme de « pop-up store » dans le Dover Street Market londonien de Rei Kawakubo. Les articles qu'ils vendent sont si exclusifs que les gens font la queue tout autour de l'immeuble pour être sûrs d'obtenir le collector qu'ils convoitent. Peu de temps après, il ouvre des boutiques BAPE futuristes faites de néons, de tapis roulants, du fameux camo BAPE et d'aménagement en plastique et chrome. Rapidement, BAPE conquiert Nagoya et Osaka, puis se lance à l'étranger avec l'ouverture du Busy Workshop à Londres en 2001. BAPE possède aujourd'hui 22 boutiques dans le monde, notamment au Japon, à Hong Kong, à Londres, New York, Taipei et Los Angeles. Avec HUMANMADE, NIGO® a créé une ligne dont chaque pièce rappelle une de ses collections précédentes. Mr BATHING APE a combiné, pour sa seconde saison, le raffinement de « Saville Row » avec la philosophie de BAPE. Ce sont des vêtements formels avec les caractéristiques uniques de BAPE et des citations amusantes. Sa constante réappropriation des classiques et de l'Americana, des blousons aux jeans, des sweats à capuche aux T-shirts, repose sur une attention immense et un maximum d'amour pour ce qu'il fait. En privilégiant toujours le meilleur goût et des normes de qualité irréprochables, sans jamais faire de publicité et refusant tout contrat de promotion avec des célébrités, NIGO® voit sans cesse augmenter l'intérêt suscité par sa griffe, soutenue par les plus grandes stars de la musique.

BEN REARDON

"I aim to create fashion that is neutral in such a way that each person can add his or her own personality to it"
DRIES VAN NOTEN

Dries Van Noten's culturally diverse style has made him one of the most successful of the 'Antwerp Six' designers who arrived at the London collections back in March 1986. His signature full skirts, soft jackets and scarves are embroidered or beaded using the traditional folkloric techniques of India, Morocco or Eastern Europe – whichever far-flung culture has caught his attention that season. Born in Antwerp, Belgium, in 1958 to a family of fashion retailers and tailors, Van Noten enrolled at the city's Royal Academy in 1975; to support his studies, he worked both as a freelance designer for various commercial fashion companies and as a buyer for his father's boutiques. Following the legendary group show in London, Van Noten sold a small selection of men's shirts to Barneys in New York and Whistles in London; these stores then requested that he make smaller sizes, for women. In the same year, Van Noten opened his own tiny shop in Antwerp, subsequently replaced by the larger Het Modepaleis in 1989. In 1991, he showed his menswear collection in Paris for the first time; a womenswear line followed in 1993. Van Noten is perhaps the most accessible of the Belgian designers, but his theory of fashion is far from conventional. He prefers to design collections 'item by item', offering his clients a sense of individuality, rather than slavishly creating a collection around one silhouette or a single theme. In 2004, he celebrated his 50th fashion show with a dinner in Paris where models walked along dining tables wearing his Spring/Summer 2005 collection; the anniversary was also marked with the publication of a book, 'Dries Van Noten 01–50'. He now has three stores and around 500 outlets worldwide. In March 2009, the Belgian designer opened a boutique in Tokyo to complement his flagship in Saint-Germain close to the Académie des Beaux-Arts de Paris, bringing the total number of Dries Van Noten stores worldwide to nine.

Dries van Notens multikultureller Stil hat ihn zu einem der erfolgreichsten Designer der „Antwerp Six" gemacht, die erstmals bei den Londoner Kollektionen 1986 in Erscheinung traten. Seine Markenzeichen sind lange Röcke, weiche Jacken und Schals, oft bestickt oder perlenverziert mit den traditionellen volkstümlichen Techniken Indiens, Marokkos oder Osteuropas – je nachdem, welches Land in der jeweiligen Saison seine Aufmerksamkeit besonders gefesselt hat. 1958 wurde van Noten im belgischen Antwerpen in eine Familie geboren, die vom Einzelhandel mit Mode und von der Schneiderei lebte. Die Ausbildung an der Royal Academy seiner Heimatstadt begann er 1975. Um sich sein Studium zu finanzieren, arbeitete er zum einen als selbstständiger Designer für verschiedene kommerziell ausgerichtete Modefirmen, zum anderen als Einkäufer für die Läden seines Vaters. Nach der legendären gemeinsamen Modenschau in London verkaufte van Noten eine kleine Auswahl von Herrenhemden an Barneys, New York, und Whistles, London. Genau diese Läden verlangten bald Hemden in kleineren Größen – für Damen. Noch im selben Jahr eröffnete van Noten auch ein winziges eigenes Geschäft in Antwerpen, aus dem er dann 1989 in Het Modepaleis – bis heute sein Flagship-Store –

umzog. 1991 präsentierte er erstmals eine Herrenkollektion in Paris; die Damenlinie folgte 1993. Obwohl sein Verständnis von Mode alles andere als konventionell ist, gelten van Notens Kreationen als die tragbarsten aller belgischen Designer. Er zieht es vor, seine Kollektionen „Stück für Stück" zu kreieren, was seinen Kunden mehr Raum für Individualität lässt, anstatt sklavisch um eine Silhouette oder ein einziges Thema herum zu entwerfen. Im Jahr 2004 feierte der Designer seine 50. Modenschau mit einem Dinner in Paris, bei dem die Models in seiner Kollektion Frühjahr/Sommer 2005 über die Tische flanierten. Aus Anlass dieses Jubiläums kam auch das Buch „Dries Van Noten 01–50" heraus. Im März 2009 eröffnete der belgische Designer eine Boutique in Tokio, quasi als Gegenstück zu seinem Flagship-Store im Pariser Saint-Germain, nahe der Académie des Beaux-Arts. Damit stieg die Zahl der Dries Van Noten Stores weltweit auf neun.

Parmi les jeunes créateurs des « Six d'Anvers » qui ont débarqué aux collections de Londres en mars 1986, Dries Van Noten, grâce à son style culturellement éclectique, est l'un de ceux qui ont rencontré le plus de succès. Selon la culture lointaine qui l'inspire pour la saison, il brode et perle ses jupes amples, ses vestes souples et ses écharpes inimitables à l'aide de techniques folkloriques traditionnelles venues d'Inde, du Maroc ou d'Europe de l'Est. Né en 1958 à Anvers dans une famille de tailleurs et de commerçants spécialisés dans l'habillement, Van Noten entre à l'Académie Royale de la ville en 1975 ; pour financer ses études, il travaille à la fois comme créateur free-lance pour diverses griffes commerciales et comme acheteur pour les boutiques de son père. À l'issue du défilé londonien légendaire des « Six d'Anvers », Van Noten vend une petite collection de chemises pour homme au grand magasin Barneys de New York et à Whistles à Londres ; les deux lui demanderont ensuite de fabriquer des tailles plus petites, pour les femmes. La même année, Van Noten ouvre une minuscule boutique à Anvers, remplacée en 1989 par le plus important Het Modepaleis, qui reste aujourd'hui sa boutique phare. En 1991, il présente pour la première fois sa collection pour homme à Paris, suivie d'une ligne pour femme en 1993. Van Noten est sans doute le plus accessible des créateurs belges, mais sa théorie de la mode n'a pourtant rien de conventionnel. Pour offrir à ses clients un certain sens de l'individualité, il préfère dessiner ses collections « pièce par pièce » plutôt que de concevoir servilement ses lignes autour d'une seule silhouette ou d'un même thème. En 2004, il célèbre son 50e défilé lors d'un dîner parisien où les mannequins parent sur les tables, vêtues de sa collection printemps/été 2005 ; cet anniversaire est également marqué par la sortie d'un livre, Dries Van Noten 01 – 50. En 2009, le créateur belge ouvre une grande boutique à Tokyo, qui s'ajoute à celle de Saint-Germain-des-Prés non loin de l'Académie des Beaux-arts de Paris, et porte le nombre de points de vente Dries Van Noten à neuf à travers le monde.

SUSIE RUSHTON

PHOTOGRAPHY EMMA SUMMERTON. FASHION DIRECTOR EDWARD ENNINFUL. MODEL RAQUEL ZIMMERMANN. MARCH 2008.

"The clothes we wear should underline the personality of the individual who wears them"
LUCAS OSSENDRIJVER · LANVIN

Born and raised in the Netherlands, Lucas Ossendrijver is today's undisputed king of menswear. Since joining Lanvin as Alber Elbaz's counterpart in 2005, his collections have slowly collected legions of fans who subscribe to the Lanvin aesthetic of fragility and lived-in quality. Evolution, not revolution, is a word that regularly comes up in interviews with Ossendrijver. Despite Lanvin not having a menswear archive for him to refer to – even though the company had produced men's tailored pieces in 1901 – Ossendrijver has powered ahead to mark Lanvin menswear with his signature pairing of trainers with a tux, this laidback attitude to luxury a manifestation of the understated yet self-confident Dutch sensibility. Ossendrijver also brought to Lanvin his extensive experience. A compatriot of Viktor & Rolf at the Arnhem Institute for the Arts, Ossendrijver briefly designed womenswear for the French brand Plein Sud before working as a freelance designer for Kenzo Homme (1997–2000), followed by a brief spell working with Kostas Murkudis. Until right before landing the position at Lanvin, Ossendrijver was head designer at Dior Homme Classic line and had previously worked for Hedi Slimane. In the time that Ossendrijver has been at Lanvin, the company has collaborated with Acne and rebranded the classic non-fashion menswear line as Lanvin 15 Faubourg.

Der in den Niederlanden geborene und aufgewachsene Lucas Ossendrijver ist heute der unumstrittene König der Herrenmode. Seit er 2005 als Alber Elbaz' Widerpart zu Lanvin kam, haben seine Kollektionen nach und nach Legionen von Fans akquiriert, die sich Lanvins fragiler Ästhetik und behaglicher Qualität verschrieben haben. Evolution, nicht Revolution, ist ein Ausdruck, der in Interviews mit Ossendrijver regelmäßig benutzt wird. Und obwohl Lanvin über kein Menswear-Archiv verfügt, aus dem er schöpfen könnte – auch wenn das Unternehmen schon 1901 Herrenkleidung maßschneiderte – hat sich Ossendrijver ins Zeug gelegt, um der Herrenmode von Lanvin seinen Stempel aufzudrücken: Turnschuhe zum Smoking. Diese lässige Haltung gegenüber Luxus wirkt wie eine Manifestation der zurückhaltenden, aber zugleich selbstbewussten niederländischen Befindlichkeit. Ossendrijver brachte bei Lanvin auch

seine umfassende Erfahrung ein. Der Landsmann von Viktor & Rolf am Arnhem Institute for the Arts entwarf kurze Zeit Damenmode für die französische Marke Plein Sud, bevor er als selbstständiger Designer für Kenzo Homme arbeitete (1997–2000). Darauf folgte ein kurzes Intermezzo bei Kostas Murkudis. Bevor er schließlich seine jetzige Position bei Lanvin einnahm, war Ossendrijver Chefdesigner der Linie Dior Homme Classic, davor hatte er auch noch für Hedi Slimane entworfen. Seit Ossendrijver dort ist, hat das Unternehmen Lanvin mit Acne kooperiert sowie der klassischen, von aktuellen Trends unabhängigen Herrenlinie unter dem Namen Lanvin 15 Faubourg ein neues Image verliehen.

Né et élevé aux Pays-Bas, Lucas Ossendrijver est aujourd'hui le roi incontesté de la mode pour homme. Depuis son arrivée chez Lanvin aux côtés d'Alber Elbaz en 2005, ses collections attirent progressivement des légions de fans qui s'approprient avec joie l'esthétique délicate et la qualité éprouvée de la maison. Dans les interviews données par Ossendrijver, le mot évolution, et non révolution, revient régulièrement. Lanvin ne possède pas d'archives de mode masculine dont il pourrait s'inspirer – bien que la maison ait produit des costumes sur mesure en 1901 – mais Ossendrijver a dynamisé la collection pour homme avec sa juxtaposition caractéristique du jogging et du smoking, cette attitude relax du luxe qui révèle une sobriété néerlandaise néanmoins pleine d'assurance. Ossendrijver apporte aussi à Lanvin sa longue expérience du métier. Diplômé de l'Arnhem Institute for the Arts comme ses compatriotes Viktor & Rolf, Ossendrijver commence par créer des vêtements pour femme pour la marque française Plein Sud pendant une brève période, travaille ensuite comme styliste free-lance pour Kenzo Homme (1997–2000), avant une collaboration de courte durée avec Kostas Murkudis. Juste avant d'être nommé chez Lanvin, Ossendrijver était styliste principal de la ligne Dior Homme Classic, après avoir travaillé pour Hedi Slimane. Depuis qu'il est chez Lanvin, la maison a collaboré avec Acne et relancé sa ligne pour homme ultra classique sous la griffe Lanvin 15 Faubourg.

KAREN HODKINSON

"The idea of creating something new out of nothing every season drives me"
BRUNO PIETERS · HUGO BOSS

Born in 1977 in Bruges, Belgium, Bruno Pieters – like so many of his fellow fashion designer compatriots – studied at the Royal Academy in Antwerp. One of his lecturers, Hieron Pessers (who also taught Kris Van Assche and Bernhard Willhelm), greatly influenced the young Pieters' sartorial technique. A perfectionist, Pieters cites craftsmanship and technique as the cornerstone of his design sensibilities; he is also not afraid to experiment with shape and proportion. After graduating in 1999, Pieters worked for Maison Martin Margiela and Christian Lacroix before launching his own-name label in 2001. In July that same year, Pieters presented a couture collection inspired by the '50s New Look suit during Paris couture week. Since 2003, Pieters has been the creative director of Belgian luxury brand Delvaux. In 2006, competing against Anne Valérie Hash and Jonathan Saunders, Pieters bagged the Swiss Textile Awards. In the following year, he was announced as winner of the Andam Award. Since June 2007, Pieters has been the art director of Hugo Boss's diffusion line Hugo. The Antwerp-based Pieters divides his time between the Belgian city and Metzingen, Germany, the heaquarters of Hugo Boss.

Der 1977 in Brügge geborene Bruno Pieters hat wie so viele seiner belgischen Kollegen an der Royal Academy of Fine Arts in Antwerpen studiert. Einer seiner Dozenten, Hieron Pessers (der auch Kris Van Assche und Bernhard Willhelm unterrichtet hat), nahm großen Einfluss auf die Schneiderkunst von Pieters. Als Pefektionist bezeichnet dieser handwerkliches Können und Technik als die Grundpfeiler seiner Fähigkeiten als Designer. Er scheut sich aber auch nicht, mit Form und Proportion zu experimentieren. Nach seinem Studienabschluss 1999 arbeitete Pieters für Maison Martin Margiela und Christian Lacroix, bevor er 2001 ein Label mit seinem eigenen Namen startete. Im Juli desselben Jahres prä-sentierte er im Rahmen der Pariser Couture-Woche eine vom New Look der 50er-Jahre inspirierte Couture-Kollektion. Seit 2003 ist Pieters Crea-tive Director der belgischen Luxusmarke Delvaux. 2006 gewann er gegen Anne Valérie Hash und Jonathan Saunders den Swiss Textile Award. Im darauffolgenden Jahr war er Preisträger des ANDAM Award. Seit Juni 2007 ist Pieters Art Director der Nebenlinie Hugo bei Hugo Boss. So teilt der Designer seine Zeit zwischen seinem Wohnsitz in Antwerpen und dem Hauptquartier von Hugo Boss in Metzingen.

Né à Bruges en 1977, le Belge Bruno Pieters – comme nombre de ses compatriotes créateurs de mode – a fait ses études à l'Académie Royale d'Anvers. L'un de ses professeurs, Hieron Pessers (dont Kris Van Assche et Bernhard Willhelm ont également suivi les cours), a grandement influencé la technique de couturier du jeune Pieters. Perfectionniste, il considère l'artisanat et la technique comme les pierres angulaires de sa créativité, mais n'a pas peur d'expérimenter dans le domaine des formes et des proportions. Après l'obtention de son diplôme en 1999, il travaille chez Maison Martin Margiela et Christian Lacroix avant de lancer sa griffe éponyme en 2001. En juillet de la même année, Bruno Pieters présente aux défilés parisiens une collection haute couture inspirée du tailleur New Look des années 50. Depuis 2003, il est directeur de la création de la marque de luxe belge Delvaux. En 2006, Pieters rafle le Swiss Textile Award devant Anne Valérie Hash et Jonathan Saunders. L'année suivante, il gagne le Andam Award. Depuis juin 2007, Bruno Pieters est le direc-teur artistique de la ligne de diffusion Hugo chez Hugo Boss. Il partage son temps entre Anvers et la ville allemande de Metzingen, quartier général d'Hugo Boss.

KAREN HODKINSON

"Because it's Saint Laurent, I think about silhouette, imagery and how I can refer to the past we have"
STEFANO PILATI · YVES SAINT LAURENT

One of the most provocative designers working this century, Stefano Pilati has forged an identifiable design signature since taking over the reins as creative director of Yves Saint Laurent in 2004. Born in Milan in 1965, Pilati's introduction into the fashion industry was part and parcel of growing up in a family of stylish women and a city where the fashion scene was thriving. From a seasonal job at the Milan shows, Pilati interned at Nino Cerruti before joining Giorgio Armani in 1993. It was here, during an 18-month stint in Armani's menswear studio – where he developed his knowledge of fabric research and development, skills he continues to perfect to this day – that Pilati's talent caught the attention of the Prada Group. In 1995, he left Armani and began working for Miu Miu and Jil Sander, where he remained for five years. In 2000, he joined Yves Saint Laurent to design women's ready-to-wear; this swiftly went on to include the men's collections as well. In 2002, Pilati was promoted to head of design for all Yves Saint Laurent product lines, including accessories, before receiving the recognition he rightly deserved and being appointed creative director of the label in 2004. Making a distinct departure from Tom Ford's high-sexed imagery, Pilati has since redefined the silhouette of the YSL woman and taken the brand slap bang into the 21st century. Under his guidance, YSL today treads the right balance between elegance and modernism, delivering clothes that are at once beautiful, comfortable and modern, while still catering exactly for what chic Parisian women demand from YSL. As well as the mainline women's and men's collections, and a massive overhaul of all the stores to reflect his own aesthetic, Pilati has introduced Edition Unisex, an elegant, casual, tailored collection of men's clothing designed for women, and Edition 24, a 50-piece line that helps fulfil the brand's promise of not only inciting desire, but serving women with a complete wardrobe for modern life. In 2010, the French house celebrated its history with a highly acclaimed retrospective at the Petit Palais in Paris.

Als einer der provozierendsten Designer dieses Jahrhunderts hat Stefano Pilati sich seit seiner „Regierungsübernahme" als Creative Director bei Yves Saint Laurent 2004 eine unverkennbare Handschrift zugelegt. Der 1965 in Mailand geborene Pilati fand den Zugang zur Modebranche nicht zuletzt dadurch, dass er in einer Familie mit lauter eleganten Frauen und in einer Stadt mit fruchtbarer Modeszene aufwuchs. Aus einem Gelegenheitsjob bei den Mailänder Modenschauen wurde ein Praktikum bei Nino Cerruti, bevor er 1993 bei Giorgio Armani anfing. Dort eignete er sich während seiner 18 Monate in Armanis Atelier für Herrenmode Kenntnisse in Materialkunde an, die er bis heute weiterentwickelt. Und dort fiel sein Talent auch der Prada-Gruppe ins Auge. So verließ er 1995 Armani und begann, für Miu Miu und Jil Sander zu arbeiten. Nach fünf Jahren in dieser Position stieg er 2000 bei Yves Saint Laurent ein, um die Prêt-à-porter-Linie für Damen zu entwerfen, wobei er allerdings blitzschnell auch die Verantwortung für die Herrenkollektionen übernahm. 2002 wurde Pilati zum Chefdesigner aller Produktlinien von Yves Saint Laurent, inklusive Accessoires, erkoren, bevor man ihm die rechtmäßig gebührende Anerkennung zukommen ließ und ihn 2004 zum Creative Director des gesamten Labels machte. Als deutliche Abkehr von Tom

Fords sexuell aufgeladener Symbolik hat Pilati seither die Silhouette der Frau bei YSL neu definiert und die Marke auf einen Schlag ins 21. Jahrhundert versetzt. Unter seiner Führung hat YSL heute den idealen Ausgleich zwischen Eleganz und Modernität gefunden und liefert Kleidung, die schön, bequem und zeitgemäß zugleich ist und noch dazu genau dem entspricht, was die schicken Pariserinnen von YSL erwarten. Außer sich um die zentralen Kollektionen für Damen und Herren und um eine Generalüberholung aller Läden nach seinen persönlichen ästhetischen Vorstellungen zu kümmern, hat Pilati inzwischen auch die Edition Unisex eingeführt. Die elegante, lässig geschneiderte Kollektion besteht aus Herrenbekleidung für Damen. Und schließlich wäre da noch die Edition 24, eine 50-teilige Linie, die das Versprechen der Marke einlöst, nicht nur Sehnsüchte zu wecken, sondern Frauen mit einer kompletten Garderobe für den modernen Alltag auszustatten. 2010 zeigte das Modehaus eine viel beachtete Yves-Saint-Laurent-Retrospektive im Pariser Petit Palais.

Stefano Pilati, l'un des plus grands provocateurs de la mode du nouveau siècle, s'est forgé une signature très identifiable depuis qu'il a repris les rênes d'Yves Saint Laurent en 2004 au poste de directeur de la création. Né à Milan en 1965, l'arrivée de Pilati dans l'industrie de la mode est intrinsèquement liée au fait d'avoir grandi parmi des femmes élégantes dans une ville où la mode florissait. Grâce à un petit job sur les défilés de Milan, Pilati obtient un stage chez Nino Cerruti, puis intègre la maison Giorgio Armani en 1993. Au cours des 18 mois qu'il passe dans l'atelier de mode masculine d'Armani – où il développe ses connaissances sur la recherche et le développement de tissus, des compétences qu'il continue de perfectionner à ce jour –, le talent de Pilati attire l'attention du groupe Prada. En 1995, il quitte Armani et travaille pendant cinq ans pour Miu Miu et Jil Sander. En 2000, il entre chez Yves Saint Laurent comme styliste de prêt-à-porter féminin et se voit rapidement confier les collections pour homme aussi. En 2002, Pilati est promu directeur de la création de toutes les lignes de produits Yves Saint Laurent, notamment les accessoires. En 2004, il reçoit la reconnaissance qu'il mérite amplement en étant nommé directeur de la création de la marque. En nette opposition avec l'image ultra sexy véhiculée par Tom Ford, Stefano Pilati a depuis redéfini la silhouette de la femme YSL et propulsé la marque en plein dans le 21e siècle. Sous sa direction, YSL trouve aujourd'hui le bon équilibre entre élégance et modernisme. La maison propose des vêtements à la fois beaux, confortables et contemporains tout en livrant aux Parisiennes chics exactement ce qu'elles attendent d'YSL. Outre les principales collections pour femme et pour homme, et un vaste relooking de toutes les boutiques afin qu'elles reflètent sa propre esthétique, Pilati a lancé Edition Unisex, une collection de tailleurs élégants et décontractés inspirée par la mode masculine, ainsi qu'Edition 24, une ligne de 50 pièces qui aide la marque à tenir ses promesses, c'est-à-dire susciter le désir tout en offrant aux femmes une garde-robe complète adaptée à la vie moderne. En 2010, la maison de mode a présenté au Petit Palais à Paris une rétrospective Yves Saint Laurent qui a remporté un succès retentissant.

HOLLY SHACKLETON

"My work is about the female body and, ultimately, my clothes are about making women feel and look beautiful"
ZAC POSEN

At a young age, Zac Posen has already earned a place in fashion history. His leather dress, designed for the Curvaceous exhibition at the Victoria & Albert Museum, was awarded the V&A Prize and acquired for the museum's permanent collection (2001). This event marked the beginning of great things for the young New York native. Born in 1980, the son of a painter, Posen enrolled in the pre-college programme at the Parsons School of Design, later joining Saint Ann's School for the Arts in Brooklyn. His fashion studies led him to Central Saint Martins in 1999, where he embarked on a BA in womenswear. However, he soon packed in his studies in order to start his own label, which was an immediate success. His glamorous signatures include bias-cut gowns, fishtail hemlines and a passion for screen-siren style. His talent was swiftly recognised by the fashion industry: he was a finalist for the ENKA International Fashion Design Award in 2002 and a nominee for the CFDA Award for new talent in both 2002 and 2003 before winning the Perry Ellis Award in 2004. That year proved to be a groundbreaking period for Posen. In April, Sean John, the fashion company backed by Sean 'Puff Daddy' Combs, announced it was making a long-term investment in Posen's label. However, it is Posen who continues to steer the label creatively, driving it forward with his vision of a strong, feminine silhouette. With Sean John's financial backing, the days when he was forced to fund his first catwalk show with the £14,000 prize from a fashion competition are a distant memory. Freed from monetary restraints, and with his sister (Alexandra Posen) leading his Tribeca studio, he is now able to concentrate on expanding his ready-to-wear collection and developing his accessories line.

Schon in jungen Jahren hat sich Zac Posen seinen Platz in der Modegeschichte gesichert. Das Lederkleid, das er für die Ausstellung „Curvaceous" im Victoria and Albert Museum entworfen hat, wurde mit dem V&A Prize ausgezeichnet und für die Dauerkollektion des Museums angekauft. Dieses Ereignis markierte für den gebürtigen New Yorker den Beginn einer großartigen Karriere. Geboren wurde er 1980 als Sohn eines Malers. An der Parsons School of Design nahm er am Pre-College-Programm teil, später schrieb er sich an der Saint Ann's School for the Arts in Brooklyn ein. Im Rahmen seines Modestudiums begann er 1999 den Bachelor-Studiengang Damenmode am Central Saint Martins in London. Bald schon brach er die Ausbildung jedoch ab, um sich voll auf die Gründung seines eigenen Labels zu konzentrieren, das sofort ein Erfolg war. Zu seinem typischen glamourösen Stil gehören diagonal geschnittene Roben, Schleppen und ganz allgemein die Liebe zum Stil der Leinwand-Diven. Sein Talent wurde innerhalb der Branche rasch erkannt: Beim ENKA

International Fashion Design Award 2002 gehörte Posen zu den Finalisten; beim CFDA-Preis für neue Talente war er 2002 und 2003 nominiert; 2004 gewann er schließlich den Perry Ellis Award. Jenes Jahr sollte ohnehin ein sehr bewegendes für Posen werden. Im April vermeldete Sean John, das Modeunternehmen von Sean „Puff Daddy" Combs, eine längerfristige Investition in Posens Label. Die kreative Richtung gibt allerdings weiterhin der Designer selbst vor, und zwar mit seiner Vision von einer starken, femininen Silhouette. Mit der finanziellen Unterstützung von Sean John sind die Zeiten, als er seine erste Catwalk-Show mit den bei einem Modewettbewerb gewonnenen 14.000 Pfund bestreiten musste, nur noch Erinnerung. Finanzieller Beschränkungen enthoben und gemeinsam mit seiner Schwester Alexandra Posen, die sein Tribeca-Atelier leitet, kann Posen sich nun auf den Ausbau seiner Prêt-à-porter-Kollektion und die Entwicklung einer Accessoire-Linie konzentrieren.

Très jeune déjà, Zac Posen a gagné sa place au panthéon de la mode. La robe en cuir qu'il a dessinée pour l'exposition « Curvaceous » du Victoria & Albert Museum lui a valu le V&A Prize et fait désormais partie de la collection permanente du musée. Cet événement marque le début d'une grande carrière pour ce jeune New-Yorkais. Né en 1980 d'un père peintre, Zac Posen s'inscrit à la prépa de la Parsons School of Design avant de partir pour la Saint Ann's School for the Arts de Brooklyn. En 1999, il débarque à Central Saint Martins où il entame un BA en mode féminine. Il interrompt ses études prématurément pour lancer sa propre griffe et rencontre un succès immédiat. Son style glamour et caractéristique se distingue par ses robes coupées en biais, ses ourlets en queue de poisson et une passion pour les sirènes du grand écran. Le monde de la mode ne tarde pas à reconnaître son talent : finaliste de l'ENKA International Fashion Design Award en 2002, nominé par le CFDA dans la catégorie nouveau talent en 2002 et 2003, il finit par remporter le prix Perry Ellis en 2004, une année révolutionnaire pour le jeune créateur. En avril, Sean John, la marque de Sean « Puff Daddy » Combs, décide d'investir à long terme dans la griffe de Posen. Malgré toutes ces réussites, il continue à diriger sa griffe avec créativité et la fait évoluer grâce à sa vision d'une silhouette féminine prononcée. Fort du soutien de Sean John, la période où il était contraint de financer son premier défilé avec les 14 000 livres gagnées dans un concours de mode n'est plus qu'un lointain souvenir. Libéré de toute contrainte économique et soutenu par sa sœur (Alexandra Posen) qui dirige son atelier de Tribeca, il peut désormais se concentrer sur l'extension de sa collection de prêt-à-porter et sur le développement de sa ligne d'accessoires.

KAREN HODKINSON

"When people think of fashion, they always prefer to see the crazy side, the clichéd side of it. But I think that's wrong. Fashion is an important part of a woman's life"
MIUCCIA PRADA · PRADA + MIU MIU

In 1971, Miuccia Prada entered the family business. Twenty years later, the highly traditional leather goods company had changed beyond all recognition. The innovation of something as simple as a nylon bag meant there was no looking back: Prada was on the way to redefining luxury, subtlety and desirability in fashion. Prada the company – led by the designer and her husband, Patrizio Bertelli, who started work with Prada in 1977 and is now CEO of the Prada Group – seems to have an uncanny ability to capture the cultural climate in fashion. This sensitivity has been unashamedly teamed with commercial savvy, which has made the brand's influence over the past decade vast and its growth enormous. From bags and shoes to the first womenswear collection (1988), the Miu Miu line for the younger customer (1993), menswear (1994), Prada Sport (1997) and Prada Beauty (2000), all are directly overseen by Miuccia Prada herself. Yet, unlike many other Leviathan brands, there is something both unconventional and idiosyncratic in Miuccia Prada's aesthetic. Much of this may be down to her contradictory character. Born in Milan in 1950, Miuccia Prada studied political science at the city's university and was a member of Italy's Communist Party, yet is said to have worn Yves Saint Laurent on the barricades. The designer, who has made The Wall Street Journal's '30 Most Powerful Women in Europe' list, also spent a period studying to be a mime artist. These dualities have led to her expert ability in balancing the contrary forces of art and commerce within the superbrand, sometimes quite literally: Prada has its own art foundation and has collaborated with the architect Rem Koolhaas on stores in New York (2001) and Los Angeles (2004). From the late '90s, the Prada Group embarked upon a policy of rapid expansion, purchasing brands including Azzedine Alaïa, Helmut Lang and Church & Co. Every presentation of men's, women's and Miu Miu collections continues to reflect the diverse cultural interests of Miuccia Prada. With associated projects, her collaboration with Rem Koolhaas is a constant inspiration.

1971 trat Miuccia Prada in das Familienunternehmen ein. Zwanzig Jahre danach hat sich die bis dahin eher traditionelle Lederwarenfabrik bis zur Unkenntlichkeit verändert. Etwas so Simples wie eine Nylonhandtasche markierte den Neuanfang. Prada gab den Begriffen Luxus, Raffinesse und Begehrlichkeit in Sachen Mode eine neue Bedeutung. Unter der Leitung der Designerin und ihres Mannes Patrizio Bertelli, der 1977 in das Unternehmen eintrat und heute Chef des Konzerns ist, beweist Prada einen untrüglichen Instinkt, wenn es darum geht, aktuelle Modeströmungen aufzunehmen. Dieses Gespür sorgte, gepaart mit dem nötigen Geschäftssinn, in den letzten zehn Jahren für das ungeheure Wachstum und den enormen Einfluss der Marke. Von den Taschen und Schuhen, der ersten Damenkollektion, dem Label Miu Miu für jüngere Kundinnen (1993) über Männermode (1994) und die Linie Prada Sport (1997) bis hin zu Prada Beauty (2000) unterstehen alle Bereiche nach wie vor Miuccia Prada. Doch ein Unterschied zu anderen großen Marken ist Miuccia Pradas Ästhetik höchst unkonventionell und individuell. Vieles davon mag auf ihren ungewöhnlichen Werdegang zurückzuführen sein. 1950 in Mailand geboren, studierte Miuccia Prada in ihrer Heimatstadt Politikwissenschaft und war Mitglied der Kommunistischen Partei. Doch

angeblich trug sie selbst auf den Barrikaden Yves Saint Laurent. Die vom Wall Street Journal zu einer der „30 mächtigsten Frauen Europas" gekürte Geschäftsfrau absolvierte auch eine Ausbildung als Pantomime. Ihre Vielseitigkeit mag dazu beitragen, dass es ihr immer wieder hervorragend gelingt, Kunst und Kommerz unter dem Dach der Supermarke miteinander zu versöhnen. Und das ist gelegentlich durchaus wörtlich zu verstehen: So betreibt Prada eine eigene Kunststiftung und ließ die Läden in New York (2001) und Los Angeles (2004) vom Stararchitekten Rem Koolhaas gestalten. Seit Ende der 1990er-Jahre setzt der Prada-Konzern auf rasche Expansion und kaufte in diesem Zuge Marken wie Azzedine Alaïa, Helmut Lang oder Church & Co. auf. Jede Präsentation einer Herren-, Damen- oder Miu-Miu-Kollektion spiegelt nach wie vor Miuccia Pradas vielfältige kulturelle Interessen. In den dazugehörigen Projekten dient ihr Rem Koolhaas als stetiger Quell der Inspiration.

Miuccia Prada rejoint l'entreprise familiale en 1971. Vingt ans plus tard, ce maroquinier ultra-classique a subi une transformation si radicale qu'il en est devenu méconnaissable. Une innovation telle que le sac en nylon prouvait bien que la maison ne regardait plus en arrière : Prada était sur le point de redéfinir le luxe, la subtilité et les avantages de la mode. Patrizio Bertelli, mari de Miuccia mais également directeur de l'entreprise, designer et actuel PDG du groupe Prada, avait commencé à travailler pour la maison en 1977. La société semble douée d'une étrange facilité à capter le climat culturel de la mode. Cette intuition se mêle sans complexe à un esprit de conquête commerciale qui n'a fait qu'augmenter l'influence de la marque ces dix dernières années et lui a permis d'enregistrer une croissance vertigineuse. Des chaussures aux sacs en passant par la première collection de vêtements pour femme (1988), la ligne Miu Miu pour les jeunes (1993), la ligne masculine (1994), Prada Sport (1997) et Prada Beauty (2000), tout est directement supervisé par Miuccia Prada en personne. Contrairement à la plupart des géants de la mode, l'esthétique de Miuccia Prada se distingue par son anti-conformisme très caractéristique. Cette ambivalence repose en grande partie sur l'esprit de contradiction de Miuccia. Née en 1950 à Milan, elle étudie les sciences politiques à l'université de la ville et s'inscrit au Parti Communiste Italien, n'hésitant pas à monter sur les barricades habillée en Yves Saint Laurent. La créatrice, incluse dans la liste des « 30 femmes les plus puissantes d'Europe » du Wall Street Journal, a également suivi une formation pour devenir mime. Ces dualités lui ont permis de réconcilier les forces contradictoires de l'art et du commerce au sein de la « supermarque », parfois même au pied de la lettre : Prada possède sa propre fondation artistique et a collaboré avec l'architecte Rem Koolhaas à la création des boutiques de New York (2001) et de Los Angeles (2004). Dès la fin des années 90, le groupe Prada a adopté une politique d'expansion rapide, rachetant des marques telles qu'Azzedine Alaïa, Helmut Lang et Church & Co. Chaque présentation des collections pour homme, pour femme et Miu Miu continue à refléter la diversité des passions culturelles de Miuccia Prada. Avec des projets communs Rem Koolhaas demeure une constante source d'inspiration.

JO-ANN FURNISS

"I don't find designing difficult, it's everything else that goes with it that's hard"
GARETH PUGH

Gareth Pugh is the Sunderland-born designer currently hammering a nail into the coffin of conventional fashion. When he graduated from Central Saint Martins in 2003, his red-and-white striped inflatable balloon costume was photographed by Nicola Formichetti for the cover of 'Dazed & Confused' in February 2004. He showed his fantastical creations in the London clubs and assisted Rick Owens at luxury furrier Revillon before receiving an invitation to show at Fashion East during London Fashion Week, where Casey Spooner walked the final look which lit up to screams and thunderous applause from an audience who felt lucky to be there to witness the birth of a new and important voice in British fashion. Pugh soon received commissions from Kylie Minogue to design for her Showgirls tour, and collaborated with Judy Blame, Nick Knight, Fischerspooner, Moët, MTV, HSBC (for a commercial), and 'i-D'. BoomBox threw a party in his honour, 'Elle' crowned him Young Designer of the Year, he modelled for Arena Homme Plus, made bespoke clothes for Beth Ditto, styled for every magazine of note, featured in exhibitions including the V&A and The Metropolitan Museum of Art, was photographed by Bruce Weber and Mario Testino, designed a Christmas tree for Topshop, guest-edited 'Time Out' and designed his own Ken doll. On top of all this, he has carved out his bleak yet elegant, aggressive but luxurious, unflinching vision of how to dress in the modern world. Each season, Pugh explores the same recurring themes, including inflatables, fur, leather, triangles, PVC and black, black and more black, quickly establishing his voice as strong and severe. Showing in Paris since September 2008, Pugh showed his first menswear collection in January 2009. His first stand-alone store opened in Hong Kong in August 2010 and, in 2011, Pugh was invited as the guest designer at Italian trade show Pitti, where he presented a special collection via video installation in collaboration with producer Ruth Hogben.

Gareth Pugh ist der in Sunderland geborene Designer, der gegenwärtig einen Nagel in den Sarg der konventionellen Mode hämmert. Nach seinem Abschluss am Central Saint Martins im Jahr 2003 wurde sein rot-weiß-gestreiftes aufblasbares Ballonkostüm von Nicola Formichetti für das Cover von „Dazed & Confused" im Februar 2004 fotografiert. Er zeigte seine fantastischen Kreationen in den Londoner Clubs und assistierte Rick Owens bei der Nobel-Pelzmarke Revillon, bevor er die Einladung erhielt, während der London Fashion Week bei Fashion East zu präsentieren, wo Casey Spooner den finalen Look präsentierte, was Kreischen und donnernden Applaus beim Publikum auslöste. Die Leute waren offenbar beglückt, Augenzeugen der Geburt einer neuen und bedeutenden Figur in der britischen Modeszene zu sein. Bald erhielt Pugh von Kylie Minogue den Auftrag, Kreationen für ihre Tour „Showgirls" zu entwerfen. Zudem arbeitete er mit Judy Blame, Nick Knight, Fischerspooner, Moët, MTV, machte einen Werbespot für HSBC und i-D. BoomBox schmiss ihm zu Ehren eine Party, Elle krönte ihn zum Young Designer of the Year, er modelte für Arena Homme Plus, fertigte Maßkleidung für Beth Ditto, stylte für alle nennenswerten Magazine, präsentierte sich in Ausstellungen, u. a. im Victoria and Albert Museum und im Metropolitan Museum of Art, wurde von Bruce Weber und Mario Testino fotografiert, gestaltete einen

Weihnachtsbaum für Topshop, war Gast-Herausgeber von Time Out und entwarf seine eigene Ken-Puppe. Abgesehen von alldem ist es ihm aber gelungen, seine raue und doch elegante, angriffslustige und zugleich luxuriöse, überaus eigenwillige Vision von Kleidung in einer modernen Welt herauszuarbeiten. Außerdem widmet sich Pugh Saison für Saison der Erforschung wiederkehrender Themen wie Aufblasbares, Pelz, Leder, Dreiecke, PVC, Schwarz, Schwarz und noch einmal Schwarz. Dabei verschaffte er sich mit starker, durchdringender Stimme rasch Gehör. Seit September 2008 präsentierte er in Paris. Im Januar 2009 zeigte er seine erste Herrenkollektion und im August 2010 eröffnete er seinen ersten eigenen Laden in Hongkong. Pugh wurde als Gastdesigner zur Pitti 2011 nach Florenz eingeladen, wo er seine Kollektion per Videoinstallation in Zusammenarbeit mit der Filmemacherin Ruth Hogben vorführte.

Originaire de Sunderland, le créateur Gareth Pugh est en train de planter le dernier clou dans le cercueil de la mode conventionnelle. Après l'obtention de son diplôme de Central Saint Martins en 2003, son costume en ballons gonflables à rayures rouges et blanches est pris en photo par Nicola Formichetti pour la couverture de Dazed & Confused en février 2004. Gareth Pugh présente alors ses créations fantasques dans les clubs londoniens. Il devient assistant de Rick Owens chez le fourreur de luxe Revillon, puis est invité à défiler dans le cadre de Fashion East pendant la London Fashion Week : le chanteur Casey Spooner clôture le défilé dans une tenue qui s'illumine soudain, déclenchant un tonnerre d'applaudissements de la part d'un public en délire qui se félicite d'être au bon endroit au bon moment pour assister à la naissance d'une importante nouvelle voix de la mode britannique. Peu de temps après, Kylie Minogue lui commande plusieurs costumes pour sa tournée Showgirls. Pugh a aussi collaboré avec Judy Blame, Nick Knight, Fischerspooner, Moët et MTV, ainsi que sur un spot publicitaire pour HSBC et i-D. BoomBox a donné une soirée en son honneur et le magazine Elle l'a couronné Young Designer of the Year. Pugh a posé dans Arena Homme Plus, créé des vêtements sur mesure pour Beth Ditto, collaboré en tant que styliste avec tous les magazines qui comptent, a vu ses créations exposées plusieurs fois, notamment au Victoria & Albert Museum et au Metropolitan Museum of Art, a été photographié par Bruce Weber et Mario Testino, a conçu un arbre de Noël pour Topshop, dirigé un numéro de Time Out et créé sa propre poupée Ken. Pour couronner le tableau, il a imprimé son infaillible vision de la mode d'aujourd'hui, à la fois austère et élégante, agressive mais luxueuse. Chaque saison, Gareth Pugh explore des thèmes récurrents tels les objets gonflables, la fourrure, le cuir, les triangles, le PVC, le noir, le noir et encore le noir, imposant à toute vitesse son style fort et rigoureux. Au rendez-vous des défilés parisiens depuis septembre 2008, Gareth Pugh présente en janvier 2009 sa première collection pour homme. En août 2010, il ouvre son propre magasin (le premier) à Hong Kong et est invité en tant que créateur au Pitti 2011 à Florence où il présente sa collection par le biais d'une installation vidéo, en collaboration avec la réalisatrice Ruth Hogben.

BEN REARDON

PHOTOGRAPHY ALLAN AMATO, STYLING SAM WILLOUGHBY. MODEL MARILYN MANSON, JULY 2007.

PHOTOGRAPHY HANS FEURER. STYLING HAVANA LAFFITTE. MODEL ALI STEVENS. JUNE 2000

"I never get bored! I often think how lucky I am just for being able to do all the things I wanted to do"
JOHN RICHMOND

'Destroy, Disorientate, Disorder' and Debenhams, the British department store: John Richmond is equal parts raring-to-rock and ready-to-wear. The music-loving Mancunian has a singular talent for reconciling anarchic punk aesthetics with elegant tailoring. Born in 1961, Richmond graduated from Kingston Polytechnic in 1982 and worked as a freelance designer for Emporio Armani, Fiorucci and Joseph Tricot before forming his first label, Richmond-Cornejo, a collaboration with designer Maria Cornejo, in 1984. In 1987, he struck out on his own. During his career, Richmond has dressed pop icons such as Bryan Adams, David Bowie, Madonna and Mick Jagger; George Michael wore Richmond's Destroy jacket in the video for 'Faith'. John Richmond designs are synonymous with the spirit of rock and the smell of leather. Today, his label comprises three clothing lines: John Richmond, Richmond X and Richmond Denim, with eyewear and underwear collections also recently launched. A business partnership with Saverio Moschillo has provided Richmond with a worldwide network of showrooms, from Naples, Rome and Paris to Munich, Düsseldorf and New York. They house his leather biker jackets, oil-printed T-shirts, acid-orange pleated skirts and long-line sweaters. Richmond's flagship store in London's Conduit Street joins two Italian shops in Milan and Bari. Then there's the Designers at Debenhams collection, the John Richmond Smart Roadster car – needless to say, a John Richmond fragrance, childrenswear collection, watches and jewellery line are also in the pipeline. Other projects include the expansion of his stores, showcasing the younger diffusion ranges – X and Denim lines – to the global market. One hundred John Richmond stores were to be opened in the world's main markets by 2011.

„Destroy, Disorientate, Disorder" und das britische Kaufhaus Debenhams: John Richmond ist zu gleichen Teilen Rock'n'Roll und Prêt-à-porter. Der Musikliebhaber aus Manchester besitzt ein einzigartiges Talent für die Versöhnung von anarchischer Punk-Ästhetik mit eleganter Schneiderkunst. 1961 geboren, beendete Richmond 1982 das Kingston Polytechnikum und designte danach zunächst als Freelancer für Emporio Armani, Fiorucci und Joseph Tricot, bevor er 1984 in Kooperation mit der Designerin Maria Cornejo sein erstes Label Richmond-Cornejo gründete. Ab 1987 versuchte er sein Glück dann wieder allein. Im bisherigen Verlauf seiner Karriere kleidete er Popikonen wie Bryan Adams, David Bowie, Madonna und Mick Jagger ein. George Michael trug in seinem Video zu „Faith" die Destroy-Jacke von Richmond. Seine Entwürfe sind Synonyme für den Spirit of Rock und den Geruch von Leder. Heute umfasst sein Label drei verschiedene Linien: John Richmond, Richmond X und Richmond Denim; kürzlich kamen noch Brillen- und Dessouskollektionen dazu. Die geschäftliche Verbindung mit Saverio Moschillo ermöglicht Richmond den Zugang zu einem weltweiten Netz von Showrooms, sei es in

Neapel oder Rom, in Paris oder München, Düsseldorf oder New York. Dort führt man seine Biker-Jacken, ölbedruckten T-Shirts, seine Faltenröcke in Neonorange und die lang geschnittenen Sweater. Richmonds neuester Flagship-Store in der Londoner Conduit Street steht in Verbindung mit zwei Läden in Italien – genauer gesagt: in Mailand und Bari. Außerdem wären da noch die Kollektion Designers at Debenhams und das Auto namens John Richmond Smart Roadster. Dass ein eigener Duft, eine Kinderkollektion sowie Uhren und Schmuck bereits in Planung sind, versteht sich da fast von selbst. Weitere Projekte umfassen die Expansion seiner Läden zur Präsentation der jüngeren Nebenlinien – X und Denim – auf dem weltweiten Markt. Im Rahmen dieses Projekts sind bis zum Jahr 2011 hundert Läden an den wichtigsten Plätzen der Welt avisiert.

Entre son slogan « Destroy, Disorientate, Disorder » et le grand magasin anglais Debenhams, on peut dire que John Richmond est à la fois rock'n'roll et prêt-à-porter. Originaire de Manchester, ce fan de musique possède un talent unique pour réconcilier esthétique anarchique punk et coupes élégantes. Né en 1961, Richmond sort diplômé de l'école polytechnique de Kingston en 1982 et travaille comme créateur free-lance pour Emporio Armani, Fiorucci et Joseph Tricot. En 1984, il fonde sa première griffe, Richmond-Cornejo, en collaboration avec la créatrice Maria Cornejo, mais décide de se lancer en solo dès 1987. Au cours de sa carrière, Richmond a habillé des icônes pop telles que Bryan Adams, David Bowie, Madonna et Mick Jagger ; George Michael a même porté son blouson Destroy dans son clip « Faith ». Les créations de John Richmond fusionnent l'esprit du rock et l'odeur du cuir. Aujourd'hui, sa griffe comprend trois lignes de mode : John Richmond, Richmond X et Richmond Denim, sans oublier le récent lancement de collections de lunettes et de sous-vêtements. Grâce à son partenariat commercial avec Saverio Moschillo, Richmond dispose d'un réseau mondial de showrooms installés à Naples, Rome, Paris, Munich, Düsseldorf et New York. Tous accueillent ses blousons de motard en cuir, ses T-shirts imprimés à l'huile, ses jupes plissées orange fluo et ses pulls aux lignes allongées. La boutique londonienne flambant neuve de Richmond dans Conduit Street vient s'ajouter aux deux boutiques italiennes de Milan et de Bari. Sans compter la collection Designers at Debenhams et la voiture John Richmond Smart Roadster. Logiquement, un parfum, une ligne pour enfant, une collection de montres et de bijoux John Richmond ne devraient plus tarder à voir le jour. Le créateur compte également étendre son réseau mondial d'enseignes pour présenter ses lignes de diffusion, X et Denim, qui ciblent une clientèle plus jeune. En effet, la marque compte ouvrir 100 boutiques sur les principaux marchés internationaux d'ici 2011.

NANCY WATERS

"As hard and painful as designing can be, it is the thing I have always been most passionate about"
NARCISO RODRIGUEZ

Narciso Rodriguez designs clothes that are sliced, cut and put together with apparently effortless finesse. They are fluid and simple, architectural and modern, easy to wear but not casual, dressed-up but not too over-the-top. Rodriguez has an impeccable list of credentials. He graduated from Parsons School of Design in 1982, and after a brief period free-lancing, joined Donna Karan at Anne Klein in 1985. He worked there for six years before moving to Calvin Klein as womenswear designer. In 1995, he relocated to Paris, where he stayed for two years with Cerruti, first as women's and men's design director, and then as creative director for the entire womenswear division. Never one to slow down the pace, in 1997 Rodriguez not only showed his debut signature line in Milan, but also became the womenswear design director at leather goods brand Loewe, a position he retained until 2001. In 2003, he received the CFDA's womenswear Designer of the Year Award and in 2004 was the recipient of the Hispanic Heritage Vision Award. Since 2001, he has concentrated on his eponymous line, which is produced and distributed by Aeffe SpA and shown at New York Fashion Week. Rodriguez's Latin roots (he was born in 1961 in New Jersey to Cuban-American parents) inspire the slick, glamorous side of his work while his experience in Europe has honed his fashion craftsmanship and tailoring expertise. This perfectly stylish balance has seduced some of the world's loveliest ladies, including Salma Hayek, Julianna Margulies and the late Carolyn Bessette, who married John F. Kennedy Jr in a Rodriguez creation. In May 2007, Rodriguez was announced winner of the Pratt Institute's Fashion Icon Award.

Narciso Rodriguez entwirft Kleider, die mit scheinbar müheloser Finesse zugeschnitten und zusammengefügt sind. Sie sind fließend und schlicht, skulptural und modern, tragbar, aber nicht alltäglich, schick, jedoch nicht überkandidelt. Die Referenzen, die der Designer vorzuweisen hat, sind tadellos. 1982 machte er seinen Abschluss an der Parsons School of Design, darauf folgte eine kurze Phase als freischaffender Designer. 1985 fing er unter Donna Karan beim Label Anne Klein an. Nach sechs Jahren wechselte er als Damenmodedesigner zu Calvin Klein. Im Jahr 1995 zog er nach Paris, wo er zwei Jahre für Cerruti tätig war, zunächst als Design Director für Damen wie für Herren und schließlich als Creative Director der gesamten Damenmode. Das Tempo ging es weiter – 1997 präsentierte Rodriguez nicht nur in Mailand die erste Kollektion seiner eigenen Linie, sondern wurde auch Design Director der Damenmode beim Lederwarenhersteller Loewe, was er bis 2001 bleiben sollte. 2003 wurde er vom Council of Fashion Designers (CFDA) zum Designer of the Year für den Bereich Damenmode gewählt; 2004 zeichnete man

ihn mit dem Hispanic Heritage Vision Award aus. Seit 2001 konzentriert sich der Designer ausschließlich auf seine eigene Linie, die von Aeffe SpA produziert und vertrieben und bei der New York Fashion Week vorgestellt wird. Seine Wurzeln (er wurde 1961 als Kind kubanisch-amerikanischer Eltern in New Jersey geboren) inspirieren Rodriguez zu den schicken glamourösen Aspekten seiner Arbeit, während die in Europa gesammelten Erfahrungen ihm im handwerklich-technischen Bereich zugute kommen. Wie perfekt sich beides ergänzt, konnte man schon an einigen der schönsten Frauen der Welt bewundern, etwa an Salma Hayek, Julianna Margulies und der inzwischen verstorbenen Carolyn Bessette, die John F. Kennedy Junior in einer Rodriguez-Kreation geheiratet hat. Im Mai 2007 wurde Rodriguez vom Pratt Institute mit dem Fashion Icon Award ausgezeichnet.

Narciso Rodriguez dessine des vêtements taillés, coupés et assemblés avec une grande finesse et une apparente facilité. Ses créations sont simples et fluides, architecturales et modernes, faciles à porter mais pas trop informelles, chic mais jamais surchargées. Rodriguez revendique une liste de références idéales : diplômé de la Parsons School of Design en 1982, il travaille en free-lance pendant une brève période avant de rejoindre Donna Karan chez Anne Klein en 1985. Il reste six ans, puis part travailler chez Calvin Klein en tant que styliste pour femme. En 1995, il s'installe à Paris où il passe deux ans chez Cerruti, d'abord comme directeur des lignes pour femme et pour homme, puis comme directeur de la création de toutes les collections féminines. N'étant pas du genre à ralentir le rythme, en 1997 Rodriguez présente non seulement sa première collection signature à Milan, mais devient également directeur de la création féminine du maroquinier Loewe, un poste qu'il occupe jusqu'en 2001. En 2003, le CFDA le couronne Womenswear Designer of the Year, puis il reçoit en 2004 le Vision Award de la fondation Hispanic Heritage. Depuis 2001, il se consacre à sa ligne éponyme, produite et distribuée par Aeffe SpA et présentée à la New York Fashion Week. Ses racines latines (il est né en 1961 dans le New Jersey de parents d'origine cubaine) inspirent le côté brillant et glamour de son travail, tandis que son expérience européenne aiguise son savoir-faire et son expertise de la coupe : un savant équilibre stylistique qui séduit certaines des plus belles femmes du monde telles que Salma Hayek, Julianna Margulies et feue Carolyn Bessette, qui avait épousé John F. Kennedy Junior dans une robe dessinée par Rodriguez. En mai 2007, le Pratt Institute lui a décerné son Fashion Icon Award.

TERRY NEWMAN

"I hope that my creations can give a little bit of joy"
SONIA RYKIEL

Sonia Rykiel is synonymous with Paris. Born in the city in 1930, she went on to encapsulate Parisian style with her chic fashion line. As an expectant mother, she had discovered that there were no sweaters available that were soft and flexible enough for her to wear through her pregnancy, so, in 1962, she created her own line of knitwear. This was so successful that she opened her first boutique in that momentous Parisian year, 1968. And, in their own way, Rykiel's designs were revolutionary. Her flattering knits – often in what was to become her trademark stripes – symbolised liberation for women's bodies from the stiff silhouette of the previous decade. She also increased the sex appeal of knits: freed from linings and hems, her dresses and sweaters were like second skins for the women who wore them. Rykiel has continued to build her very own French Empire since the 1970s. She recognised the wisdom of establishing a beauty line early on, launching a perfume in 1978 and cosmetics in 1987. Completely independent, Rykiel's business is very much a family affair. Husband Simon Bernstein is her business partner and daughter Nathalie Rykiel has been involved in the company since 1975. With such support, Sonia Rykiel has the freedom to do other things. Today, Madame Rykiel is something of a French institution. She has written novels, decorated hotels, sung a duet with Malcolm McLaren and even had a rose named after her. And the accolades keep on coming. Rykiel has been awarded an Oscar by the Fashion Group International and in December 2001, the French government named her Commandeur de l'Ordre National du Mérite. Now in her eighties, the grande dame of French fashion shows no signs of giving up. Her creations are impossibly sexy, impossibly shiny and impossibly decadent, and in Spring/Summer 2009, Sonia celebrated 40 years in the fashion game with a surprise tribute catwalk show organised by daughter Nathalie. Out came a procession of 30 girls rocking out 'Tribute' dresses designed by Rykiel's friends, peers and fashion designers including Martin Margiela, Jean Paul Gaultier, Karl Lagerfeld and Alber Elbaz in a breathless ode to the brilliant flame-haired queen of knits. Long may she reign.

Sonia Rykiel gilt inzwischen als Synonym für Paris, wo sie 1930 geboren wurde. Später gelang es ihr, die Pariser Eleganz in ihrer schicken Modelinie auf den Punkt zu bringen. Als werdende Mutter hatte sie 1962 feststellen müssen, dass es keine Pullover gab, die für eine Schwangerschaft weich und elastisch genug waren, also entwarf sie kurzerhand ihre eigene Strickkollektion. Der Erfolg war so groß, dass Rykiel im für Paris so bedeutsamen Jahr 1968 ihre erste Boutique in der Stadt eröffnete. Und auf ihre Weise waren auch die damaligen Kreationen von Sonia Rykiel revolutionär. Ihre Stricksachen – oft mit Streifen, die ihr Markenzeichen werden sollten – symbolisierten die Befreiung des weiblichen Körpers von der starren Silhouette des vorangegangenen Jahrzehnts. Sie steigerte auch den Sexappeal von Strick: frei von Futter und Säumen, wirkten ihre Kleider und Pullover wie eine zweite Haut ihrer Trägerin. Seit den 1970er-Jahren baut Rykiel kontinuierlich an ihrem ganz privaten französischen Imperium. Früh erkannte sie den Wert eigener Beautyprodukte und brachte 1978 einen ersten Duft, 1987 die ersten Kosmetika unter ihrem Namen heraus. Das völlig autarke Unternehmen ist ein Familienbetrieb. Ehemann Simon Bernstein ist ihr Geschäftspartner, Tochter Nathalie Rykiel seit 1975 in die Firma integriert. Dieser Rückhalt gibt Rykiel die Freiheit, auch andere Dinge als Mode zu machen. Inzwischen gilt Madame Rykiel als eine Art Institution. Sie hat Romane veröffentlicht, Hotels eingerichtet, ein Duett mit Malcolm McLaren gesungen, ja sogar eine Rose ist nach ihr benannt. Und die Reihe der Auszeichnungen reißt nicht ab: So erhielt Rykiel von der Fashion Group International einen Oscar; im Dezember 2001 ehrte die französische Regierung sie mit dem Titel Commandeur de l'Ordre National du Mérite. Auch wenn sie inzwischen in den Siebzigern ist, setzt sich die Grande Dame der französischen Mode noch nicht zur Ruhe. Ihre Kreationen sind sexy, schön und dekadent. Anlässlich von Frühjahr/Sommer 2009 feierte Sonia Rykiel ihre 40 Jahre im Modezirkus mit einer Überraschungs-Catwalk-Show, die Tochter Nathalie ihr zu Ehren organisiert hatte: eine Präsentation von „Tribute"-Kleidern, die Rykiels Freunde, Weggefährten und Modedesigner wie Martin Margiela, Jean Paul Gaultier, Karl Lagerfeld und Alber Elbaz kreiert hatten. Das Ganze war eine atemlose Ode an die Königin des Strick mit ihren flammend roten Haaren. Möge sie noch lange regieren!

Sonia Rykiel est synonyme de Paris. Née en 1930 dans la capitale, elle saisit la quintessence du style parisien dans ses collections de mode très chic. Pendant sa grossesse, elle n'arrive pas à trouver de pulls assez souples pour son ventre de femme enceinte, ce qui l'incite à créer sa propre ligne de maille en 1962. Elle remporte un tel succès qu'elle ouvre sa première boutique dès 1968, une année de bouleversement pour les Parisiens. À leur façon, les créations Rykiel sont tout aussi révolutionnaires : ses tricots flatteurs, souvent déclinés dans ce qui deviendra ses rayures signature, symbolisent l'émancipation des femmes, libérant leurs corps de la silhouette rigide imposée par la décennie précédente. Elle rehausse également le sex-appeal de la maille ; dépourvus de doublures et d'ourlets, ses robes et ses pulls enveloppent celles qui les portent comme une seconde peau. Depuis les années 70, Sonia Rykiel ne cesse de développer son propre empire français. Elle comprend très tôt l'intérêt de créer une ligne de beauté et lance un parfum en 1978, puis une gamme de maquillage en 1987. Entièrement indépendante, l'entreprise de Sonia Rykiel reste avant tout familiale. Son mari Simon Bernstein y est associé et sa fille Nathalie Rykiel y travaille depuis 1975. Forte d'un tel soutien, Sonia trouve le temps de se consacrer à d'autres passions. Aujourd'hui, Madame Rykiel est devenue une sorte d'institution française. Elle a écrit des romans, décoré des hôtels, chanté un duo avec Malcolm McLaren et revendique même une rose à son nom. Et les distinctions ne cessent de pleuvoir. Sonia Rykiel a reçu un Oscar du Fashion Group International, et le gouvernement français l'a adoubée commandeur de l'Ordre National du Mérite en décembre 2001. Et la grande dame de la mode française n'a aucune envie d'abandonner. Ses créations sont incroyablement sexy, voyantes et décadentes. Pour le printemps/été 2009, un défilé surprise organisé par sa fille Nathalie rendait hommage aux 40 ans de carrière de Sonia : 30 filles ont paradé dans des robes « Tribute » conçues par les amis et pairs de Sonia Rykiel, des créateurs de mode parmi lesquels Martin Margiela, Jean Paul Gaultier, Karl Lagerfeld et Alber Elbaz, dans une ode époustouflante à la reine de la maille aux cheveux de feu. Longue vie à la reine !

LAUREN COCHRANE

"The simpler the better"
JONATHAN SAUNDERS + POLLINI

The exuberant prints shown in his graduate collection were an instant hit and took many a fashion critic's breath away. Using traditional silk-screening techniques, Jonathan Saunders is now synonymous with geometric patterns and colour. Within a year of graduating from Central Saint Martins (MA with distinction in printed textiles) in 2002, Scottish-born Jonathan Saunders – the son of two ministers from Rutherglen – made his runway debut at London Fashion Week. Since then, Saunders' brilliant fusion of print and silhouette has been in great demand and he has gone on to consult for other major fashion houses such as Alexander McQueen, Chloé and Pucci. His namesake line has at the same time been growing in stature, stocked by prestigious stores such as Harrods and Harvey Nichols in London and Neiman Marcus in the United States. He showed for the first time in New York in February 2008, joining a string of British fashion designers like Matthew Williamson and Preen on the New York schedule, to build on his international business. In 2008, he was named creative director of the fashion house Pollini where he continues to be a master of print and colour.

Die überbordenden Print-Muster seiner Abschlusskollektion waren ein unmittelbarer Erfolg und nahmen vielen Modejournalisten den Atem. Durch seine Anwendung traditioneller Siebdrucktechnik gilt Jonathan Saunders' Name heute als Synonym für geometrische Muster und Farbe. Nur ein Jahr nach seinem Abschluss am Central Saint Martins (MA mit Prädikat im Fach Bedruckte Textilien) 2002 gab der in Schottland gebore-ne Jonathan Saunders – Sohn einer Pfarrersfamilie aus Rutherglen – sein Laufsteg-Debüt bei der London Fashion Week. Seit damals ist Saunders' brillante Verbindung von Muster und Silhouette extrem gefragt, und er hat sich einen Namen als Berater großer Modehäuser wie Alexander McQueen, Chloé und Pucci gemacht. Parallel dazu hat die nach ihm selbst

benannte Linie an Ansehen gewonnen und ist inzwischen in Nobelkauf-häusern wie Harrods und Harvey Nichols in London und Neiman Marcus in den USA vorrätig. In New York präsentierte er erstmals im Februar 2008 und trat damit einer Riege britischer Designer wie Matthew Wil-liamson und Preen im New Yorker Kalender bei, um seine internationalen Geschäfte auszubauen. 2008 wurde er zum Creative Director des Mode-hauses Pollini ernannt, wo er seinen Ruf, ein Meister des Drucks und der Farbe zu sein, weiter ausbaut.

Les imprimés exubérants que présente Jonathan Saunders dans sa collec-tion de fin d'études remportent un succès immédiat et époustouflent plus d'un critique de mode. Fan des techniques de sérigraphie traditionnelles, son nom est aujourd'hui synonyme de couleur et de motifs géométriques. Un an après avoir décroché son diplôme à Central Saint Martins (un MA en textiles imprimés obtenu avec mention en 2002), cet Écossais élevé par des parents pasteurs à Rutherglen défile déjà à la London Fashion Week. Depuis, sa fusion extrêmement brillante entre imprimé et silhouette est très demandée. Saunders a aussi travaillé comme consultant auprès de grandes maisons de mode telles Alexander McQueen, Chloé et Pucci. Parallèlement, sa collection éponyme prend de plus en plus d'ampleur, désormais distribuée par des détaillants aussi prestigieux qu'Harrods et Harvey Nichols à Londres, et Neiman Marcus aux États-Unis. Son premier défilé new-yorkais officiel a eu lieu en février 2008 aux côtés d'autres créateurs britanniques comme Matthew Williamson et Preen, ce qui lui a permis de développer son activité à l'international. En 2008, il a été nommé directeur de la création de la maison Pollini où il continue de se construire une réputation de maître de l'imprimé et des couleurs.

KAREN HODKINSON

"I like to look at fashion from a scientific way, that still remains true to its purpose"
MARIOS SCHWAB

Marios Schwab is the embodiment of a cosmopolitan. The 30-year-old half-Greek half-Austrian designer lived in Athens and Berlin before moving to London. At the renowned German fashion institution Esmod, Schwab graduated with distinction and Best Student Award, after which he moved to London and graduated with an MA in womenswear fashion from Central Saint Martins in 2003. By this time his childhood ambition to be a ballet dancer was far behind him. His label was launched in 2005 and after showing for two seasons with Fashion East, Schwab debuted on schedule at London Fashion Week for Spring/Summer 2007 to high critical acclaim. Describing the little black dress as his design signature, his dresses have been worn by Kate Moss, Hilary Duff, Kylie Minogue and Clemence Poesy. Awarded Best New Designer at the British Fashion Awards in 2006, Schwab won the Swiss Textiles Award the next year. In 2008, Schwab collaborated with Swarovski for the Runway Rocks show, and continues to show in London. His designs are sold worldwide from Browns and Dover Street Market to Maria Luisa and Barneys.

Marios Schwab ist die Verkörperung eines Kosmopoliten. Der 30-Jährige ist zur Hälfte Grieche, zur Hälfte Österreicher und lebte in Athen und Berlin, bevor er seinen Wohnsitz nach London verlegte. Er absolvierte die renommierte deutsche Modeschule Esmod mit Auszeichnung und dem Best Student Award. Anschließend ging er nach London, wo er am Central Saint Martins einen Master in Womenswear Fashion erwarb. Seinen Kindheitstraum, Tänzer zu werden, hatte er zu diesem Zeitpunkt schon weit hinter sich gelassen. 2005 gründete er sein eigenes Label, und nachdem er zwei Saisons lang bei der Fashion East vertreten gewesen war, gab er ein viel beachtetes Debüt im offiziellen Kalender

der London Fashion Week mit seiner Kollektion für Frühjahr/Sommer 2007. Das kleine Schwarze gilt als sein Markenzeichen, und so sieht man seine Kleider unter anderem an Kate Moss, Hilary Duff, Kylie Minogue und Clemence Poesy. Bei den British Fashion Awards 2006 wurde er als Best New Designer ausgezeichnet. Im Jahr darauf gewann Schwab den Swiss Textiles Award. 2008 arbeitete er gemeinsam mit Swarovski an der Show „Runway Rocks". Darüber hinaus präsentiert Schwab weiterhin in London. Seine Kollektionen werden weltweit in exklusiven Boutiquen verkauft.

Marios Schwab est le cosmopolite par excellence. Mi-grec, mi-autrichien, ce styliste de 30 ans a vécu à Athènes et à Berlin avant de venir s'installer à Londres. De la célèbre école de mode allemande Esmod, Schwab sort diplômé avec les honneurs du jury et le prix de meilleur étudiant. C'est à ce moment-là qu'il part vivre à Londres, où il décroche en 2003 un MA en mode féminine de Central Saint Martins. S'il rêvait de devenir danseur classique quand il était petit, ces ambitions sont désormais loin derrière lui. Schwab lance sa griffe en 2005, puis, après deux saisons dans le cadre des défilés Fashion East, il fait ses débuts officiels aux collections printemps/été 2007 de la London Fashion Week devant une critique enthousiasmée. Avec la petite robe noire comme signature créative, ses modèles ont été portés par Kate Moss, Hilary Duff, Kylie Minogue et Clemence Poesy. Couronné Best New Designer aux British Fashion Awards en 2006, Schwab remporte le Swiss Textiles Award l'année suivante. En 2008, il collabore avec Swarovski pour le défilé Runway Rocks et continue à présenter ses collections à Londres. Ses collections sont vendues à travers le monde entier dans des boutiques exclusives de mode.

KAREN HODKINSON

"I love creating and I hate the empty feeling when it's done"
JEREMY SCOTT

Jeremy Scott's story is the stuff of fairy tales and syndicated game shows. Born in 1974 and raised in Kansas City, Missouri, Scott was the boy who read Italian 'Vogue' between classes and wrote about fashion in French essays. After graduating from New York's Pratt Institute, the 21-year-old made a pilgrimage to Paris, where his collection, made out of paper hospital gowns, went down in fashion folklore. His first formal runway presentation in October 1997, 'Rich White Women', presenting asymmetrically cut trousers and multifunctional T-shirts, established Scott as a substantial Parisian presence. But controversy clings to the designer like a Pierre Cardin teddy bear brooch. Later collections took inspiration from sci fi B-movies, soap operas and games shows, along the way establishing key details of the Scott aesthetic: attention to volume, obsession with logos (including bestselling back-to-front Paris print), bold prints, pop imagery and healthy doses of humour. In autumn 2001, Scott relocated to Los Angeles, a city that has welcomed his über-trash style with open arms, to such an extent that he achieved one of his long-term ambitions, appearing on the American classic soap opera 'The Young and the Restless' playing, who else, himself! Scott continues to show in both New York and Paris switching back and forth between the worlds of urban and chic. Scott's colourful, optimistic vision has developed into strong collaborations. In 2006, he began a collaborative relationship adorning the iconic Longchamp pliage bag with bold graphic imagery such as his telephone and boot stomp prints. In 2008, Adidas launched a Jeremy Scott collection of clothing and shoes. Winged high tops and trainers with plush teddy bear heads sprouting out of them have become not only bestsellers but icons of the brand itself. In spring 2010, Jeremy Scott for Swatch was launched with a celebratory billboard of Scott and Swatch hovering above Times Square. His artistic energy continues to inspire his many celebrity fans, from Madonna and Beth Ditto to Rihanna and Katy Perry. As Scott himself might say, vive l'avant-garde!

Jeremy Scotts Biografie klingt wie der Stoff, aus dem Märchen sind. Oder Fernsehshows. Der 1974 geborene und in Kansas City, Missouri, aufgewachsene Scott las tatsächlich schon als Schüler in der Pause die italienische Vogue und schrieb in Französisch Aufsätze über Mode. Nach einem Abschluss am New Yorker Pratt Institute pilgerte der damals 21-Jährige nach Paris, wo seine Kollektion aus papierenen Krankenhaushemden in die Modegeschichte einging. Scotts erste offizielle Laufsteg-Schau präsentierte im Oktober 1997 unter dem Titel „Rich White Women" asymmetrisch geschnittene Hosen und multifunktionale T-Shirts, mit denen der Designer sich in der Pariser Szene etablierte. Doch haftet ihm Widersprüchlichkeit wie eine Teddybär-Brosche von Pierre Cardin an. Spätere Kollektionen waren von zweitklassigen Science-Fiction-Filmen, Soap-Operas und Spielshows inspiriert, setzten aber dennoch Maßstäbe für Scotts Ästhetik: Volumen, eine Passion für Logos (inklusive des Bestsellers in Gestalt eines umlaufenden Parisdrucks), freche Prints, poppige Bilder und eine gesunde Portion Humor. Im Herbst 2001 verlegte Scott seinen Wohnsitz nach Los Angeles – in die Stadt, die seinen extrem kitschigen Stil mit solcher Begeisterung aufgenommen hatte. Die Resonanz war so groß, dass ein lang gehegter Wunsch Scotts in Erfüllung ging: Er spielte sich selbst in der typisch amerikanischen Serie „Schatten der

Leidenschaft". Seine Kollektionen zeigt Scott weiterhin in New York und Paris, sie bewegen sich zwischen lässig und extravagant. Aus seiner farbenfroh optimistischen Vision haben sich intensive Kooperationen entwickelt. So verzierte er 2006 die berühmte Longchamps-Tasche Pliage mit auffälligen grafischen Darstellungen wie der seines Telefons und Stiefelabdrücken. 2008 brachte Adidas eine Jeremy-Scott-Kollektion mit Kleidung und Schuhen heraus. Die geflügelten High-Top-Sneaker und Turnschuhe, aus denen Plüschteddybärenköpfe ragten, wurden nicht nur zu Verkaufsschlagern, sondern zu einem Symbol der Marke. Scotts Zusammenarbeit mit dem Uhrenhersteller Swatch wurde im Frühjahr 2010 mit einer riesigen Plakatwand über dem Times Square eingeläutet. Seine künstlerische Energie dient weiterhin vielen prominenten Fans als Inspiration, von Madonna über Beth Ditto bis hin zu Rihanna und Katy Perry. Getreu Scotts Motto: Vive l'avant-garde!

L'histoire de Jeremy Scott est une affaire de contes de fées et de jeux télévisés. Né en 1974, il grandit à Kansas City dans le Missouri, où il est bien le seul à lire le Vogue italien entre les cours et à disserter sur la mode dans ses rédactions de français. Une fois diplômé du Pratt Institute de New York à 21 ans, Scott part en pèlerinage à Paris. La collection qu'il y présente marque un véritable tournant dans l'histoire de la mode, avec ses robes d'hôpitaux en papier. En octobre 1997, lors de son premier défilé officiel intitulé « Rich White Women », il présente des pantalons asymétriques et des T-shirts multifonctions qui assoient définitivement sa présence sur la scène parisienne. Mais la controverse s'accroche à lui comme une broche-nounours de Pierre Cardin. Les collections suivantes s'inspirent de films de science-fiction de série B, de soaps-opéras et de jeux télévisés et certains détails-clés parviennent à imposer l'esthétique de Scott : l'attention portée au volume, l'obsession des logos (notamment l'imprimé intégral « Paris » qui s'est très bien vendu), les imprimés insolents, les images pop et une bonne portion d'humour. À l'automne 2001, Scott s'installe à Los Angeles, une ville qui accueille son style ultra-trash à bras ouverts. À tel point qu'il réalise l'un de ses plus vieux rêves : il joue son propre rôle dans le feuilleton typiquement américain Les Feux de l'Amour. Scott continue à présenter à la fois à New York et à Paris des collections qui oscillent entre nonchalance et extravagance. Son optimisme multicolore s'exprime aussi à travers d'importantes collaborations. Ainsi, en 2006, il décore le célèbre sac Longchamps Pliage avec des applications graphiques ostensibles comme l'empreinte de son téléphone et de ses bottes. En 2008, Adidas lance une collection de vêtements et de chaussures signée Jeremy Scott. Les sneakers hautes avec des ailes et les baskets d'où surgissent des têtes d'ours en peluche ne sont pas seulement des gros succès commerciaux mais deviennent également le symbole de la marque. La collaboration de Scott avec le fabricant de montres Swatch est annoncée au printemps 2010 avec renfort d'un immense mur-affiche surplombant le Times Square. Son énergie artistique continue d'inspirer ses nombreuses et célèbres admiratrices, qu'il s'agisse de Madonna, Beth Ditto, Rihanna ou Katy Perry. Comme le dirait Scott lui-même, « vive l'avant-garde » !

GLENN WALDRON

"The collections have been part of the process of growing up"
RAF SIMONS · JIL SANDER

Although he is now one of the indisputable kings of menswear, Raf Simons (born 1968) never took a single fashion course. Instead, he studied industrial design in Genk, Belgium, close to his hometown Neerpelt. Nevertheless, he took an internship at the Walter van Beirendonck Antwerp office while still at school, citing fashion as a major point of interest. Afterwards, Simons started working as a furniture designer. In 1995, after moving to Antwerp and meeting up with Linda Loppa, head of the fashion department at the city's Royal Academy, he decided to switch career. Obsessed both by traditional, formal menswear and the rebellious dress codes of present and past youth cultures, Simons distilled a groundbreaking new style from these inspirations. From his first collection for Autumn/Winter 1995 on, he drew a tight, linear silhouette executed in classical materials that encapsulated references like English schoolboys, gothic music, punk, Kraftwerk and Bauhaus architecture. Despite international acclaim, Raf Simons surprisingly shut down his company after presenting his Autumn/Winter 1999 collection, in order to take a sabbatical. After sealing a close co-operation with Belgian manufacturer CIG, Simons returned for Autumn/Winter 2000 with a new, multilayered and radical look, worn as ever by non-professional models scouted on the streets of Antwerp. These teenage boys were the subject of a collaboration with David Sims, resulting in photographs compiled in a book ('Isolated Heroes', 1999). Raf Simons designed the Ruffo Research men's collections for two seasons in 1999. Since October 2000, he has taught fashion at the University of Applied Arts in Vienna, and in February 2001, he guest edited an issue of 'i-D'. In 2003, Simons curated two exhibitions (The Fourth Sex at Pitti Immagine, Florence, and Guided by Heroes in Hasselt, Belgium) and collaborated with Peter Saville on his Autumn/Winter 2003 collection, Closer. In May 2005, it was announced that Simons would take over as creative director at Jil Sander – Simons dedicated the Autumn/Winter 2009 collection to Sander. Following the closing of the original Hamburg Studio, Rashahana, the new Japanese owners of the label, moved all staff to Milan. 2010 marks Raf Simons' 15th anniversary in the fashion industry.

Auch wenn er heute zu den unumstrittenen Königen der Herrenmode zählt, hat der 1968 in Neerpelt geborene Raf Simons nie auch nur ein einziges Seminar zum Thema Mode besucht. Stattdessen studierte er im belgischen Genk Industriedesign. Allerdings absolvierte er noch als Schüler ein Praktikum im Antwerpener Atelier von Walter van Beirendonck und interessierte sich bereits damals sehr für Mode. Zunächst arbeitete Simons als Möbeldesigner. Nachdem er nach Antwerpen gezogen war und dort Linda Loppa, die Leiterin der Modefakultät an der Königlichen Akademie, kennengelernt hatte, beschloss er 1995 umzusatteln. Fasziniert von der traditionellen klassischen Herrenmode und den rebellischen Dresscodes der Jugendlichen verschiedenster Generationen, destillierte Simons aus diesen Inspirationen einen bahnbrechenden neuen Stil. Schon in seiner ersten Kollektion, Herbst/Winter 1995, entschied er sich für eine schmale, lineare Silhouette aus klassischen Materialien mit Bezügen zu englischen Schuluniformen, Gothic Music, Punk, Kraftwerk und Bauhausarchitektur. Trotz internationaler Anerkennung schloss Simons seine Firma nach der Präsentation seiner Kollektion für Herbst/Winter 1999, um sich eine Auszeit zu gönnen. Nachdem die enge Zusammenarbeit mit dem belgischen Hersteller CIG

besiegelt war, kehrte Simons für die Saison Herbst/Winter 2000 mit einem neuen, radikalen Look aus vielen Lagen zurück. Den präsentierten wie immer Amateur-Models, die man auf den Straßen von Antwerpen angeworben hatte. Um eben diese Teenager-Jungs ging es auch bei einem Projekt mit David Sims, das in dem Fotoband „Isolated Heroes" (1999) dokumentiert ist. Im Jahr 1999 entwarf Simons bei Ruffo Research die Herrenkollektionen für zwei Saisons. Seit Oktober 2000 lehrt er Mode an der Universität für Angewandte Kunst in Wien. Als Gastredakteur wirkte er im Februar 2001 an einer Ausgabe von i-D mit. 2003 war Simons Kurator von zwei Ausstellungen („The Fourth Sex" in der Fondazione Pitti Immagine in Florenz und „Guided by Heroes" im belgischen Hasselt) und erarbeitete zusammen mit Peter Saville seine Kollektion „Closer" für Herbst/Winter 2003. Im Mai 2005 gab Jil Sander bekannt, dass Raf Simons die Aufgaben des Creative Director übernehmen würde. Seine Kollektion für Herbst/Winter 2009 widmete der Designer Jil Sander. Nach der Schließung des Hamburger Studios verlegte der neue japanische Eigentümer des Labels das Unternehmen nach Mailand. Es war Raf Simons 15. Jahr in der Modebranche.

Bien qu'il soit sans conteste l'un des rois de la mode pour homme, Raf Simons (né en 1968) n'a jamais suivi la moindre formation en mode. En fait, il a étudié le design industriel à Genk, près de sa ville natale de Neerpelt en Belgique. Pendant ses études, il fait toutefois un stage au bureau anversois de Walter van Beirendonck, car la mode figure parmi ses principaux centres d'intérêt. Ensuite, Simons commence à travailler comme designer de meubles. En 1995, après avoir emménagé à Anvers et rencontré Linda Loppa, directrice du département mode de l'Académie Royale de la ville, il décide de changer de carrière. Obsédé à la fois par la mode masculine classique et les codes vestimentaires de la jeunesse rebelle d'hier et d'aujourd'hui, Simons puise dans ces inspirations et invente un nouveau style révolutionnaire. Dès sa première collection à l'automne/hiver 1995, il définit une silhouette étroite et linéaire, façonnée dans des matières classiques pleines de références aux collégiens anglais, à la musique gothique, au punk, à Kraftwerk ou encore à l'architecture Bauhaus. Malgré un succès international, contre toute attente, Raf Simons ferme sa maison après avoir présenté sa collection automne/hiver 1999, décidant de prendre un congé sabbatique. Il signe ensuite un accord d'étroite coopération avec le fabricant belge CIG, puis revient à l'automne/hiver 2000 avec un nouveau look radical comme multiples facettes, présenté comme toujours sur des mannequins non professionnels recrutés dans les rues d'Anvers. Ces adolescents font d'ailleurs l'objet d'une collaboration avec David Sims, qui sort un livre de photographies (Isolated Heroes, 1999). Par ailleurs, Raf Simons conçoit deux collections masculines pour Ruffo Research en 1999. Depuis octobre 2000, il enseigne la mode à l'Université des Arts Appliqués de Vienne et a été invité au comité de rédaction du numéro de février 2001 du magazine i-D. En 2003, il organise deux expositions (« The Fourth Sex » au Pitti Immagine de Florence et « Guided by Heroes » à Hasselt, Belgique) et collabore avec Peter Saville sur « Closer », sa collection automne/hiver 2003. En mai 2005, la maison Jil Sander annonce le recrutement de Raf Simons au poste de directeur de la création. Il dédie la collection automne/hiver 2009 à la créatrice dont la maison porte le nom.

PETER DE POTTER

"The perpetual 'restart' of fashion is very interesting and this permanent evolution is what pushes me to stay in this profession"
MARTINE SITBON · RUE DU MAIL

Martine Sitbon is a designer whose eye roves the globe for inspiration, referencing and subverting an eclectic mix of cultures while never exploiting her exotic upbringing. The child of an Italian mother and French father, Sitbon was born in Casablanca in 1951. At the age of ten, she moved to Paris, where she experienced first-hand the social transformations the city went through in the late '60s. She studied at the famed Studio Berçot, graduating in 1974 before travelling. After spending seven years rummaging through Hong Kong, Mexico, India, New York and Milan, she later fed this blend of the exotic and urban into her designs. In 1985, Sitbon launched her own label and presented her first show in Paris with a collection that famously gathered together monks' hoods, pastel colours, bloomers and a Velvet Underground soundtrack. Black may be key to the palette of the artistic intelligentsia, but Sitbon has enticed them with combinations of sober shades that threaten to clash head-on, but swerve just at the last minute. Her coolly dishevelled clothing often uses elements of leather and masculine tailoring to juxtapose the flea-market femininity of velvets, silks and satins. These contrasting combinations saw her recruited by Chloé in 1988 to design the label's womenswear line, a collaboration that lasted for nine seasons. In 1996, Sitbon opened her first boutique, in Paris. From 2001 to 2002, Sitbon was head designer for womenswear at Byblos. Now concentrating on her own-label menswear and womenswear, Sitbon remains the choice for those who love fashion's more eclectic side. Sitbon stopped showing in Paris from 2004 to 2007, when she presented her first edition of Rue du Mail together with her partner, Marc Ascoli. Within three seasons, the collection – comprising Sitbon's signature of beautifully sculpted asymmetric silhouettes, intelligent mix of muted colours and contrasting textures from satin to canvas – thrilled her fans as well as her young Hong Kong backer.

Martine Sitbon ist eine Designerin, die rund um den Globus nach Inspiration, Bezugspunkten und Subversion für einen eklektischen Mix der Kulturen sucht, ohne dafür ihre exotische Herkunft auszuschlachten. Sie wurde 1951 als Kind einer italienischen Mutter und eines französischen Vaters in Casablanca geboren. Als sie zehn Jahre alt war, zog sie mit ihrer Familie nach Paris, wo sie die gesellschaftlichen Umwälzungen Ende der 1960er aus unmittelbarer Nähe miterlebte. Sie studierte bis 1974 am berühmten Studio Berçot, um danach auf Reisen zu gehen. Nach sieben Jahren, die sie in Hongkong, Mexiko, Indien, New York und Mailand verbracht hatte, ließ sie diese Melange aus exotischen und urbanen Eindrücken in ihre Kreationen einfließen. 1985 präsentierte Sitbon ihr eigenes Label und ihre erste Schau in Paris mit einer denkwürdigen Kollektion aus Mönchskutten, Pastellfarben, Pumphosen und einem Soundtrack von Velvet Underground. Schwarz mag die dominierende Farbe der Künstler-Intelligenzia sein, doch Sitbon lockte sie mit Kombinationen sachlicher Farbtöne, die sich zu beißen scheinen, im letzten Augenblick aber doch noch harmonieren. Für ihre auf eine coole Art wirren Kleider benutzt sie oft Elemente aus der Leder- und Herrenschneiderei, die sie mit der Weiblichkeit von Flohmarktfunden aus Samt, Seide und Satin konfrontiert. Diese gegensätzlichen Kombinationen brachten sie 1988 zu Chloé,

wo sie die Damenlinie des Labels entwarf. Eine Partnerschaft, die neun Saisons lang hielt. 1996 eröffnete Sitbon ihre erste Pariser Boutique. Als Chefdesignerin der Damenmode war sie von 2001 bis 2002 für Byblos tätig. Heute konzentriert sich Sitbon ausschließlich auf die Damen- und Herrenmode ihres eigenen Labels und empfiehlt sich damit allen, die die eklektische Seite der Mode lieben. Von 2004 bis 2007 präsentierte Sitbon nicht in Paris. Erst mit ihrer ersten Kollektion für Rue du Mail gemeinsam mit ihrem Partner Marc Ascoli kehrte sie zurück. Innerhalb von drei Saisons begeisterte die Kollektion – mit den für Sitbon so typischen wunderbar skulpturalen asymmetrischen Silhouetten, einer intelligenten Mischung gedämpfter Farben und kontrastierenden Materialien von Satin bis Segeltuch – ihre Fans ebenso wie ihren jungen Sponsor aus Hongkong.

La créatrice Martine Sitbon parcourt le monde en quête d'inspiration, faisant référence de façon subversive à un mélange éclectique de cultures sans jamais exploiter ses propres origines exotiques. Martine Sitbon naît en 1951 à Casablanca d'une mère italienne et d'un père français. Elle arrive à Paris à l'âge de dix ans, où elle assiste aux premières loges aux transformations sociales que subit la capitale française jusqu'à la fin des années 60. Elle sort diplômée du célèbre Studio Berçot en 1974, puis part en voyage pour enrichir les compétences techniques qu'elle a déjà acquises d'un aspect multiculturel et de sa passion des tissus luxueux. Après sept années de découvertes entre Hong Kong, le Mexique, l'Inde, New York et Milan, elle insuffla plus tard ce mix exotique et urbain à ses créations. En 1985, Martine Sitbon lance sa propre griffe et présente son premier défilé à Paris avec une collection restée dans les annales qui mêle capuches monastiques, couleurs pastel, salopettes et musique du Velvet Underground. Le noir a beau être essentiel aux yeux de l'intelligentsia artistique, Martine Sitbon la convertit à d'autres couleurs sobres dans des combinaisons pas nécessairement harmonieuses, mais qui évitent toutefois le chaos chromatique. Ses vêtements tranquillement désordonnés conjuguent souvent des éléments du cuir et des costumes pour homme avec la féminité vintage des velours, des soies et des satins. Ces combinaisons contrastées attirent l'attention de la maison Chloé, qui embauche Martine Sitbon en 1988 pour dessiner sa ligne pour femme, une collaboration qui durera neuf saisons. En 1996, la créatrice ouvre sa première boutique à Paris. En 2001 et 2002, elle travaille comme styliste principale de la collection pour femme de Byblos. Aujourd'hui, Martine Sitbon se consacre à sa propre griffe pour homme et pour femme. Elle reste une créatrice de choix pour tous ceux qui privilégient le côté plus éclectique de la mode. Elle cesse de présenter ses collections à Paris entre 2004 et 2007, une année qui voit le lancement de la première édition « Rue du Mail » en partenariat avec Marc Ascoli. En l'espace de trois saisons, cette collection qui reprend les signatures de Martine Sitbon – silhouettes asymétriques magnifiquement sculptées, mélange intelligent de couleurs sourdes, textures contrastées du satin à la toile – suscite l'enthousiasme de ses fans comme celui de son jeune financier de Hong Kong.

LIZ HANCOCK

"The thing I'm most interested in is continuity. I've always worked hard at not being today's flavour"
PAUL SMITH

A serious accident while riding his bike put paid to Paul Smith's dream of becoming a professional racing cyclist. However, this mishap propelled him to pursue a career involving his other passion: fashion. In 1970, Smith (born Nottingham, 1946) opened a store in his native city, selling his own early designs that reflected the types of clothing he loved but was unable to buy anywhere else. Studying fashion design at evening classes, and working closely with his wife, Pauline Denyer, a graduate of the Royal College of Art, by 1976 he was showing a full range of menswear in Paris. Carving out a distinctive look that combined the best of traditional English attire often with unusual or witty prints, Smith blazed a trail throughout the late '70s. His progress continued into the '80s – when he put boxer shorts back on the fashion map – and beyond, with stores opened in New York (1987), and Paris (1993). The designer now has a staggering 200 shops in Japan, and also offers a range of womenswear (launched in 1994) and clothing for kids, in addition to accessories, books, jewellery, fragrances, pens, rugs and china. In 2001, Smith was knighted, and despite the success and breadth of his company – wholesaling to 75 countries around the globe and 17 shops in England – his hands-on involvement remains integral to its success. Commercial accomplishments aside, Smith's aesthetic has retained its idiosyncrasies. Paul Smith's global expansion continues to reach the first decade of the 21st century. While established in Asia and Europe, his unique aesthetic has also grown in America from East Coast New York to West Coast LA and San Francisco. The PS is in his personal touch, as the perfect shopkeeper.

Ein schwerer Unfall beendete Paul Smiths Traum von einer Karriere als Radrennfahrer. Allerdings veranlasste ihn dieses Missgeschick, aus seiner zweiten Passion – der Mode – eine Karriere zu machen. Der 1946 in Nottingham geborene Smith eröffnete 1970 in seiner Heimatstadt einen Laden, wo er seine frühen eigenen Entwürfe verkaufte – lauter Dinge, die er selbst gern getragen hätte, aber nirgends auftreiben konnte. In Abendkursen studierte er Modedesign und arbeitete außerdem eng mit seiner Frau Pauline Denyer, einer Absolventin des Royal College of Art, zusammen. 1976 konnte Smith eine komplette Herrenkollektion in Paris präsentieren. Sein ausgeprägt individueller Look vereinte die Vorzüge der traditionellen englischen Schneiderkunst mit oft ungewöhnlichen oder witzigen Mustern und hinterließ in den 1970er-Jahren deutliche Spuren. Die positive Entwicklung hielt bis in die 1980er-Jahre an – als er die Boxershorts wieder im allgemeine Modebewusstsein zurückbrachte – und darüber hinaus, mit Neueröffnungen von Läden in New York (1987) und Paris (1993). Inzwischen besitzt der Designer unglaubliche 200 Shops in Japan, wo er auch eine Damenkollektion (seit 1994), Kindersachen sowie Accessoires, Bücher, Schmuck, Düfte, Schreibgeräte, Teppiche und

Porzellan führt. Im Jahr 2001 wurde Smith zum Ritter geschlagen, und trotz des Erfolges und der großen Produktpalette seines Unternehmens – man beliefert Großhändler in 75 Ländern rund um den Globus und 17 Shops in England – ist nach wie vor sein ganz persönliches Engagement integraler Bestandteil des Gelingens. Abgesehen von seinen kommerziellen Talenten hat sich Smith in seiner Ästhetik auch Eigenheiten bewahrt. Paul Smiths weltweite Expansion geht auch im 21. Jahrhundert weiter. Nachdem er sich in Asien und Europa bereits etabliert hat, setzt sich seine unverwechselbare Ästhetik nun auch in Amerika, von New York bis nach Los Angeles und San Francisco zunehmend durch. Sein Erfolgsrezept ist dabei wohl das persönliche Engagement des perfekten Geschäftsmannes.

Un grave accident de vélo met un terme aux premières ambitions du jeune Paul Smith, qui rêvait de devenir cycliste professionnel, mais cette mésaventure le conduit à se consacrer à son autre passion : la mode. En 1970, Smith (né en 1946) ouvre une boutique dans sa ville natale de Nottingham où il vend ses premières créations qui reflètent le type de vêtements qu'il adore mais qu'il n'arrive à trouver nulle part. Étudiant la mode en cours du soir tout en travaillant en étroite collaboration avec Pauline Denyer, son épouse diplômée du Royal College of Art, il développe si bien son entreprise qu'il finit par présenter une collection pour homme complète à Paris dès 1976. Forgeant un look original qui combine le meilleur du style anglais traditionnel à des imprimés souvent insolites ou pleins d'esprit, Paul Smith reste sur cette lancée jusqu'à la fin des années 70. Il poursuit son ascension pendant les années 80 et au-delà, époque à laquelle il remet les boxer shorts au goût du jour, avec l'ouverture de nouvelles boutiques à New York (1987) et à Paris (1993). Aujourd'hui, le créateur ne compte pas moins de 200 points de vente au Japon et propose également une ligne pour femme (lancée en 1994) ainsi qu'une collection pour enfant, sans mentionner les accessoires, les livres, les bijoux, les parfums, les stylos, les tapis et la porcelaine Paul Smith. En 2001, Paul Smith est fait Chevalier de Sa Majesté, et malgré l'immense succès et la diversification de son entreprise, qui vend dans 75 pays à travers le monde, dont 17 boutiques en Angleterre, son approche pratique reste un facteur essentiel de sa réussite. Outre ces exploits commerciaux, l'esthétique de Smith conserve ses traits distinctifs. L'expansion mondiale de l'entreprise Paul Smith poursuit son cours pendant la première décennie du 21e siècle. Bien établi en Asie et en Europe, son esthétique unique s'implante aussi aux États-Unis, de New York sur la côte est à L.A. et San Francisco sur la côte ouest. La touche personnelle de Paul Smith, c'est aussi de représenter le parfait commerçant.

JAMES ANDERSON

PHOTOGRAPHY LARRY DUNSTAN STYLING RICHARD SIMPSON OCTOBER 2001

"People who go to my fashion shows kinda go to a rock concert"
ANNA SUI

Anna Sui's singularity lies in her ability to weave her own passions into her work. Her creations are intricate pastiches of vintage eras and knowing nods to music and popular culture – from '60s Portobello to downtown rockers and B-Boys. Her love of fashion began early. Growing up in a sleepy suburb of Detroit, Sui spent her days styling her dolls and collating her 'genius files', a source book of magazine clippings that she continues to reference today. In the 1970s, she began studying at Parsons School of Design in New York, where she became a regular on the underground punk scene and where she met photographer Steven Meisel, a long-time friend and collaborator. Sui spent the remainder of the '70s designing for a string of sportswear companies. Then, in 1980, she presented a six-piece collection at the Boutique Show, receiving an immediate order from Macy's. Sui made her runway debut proper in 1991; the collection was a critically acclaimed homage to her heroine, Coco Chanel. And by the early '90s, her self-consciously maximalist look was helping to pave the way for designers like Marc Jacobs, sparking a revival in the New York fashion scene. In 1992, she won the CFDA Perry Ellis Award for New Fashion Talent. Sui encapsulated the grunge spirit of the times, with Smashing Pumpkins guitarist James Iha – a close friend – appearing in her Winter 1995 California Dreaming show, and Courtney Love famously adopting Sui's classic baby-doll dresses. Sui now has stores in New York, LA, Taiwan, Hong Kong, Shanghai, Tokyo and Osaka, and has added denim, sportswear, shoes and accessories to her brand. Her kitsch cosmetics and best-selling fragrances, with distinctive rose-embossed packaging, have all helped to establish her as an important designer and shrewd businesswoman with an eccentric spirit and limitless sense of fun. In 2006, a limited-edition Anna Sui Boho Barbie was launched with Mattel. 2010 saw the launch of Sui's first book, a retrospective chronicling the past 20 years of her runway, editorial and celebrity experiences.

Anna Suis Einzigartigkeit liegt darin begründet, dass sie spielerisch ihre eigenen Leidenschaften in ihre Arbeit hineinwebt. Ihre Kreationen sind aufwendige Imitationen von Vintage vergangener Epochen und Anspielungen auf Musik und Popkultur – vom Portobello der 1960er-Jahre bis zu den Vorstadtrockern und B-Boys. Ihre Liebe zur Mode entwickelte sich früh. Während ihrer Kindheit in einem verschlafenen Vorort von Detroit verbrachte Sui viel Zeit mit dem Stylen ihrer Puppen und dem Anlegen ihrer „Genius Files", einer Sammelmappe mit Zeitungsausschnitten, auf die sie bis heute zurückgreift. In den 1970ern begann sie ihr Studium an der Parsons School of Design in New York, wo sie treues Mitglied der Underground-Punk-Szene wurde und den Fotografen Steven Meisel kennenlernte, der ihr langjähriger Freund und Kollege werden sollte. Den Rest der 1970er-Jahre verbrachte Sui mit dem Designen von Sportswear für diverse Firmen. 1980 präsentierte sie dann auf der Boutique Show eine sechsteilige Kollektion, die sofort von Macy's geordert wurde. Ihr offizielles Laufsteg-Debüt gab Sui schließlich 1991. Ihre damalige, von den Kritikern gefeierte Kollektion war eine Hommage an ihr Idol Coco Chanel. Ihr selbstbewusster maximalistischer Look bahnte Anfang der 1990er-Jahre Designern wie Marc Jacobs den Weg und sorgte für eine Neubelebung der New Yorker Modeszene. 1992 gewann sie den Perry Ellis Award for New Fashion Talent der CFDA. Sui griff den Grunge-

Stil der damaligen Zeit auf, insbesondere als der Gitarrist der Smashing Pumpkins, James Iha – ein enger Freund der Designerin – in ihrer Schau „California Dreaming" im Winter 1995 auftrat und Courtney Love öffentlichkeitswirksam Suis klassische Babydoll-Kleider für sich entdeckte. Heute betreibt Sui eigene Läden in New York, L.A., Taiwan, Hongkong, Shanghai, Tokio und Osaka und hat ihr Programm um Jeans, Sportswear, Schuhe sowie Accessoires erweitert. Nicht zuletzt haben ihre kitschig gestalteten Kosmetika und bestens verkäuflichen Düfte mit der typischen rosenverzierten Verpackung dazu beigetragen, sie als wichtige Designerin und kluge Geschäftsfrau mit exzentrischem Geschmack und grenzenlosem Sinn für Humor zu etablieren. 2006 brachte Mattel als limitierte Sonderedition eine Anna Sui Boho Barbie auf den Markt. 2010 erschien Suis erstes Buch, in dem sie über ihre Erfahrungen aus 20 Jahren Model-Alltag, den Umgang mit Medien und Prominenten schreibt.

La singularité d'Anna Sui réside dans son talent ludique à intégrer ses propres passions dans son travail. Ses créations sont autant de pastiches élaborés des époques vintage que des clins d'œil entendus à la musique et à la culture pop, du Portobello des années 60 aux rockers et B-Boys d'aujourd'hui. Élevée dans une triste banlieue de Detroit, Anna Sui passe ses journées à habiller ses poupées et à compiler ce qu'elle appelle ses « genius files », un album de photos découpées dans les magazines de mode dont elle se sert encore aujourd'hui. Pendant les années 70, elle entame des études à la Parsons School of Design de New York, où elle fraye avec la scène punk underground et rencontre le photographe Steven Meisel, qui deviendra son ami et collaborateur. Jusqu'à la fin des années 70, Anna Sui occupe plusieurs postes de styliste dans le sportswear. Puis, en 1980, elle présente au Boutique Show une petite collection de six pièces immédiatement achetée par Macy's. Anna Sui fait ses véritables débuts lors d'un premier défilé en 1991, avec une collection créée en hommage à son héroïne Coco Chanel et plébiscitée par la critique. Au début des années 90, son look délibérément maximaliste ouvre la voie à des créateurs tels que Marc Jacobs et déclenche le renouveau de la mode new-yorkaise. En 1992, elle remporte le prix Perry Ellis décerné aux nouveaux talents par le CFDA. Anna Sui saisit parfaitement l'esprit grunge de l'époque : son grand ami James Iha, guitariste des Smashing Pumpkins, défile pour sa collection « California Dreaming » de l'hiver 1995 et Courtney Love adopte ses petites robes de baby doll. Anna Sui possède actuellement des boutiques à New York, Los Angeles, Taïwan, Hong Kong, Shanghai, Tokyo et Osaka. Sa marque s'est enrichie d'une ligne de pièces en denim, d'une gamme sportswear, de chaussures et d'accessoires. Dans leurs flacons roses originaux, ses produits de maquillage kitsch et ses parfums à succès ont contribué à faire d'elle une créatrice qui compte, une femme d'affaires avisée à l'esprit excentrique et au sens de l'humour illimité. En 2006, elle a sorti une poupée Barbie « bohemian chic » Anna Sui en édition limitée avec Mattel. En 2010 paraît le premier ouvrage de Sui dans lequel elle décrit son expérience acquise pendant les vingt ans de sa carrière de mannequin et où elle raconte les relations avec les médias et les VIP.

AIMEE FARRELL

PORTRAIT JOSHUA JORDAN. PHOTOGRAPHY YELENA YEMCHUK. STYLING SORAYA DAYANI. MODEL JP. OCTOBER 2004.

"I cannot deny the difficulty involved in creating designs. But I think I continue creating them because I enjoy it"
JUN TAKAHASHI · UNDERCOVER

Founded by Japanese designer Jun Takahashi in 1994, the Undercover label now includes some seriously discerning types among its fanbase, not least Rei Kawakubo, who in 2004 had Takahashi design a selection of blouses to sell in the Comme des Garçons store in Tokyo. Born in Kiryu, in 1969, and a graduate of the Bunka Academy, Takahashi began making clothes while studying to wear himself, frustrated at not being able to find anything he liked in shops. His confidence and individuality sets him apart from many young Japanese designers, who are happy to rely on easily digestible, graphic-led T-shirts and slogans. Takahashi's approach is more complex and distinctive, and has been variously described as 'thrift-shop chic' or 'subversive couture'. Considering his belief that life is as much about pain as it is about beauty, it is not surprising that the resulting Undercover aesthetic makes for an anarchic collision of the violent (slashed, ripped and restitched fabrics) and the poetic (chiffon, lace and faded floral prints). Further clues to the designer's mindset are found in his fondness for defiant English punk bands – while still a student, he was a member of the Tokyo Sex Pistols. Having won the prestigious Mainichi Fashion Grand Prize in 2001 and made his Paris catwalk debut with his Spring/Summer 2003 collection, Takahashi today continues to up the ante. Undercover is now split into five lines – Undercover, Undercoverism, Undakovit, Undakovrist and Undakovr, all of which are sold through a flagship store in Tokyo's fashionable Omotesando district. Further Undercover stores have opened in Paris and Milan, while global stockists continue to grow (in tandem with appreciative converts to the label). In 2008, Takahashi and NIGO®(of A Bathing Ape) reconstructed their No Label store within Dover Street Market, London. The following year, Undercover was invited to present their collection in the famous Boboli Gardens in Florence during Pitti Imagine. Takahasi has recently been appointed as the new designer collaborator for Uniqlo, succeeding Jil Sander.

Das 1994 vom japanischen Designer Jun Takahashi gegründete Label Undercover kann einige wirklich scharfsichtige Leute zu seinen Fans zählen. Etwa Rei Kawakubo, die Takahashi im Jahr 2004 eine Auswahl von Blusen entwerfen und anschließend im Laden von Comme des Garçons in Tokio verkaufen ließ. Der 1969 in Kiryu geborene Absolvent der Bunka-Akademie begann schon im College-Alter, seine Kleidung selbst zu entwerfen – aus Ärger darüber, dass er in keinem Laden etwas fand, das ihm zusagte. Sein Selbstvertrauen und seine Individualität unterscheiden ihn von vielen japanischen Jungdesignern, die sich nur zu gern auf eine leichte Kost aus grafisch gestalteten T-Shirts und Slogans verlassen. Takahashis Zugang ist komplexer und unverwechselbar, er wurde schon mit Begriffen wie „Thrift-shop Chic" oder „subversive Couture" versehen. Gemäß seiner Überzeugung, wonach Schmerz genauso Teil des Lebens ist wie Schönheit, kollidieren in der Ästhetik von Undercover folgerichtig gewalttätige Elemente (aufgeschlitzter, zerrissener und geflickter Stoff) mit poetischen (Chiffon, Spitze und verblichene Blumenmuster). Weiteren Aufschluss über die Denkweise des Designers gibt sein Faible für aufmüpfige englische Punkbands – in seiner Studentenzeit war er selbst Mitglied der Hommage-Band Tokyo Sex Pistols. Nachdem er 2001

den Hauptpreis beim prestigeträchtigen Mainichi Fashion Grand Prize gewonnen und mit der Kollektion für Frühjahr/Sommer 2003 sein Debüt auf dem Pariser Catwalk gegeben hat, ist Takahashi heute dabei, seinen Marktwert weiter zu steigern. Undercover umfasst inzwischen fünf Linien – Undercover, Undercoverism, Undakovit, Undakovrist und Undakovr –, die allesamt im Flagship-Store in Tokios Trendviertel Omotesando verkauft werden. Weitere Undercover-Läden wurden in Paris und Mailand eröffnet. Außerdem wächst parallel zur Zahl der dankbaren Anhänger des Labels auch die der interessierten Großhändler in aller Welt. 2008 gestalteten Takahashi und NIGO® (von A Bathing Ape) ihren ‚No Label'-Laden im Londoner Dover Street Market um. Im darauffolgenden Jahr wurde Undercover eingeladen, seine Kollektion im Rahmen der Pitti Immagine in den berühmten Boboli-Gärten in Florenz zu präsentieren. Takahashi wurde kürzlich als Nachfolger von Jil Sander zum neuen Designer der Modekette Uniqlo ernannt.

Fondée en 1994 par le créateur japonais Jun Takahashi, la griffe Undercover compte aujourd'hui parmi ses fans des personnages au goût très avisé, notamment Rei Kawakubo qui, en 2004, a demandé au jeune styliste de lui dessiner une sélection de chemisiers pour les vendre dans la boutique Comme des Garçons de Tokyo. Né en 1969 à Kiryu et diplômé de la Bunka Academy, Jun Takahashi est encore étudiant quand il commence à confectionner ses propres vêtements, frustré de ne pas trouver ce qu'il aime dans les magasins. Son assurance et son individualité le distinguent de la plupart des autres jeunes créateurs japonais, qui se contentent souvent de proposer des T-shirts à l'esprit graphique et aux slogans facilement consommables. L'approche de Takahashi est bien plus complexe et originale, souvent décrite comme du « chic d'occasion » ou de la « couture subversive ». Comme Takahashi croit que la vie est autant faite de douleur que de beauté, rien de surprenant à ce que l'esthétique d'Undercover propose une collision anarchique entre violence (tissus taillladés, déchirés et recousus) et poésie (mousseline, dentelle et imprimés floraux passés reflétant l'état d'esprit et la prédilection du créateur pour les groupes punk anglais provocants : étudiant, il était membre des Tokyo Sex Pistols, formés en hommage au groupe britannique. Après avoir remporté le prestigieux Mainichi Fashion Grand Prize en 2001 et fait ses débuts à Paris avec sa collection printemps/été 2003, Jun Takahashi ne cesse de faire monter les enjeux. Undercover se divise désormais en cinq lignes : Undercover, Undercoverism, Undakovit, Undakovrist et Undakovr, toutes vendues par sa boutique indépandante à Omotesando, quartier branché de Tokyo. D'autres boutiques Undercover ont ouvert à Paris et Milan alors que les distributeurs internationaux continuent à se développer, en tandem avec les admirateurs de la griffe. En 2008, Takahashi et NIGO® (de A Bathing Ape) reconstruient leur boutique « No Label » au sein du Dover Street Market de Londres. L'année suivante, la marque Undercover a été invitée à présenter sa collection dans le fameux Jardin de Boboli pendant le salon Pitti Imagine de Florence. Récemment, Takahashi a succédé à Jil Sander comme designer de la chaîne de distribution Uniqlo.

JAMES ANDERSON

"I like to imagine being in the skin of women"
OLIVIER THEYSKENS

He lives in a 19th-century brothel in Brussels, owns the head of a stuffed giraffe and makes macabre clothes riddled with sexual and religious connotations – but designer Olivier Theyskens is not as dark as he seems. He cried at 'ET', is David Attenborough's number one fan and would rather stay at home cooking than go out to some celeb-packed party. Theyskens fans include Smashing Pumpkins' Melissa Auf der Maur, who has catwalked for him, but the Belgian first made headline news when Madonna sent a personally faxed request on his 21st birthday. Born in Brussels in 1977, Theyskens dropped out of the city's Ecole Nationale Supérieure des Arts Visuels de la Cambre in January 1997 but presented his debut collection, Gloomy Trips, that August. Six months later, Madonna wore one of the dresses to the Oscars and a star was born. Theyskens' Gothic image was engendered on the catwalk: clothes were embroidered with real hair or decorated with dead skulls and stuffed birds, while his signature voluminous dresses, scarred with hook fasteners, made models look like beautiful Victorian governesses. In 2002, he joined the House of Rochas as artistic director – his first collection in March 2003 marked the return of Rochas as a fashion force. In 2005, Theyskens was given the Fashion Group's Star Honoree Award at the Night of Stars and, in the following year, he won Best International Designer at the CFDA Fashion Awards. Olivier Theyskens joined Nina Ricci in 2006, but left the design house in 2009. For Spring 2011, Theyskens was asked by CEO Andrew Rosen to design a capsule collection for Theory. So successful was the collection, the company formally announced Theyskens as Artistic Director.

Er lebt in einem ehemaligen Bordell aus dem 19. Jahrhundert in Brüssel, besitzt den ausgestopften Kopf einer Giraffe und macht makabre Mode voller sexueller und religiöser Anspielungen. Trotzdem ist der Designer Olivier Theyskens gar kein so düsterer Mensch wie es vielleicht auf den ersten Blick scheint. Er weint bei „E. T.", ist der größte Bewunderer von David Attenborough und bleibt lieber zu Hause, um zu kochen, als auf irgendeine Promi-Party zu gehen. Zu Theyskens' Fans gehört unter anderem Melissa Auf der Maur. Die ehemalige Bassistin der Smashing Pumpkins hat für den Designer auch schon bei Schauen gemodelt. In die Schlagzeilen kam der Belgier jedoch erstmals, als Madonna ihm an seinem 21. Geburtstag höchstpersönlich eine Bestellung faxte. Der 1977 in Brüssel geborene Theyskens brach zwar im Januar 1997 sein Studium an der Ecole Nationale Supérieure des Arts Visuels de la Cambre in seiner Heimatstadt ab, präsentierte jedoch schon im August desselben Jahres seine Debütkollektion „Gloomy Trips". Sechs Monate später trug Madonna eines dieser Kleider zur Oscar-Verleihung und machte dessen Designer damit über Nacht zum Star. Theyskens' Image als Gothic-Fan

entstand auf dem Catwalk: durch Stoffe, die mit echten Haaren bestickt waren, Totenköpfe und ausgestopfte Vögel als Dekoration. Gleichzeitig ließen seine typisch voluminösen, mit zahllosen Häkchen versehenen Kleider die Models wie wunderschöne viktorianische Gouvernanten aussehen. 2002 wurde er Art Director im Hause Rochas. Seine erste Kollektion im März 2003 bedeutete die Rückkehr Rochas' als Marke von Rang. Im Jahr 2005 wurde Theyskens von der Fashion Group im Rahmen der Night of Stars als Star Honoree ausgezeichnet. Im darauf folgenden Jahr schnitt er bei den CFDA Fashion Awards als Best International Designer ab. Von 2006 bis 2009 war Theyskens für Nina Ricci tätig. Andrew Rosen, geschäftsführendes Vorstandsmitglied von Theory, bat Theyskens, für das Frühjahr 2011 eine Sonderkollektion zu entwerfen, die so erfolgreich war, dass das Unternehmen Theyskens zum Artistic Director machte.

Certes, Olivier Theyskens vit dans un bordel bruxellois du 19ᵉ siècle, possède une tête de girafe empaillée et crée des vêtements macabres aux connotations sexuelles et religieuses évidentes ; pourtant, ce créateur n'est pas aussi sombre qu'il y paraît. En larmes devant E.T. et fan numéro un de David Attenborough, il préfère rester chez lui et faire la cuisine plutôt que de courir les soirées people. Theyskens compte des fans célèbres, tels que Melissa Auf der Maur, du groupe Smashing Pumpkins, qui a défilé pour lui. Le Belge a même fait la une des journaux lorsque Madonna lui a faxé une commande le jour de son 21ᵉ anniversaire. Né à Bruxelles en 1977, Theyskens interrompt ses études à l'École Nationale Supérieure des Arts Visuels de la Cambre en janvier 1997 et présente sa première collection, « Gloomy Trips », dès le mois d'août suivant. Six mois plus tard, Madonna porte l'une de ses robes à la cérémonie des Oscars : une étoile est née. L'image gothique de Theyskens trouve son origine sur les podiums de ses défilés : il présente des vêtements brodés de vrais poils ou décorés de crânes et d'oiseaux empaillés, tandis que ses robes volumineuses si caractéristiques, déformées par des crochets, donnent aux mannequins un air de gouvernantes de l'ère victorienne. En 2002, il devient directeur artistique de Rochas : sa première collection en mars 2003 marque le retour en force de cette vénérable maison de mode. En 2005, Theyskens reçoit le prix Star Honoree du Fashion Group lors de la Night of Stars, et l'année suivante, il remporte le titre de Best International Designer du CFDA. Olivier Theyskens rejoint ensuite la maison Nina Ricci au poste de directeur artistique, mais démissionne en 2009. Andrew Rosen, président du comité de direction de Theory, demande alors à Theykens de créer une collection spéciale pour le printemps 2011 ; son succès est tel que l'entreprise a choisi Theykens comme directeur artistique.

"The starting point for each new collection is the previous collection"
JUSTIN THORNTON & THEA BREGAZZI · PREEN

Preen is Justin Thornton and Thea Bregazzi (both born in 1969). The pair grew up on the Isle of Man, meeting at the age of just 18 while both were studying for an art foundation course. However, the duo – and couple – did not start designing together until their island upbringing was in the past. Both attended fashion college on the mainland before setting out on their own after graduating. Thornton designed for Helen Storey's innovative Second Life collection and Bregazzi started styling. It was Storey who brought them back together, asking them to jointly consult on her Autumn/Winter 1996 collection. The formation of Preen was the next logical step. The duo launched their first stand-alone collection in 1997, creating a buzz around individually crafted, deconstructed pieces that fused Victoriana with streetwear elements in a sharp, tailored silhouette. Construction and deconstruction have fascinated the couple ever since. Darlings of the style press during their formative years, Preen have developed their deconstruction tendencies, consistently providing alternatives to classic tailoring. Inspirations include circus performers, Pearly Kings and Queens and ballgowns. Such eccentricity had somewhat mystified fashion critics until their Spring/Summer 2003 collection. Shown at London Fashion Week, the duo softened their gritty, streetwear look for gentler shapes inspired by seminal fashion movie 'Belle de Jour' and even '70s rag doll Holly Hobby. They gained celebrity fans including American 'Vogue''s Anna Wintour, Claudia Schiffer and Gwyneth Paltrow. Their menswear line, launched in 2003, has been well received. Ewan McGregor and David Bowie are fans. Now a fixture on New York Fashion Week's calendar (since 2007), they have also shown for the first time (Preen Line Autumn/Winter 2008) at Copenhagen Fashion Week.

Preen, das sind Justin Thornton und Thea Bregazzi, beide Jahrgang 1969. Das Paar wuchs auf der Isle of Man auf und lernte sich mit gerade mal 18 Jahren als Teilnehmer an einem Kunstseminar kennen. Mit den gemeinsamen Entwürfen begann das berufliche wie private Team jedoch erst, nachdem es die Insel verlassen hatte. Beide besuchten eine Modeschule auf dem Festland und gingen nach dem Abschluss erst einmal getrennte Wege. Thornton entwarf für Helen Storeys innovative Kollektion „Second Life", während Bregazzi zunächst als Stylistin arbeitete. Es war Storey, die die beiden wieder zusammenbrachte, als sie sie als Berater für ihre Kollektion Herbst/Winter 1996 engagierte. Die Gründung von Preen war dann nur noch der nächste logische Schritt. Die erste eigene Kollektion lancierte das Duo 1997. Ihre individuell gearbeiteten, dekonstruktiven Kreationen vereinten Aspekte viktorianischer Mode mit Streetwear-Elementen in klar umrissenen Silhouetten. Das Thema Konstruktion und Dekonstruktion fasziniert die beiden Designer seit jeher. Als Liebling der Modepresse in den Anfangsjahren hat Preen die Neigung zur Dekonstruktion inzwischen weiter ausgebaut und bietet konsequent Alternativen zu klassisch geschneiderter Kleidung an. Als

Inspiration dienen dabei Zirkuskünstler, Pearly Kings and Queens sowie Ballroben. Diese Exzentrik bezauberte alle Kritiker. Seit seiner Kollektion für Frühjahr/Sommer 2003 hat das Designerpaar jedoch begonnen, den gewagten Streetwear-Look im Stil von „Belle de Jour" und der Lumpenpuppe Holly Hobby aus den 1970er-Jahren etwas abzuschwächen. Zu den prominenten Anhängern des Labels gehören Anna Wintour von der amerikanischen Vogue, Claudia Schiffer und Gwyneth Paltrow. Die 2003 vorgestellte Herrenlinie wurde ebenfalls wohlwollend aufgenommen. Hier zählen Ewan McGregor und David Bowie zu den Fans. Nachdem es fixer Bestandteil der New York Fashion Week geworden war (seit 2007), präsentierte sich das Label (mit Preen Line Herbst/Winter 2008) erstmals auch bei der Copenhagen Fashion Week.

Preen, c'est Justin Thornton et Thea Bregazzi (tous deux nés en 1969). Bien qu'ils aient tous deux grandi sur l'île de Man, ils se rencontrent seulement à l'âge de 18 ans dans une école d'art. Néanmoins, ce duo qui forme aussi un vrai couple dans la vie ne collaborera pas avant d'avoir laissé derrière lui son enfance passée sur l'île. Ils suivent des études de mode sur le continent et se lancent après l'obtention de leurs diplômes. Justin Thornton dessine pour la collection innovante « Second Life » de Helen Storey tandis que Thea Bregazzi travaille dans le stylisme. C'est justement Helen Storey qui les réunit lorsqu'elle leur demande de travailler ensemble en tant que consultants sur sa collection automne/hiver 1996. Logiquement, l'étape suivante voit la création de leur griffe Preen. Le duo lance sa première collection en 1997 et tout le monde ne parle plus que de leurs pièces déconstruites de production artisanale qui fusionnent l'époque victorienne à des éléments streetwear au sein d'une silhouette bien définie. Depuis, le couple reste fasciné par les questions de construction et de déconstruction. Chouchous de la presse spécialisée pendant leurs années de formation, ils développent à travers Preen leur tendance déconstructionniste et ne cessent de proposer des alternatives aux coupes classiques. Entre autres, ils s'inspirent des artistes de cirque, des « Pearly Kings and Queens » et des robes de bal, une excentricité qui laissera les critiques de mode dubitatifs jusqu'à leur collection printemps/été 2003 présentée à la London Fashion Week, où leur look streetwear dérangeant s'adoucit grâce à des formes plus faciles inspirées de Belle de Jour et même de la poupée en chiffon Holly Hobby des années 70. Ils séduisent des clientes célèbres telles qu'Anna Wintour du Vogue américain, Claudia Schiffer et Gwyneth Paltrow. Leur ligne pour homme lancée en 2003 a été bien accueillie : Ewan McGregor et David Bowie en sont fans. Désormais rendez-vous régulier du calendrier de la New York Fashion Week (depuis 2007), Preen a défilé pour la toute première fois à la Semaine de la mode de Copenhague (collection automne/hiver 2008).

LAUREN COCHRANE

"Sometimes I don't even design the product, I just invent a new process instead"
AITOR THROUP

DESIGN ABOUT TOWN SHOOT AITOR THROUP MODEL TOM. FEBRUARY 2007.

Born in 1980 in Buenos Aires, Aitor Throup moved to Burnley, Lancashire, by way of Spain. A passion for technologically advanced garments (from labels such as Stone Island and CP Company), drawing and designing comic book characters led him to a BA in fashion design at Manchester Metropolitan University. The importance he places on narrative was apparent in his graduate collection from the RCA – entitled When Football Hooligans Become Hindu Gods, the collection comprised military elements and Hindu symbolism. Throup's design philosophy is one that is more organic than methodical, which always starts with the human form. Throup then allows his creations to evolve naturally, using a three-stage construction process of "drawing, sculpture, garment" instead of a more conventional construction. At ITS#FIVE (International Talent Support) in 2006, Throup won the Collection of the Year Award and the i-D Styling Award, and went on to exhibit twice at London Fashion Week's MAN show. In 2008, Throup presented his first instalment of an ongoing seasonal Anatomy Series collaboration with Stone Island at Milan Fashion Week and exhibited a special collaboration with CP Company. More recently, the football-obsessed Throup was appointed creative consultant for the British football brand Umbro which led to his involvement in the concept and design of both the 'home' and 'away' football kits worn by England at the 2010 World Cup. With Throup now working with his favourite brands from boyhood, he has come full circle.

1980 in Buenos Aires geboren, kam Aitor Throup über Spanien nach Burnley, Lancashire. Dank seines Faibles für High-Tech-Kleidung (von Labels wie Stone Island und C.P. Company) sowie für das Zeichnen und Entwerfen von Comicfiguren brachte er es zu einem Bachelor im Fach Modedesign an der Manchester Metropolitan University. Die Bedeutung, die er den Geschichten hinter seinen Kreationen beimisst, war an seiner Abschlusskollektion an der RCA ablesbar, die er „When Football Hooligans Become Hindu Gods" betitelte; folgerichtig waren darin militärische Elemente mit Hindu-Symbolismus kombiniert. Throups Design-Philosophie ist eher organisch als methodisch und hat ihren Ursprung stets in der menschlichen Gestalt. In der Folge gestattet er seinen Kreationen, sich im Verlauf eines dreistufigen Prozesses – Zeichnung, Plastik, Kleidungsstück – quasi natürlich zu entwickeln. Bei ITS#FIVE (International Talent Support) gewann Throup 2006 den Collection of The Year Award sowie den

i-D Styling Award. Danach präsentierte er zweimal bei der Show MAN im Rahmen der London Fashion Week. 2008 zeigte Throup auf der Mailänder Modewoche seinen ersten Beitrag einer noch laufenden saisonalen Zusammenarbeit mit Stone Island unter dem Titel „Anatomy Series". Außerdem war dort das Ergebnis einer einmaligen Kooperation mit C.P. Company zu sehen. Erst kürzlich wurde der fußballversessene Throup zum kreativen Berater der britischen Fußball-Marke Umbro ernannt, nachdem er bereits vorher an den Entwürfen für die englischen Heim- und Auswärtstrikots für die Fußballweltmeisterschaft 2010 beteiligt gewesen war. Nachdem er nun für die Lieblingsmarken seiner Jugend tätig ist, hat sich für den Designer damit der Kreis geschlossen.

Né à Buenos Aires en 1980, Aitor Throup s'installe à Burnley dans le Lancashire après un détour par l'Espagne. Passionné par les vêtements technologiques (comme ceux des griffes Stone Island et C.P. Company), par le dessin et la création de personnages de bande dessinée, il suit un BA en création de mode à la Metropolitan University de Manchester. L'importance qu'il accorde au récit transparaît dans sa collection de fin d'études au Royal College of Arts, intitulée « When Football Hooligans Become Hindu Gods », elle présente des éléments militaires et des symboles hindouistes. La philosophie créative de Throup est plus organique que méthodique, puisque tout part toujours de la forme humaine. Il laisse ensuite ses créations évoluer naturellement à travers un processus de construction en trois étapes – « dessin, sculpture, vêtement » – au lieu d'adopter une structure plus conventionnelle. Au concours ITS#FIVE (International Talent Support), Throup remporte le Collection of The Year Award en 2006 et l'i-D Styling Award, puis présente deux collections aux défilés masculins de la London Fashion Week. En 2008, Throup expose une première installation issue de sa collaboration « Anatomy Series » permanente avec Stone Island à la Semaine de la mode de Milan, ainsi qu'un autre projet spécial conçu avec C.P. Company. Récemment, cet obsédé de football est devenu consultant en stylisme pour la griffe de sportswear anglaise Umbro et ce, après avoir participé au préalable à la conception et au dessin des maillots de l'équipe nationale anglaise (domicile et extérieur) pour la Coupe du Monde 2010. Maintenant qu'il travaille avec les marques qu'il adorait dans sa jeunesse, Throup revient à ses premières amours.

KAREN HODKINSON

"My definition of beauty is something between extremely ugly and extremely fantastic"
RICCARDO TISCI · GIVENCHY

In September 2004, Riccardo Tisci presented a show unconventional for high-gloss Milan Fashion Week: supermodels wearing intricately ruched and tiered black gowns moving around a smoky, atmospheric set littered with disused car parts and large black balls. Born in Italy (1974), Tisci moved to London at the age of 18 and graduated from Central Saint Martins in 1999. The following year, he moved back to Italy, where he developed a small collection of dresses and T-shirts for the London boutique Kokon To Zai. British 'Vogue' photographed them and Björk bought some, but production was a low-key affair with everything handmade by the designer's mother and eight sisters. In 2002, Tisci was appointed creative director of the Italian fashion house Coccapani, where he designed four well-received collections. During the same period, he designed the first Puma Rudolf Dassler Schuhfabrik collection, injecting his sense of playful volume into women's sports pieces. 2004 was set to be his big breakthrough year – the designer won a contract with Ruffo Research, but after a few months, the company behind the brand put the project on hold, forcing Tisci to reconsider his plans. It was then that he launched his own label. The 12 outfits presented in September 2004 and modelled by the likes of Karen Elson and Mariacarla Boscono – the latter, his muse and best friend – were just a taste of things to come. In March 2005, Tisci was presented with his greatest challenge to date when he was named the new creative director of womenswear at Givenchy (menswear was added in 2008). The Italian has since shelved his eponymous line in favour of concentrating all his energy on the grand Parisian couture house. Tisci is the fourth designer to head up the LVMH-owned brand since founder Hubert de Givenchy retired from fashion in 1995.

Im September 2004 präsentierte Riccardo Tisci eine für die ansonsten auf Hochglanz abonnierte Mailänder Modewoche reichlich ungewohnte Show: Supermodels in kompliziert gerüschten, aus mehreren Lagen bestehenden schwarzen Roben bewegten sich auf einem rauchigen, atmosphärisch dichten Set, auf dem alte Autoteile und große schwarze Bälle herumlagen. Der 1975 in Italien geborene Tisci zog mit 18 nach London und machte 1999 seinen Abschluss am Central Saint Martins. Im darauffolgenden Jahr ging er zurück nach Italien, wo er eine kleine Kollektion aus Kleidern und T-Shirts für die Londoner Boutique Kokon To Zai entwarf. Die britische Vogue fotografierte diese, und Björk kaufte ein paar Teile. Das Ganze war jedoch ein Low-Budget-Projekt – alles handgenäht von der Mutter des Designers und seinen acht Schwestern. 2002 ernannte das italienische Modehaus Coccapani Tisci zu seinem Chefdesigner. Er entwarf vier Kollektionen, die alle sehr gut aufgenommen wurden. Im selben Zeitraum designte Tisci auch die erste Kollektion „Puma Rudolf Dassler Schuhfabrik", bei der sein Gespür für verspielte Fülle sich in Sportmode für Damen niederschlug. 2004 war dann das Jahr des großen Durchbruchs – der Designer ergatterte zunächst einen Vertrag mit Ruffo Research. Nach ein paar Monaten setzte das Unternehmen hinter der Marke das Projekt jedoch aus, was Tisci dazu zwang, seine Pläne zu überdenken. So kam es, dass er sein eigenes Label lancierte. Die zwölf Outfits, die im September 2004 von Models wie Karen Elson und Mariacarla Boscono – Letztere ist die Muse und beste Freundin des Designers – präsentiert wurden, waren nur ein Vorgeschmack dessen, was noch kommen sollte. Denn im März 2005 stellte sich Tisci seiner bisher größten Herausforderung, als er zum neuen Creative Director der Damenmode (die Herrenmode kam 2008 hinzu) bei Givenchy ernannt wurde. Die nach ihm benannte Linie lässt der Italiener im Moment ruhen, um all seine Energie für das große Pariser Modehaus aufzuwenden. Tisci ist der vierte Designer an der Spitze der Couture-Marke im Besitz von LVMH, seit sich ihr Gründer Hubert de Givenchy 1995 aus dem Modegeschäft zurückzog.

En septembre 2004, Riccardo Tisci présente un défilé tout à fait inattendu pour la très glamour Milan Fashion Week : des top models vêtues de robes noires décorées de volants et de ruchés complexes défilent autour d'un décor atmosphérique et enfumé, jonché de vieilles pièces détachées automobiles et de grands ballons noirs. Né en Italie (1974), Riccardo Tisci débarque à Londres à l'âge de 18 ans et sort diplômé de Central Saint Martins en 1999. L'année suivante, il revient en Italie pour développer une petite collection de robes et de T-shirts commandée par la boutique londonienne Kokon To Zai. Le Vogue anglais les photographie et Björk achète quelques pièces, mais la production reste modeste puisque tout est fait à la main par la mère et les huit sœurs du créateur. En 2002, Tisci est nommé directeur de la création de la maison italienne Coccapani, où il conçoit quatre collections plutôt bien accueillies. Au cours de cette période, il dessine également la première collection « Puma Rudolf Dassler Schuhfabrik », à laquelle il insuffle son sens ludique du volume dans des créations sport pour femme. C'est en 2004 qu'il perce enfin pour de bon : il remporte un contrat avec Ruffo Research mais au bout de quelques mois, l'entreprise qui possède la marque suspend le projet et contraint Tisci à revoir ses plans ; il décide alors de lancer sa propre griffe. Les douze tenues présentées en septembre 2004 sur les mannequins telles que Karen Elson et Mariacarla Boscono, sa muse et meilleure amie, n'offrent qu'un avant-goût des collections à venir. En mars 2005, Riccardo Tisci doit relever son plus grand défi à ce jour lorsqu'il est nommé directeur de la création des lignes pour femme de Givenchy (les lignes pour homme viennent s'y ajouter seulement en 2008). L'Italien met sa griffe éponyme en sommeil afin de consacrer toute son énergie à cette grande maison parisienne de haute couture. Depuis que son fondateur Hubert de Givenchy a pris sa retraite en 1995, Tisci est le quatrième créateur à superviser la marque de LVMH.

PHOTOGRAPHY KERRY HALLIHAN. STYLING ALASTAIR MCKIMM. MODEL MARIACARLA BOSCONO. NOVEMBER 2007.

"What inspires me is whatever helps you to get away from mental pollution"
JEAN TOUITOU • APC

You'll never see an APC creation waltzing down a catwalk accessorised with a pair of horns. Instead, the subtle fashion brand has a coded elegance that attracts discerning customers drawn to its perfect jeans, shrunken blazers, sunglasses and radical T-shirts. In addition to clothing, there's the treasure trove of APC 'things' on offer each season: guitar plectrums, books (such as their edition of Charles Anastase illustrations), shaving oil, candles, olive oil. And it's all the brainchild of Jean Touitou, who was born in Tunis in 1951 and graduated from the Sorbonne in Paris with a history degree and no intention whatsoever of becoming a fashion designer. It was entirely by accident that he landed his first job with Kenzo, which was followed by gigs at agnès b. and Irié before he finally decided to go his own way in 1987 with the launch of APC (Atelier de Production et de Création). Touitou began with menswear, and quickly followed with a womenswear collection, debuting the year after. In 1991, the first APC shop opened in Japan and today the company has stores in Hong Kong, New York, Berlin and Paris, plus a comprehensive online service. Collaboration is important to Touitou, and over the years he has partnered Margiela, Martine Sitbon, Eley Kishimoto and Gimme 5 for innovative limited-edition projects. Jessica Ogden designs a childrenswear line and, since 2004, also the mini Madras collection of beachwear inspired by Indian textiles. The company also has a music division: Marc Jacobs and Sofia Coppola, among others, have put their names to compilations on the APC music label, and dance albums, punk-jazz and French-Arabic CDs have all been released to further express the brand's originality. In 2009, Touitou opened a boutique on London's Dover Street as well as a second store on East London's Redchurch Street in 2011, a kindergarten in Paris's rue de Fleurus (designed by Laurent Daroo) and created a new classic jean with Supreme in New York. APC continues to infiltrate fashion with Touitou's personal political sensibility and catching the zeitgeist remains Touitou's driving force.

Sie werden nie eine Kreation von APC auf dem Laufsteg vorgeführt bekommen, die als Accessoire mit einem Paar Hörner versehen ist. Stattdessen propagiert diese feinsinnige Modemarke eine verschlüsselte Eleganz, die aufmerksame Kunden mit perfekten Jeans, kleinen Blazern, Sonnenbrillen und radikalen T-Shirts anzieht. Neben Kleidern gibt es bei APC in jeder Saison auch noch eine Art Schatzkiste mit den verschiedensten Dingen: Gitarrenplektren, Bücher (etwa die firmeneigene Edition von Charles Anastases Illustrationen), Rasieröl, Kerzen, Olivenöl. Das sind alles die Ideen von Jean Touitou, der 1951 in Tunis geboren wurde, an der Pariser Sorbonne einen Abschluss in Geschichte machte und nie vorhatte, Modedesigner zu werden. Sein erster Job bei Kenzo war ein absoluter Zufall. Danach folgten Engagements bei agnès b. und Irié, bevor er sich 1987 entschloss, eigene Wege zu gehen und APC (Atelier de Production et de Création) gründete. Touitou begann mit Herrenmode, gab aber schon ein Jahr später mit einer Kollektion sein Debüt in der Damenmode. 1991 eröffnete der erste APC-Laden in Japan. Inzwischen besitzt die Firma eigene Geschäfte in Hongkong, New York, Berlin und Paris sowie einen umfassenden Online-Shop. Kooperation ist Touitou ungeheuer wichtig,

und so hat er im Lauf der Jahre bereits mit Margiela, Martine Sitbon, Eley Kishimoto und Gimme 5 im Rahmen von innovativen Projekten mit limitierten Auflagen zusammengearbeitet. Jessica Ogden entwirft die Kinderkollektion und seit 2004 auch die von indischen Textilien inspirierte kleine Madras-Linie für Beachwear. Zum Unternehmen gehört auch eine Musikabteilung. Unter anderem haben Marc Jacobs und Sofia Coppola Compilations beim Musiklabel APC veröffentlicht. Dance-Alben, Punk-Jazz und CDs mit franco-arabischer Musik unterstreichen allesamt die Originalität der Marke. 2009 eröffnete Touitou in London einen Laden in der Dover Street, einen weiteren 2011 in der Redchurch Street in East London, in Paris einen Kindergarten in der Rue de Fleurus (nach Entwürfen von Laurent Daroo),und er kreierte gemeinsam mit Supreme eine neue klassische Jeans in New York. APC beeinflusst die Mode weiterhin mit Touitous ganz persönlicher politischer Sensibilität, wobei die Reflexion des Zeitgeists nach wie vor Triebfeder dieses Designers ist.

On ne verra jamais une création APC valser toutes griffes dehors le long d'un podium. Au contraire, la mode subtile que propose cette marque se distingue par son élégance codée qui attire les clients les plus exigeants, séduits par ses jeans parfaitement coupés, ses petits blazers, ses lunettes de soleil et ses T-shirts à slogan. Outre les vêtements, APC propose chaque saison ses dernières « trouvailles » : plectres de guitare, livres (tels que l'édition APC des illustrations de Charles Anastase), huile de rasage, bougies ou huile d'olive. Des idées tout droit sorties du cerveau de Jean Touitou, né en 1951 à Tunis. Diplômé de la Sorbonne en histoire, il n'a jamais cherché à devenir styliste. C'est donc par pur hasard qu'il se retrouve chez Kenzo, avant de partir travailler chez agnès b. et Irié. Il finit par lancer sa propre griffe en 1987 et la baptise APC (Atelier de Production et de Création). Touitou propose d'abord une ligne pour homme, rapidement suivie d'une collection pour femme au début de l'année suivante. En 1991, la première boutique APC ouvre ses portes au Japon. Aujourd'hui, l'entreprise possède des points de vente à Hong Kong, New York, Berlin et Paris, sans oublier son service de vente sur Internet. La collaboration revêt beaucoup d'importance aux yeux de Jean Touitou qui, au fil des années, s'est associé à Margiela, Martine Sitbon, Eley Kishimoto et Gimme 5 pour travailler sur des projets innovants en édition limitée. Jessica Ogden, qui dessine la ligne pour enfant d'APC, conçoit également depuis 2004 la collection de maillots de bain à mini-carreaux Madras, inspirée des textiles indiens. L'entreprise s'est également diversifiée dans la musique : Marc Jacobs et Sofia Coppola, entre autres, ont proposé leurs titres sur les compilations du label d'APC dont les albums électro, punk-jazz et franco-arabes expriment la grande originalité de la marque. En 2009, Jean Touitou a ouvert une boutique dans Dover Street à Londres, une autre en 2011 dans la Redchurch Street de East London, une crèche rue de Fleurus à Paris (conçue par Laurent Daroo) et créé un nouveau classique du jean avec Supreme à New York. APC continue à infiltrer la sensibilité politique de son créateur dans l'univers de la mode ; saisir l'air du temps reste le grand moteur de Touitou.

TERRY NEWMAN

"I cannot live without design. I am design-addicted"
GIAMBATTISTA VALLI

In March 2005, Giambattista Valli showed his first eponymous collection in Paris. His debut emphasised polished pieces such as curvy tuxedos or tiny cocktail frocks in scarlet chiffon or black tulle. The Italian designer (born in Rome, 1966) already had an impressive CV by that time, however, with a role as artistic director of Emanuel Ungaro's ready-to-wear collections as his highest-profile appointment to date. Valli, who grew up in Rome, cites quintessential glamorous movie icons such as Claudia Cardinale, Marilyn Monroe and Rita Hayworth as early influences. His formal studies focused more squarely on fashion from 1980 when he studied at Rome's School of Art, followed by fashion training at the European Design Institute (1986) and an illustration degree at Central Saint Martins in London (1987). In 1988, Valli worked for seminal Roman designer Roberto Capucci, moving to Fendi as a senior designer of the Fendissime line in 1990; in 1995, he was appointed senior designer at Krizia. The following year, through a mutual friend, Valli met Emanuel Ungaro. The master couturier named Valli head designer of his ready-to-wear collections in 1997, eventually promoting him to the position of creative director of Ungaro ready-to-wear two years later. At Ungaro, Valli translated the established house codes of tumbling ruffles, tropical-flower colours and elegantly draped, ultra-feminine gowns for a younger generation of jet-setting glamour girls. His own line, Giambattista Valli, today attracts an international, glamorous crowd, including Penelope Cruz, Sarah Jessica Parker, Natalie Portman and Tilda Swinton. Giambattista Valli has also become fashion's go-to label for head-turning accessories (in particular show-stopping high heels and bags). 2008 saw Valli sign a deal with top Italian fur manufacturer Ciwi Furs to design his own line of fur coats and jackets, and another one with skiwear label Moncler. Today there are more than 220 Giambattista Valli selling points in 45 countries worldwide. In July 2011, the designer showed his very first haute couture collection in Paris, hailed by journalists as a significant achievement.

Im März 2005 präsentierte Giambattista Valli in Paris seine erste Kollektion unter eigenem Namen. Im Mittelpunkt standen Hingucker wie figurbetonte Smokings oder winzige Cocktailkleidchen aus dunkelrotem Chiffon oder schwarzem Tüll. Der 1966 in Rom geborene und aufgewachsene Designer hatte zu diesem Zeitpunkt bereits eine eindrucksvolle Vita vorzuweisen. Die höchste Position, die er bisher innehatte, war die des künstlerischen Direktors der Prêt-à-porter-Kollektionen bei Emanuel Ungaro. Als früheste Einflüsse gibt der Designer glamouröse Filmdiven wie Claudia Cardinale, Marilyn Monroe und Rita Hayworth an. Seine offizielle Ausbildung konzentrierte sich jedoch auf die Mode ab 1980, als er an der Kunsthochschule in Rom studierte, dann am European Design Institute (1986) und schließlich noch einen Abschluss im Fach Illustration am Central Saint Martins in London (1987) machte. 1988 begann Valli für den aufstrebenden römischen Designer Roberto Capucci zu arbeiten, bis er 1990 als Senior Designer der Linie Fendissime zu Fendi wechselte. 1995 wurde er Senior Designer im Hause Krizia. Schon im folgenden Jahr lernte er über einen gemeinsamen Freund Emanuel Ungaro kennen. 1997 machte der Meister-Couturier Valli zunächst zum Chefdesigner seiner Prêt-à-porter-Kollektionen und zwei Jahre später zum Creative Director desselben Bereichs. Bei Ungaro übersetzte der Designer den eta-

blierten Stil des Hauses mit seinen Rüschenkaskaden, Farben tropischer Blumen und elegant drapierten, ultra-femininen Roben für eine jüngere Generation von Glamour-Girls des Jetset. Ein Thema, dem er auch bei seiner eigenen Marke Giambattista Valli treu geblieben ist, die heute internationale Stars wie Penelope Cruz, Sarah Jessica Parker, Natalie Portman und Tilda Swinton anspricht. Giambattista Valli hat sich außerdem zu einem Label entwickelt, an dem man nicht vorbeikommt, wenn man aufsehenerregende Accessoires sucht (insbesondere High Heels und Taschen). 2008 kam Valli zum einen mit der italienischen Nobel-Pelzmarke Ciwi Furs ins Geschäft, für die er eine eigene Linie mit Pelzmänteln und Jacken kreierte, zum anderen mit dem Skimoden-Hersteller Moncler. Weltweit gibt es heute mehr als 220 Läden in 45 Ländern, die Giambattista Valli verkaufen. Im Juli 2011 zeigte er in Paris seine von der Presse als herausragende Leistung gefeierte erste Haute Couture-Kollektion.

En mars 2005, Giambattista Valli présente sa première collection éponyme à Paris. Ses débuts mettent en scène des pièces telles que des smokings aux lignes arrondies et de minuscules robes de cocktail en mousseline écarlate ou en tulle noir. À ce stade, le créateur italien (né en 1966 à Rome) affiche déjà un CV impressionnant, dont la plus prestigieuse référence reste son poste de directeur artistique des collections de prêt-à-porter d'Emanuel Ungaro. Giambattista Valli, qui a grandi à Rome, dit avoir été largement influencé par les stars les plus glamour du grand écran comme Claudia Cardinale, Marilyn Monroe et Rita Hayworth. Il oriente plus sérieusement sa formation vers la mode dès 1980 en s'inscrivant d'abord à l'école d'art de sa ville, puis en suivant des études de mode à l'European Design Institute (1986) avant de sortir diplômé en illustration de Central Saint Martins à Londres (1987). En 1988, Valli travaille pour l'influent créateur romain Roberto Capucci, puis pour Fendi en tant que styliste senior de la ligne Fendissime en 1990 ; en 1995, il est nommé styliste senior chez Krizia. L'année suivante, Valli rencontre Emanuel Ungaro par le biais d'un ami commun. Le maître couturier le nomme styliste principal de ses collections de prêt-à-porter en 1997, puis le promeut au poste de directeur de la création du prêt-à-porter Ungaro deux ans plus tard. Chez Ungaro, Valli traduit les codes bien établis de la maison – cascades de volants, couleurs de fleurs tropicales et robes très féminines aux drapés élégants – à l'intention d'une plus jeune génération de filles chics et branchées. Il continue à exploiter ce thème dans sa griffe éponyme qui séduit désormais des clientes internationales aussi glamour que Penelope Cruz, Sarah Jessica Parker, Natalie Portman et Tilda Swinton. Les fashionistas privilégient aussi la marque Giambattista Valli quand elles cherchent des accessoires qui ne passent pas inaperçus (en particulier les talons aiguille et les sacs extravagants). En 2008, Valli signe un contrat avec le grand fabricant italien de fourrures Ciwi Furs pour dessiner sa propre ligne de manteaux et de vestes en fourrure, ainsi qu'un accord avec la marque de vêtements de ski Moncler. Aujourd'hui, on compte plus de 220 points de vente Giambattista Valli dans 45 pays à travers le monde. En juillet 2011, il présente à Paris sa première collection de haute couture qui est accueillie par la presse comme une « performance exceptionnelle ».

SUSIE RUSHTON

"Fashion is a language"
AN VANDEVORST & FILIP ARICKX · AF VANDEVORST

AF Vandevorst, the Belgian design duo of An Vandevorst (born 1968) and Filip Arickx (born 1971) view fashion as nothing less than a way to communicate the inner workings of the mind. The husband-and-wife design team met in 1987 at the Royal Academy in Antwerp. On graduating, Vandevorst worked as an assistant to Dries Van Noten. Meanwhile, Arickx, who worked for Dirk Bikkembergs for three years as a teenager, completed military service after leaving the Academy, and then worked as a freelance designer and stylist. Together, they established their own label in 1997, and presented their first collection in Paris for Autumn/Winter 1998. The label quickly came to the attention of both the fashion press and establishment; after only their second collection, they were awarded Paris Fashion Week's Venus de la Mode award for Le Futur Grand Créateur, a prestigious prize for newcomers. For the Spring/Summer and Autumn/Winter 2000 seasons, the pair were invited to design the Ruffo Research collection, an opportunity periodically offered to young designers by the Italian leather house Ruffo. AF Vandevorst clothes convey a slouchy confidence, and a version of femininity that evokes a sexy yet intellectual cool. Traditional clothing (horse-riding equipment, kimonos, frock coats) is often referenced, reworked and refined until it sits slightly left-of-centre; a medical-style red cross is their enduring symbol. For collection themes, they often favour the unexpected, as for Autumn/Winter 2003, when honey bees provided inspiration. Following no set colour palette, AF Vandevorst stray from muted tones into brights. The label has expanded to encompass footwear, accessories and lingerie and the couple found time to curate an exhibition at MoMu (The Antwerp Fashion Museum) in 2005. In 2008, the duo celebrated their 10th anniversary.

Für AF Vandevorst, das belgische Designerduo An Vandevorst (Jahrgang 1968) und Filip Arickx (Jahrgang 1971), ist Mode nichts Geringeres als eine Möglichkeit, die Vorgänge des Geistes sichtbar zu machen. Das Ehepaar lernte sich 1987 an der Königlichen Akademie in Antwerpen kennen. Nach ihrem Abschluss arbeitete Vandevorst zunächst als Assistentin für Dries van Noten. Arickx hatte schon als Teenager drei Jahre lang bei Dirk Bikkembergs gejobbt und absolvierte nach der Akademie erst einmal seinen Wehrdienst. Anschließend arbeitete er als freischaffender Designer und Stylist. Das gemeinsame eigene Label gründeten die beiden 1997. Ihre erste Kollektion, Herbst/Winter 1998, präsentierten sie in Paris. Rasch gewannen sie die Aufmerksamkeit sowohl der Presse als auch des Fashion Establishments. So wurden sie bereits für ihre zweite Kollektion im Rahmen der Pariser Modewoche mit der Vénus de la Mode als Le Futur Grand Créateur ausgezeichnet, einem prestigeträchtigen Preis für Newcomer. Für Frühjahr/Sommer sowie Herbst/Winter 2000 erhielt das Paar den Auftrag, die Kollektion für Ruffo Research zu entwerfen. Der italienische Lederwarenhersteller Ruffo bietet jungen Designern regelmäßig diese Gelegenheit. Die Entwürfe von AF Vandevorst drücken lässiges Selbstvertrauen aus, zugleich wirken sie auf eine Weise feminin, die sexy, aber zugleich intellektuell und cool rüberkommt. Traditionelle Kleidung (Reitkleidung, Kimonos, Gehröcke) wird oft zitiert, umgearbeitet und leicht verfremdet. Symbol des Labels ist seit jeher ein rotes Kreuz wie im medizinischen Bereich. Als Themen ihrer Kollektionen wählen die Designer oft Ungewöhnliches, wie die Bienen im Herbst/Winter 2003. Was die Farben angeht, ist man bei AF Vandevorst völlig ungebunden und bedient sich mal bei den gedämpften und mal bei den kräftigen Tönen. Man erweiterte die Produktpalette des Labels um Schuhe, Accessoires und Dessous. Im Jahr 2005 kuratierte das Ehepaar zudem eine Ausstellung im MoMu (dem Antwerpener Mode-Museum). Sein zehnjähriges Bestehen feierte das Label 2008.

AF Vandevorst, le duo de créateurs belges formé par An Vandevorst (née en 1968) et Filip Arickx (né en 1971), considère la mode comme rien de moins qu'un moyen de révéler les rouages cachés de l'esprit. Aujourd'hui mariés, ils se sont rencontrés en 1987 à l'Académie Royale d'Anvers. Une fois diplômée, An Vandevorst travaille comme assistante pour Dries Van Noten, tandis que Filip Arickx, qui avait fait ses classes pendant trois ans auprès de Dirk Bikkembergs, effectue son service militaire après avoir quitté l'Académie et avant de travailler comme créateur et styliste en free-lance. Ensemble, ils fondent leur propre griffe en 1997 et présentent une première collection à Paris lors des défilés automne/hiver 1998. Leur travail attire rapidement l'attention de la presse et du monde de la mode ; dès leur deuxième collection, le duo reçoit le prix du Futur Grand Créateur des Vénus de la Mode, récompense prestigieuse décernée aux nouveaux talents pendant la Semaine de la Mode de Paris. Pour les saisons printemps/été et automne/hiver 2000, ils sont invités à dessiner la collection Ruffo Research, une opportunité que le grand maroquinier italien Ruffo offre régulièrement aux jeunes créateurs. Des vêtements AF Vandevorst émanent une confiance désinvolte et une féminité originale témoignant d'une attitude cool, sexy mais néanmoins intello. Les collections font souvent référence aux costumes traditionnels (tenues d'équitation, kimonos, fracs), retravaillés et raffinés jusqu'à leur conférer une asymétrie légèrement décalée sur la gauche, avec une croix rouge d'inspiration médicale comme symbole récurrent. Pour les thèmes de leurs collections, ils privilégient souvent l'inattendu, comme pour la saison automne/hiver 2003 inspirée par les abeilles. Ne suivant aucune palette de couleurs prédéfinie, AF Vandevorst vagabonde des tons les plus neutres aux plus vifs. La griffe s'étoffe de collections de chaussures, d'accessoires et de lingerie, et en 2005, le couple trouve même le temps d'organiser une exposition au MoMu (le Musée de la Mode d'Anvers). Le duo a célébré son 10e anniversaire en 2008.

LIZ HANCOCK

"I am always driven to push forward, searching for what is modern. That is what motivates me"

DONATELLA VERSACE

Donatella Versace (born 1959) is a goddess of fashion. The female figurehead of one of the few remaining family-run fashion houses, she presides over seven brands under the Versace name. Her flamboyant, party-girl image has become synonymous with Versace itself. Gianni (born 1946) and Donatella grew up in Reggio Calabria, southern Italy. While her much older brother moved to Milan to seek his fashion fortune, Donatella studied for a degree in languages at the University of Florence. While there, her brother's career took off. After working for Callaghan and Genny, he set up his solo label in 1978. Suggesting the family's love for bright colours, body-hugging shapes and a large dose of glamour, it was a great success. The two worked together for much of the '80s and '90s, with Donatella concentrating on the sumptuous advertising images for which Versace is known to this day. She also set up the children's line, Young Versace, in 1993 and worked as head designer on the diffusion label, Versus. When Gianni was tragically killed in 1997, his sister became chief designer. She met the challenge. Versace was brought into the 21st century by fusing Gianni's very Italian glamour with Donatella's own rock'n'roll instincts. Versace is continually in the public eye, not least because of its – and Donatella's – famous friends. Jon Bon Jovi, Courtney Love and Elizabeth Hurley are all devoted Versace fans. Madonna even posed as a sexy secretary in Versace's Spring/Summer 2005 ad campaign. Donatella is also responsible for extending the brand's range, setting up both a cosmetics line and Palazzo Versace, the first six-star Versace hotel, which opened on the Gold Coast of Australia in 2000. As well as clothing, accessories, fragrances, jewellery and timepieces, there is now a Versace home furnishings collection, as well as an interior design facility for private jets and helicopters, and even a limited-edition Versace Lamborghini sports car. Donatella Versace is 20 per cent owner of Gianni Versace SpA and holds the position of creative director and vice-president of the board, while her daughter, Allegra, is 50 per cent owner. Versace is teaming up with serial high street collaborators H&M with an exciting new line launching in Winter 2011.

Die 1959 geborene Donatella Versace ist eine Modegöttin. Als weibliche Galionsfigur eines der wenigen noch in Familienbesitz befindlichen Modehäuser herrscht sie über sieben Marken mit dem Namen Versace. Ihr schillerndes Image als Party-Girl ist zum Synonym für Versace selbst geworden. Gianni (Jahrgang 1946) und Donatella wuchsen im süditalienischen Reggio Calabria auf. Während ihr deutlich älterer Bruder nach Mailand zog, um sein Glück in der Mode zu suchen, studierte Donatella an der Universität von Florenz Sprachen. In jener Zeit nahm die Karriere des Bruders ihren Anfang. Nachdem er zunächst für Callaghan und Genny gearbeitet hatte, gründete er 1978 sein eigenes Label. Gemäß der familiären Vorliebe für kräftige Farben, figurbetonte Schnitte und eine große Portion Glamour wurde es ein immenser Erfolg. Die beiden arbeiteten in den 1980er- und 1990er-Jahren über weite Strecken zusammen, wobei Donatella sich stark auf die prachtvollen Werbeauftritte konzentrierte, für die Versace bis heute bekannt ist. Sie gründete aber auch 1993 die Kinderlinie Young Versace und fungierte als Hauptdesignerin der Nebenlinie Versus. Nach Giannis tragischem Tod im Jahr 1997 wurde seine Schwester Chefdesignerin. Sie meisterte diese Herausforderung und führte Versace ins 21. Jahrhundert, indem sie Giannis sehr italienischen Glamour mit ihren eigenen Rock'n'Roll-Instinkten verband. Das Haus Versace steht nach wie vor im Blickpunkt des öffentlichen Interesses, nicht zuletzt wegen seiner und ihrer prominenten Freunde. Jon Bon Jovi, Courtney Love und Elizabeth Hurley sind allesamt treue Versace-Fans. In der Werbekampagne für Frühjahr/Sommer 2005 spielt sogar Madonna eine sexy Sekretärin. Donatella verantwortet übrigens auch die Erweiterung des Spektrums von Versace, etwa mit eigenen Kosmetika und dem ersten Sechs-Sterne-Hotel der Marke, dem 2000 an der australischen Gold Coast eröffneten Palazzo Versace. Neben Kleidung, Accessoires, Düften, Schmuck und Uhren gibt es nun auch noch eine Wohnkollektion sowie eine Abteilung für die Inneneinrichtung von Privatjets und Helikoptern und mit Versace Lamborghini sogar eine Sonderedition von Sportwagen. Donatella Versace hält 20 % an der Gianni Versace SpA. Zudem ist sie Creative Director und stellvertretende Aufsichtsratschefin. Ihre Tocher Allegra besitzt 50 % der Gianni Versace SpA. Im Winter 2011 bietet Versace über den Filialisten H&M eine exklusive Kollektion an.

Donatella Versace (née en 1959) est une déesse de la mode. Figure féminine de l'entreprise familiale, elle supervise les sept marques de la griffe Versace. Sa flamboyante image de fêtarde est même synonyme de Versace. Gianni (né en 1946) et Donatella ont grandi à Reggio Calabria, une ville du sud de l'Italie. Lorsque son frère s'installe à Milan pour travailler dans la mode, Donatella étudie les langues à Florence. La carrière de son frère décolle et après avoir travaillé pour Callaghan et Genny, il crée sa propre griffe en 1978. La passion familiale pour les couleurs vives, les formes moulantes et le glamour remporte un vif succès. Ils travaillent ensemble pendant la majeure partie des années 80 et 90, Donatella se concentrant sur les somptueuses images publicitaires qui feront la gloire de Versace. En 1993, elle lance la ligne pour enfant Young Versace et travaille comme styliste principale sur la ligne Versus. Après l'assassinat tragique de Gianni en 1997, sa sœur devient directrice de la création. Versace entre dans le 21e siècle en fusionnant le glamour italien de Gianni avec les instincts rock'n'roll de Donatella. La marque Versace occupe constamment le devant de la scène, aussi grâce à ses amis célèbres : Jon Bon Jovi, Courtney Love et Elizabeth Hurley, fans dévoués de Versace. Madonna accepte de jouer le rôle d'une secrétaire sexy pour la campagne publicitaire printemps/été 2005. Donatella réussit aussi à étendre l'offre de la marque, avec le lancement d'une ligne de maquillage et de Palazzo Versace, premier hôtel Versace six étoiles ouvert sur la Gold Coast australienne en 2000. Outre les lignes de vêtements, d'accessoires, de parfums, de bijoux et de montres, Versace compte désormais une collection de meubles, un service de design d'intérieur pour jets privés et hélicoptères, et même une Lamborghini Versace en édition limitée. Donatella Versace assume les fonctions de directrice de la création et de vice-présidente du conseil d'administration de Gianni Versace SpA, dont elle détient 20 % des parts. Sa fille, Allegra, en possède 50 %. En hiver 2011, Versace a proposé une collection exclusive par le biais des magasins de la chaîne de distribution H&M.

LAUREN COCHRANE

DONATELLA VERSACE

"I'm always most productive when I'm around people I admire who inspire and challenge me"
STUART VEVERS · LOEWE

The career of Stuart Vevers (born in Carlisle, England) so far is one of hard graft rather than chance or luck. Stating that "fashion is about hard work" was the most useful thing he learned from his student days at the University of Westminster, Vevers' first job after leaving college in 1996 was with Calvin Klein in New York. Milan beckoned two years later; at Bottega Veneta, Vevers was in charge of accessories. While still at Bottega Veneta, Vevers started working with Luella Bartley – Bartley is part of Vevers' fashion gang, which includes Giles Deacon and Katie Grand. The collaboration lasted eight years and Vevers is also godfather to Bartley's second child. Next came his appointment as Givenchy's accessory designer for both ready-to-wear and couture. From 2002, Vevers juggled Givenchy, Luella, a two-season stint on his own line and work as Louis Vuitton's accessories designer – as a member of Marc Jacobs' creative team, Vevers concentrated on bags. At the end of 2004, Vevers returned to London and became Mulberry's design director. Instrumental to the brand's turnaround, his handbag hits include the Emmy, Agyness and Mabel. He won the British Fashion Council's Accessory Designer of the Year Award in 2006. Then, in 2007, Vevers replaced Jose Enrique Ona Selfa to become Loewe's creative director. Now based in Madrid, Stuart has managed to keep the heritage of the 165-year-old Spanish luxury brand while modernising its most iconic styles and its work with leather. Stuart has produced six ready-to-wear collections to date, working with leather in fresh and modern ways and reworking iconic handbags styles such as the Amazona and the Flamenco.

Die Karriere des im englischen Carlisle geborenen Stuart Vevers ist bislang eher von harter Arbeit als von Zufall oder Glück bestimmt gewesen. Nach eigener Aussage gilt ihm der Satz „Mode ist harte Arbeit" als das Nützlichste, was er als Student an der University of Westminster gelernt hat. Den ersten Job nach seinem Hochschulabschluss 1996 bekam Vevers bei Calvin Klein in New York. Zwei Jahre später lockte Mailand, wo er bei Bottega Veneta für die Accessoires verantwortlich war. Noch während dieser Zeit begann Vevers mit Luella Bartley zu arbeiten – Bartley gehört ebenso wie Giles Deacon und Katie Grand zu Vevers' Mode-Clique. Ihre Kooperation dauerte acht Jahre, in denen Vevers sogar Pate von Bartleys zweitem Kind wurde. Als Nächstes folgte die Ernennung zum Accessoire-Designer bei Givenchy, sowohl für Prêt-à-porter wie für die Couture. Ab 2002 jonglierte Vevers Givenchy, Luella, eine zwei Saisons dauernde Schicht für seine eigene Linie und einen Job als Accessoire-Designer bei Louis Vuitton – als Mitglied von Marc Jacobs' Kreativteam konzentrierte

er sich auf Taschen. Ende 2004 kehrte Vevers als Design Director von Mulberry nach London zurück. Mit seinen Handtaschen-Hits Emmy, Agyness und Mabel war er maßgeblich an der Kehrtwende der Marke beteiligt. 2006 gewann er die Auszeichnung Accessory Designer of the Year des British Fashion Council. 2007 folgte Vevers Jose Enrique Ona Selfa auf den Posten des Creative Directors bei Loewe. Nun lebt er in Madrid und hat das Erbe der mehr als 165 Jahre alten spanischen Luxusmarke zu bewahren, indem er die alten Styles modernisiert und die Tradition hochwertiger Lederarbeit fortführt. Stuart hat bereits sechs Kollektionen produziert, seine Handtaschen sind Neuauflagen alter Modelle in frischem und modernem Look wie die Modelle Amazon und Flamenco.

À ce jour, la carrière de Stuart Vevers (né à Carlisle en Angleterre) tient plus du labeur que du hasard ou de la chance. « La mode, c'est du travail acharné », telle est la phrase qu'il cite comme la chose la plus utile qu'il ait apprise pendant ses études à l'Université de Westminster. Après avoir quitté la fac en 1996, il décroche son premier job chez Calvin Klein à New York, puis deux ans plus tard, part pour Milan où il est en charge des accessoires chez Bottega Veneta. C'est pendant cette période qu'il commence à travailler avec Luella Bartley, qui fait partie de sa bande aux côtés de Giles Deacon et Katie Grand. Leur collaboration durera huit ans ; Vevers est aussi le parrain du second fils de Luella Bartley. Il devient ensuite créateur d'accessoires chez Givenchy, pour le prêt-à-porter et la haute couture. À partir de 2002, Stuart Vevers jongle entre Givenchy, Luella, un travail de deux saisons sur sa propre collection et une collaboration comme créateur d'accessoires chez Louis Vuitton dans l'équipe créative de Marc Jacobs, où il se concentre sur les sacs. Fin 2004, Vevers revient à Londres et décroche la direction de la création de Mulberry. Ses sacs à main Emmy, Agyness et Mabel, entre autres, jouent un rôle crucial dans le renouveau de la marque et remportent un succès éclatant. En 2006, Vevers est élu Accessory Designer of the Year par le British Fashion Council. L'année suivante, il remplace Jose Enrique Ona Selfa à la direction de la création de Loewe et s'installe à Madrid. Il se doit désormais de conserver l'héritage de la marque de luxe espagnole, qui a aujourd'hui 165 ans, en modernisant les anciens styles et en perpétuant la tradition d'un travail du cuir de très grande qualité. Stuart a d'ores et déjà conçu six collections, ses sacs à main sont des rééditions d'anciens modèles, agrémentées d'un look frais et moderne à l'instar des modèles « Amazone » et « Flamenco ».

KAREN HODKINSON

292

"Create clothes that have a familiarity and wearability, but constantly push the limits of how people perceive the latter"
ALEXANDER WANG

Since his debut on the New York fashion scene in 2006, Alexander Wang has cemented his reputation as the go-to brand for cool, stylish clothes for cool, stylish girls. Born and raised in San Francisco, California, to a Chinese-American family, Wang moved to New York at the age of 18 to study fashion at Parsons School of Design. During this time, he undertook a number of internships, including placements at Marc Jacobs, 'Teen Vogue', American 'Vogue' and Derek Lam, before deciding to drop out of university in 2006 and launch himself as a fully independent fashion designer. Wang debuted his eponymous womenswear collection of cashmere knits one year later to instant critical acclaim, and by his sophomore collection, for Autumn/Winter 2007, the young designer had been touted as one of the most exciting designers of a new generation. Believing a T-shirt and jeans can be just as sexy as an evening gown, Wang has since cultivated a design signature of slouchy tees, layered dresses and trousers that perfectly merge his Californian upbringing with his current downtown New York living. His simple yet chic clothes are widely acknowledged as the garments of choice for supermodels off-duty, and he counts many of the big-name girls as his best friends. Wang continue to cultivate his grunge-meets-glamour aesthetic by launching a slick accessories line of high heels and bags, and a diffusion line of T-shirts called T by Alexander Wang. Today Alexander Wang sells to over 150 boutiques and retail stores worldwide with his first flagship store opening in March 2011 in Soho, New York, while his accolades include a nomination for the 2008 CFDA Swarovski Womenswear Designer of the Year Award, a place amongst the top ten finalists for the Vogue/CFDA Fashion Fund and the prestigious Ecco Domani Emerging Designer Award. Long may his success continue.

Seit seinem Debüt in der New Yorker Modeszene 2006 hat Alexander Wang seinen Ruf gefestigt, das Label schlechthin zu sein, das coole Klamotten für coole Mädchen liefert. Als Spross einer chinesisch-amerikanischen Familie wurde Wang in San Francisco geboren, wo er auch aufwuchs. Mit 18 ging er zum Modestudium an der Parsons School of Design nach New York. Er absolvierte eine Reihe von Praktika, unter anderem bei Marc Jacobs, Teen Vogue, bei der amerikanischen Vogue und bei Derek Lam, bevor er sich 2006 entschied, die Universität zu verlassen, um sich als komplett unabhängiger Designer zu versuchen. Sein Debüt gab Wang im Jahr darauf mit einer Strickkollektion aus Kaschmir für Damen, die auf Anhieb begeistert aufgenommen wurde. Als seine zweite Kollektion, für Herbst/Winter 2007, herauskam, wurde der junge Modemacher bereits lautstark als einer der aufregendsten Designer einer neuen Generation gefeiert. Mit der Einstellung, dass ein T-Shirt und Jeans ebenso sexy sein können wie eine Abendrobe, hat Wang seither seine eigene Handschrift in Form von lässigen T-Shirts, Lagenkleidern und Hosen kultiviert, die allesamt auf perfekte Weise seine kalifornische Herkunft mit seinem gegenwärtigen Zuhause in Downtown New York in Einklang bringen. Seine schlichten, aber trotzdem schicken Sachen gelten weithin als Lieblingsfreizeitkleidung von Supermodels. Daher zählen viele der Mädchen mit großen Namen zu seinen besten Freundinnen. Wang bleibt weiterhin seiner „Grunge meets glamour"-Ästhetik treu, und zwar in Gestalt einer kleinen Accessoirelinie mit High Heels und Taschen sowie einer T-Shirt-Nebenkollektion namens T by Alexander Wang. Inzwischen verkauft Alexander Wang seine Kreationen in mehr als 150 Boutiquen und Kaufhäusern weltweit und seit März 2011 in seinem ersten Flagship-Store in Soho, New York. Zu seinen Auszeichnungen zählen die Nominierung bei der CFDA für den Swarovski Womenswear Designer of the Year Award 2008, ein Platz unter den zehn Finalisten für den Vogue/CFDA Fashion Fund und der renommierte Ecco Domani Emerging Designer Award. Möge sein Erfolg von langer Dauer sein.

Depuis ses débuts à New York en 2006, Alexander Wang a imposé sa marque de vêtements comme celle des filles cool et branchées. Né dans une famille sino-américaine à San Francisco en Californie, Wang s'installe à New York dès ses 18 ans pour étudier la mode à la Parsons School of Design. Pendant ses études, il effectue plusieurs stages, notamment chez Marc Jacobs, Teen Vogue, Vogue et Derek Lam. En 2006, il décide d'arrêter ses études pour se lancer à son compte. Un an plus tard, Wang présente une première collection éponyme de maille en cachemire pour femme qui enchante immédiatement la critique. L'année suivante, sa deuxième collection pour la saison automne/hiver 2007 incite la presse à le décrire comme l'un des créateurs les plus fascinants de la nouvelle génération. Convaincu qu'un T-shirt et un jean peuvent être aussi sexy qu'une robe du soir, Alexander Wang cultive depuis un style signature fait de T-shirts informes et de robes superposées sur des pantalons qui fusionne à la perfection ses origines californiennes avec sa vie actuelle dans le downtown new-yorkais. Quand elles ne sont pas de service, les top-modèles adorent porter ses vêtements simples mais chics, et Wang compte les plus célèbres d'entre elles parmi ses meilleures amies. Il continue d'explorer son esthétique à la fois grunge et glamour en lançant une impeccable collection de sacs et de chaussures à talons, ainsi qu'une ligne de diffusion proposant des T-shirts, « T by Alexander Wang ». Aujourd'hui, sa marque est distribuée dans plus de 150 boutiques et grands magasins à travers le monde et est présente à New York depuis mars 2011 dans sa première boutique phare à Soho. Nommé pour le prix CFDA Swarovski Womenswear Designer Of The Year en 2008, il figurait aussi parmi les dix derniers finalistes du Vogue/CFDA Fashion Fund et du prestigieux Ecco Domani Emerging Designer Award. Et ce n'est qu'un début !

HOLLY SHACKLETON

PHOTOGRAPHY AMY TROOST. STYLING ALASTAIR MCKIMM. MODEL LIU WEN. JUNE/JULY 2009.

PHOTOGRAPHY DANIEL JACKSON. STYLING ALASTAIR MCKIMM. MODEL KARLIE KLOSS. JANUARY 2008.

"I do what I do and those who sympathise with my work will wear it"
JUNYA WATANABE

Junya Watanabe (born Tokyo, 1961) is the much-fêted protégé of Rei Kawakubo. Graduating from Bunka Fashion College in 1984, he immediately joined Comme des Garçons as a pattern-cutter. By 1987, he was designing their Tricot line. He presented his first solo collection in 1992 at the Tokyo collections; a year later, he showed at Paris Fashion Week. Although designing under his own name, he is still employed by Comme des Garçons, who fund and produce the collections. Despite an obvious debt to Rei Kawakubo in his work, Watanabe still stands apart from his mentor and friend with a vision that is indisputably his own. He has often used technical or functional fabrics, creating clothes that still retain a sense of calm and femininity. This was displayed most explicitly at his Autumn/Winter 1999 show, where the catwalk was under a constant shower of water: rain seemed to splash off the outfits, which were created in fabric by the Japanese company Toray, who develop materials for extreme conditions. Despite the wealth of creativity on display, Watanabe's clothes were a response to more fundamental issues: a practical answer to conditions and lifestyles. In contrast to this, Watanabe's designs are also an exercise in sensitivity and, through his remarkably complex pattern cutting, his sculptural clothing presents a virtually unrivalled delicacy. In 2001, Watanabe presented his first menswear collection in Paris. Today, he is one of the most celebrated designers in Paris fashion.

Der 1961 in Tokio geborene Junya Watanabe ist der viel gefeierte Protegé von Rei Kawakubo. Unmittelbar nach seinem Abschluss am Bunka Fashion College 1984 fing er als Zuschneider bei Comme des Garçons an. 1987 entwarf er bereits die Nebenlinie Tricot des japanischen Modehauses. Die erste Solokollektion präsentierte Watanabe dann 1992 in Tokio, ein Jahr später war er auf der Pariser Modewoche vertreten. Auch wenn er inzwischen unter eigenem Namen entwirft, ist der Japaner noch Angestellter des Unternehmens Comme des Garçons, das seine Kollektionen auch finanziert und produziert. Obwohl er in seiner Arbeit von Rei Kawakubo entscheidend beeinflusst wurde, unterscheidet sich Watanabe doch mit einer zweifellos eigenständigen Vision von seiner Mentorin und Freundin. Oft benutzt er Mikrofasern und andere funktionale Stoffe für seine Kreationen, die dennoch eine Aura von Gelassenheit und Weiblichkeit besitzen. Am deutlichsten wurde dies bisher bei seiner Schau für Herbst/Winter 1999, als er den Catwalk ununterbrochen beregnen ließ.

Das Wasser schien von den Outfits abzuperlen, die aus einem Material der japanischen Firma Toray gefertigt waren. Dieses Unternehmen ist auf die Herstellung von Geweben für Extrembedingungen spezialisiert. Doch trotz dieser originellen Präsentation waren die Kreationen von Watanabe eine Reaktion auf fundamentalere Herausforderungen, nämlich eine praktische Antwort auf verschiedene Lebensumstände und -stile. Zugleich ist die Mode des Japaners aber auch eine Art Sensitivitätstraining, und dank seiner bemerkenswert komplexen Schnitte sind die skulpturalen Entwürfe auch von einer unvergleichlichen Zartheit. 2001 präsentierte Watanabe seine erste Herrenkollektion in Paris. Heute ist er einer der meistgefeierten Designer der Pariser Modeszene.

Junya Watanabe (né en 1961 à Tokyo) est le célèbre protégé de Rei Kawakubo. Diplômé du Bunka Fashion College en 1984, il commence immédiatement à travailler chez Comme des Garçons en tant que traceur de patrons. En 1987, il dessine déjà pour la ligne Tricot. Il présente sa première collection en solo aux défilés de Tokyo ; un an plus tard, il est invité à la Semaine de la Mode de Paris (bien qu'il dessine sous son propre nom, Watanabe est toujours employé par Comme des Garçons, qui finance et produit ses collections). Très marqué par l'influence de Rei Kawakubo, le travail de Watanabe se distingue toutefois de celui de son amie et mentor grâce à une approche indiscutablement personnelle. Les vêtements qu'il taille souvent dans des tissus techno et fonctionnels n'en sont pas moins empreints de calme et de féminité. Son talent apparaît de façon explicite à l'occasion de son défilé automne/hiver 1999, où les mannequins défilent sur un podium constamment aspergé d'eau : les gouttes de pluie rebondissent sur les vêtements coupés dans un tissu produit par Toray, une entreprise japonaise qui développe des matériaux résistant aux conditions extrêmes. Bien qu'ils démontrent l'immense créativité de Watanabe, ses vêtements apportent avant tout une réponse à des problèmes plus fondamentaux, une solution pratique aux divers climats et modes de vie. Ils témoignent également de la grande sensibilité du créateur qui, grâce à des coupes d'une remarquable complexité, confère à ses pièces sculpturales une délicatesse incomparable. En 2001, Watanabe présente sa première collection pour homme à Paris. Il est aujourd'hui l'un des créateurs les plus en vue de la scène parisienne.

MARCUS ROSS

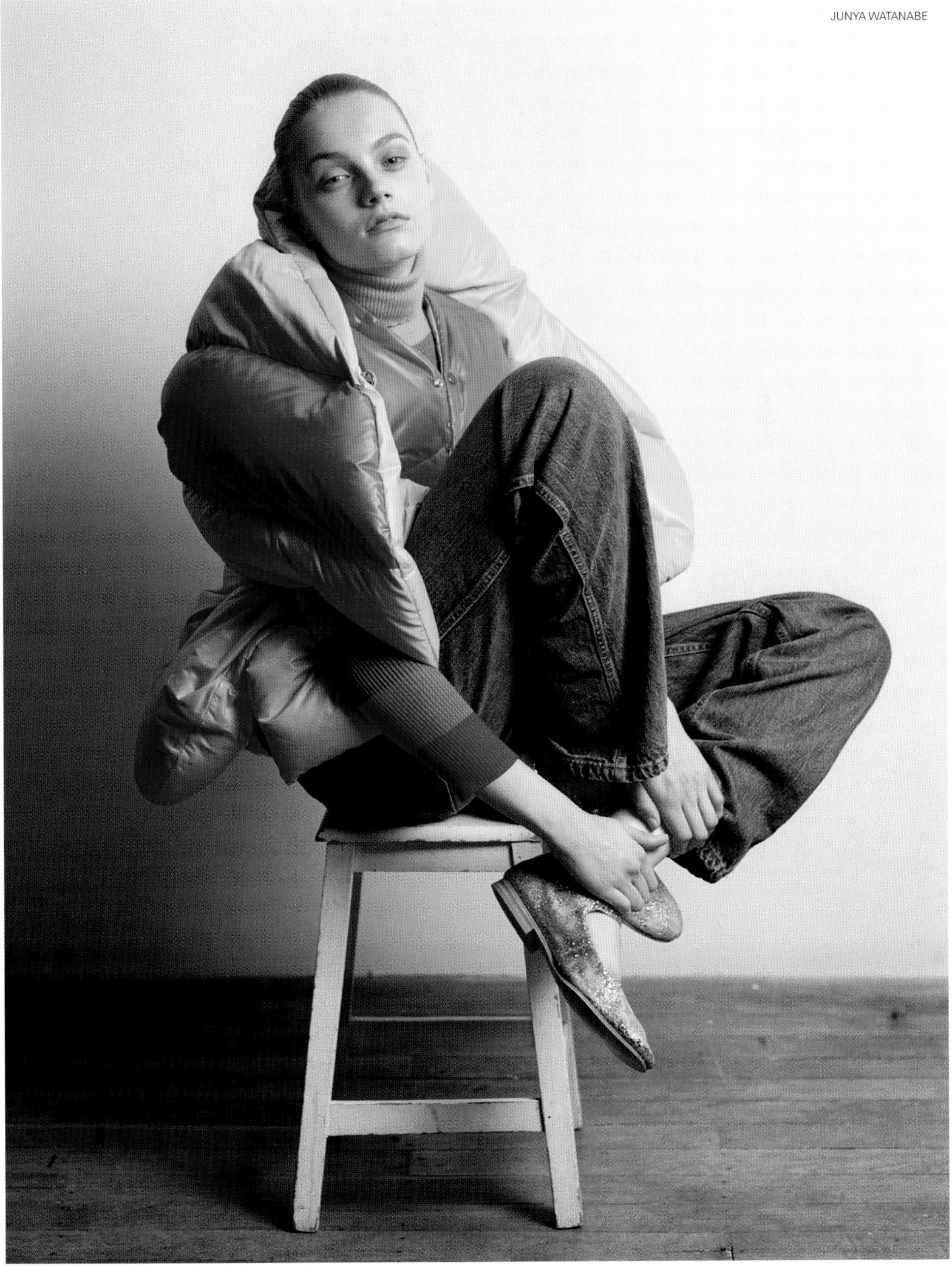

"Power is sexy. I like the men and women that I dress to look important"
VIVIENNE WESTWOOD

Vivienne Westwood is a legend in her own lifetime, a designer who inspires many other designers and who makes clothes that delight her loyal customers. Born in Derbyshire in 1941, she first became a household name when, in partnership with Malcolm McLaren, she invented the punk uniform. Let It Rock, SEX, Seditionaries, Pirates, and Buffalo Girls were all early collections they created together at their shop in World's End, Chelsea. All became classics and served to challenge common preconceptions of what fashion could be. Since severing business ties with McLaren, Westwood has gone on to become one of the most revered figures within the fashion industry. She has achieved all this without any formal training. In the '80s, she was hailed by 'Women's Wear Daily' as one of the six most influential designers of all time, and in 2004 the Victoria & Albert Museum launched a travelling retrospective exhibition defining her iconic status. There is an intellectual method to the madness of her creative energy. Historical references, techniques and fabrics are intrinsic to her approach to design. Her subversive shapes and constructions have consistently proved to be ahead of their time. Awarded an OBE 15 years after being arrested on the night of the Queen's Silver Jubilee, she has now become a part of the establishment she continues to oppose. Today she shows her ready-to-wear women's collection in Paris and a menswear collection, MAN, in Milan. While the interest in vintage Westwood has never been more intense, her diffusion line Anglomania regularly references pieces from her earlier collections. Westwood also has three bestselling perfumes – Libertine, Boudoir and Anglomania – and has shops all over the world. Westwood wrote a cultural manifesto called 'Active Resistance to Propaganda' as a call to arms for all intellectuals against passive acceptance of propaganda and obsessive consumption. In 2008, Westwood showed her Red Label in London after almost a decade of absence from London Fashion Week and called on other British brands that now only show abroad to follow her example. 2011 saw the Queen of Punk celebrate 40 years in the fashion industry.

Vivienne Westwood ist schon zu Lebzeiten eine Legende – eine Designerin, die viele andere Modeschöpfer inspiriert und mit ihren Entwürfen eine treue Kundschaft entzückt. Geboren wurde sie 1941 in Derbyshire. Erstmals machte sie sich einen Namen, als sie gemeinsam mit Malcolm McLaren die Punk-Uniform erfand. Let It Rock, SEX, Seditionaries, Pirates und Buffalo Girls sind frühe Kollektionen, die sie zusammen in ihrem Laden World's End in Chelsea entwarfen. Sie wurden allesamt zu Klassikern und stellten gängige Vorurteile darüber, was Mode sein könnte, infrage. Nachdem sie die Geschäftsbeziehung mit McLaren beendet hatte, wurde Westwood zu einer der meistgeachteten Figuren der Branche. Erreicht hat sie all das ohne jegliche konventionelle Ausbildung. In den 1980er-Jahren erkor Women's Wear Daily sie zu einem der sechs einflussreichsten Designer aller Zeiten. 2004 präsentierte das Victoria and Albert Museum eine Retrospektive rund um ihren Status als Mode-Ikone. Westwoods kreative Arbeitswut hat intellektuelle Methode. So sind historische Bezüge, Techniken und Materialien wesentliche Elemente ihres Designkonzepts. Ihre subversiven Silhouetten und Konstruktionen sind ihrer Zeit immer voraus. 15 Jahre nachdem sie in der Nacht des silbernen Thronjubiläums der Queen verhaftet worden war, zeichnete man sie als Officer of the Order of the British Empire aus. Inzwischen ist sie selbst Teil des Estab-

lishments, gegen das sie aber nach wie vor ankämpft. Heute zeigt sie ihre Prêt-à-porter-Kollektion für Damen in Paris und eine Herrenkollektion namens MAN in Mailand. Während das Interesse an ihren Vintage-Teilen so groß ist wie noch nie, nimmt sie in ihrer Nebenlinie Anglomania selbst regelmäßig Bezug auf Entwürfe aus früheren Kollektionen. Westwood hat auch bereits drei Düfte auf den Markt gebracht, die sich als Bestseller erwiesen: Libertine, Boudoir und Anglomania. Ihre Läden findet man auf der ganzen Welt. Die Designerin hat ein gesellschaftskritisches Manifest namens „Active Residence to Propaganda" geschrieben. Darin ruft sie alle Intellektuellen gegen das passive Hinnehmen von Propaganda und obsessivem Konsum zu den Waffen. 2008 präsentierte sie nach fast einem Jahrzehnt Abwesenheit bei der London Fashion Week ihr Red Label in der Hauptstadt. Zugleich rief sie andere britische Marken, die ihre Kollektionen bis dato nur im Ausland zeigten, dazu auf, ihrem Beispiel zu folgen. Mittlerweile ist die „Queen of Punk" 40 Jahre im Geschäft.

Vivienne Westwood est une légende vivante, une créatrice qui inspire de nombreux autres stylistes et dont les vêtements font le bonheur de ses fidèles clients. Née en 1941 dans le Derbyshire, elle devient d'abord célèbre dans toute l'Angleterre pour l'uniforme punk qu'elle invente avec Malcolm McLaren. Let It Rock, SEX, Seditionaries, Pirates et Buffalo Girls sont autant de collections qu'ils créent ensemble dans leur première boutique du World's End à Chelsea. Toutes sont devenues des classiques et ont servi à remettre en question les idées préconçues sur ce que la mode doit être. Depuis qu'elle a mis un terme à ses relations d'affaires avec McLaren, Vivienne Westwood est devenue l'un des personnages les plus révérés par le monde de la mode, et ce, sans la moindre formation. Dans les années 80, Women's Wear Daily la classe parmi les six créateurs les plus influents de l'époque. En 2004, le Victoria & Albert Museum lance une grande rétrospective itinérante qui assoit son statut d'icône. On distingue de la méthode et de l'intellect dans la folie de son énergie créative. Références, techniques et tissus historiques font partie intégrante de son approche de la mode. Ses formes et ses constructions subversives se sont toujours avérées très en avance sur leur temps. Décorée Officier de l'Empire britannique 15 ans après son arrestation, la nuit du jubilé d'argent de la reine, elle fait désormais partie de l'establishment auquel elle continue pourtant de s'opposer. Aujourd'hui, elle présente sa collection de prêt-à-porter pour femme à Paris et sa collection pour homme, MAN, à Milan. Alors que l'intérêt pour les pièces Westwood vintage n'a jamais été aussi intense, sa ligne secondaire Anglomania fait régulièrement référence aux vêtements de ses anciennes collections. Vivienne Westwood a également lancé trois parfums à succès, Libertine, Boudoir et Anglomania, et possède des boutiques dans le monde entier. Elle a rédigé un manifeste culturel intitulé Active Residence to Propaganda, un appel aux armes lancé à tous les intellectuels pour combattre l'acceptation passive de la propagande et de la consommation obsessionnelle. En 2008, Vivienne Westwood a présenté sa collection « Red Label » dans la capitale britannique après presque dix ans d'absence de la London Fashion Week, montrant l'exemple à d'autres marques anglaises qui ne défilent désormais plus qu'à l'étranger. Entre-temps, la « Queen of Punk » est active dans la branche depuis 40 ans.

TERRY NEWMAN

PHOTOGRAPHY MARIUS HANSEN. MODELS WORLD'S END STAFF, VIVIENNE WESTWOOD AND AGYNESS DEYN. MAY 2008.

"The most important lesson I've learned is, be kind"
BERNHARD WILLHELM

Since graduating from Antwerp's Royal Academy back in 1998, Bernhard Willhelm has created an original, beautiful and completely off-the-wall universe. During his time at college, Willhelm assisted the cream of fashion avant-garde, including Walter Van Beirendonck, Alexander McQueen, Vivienne Westwood and Dirk Bikkembergs and the lineage and experience passed on from working with these designers is more than evident in his designs. Willhelm launched his womenswear in 1999, followed in quick succession by menswear in 2000, before settling in Paris in 2002, a place this native German still calls home. Recurring themes include his twisted take on European tradition, with lederhosen and bratwurst appearing as clothing embellishments whilst Western themes like McDonalds and American football have provided inspiration at various points in his career. From 2002 to 2004, Willhelm directed the Italian house of Capucci, along with support from Tara Subkoff of Imitation of Christ and Sybilla, where he launched their first Prêt-à-Porter collection. Working across media, Willhelm has shown exhibitions including a solo show at the Groninger Museum 2009–2010, published books, designed school uniforms, launched a shoe line with Camper and a clothing line with Yoox, art-directed record covers, starred on magazine covers, and collaborated with tastemakers, including Björk and Nick Knight. His work challenges stereotypes and is characterised by storytelling, none more so than for his 'Bernhard Willhelm: Het Totaal Rappel' exhibition at the Antwerp Academy. The exhibition saw Willhelm create installations specific to each collection in collaboration with Swiss artists Taiyo Onorato and Nico Krebs, who worked with Willhelm on his brilliant look books and showroom presentations. The result was phenomenal. Glitter worlds, wooden mazes and computer graphics presented a complete and unflinching setting for his consistently brilliant designs, proving once again that Bernhard Willhelm will always be five steps ahead of the game. Willhelm and team temporarily relocated to Mexico during summer 2011.

Seit seinem Abschluss an der Antwerpener Royal Academy im Jahr 1998 hat Bernhard Willhelm ein originelles, wunderschönes und total verrücktes Universum erschaffen. Während des Studiums assistierte Willhelm bei der Crème de la Crème der Modeavantgarde, u. a. bei Walter van Beirendonck, Alexander McQueen, Vivienne Westwood und Dirk Bikkembergs. Die Erfahrung, die er aus der Arbeit mit diesen Designern gewonnen hat, ist seinen Kreationen deutlich anzusehen. Damenmode präsentierte Willhelm erstmals 1999, rasch gefolgt von einer Herrenkollektion im Jahr 2000, bevor er sich schließlich 2002 in Paris niederließ, wo sich der gebürtige Deutsche nach wie vor zu Hause fühlt. Wiederkehrende Themen bei ihm sind die eigenwillige Auseinandersetzung mit der europäischen Tradition. Da tauchen Lederhosen und Bratwürste als Zierrat auf, während an anderen Stellen seiner Karriere auch schon McDonalds und American Football als Inspiration dienten. Von 2002 bis 2004 war Willhelm Chef des italienischen Modehauses Capucci, wo er die erste Prêt-à-porter-Kollektion herausbrachte. Bei seiner Arbeit quer durch alle Medien hat Willhelm bereits Ausstellungen präsentiert (einschließlich einer Einzelausstellung im Groninger Museum 2009-2010), Bücher publiziert, Schuluniformen entworfen, eine Schuh-Linie bei Camper und Klei-

der für Yoox designt, als Art Director Plattencover entworfen, für Zeitschriftentitel posiert und mit Trendfiguren wie Björk und Nick Knight zusammengearbeitet. Seine Arbeit stellt Stereotypen infrage und erzählt immer eine Geschichte, was nirgends deutlicher wurde als bei seiner Ausstellung „Bernhard Willhelm: Het Totaal Rappel" in der Antwerpener Akademie. Er schuf dafür Installationen für die jeweiligen Kollektionen, und zwar in Zusammenarbeit mit den Schweizer Künstlern Taiyo Onorato und Nico Krebs, die Willhelm schon bei seinen brillanten Look Books und Showroom-Präsentationen unterstützt haben. Das Resultat war phänomenal: Glitzerwelten, Holzlabyrinthe und Computergrafiken lieferten die Bühne für seine durchwegs überragenden Entwürfe. Womit wieder einmal der Beweis erbracht wäre, dass Willhelm allen anderen stets fünf Schritte voraus ist. Während des Sommers 2011 siedelte Willhelm mit seinem Team vorübergehend nach Mexiko um.

Depuis qu'il a décroché son diplôme de l'Académie Royale d'Anvers en 1998, Bernhard Willhelm s'est créé un univers original, magnifique et totalement désaxé. Pendant ses études, il travaille comme assistant pour la crème de l'avant-garde de la mode, notamment Walter Van Beirendonck, Alexander McQueen, Vivienne Westwood et Dirk Bikkembergs. Les valeurs et l'expérience qu'il acquiert auprès de ces couturiers transparaissent de façon tout à fait flagrante dans ses créations. En 1999, Willhelm lance sa ligne pour femme, rapidement suivie d'une collection pour homme en l'an 2000. Il s'installe à Paris en 2002, une ville où cet Allemand d'origine se sent encore aujourd'hui comme chez lui. Ses sujets de prédilection incluent une vision décalée de la tradition européenne, comme en témoigne l'utilisation de culottes tyroliennes en cuir et de saucisses grillées décoratives sur ses vêtements, et les thèmes occidentaux tels McDonald's et le football américain, qui l'ont inspiré à diverses reprises au cours de sa carrière. Entre 2002 et 2004, Willhelm dirige la maison italienne Capucci et lance la première collection de prêt-à-porter de la marque. Artiste multidisciplinaire, il a fait l'objet de plusieurs expositions (y compris une exposition personnelle au Groninger Museum en 2009 - 2010), publié des livres, conçu des uniformes scolaires, lancé une ligne de chaussures avec Camper, une collection de vêtements avec Yoox, créé des couvertures de disques, posé à la une de plusieurs magazines et collaboré avec des prescripteurs de tendances comme Björk et Nick Knight. Son travail remet en question les stéréotypes et repose principalement sur la narration, comme l'illustrait son exposition « Bernhard Willhelm : Het Totaal Rappel » à l'Académie d'Anvers : Willhelm y montrait des installations consacrées à chacune de ses collections, en collaboration avec les artistes suisses Taiyo Onorato et Nico Krebs qui avaient travaillé avec lui sur ses fabuleux look books et ses défilés. Le résultat fut phénoménal: mondes scintillants, dédales en bois et graphisme numérique formaient un décor total et implacable pour ses créations toujours réussies, et prouvaient une fois de plus que Bernhard Willhelm aura toujours cinq longueurs d'avance sur les autres. Durant l'été 2011, Willhelm s'est installé avec son équipe provisoirement au Mexique.

BEN REARDON

PHOTOGRAPHY TESH. FASHION DIRECTOR EDWARD ENNINFUL. DECEMBER 2001/JANUARY 2002.

PHOTOGRAPHY SIMON THISLETON. STYLING SIMON FOXTON. MODEL KARL. AUGUST 2008.

"Colour is the thing I'm best known for. If people pigeonhole me, so what? Long live the pink dress!"
MATTHEW WILLIAMSON

Matthew Williamson uses colour in a way very few designers dare match. He routinely splashes ultra pinks, fluorescent yellows and acid greens with an energising flourish onto women's day and eveningwear. This has become his signature style since the debut of his first collection, Electric Angels, in 1997 – a combination of kaleidoscopic bias-cut dresses and separates, sometimes embroidered and fused with a bohemian edge. Modelled by friends Jade Jagger, Kate Moss and Helena Christensen, it was a presentation that affirmed the London-based designer's influences: fame, glamour and India (Williamson's garments often read like a travel diary, tracing his love of exotic destinations). Since that first collection, it's been the intricate detail, contemporary styling and sexy silhouettes that have kept the applause coming. Born in Chorlton, Manchester, in 1971, Williamson graduated from Central Saint Martins in 1994 and set up his own label in 1996 after spending two years as consultant at UK mass-market chain Monsoon. 2002 saw the launch of a homeware range and a move to show his womenswear collections at New York Fashion Week. A first foray into perfume and home fragrance – a collaboration with perfumer and friend Lyn Harris – saw the creation of the limited-edition perfume Incense. The first Matthew Williamson flagship store opened in 2004 on London's Bruton Street. Williamson took over as creative director at the Italian house Emilio Pucci in 2005. But in September 2008, he returned to London full-time in order to focus on his own label's ventures and expansion. In September 2007, Williamson celebrated his label's 10th anniversary with a one-off show at London Fashion Week and an exhibition dedicated to his retrospective, titled Matthew Williamson – 10 Years in Fashion, at the Design Museum (London). Williamson was awarded the Möet & Chandon Fashion Tribute (2005) and the Red Carpet Designer of the Year at the British Fashion Awards (2008). In October 2010, Williamson signed a new licensing deal with MBFG, and a new diffusion line, Muse, is expected in stores for Autumn 2011.

Matthew Williamson kombiniert Farben mit einem Wagemut, den nur sehr wenige Designer aufbringen. Mit kräftigem Schwung verteilt er knallige Pinktöne, Neongelb und -grün auf Alltags- und Abendmode für Damen. Das ist sein Markenzeichen seit dem Debüt 1997 mit seiner ersten Kollektion „Electric Angels": einer Kombination von diagonal geschnittenen kaleidoskopischen Kleidern und Einzelteilen, teilweise bestickt oder mit einem Touch Bohème versehen. Die Models damals waren seine Freundinnen Jade Jagger, Kate Moss und Helena Christensen, und die Schau bestätigte die Einflüsse auf den in London lebenden Designer: Prominenz, Glamour und Indien (seine Kleider lesen sich oft wie ein Reisetagebuch, das seine Vorliebe für exotische Ziele dokumentiert). Nach jener ersten Kollektion waren jedoch raffinierte Details, zeitgemäßes Styling und sexy Silhouetten für den anhaltenden Applaus verantwortlich. Der 1971 in Manchester geborene Williamson machte 1994 seinen Abschluss am Central Saint Martins und gründete 1996 sein eigenes Label, nachdem er zwei Jahre lang als Berater für die britische Modekette Monsoon gearbeitet hatte. 2002 kam noch eine Homeware-Kollektion dazu. In New York präsentierte er im Rahmen der Modewoche seine Damenkollektionen. Ein ers-

tes Hineinschnuppern in den Markt der Düfte und Home Fragrances war die Zusammenarbeit mit der Parfümeurin und Freundin Lyn Harris bei der Kreation des in limitierter Auflage auf den Markt gebrachten Parfüms Incense. Den ersten nach ihm benannten Flagship-Store eröffnete Williamson 2004 in der Londoner Bruton Street. 2005 übernahm er die Position des Creative Directors beim italienischen Modehaus Emilio Pucci. Im September 2008 kehrte er jedoch nach London zurück, um sich voll auf die Projekte und die Expansion seines eigenen Labels zu konzentrieren. Exakt ein Jahr zuvor hatte Williamson das 10-jährige Bestehen seiner Marke mit einer einzigartigen Show bei der London Fashion Week sowie der Ausstellung „Matthew Williamson – 10 Years in Fashion" im Londoner Design Museum gefeiert. An Auszeichnungen kann der Designer den Möet & Chandon Fashion Tribute (2005) und den Titel Red Carpet Designer of the Year im Rahmen der British Fashion Awards (2008) vorweisen. Im Oktober 2010 unterzeichnete Williamson ein Lizenzabkommen mit MBFG. Seine Zweitlinie („Muse") wird im Herbst 2011 in den Läden erwartet.

Matthew Williamson utilise la couleur comme peu d'autres osent le faire. Il éclabousse avec panache et énergie ses tenues féminines de jour et de soir de rose flashy, jaune fluo et vert acidulé. Depuis sa première collection « Electric Angels » en 1997, ce style s'est imposé en signature ; une combinaison de robes et séparés kaléidoscopiques coupés en biais, parfois brodés, au look un peu bohème. Grâce à ses amies mannequins Jade Jagger, Kate Moss et Helena Christensen, ce défilé confirme les influences du créateur londonien : gloire, glamour et Inde (ses vêtements se lisent comme des carnets de voyage témoignant de sa passion pour les destinations exotiques). Depuis cette première collection, son succès est croissant grâce aux détails complexes, au style contemporain et à la silhouette sexy. Né en 1971 à Manchester, Williamson sort diplômé de Central Saint Martins en 1994. Après avoir travaillé pendant deux ans comme consultant pour la chaîne de distribution britannique Monsoon, il crée sa propre griffe en 1996. En 2002, il lance une gamme d'articles et présente ses collections pour femme à la New York Fashion Week. Une première incursion dans les domaines parfum et parfum d'intérieur, fruit d'une collaboration avec son amie parfumeuse Lyn Harris, voit la création d'une fragrance en édition limitée, « Incense ». La première boutique indépendante Matthew Williamson a ouvert en 2004 sur la Bruton Street à Londres. En 2005, le créateur britannique devient directeur de la création de la maison italienne Emilio Pucci, qu'il quitte en septembre 2008 pour revenir à Londres et se concentrer à fond sur les projets et l'expansion de sa propre griffe. En septembre 2007, Williamson célèbre le 10e anniversaire de sa marque lors d'un défilé exceptionnel pendant la London Fashion Week et à travers une rétrospective intitulée « Matthew Williamson – 10 Years in Fashion » au Design Museum (Londres). Matthew Williamson est lauréat du Möet & Chandon Fashion Tribute (2005) et présente Red Carpet Designer of the Year des British Fashion Awards (2008). En octobre 2010, Williamson signe un accord de licence avec MBFG, une seconde ligne « Muse » est attendue dans les magasins à l'automne 2011.

TERRY NEWMAN

"You can say that designing is quite easy; the difficulty lies in finding a new way to explore beauty"
YOHJI YAMAMOTO

Famed for his abstract silhouettes, flat shoes and unswerving loyalty to the colour black, Yohji Yamamoto is one of the most influential fashion designers working today. Yamamoto's clothing combines intellectual rigour with breathtaking romance; in his hands, stark and often extremely challenging modernity segues with references to Parisian haute couture. Born in Japan in 1943, Yamamoto was brought up by his seamstress mother following his father's death in the Second World War. It was in an attempt to please his mother that he initially studied law at Tokyo's Keio University, later switching to fashion at the Bunka school, where he graduated in 1969. Yamamoto established his own label in 1971 under the name Y's, holding his first show in Tokyo in 1977. By the time he had made his Paris debut in 1981 with his eponymous brand Yohji Yamamoto, along with his girlfriend at the time, Rei Kawakubo of Comme des Garçons, his label was already a commercial success back in Japan. Yamamoto sent out models wearing white make-up and asymmetric black clothing, and the establishment dubbed his look 'Hiroshima Chic'. His womenswear and menswear – the latter shown in Paris for the first time in 1984 – became a status symbol for urban creative types. He now has over 223 retail outlets worldwide, a groundbreaking collaboration with Adidas (Y-3). His first major solo exhibition was held in 2005 at the Musée de la Mode in Paris. Yamamoto is also a karate black belt and chief organiser of the Worldwide Karate Association. 2011 marked the opening of four Yohji Yamamoto exhibitions in London; the first UK retrospective at the V&A reuniting about 80 pieces from womenswear and menswear for the first time: Yohji's Women and Yohji Making Waves are both at the Wapping Project and Yohji Yamamoto at Work is at the fashion space of the London College of Fashion. The same year, he also received the rank of Commander in the National Order of Merit from the president of the French Republic, and published his first autobiography 'My Dear Bomb'.

Yohji Yamamoto ist berühmt für seine abstrakten Silhouetten, flachen Schuhe und die unverbrüchliche Treue zur Farbe Schwarz. Zudem ist er einer der einflussreichsten Modedesigner der Gegenwart. Seine Kleider verbinden intellektuelle Schärfe mit atemberaubender Romantik. Unter seinen Meisterhänden verträgt sich absolute und oft extrem anspruchsvolle Modernität mit Bezügen zur Pariser Haute Couture. Yamamoto wurde 1943 in Japan geboren, und nachdem sein Vater im Zweiten Weltkrieg umgekommen war, sorgte seine Mutter als Näherin für den Lebensunterhalt. Auf Wunsch seiner Mutter studierte er zunächst Jura an der Tokioter Keio-Universität, wechselte dann aber zum Modestudium an die Bunka School, wo er 1969 seinen Abschluss machte. 1971 gründete Yamamoto sein eigenes Label unter dem Namen Y's. Die erste Schau fand 1977 in Tokio statt. Als er 1981 gemeinsam mit seiner damaligen Freundin Rei Kawakubo von Comme des Garçons sein Debüt unter eigenem Namen in Paris gab, war seine Marke Yohji Yamamoto zu Hause in Japan bereits ein kommerzieller Erfolg. Yamamoto schickte die Models mit weißem Make-up und asymmetrischen schwarzen Kleidern auf den Laufsteg, woraufhin das Mode-Establishment diesen Look mit dem Etikett „Hiroshima Chic" versah. Bald waren sowohl seine Damen- wie seine

Herrenmode – letztere wurde erstmals 1984 in Paris präsentiert – Statussymbole kreativer Stadtmenschen. Inzwischen verfügt er über 223 Einzelhandelsgeschäfte weltweit, dazu kommt noch eine wegweisende Kooperation mit Adidas (Y-3). Seine erste große Einzelausstellung war 2005 im Pariser Musée de la Mode zu sehen. Yamamoto ist auch Träger des schwarzen Karategürtels und Chef-Organisator der Worldwide Karate Association. 2011 eröffneten vier Yamamoto-Ausstellungen in London: die erste britische Retrospektive im Victoria and Albert Museum vereinigte erstmalig etwa 80 Exponate aus den Damen- und Herrenkollektionen, „Yohji's Women" sowie „Yohji Making Waves" waren im Wapping Project zu sehen und „Yohji Yamamoto at Work" im College of Fashion. Im selben Jahr ernannte der französische Präsident Yamamoto zum Offizier der Ehrenlegion, und es erschien seine Autobiografie unter dem Titel „My Dear Bomb".

Réputé pour ses silhouettes abstraites, ses chaussures plates et son inébranlable loyauté envers la couleur noire, Yohji Yamamoto est l'un des créateurs de mode les plus influents actuellement en exercice. La mode de Yamamoto combine rigueur intellectuelle et romantisme échevelé ; dans ses mains expertes, une modernité austère et souvent extrêmement provocatrice s'adoucit de références à la haute couture parisienne. Né en 1943 au Japon, Yamamoto grandit seul auprès de sa mère couturière, son père étant mort pendant la Seconde Guerre mondiale. C'est en cherchant à faire plaisir à sa mère qu'il entre à l'université Keio de Tokyo pour étudier le droit, qu'il abandonnera plus tard au profit d'un cours de mode à l'école Bunka, dont il sort diplômé en 1969. Yamamoto fonde sa propre griffe en 1971 sous le nom de Y's et présente son premier défilé à Tokyo en 1977. Lorsqu'en 1981, il fait ses débuts parisiens sous son propre nom aux côtés de sa petite amie de l'époque, Rei Kawakubo de Comme des Garçons, sa griffe remporte déjà un grand succès commercial au Japon. Il fait défiler des mannequins au visage entièrement peint en blanc et portant d'étranges vêtements noirs asymétriques, ce qui incite l'establishment à qualifier son look de « Hiroshima Chic ». Ses collections pour homme comme pour femme (sa ligne féminine étant présentée pour la première fois à Paris en 1984) deviennent un symbole de statut pour les jeunes urbains créatifs. Il compte aujourd'hui à son actif plus de 223 points de vente à travers le monde, une collaboration révolutionnaire avec Adidas (Y-3). Sa première grande expo y solo, a été organisée en 2005 au musée de la Mode de Paris. Yamamoto est également ceinture noire de karaté et organisateur en chef de l'Association Mondiale de Karaté. En 2011, quatre expositions Yamamoto sont présentées à Londres : la première rétrospective britannique au Victoria & Albert Museum réunissait pour la première fois quelque 80 modèles issus des collections pour femme et pour homme, « Yohji's Women » et « Yohji Making Waves » se trouvaient au Wapping Project et « Yohji Yamamoto at Work » au College of Fashion. La même année, le Président de la république française décore Yamamoto chevalier de l'Ordre des Arts et des Lettres et son autobiographie paraît sous le titre de « My Dear Bomb ».

SUSIE RUSHTON

PORTRAIT CLAUDIO DELLIOLIO. PHOTOGRAPHY DUSAN RELJIN. STYLING HAVANA LAFFITTE. MODEL MARIACARLA BOSCONO. SEPTEMBER 2003.

PHOTOGRAPHY KAYT JONES. STYLING KANAKO B KOGA. MODEL LAUREN. APRIL 2003.

YOHJI YAMAMOTO

PHOTOGRAPHY DANIEL JACKSON. STYLING MARIE CHAIX. MODEL LARA STONE. APRIL 2007.

"It's really amazing when you see your designs on the streets"
ITALO ZUCCHELLI · CALVIN KLEIN

When Calvin Klein stepped down in 2003, Italo Zucchelli assumed the role of design director of the brand's menswear collections, following four seasons of working directly with Klein. The Spring/Summer 2004 collection, shown in 2003, was Zucchelli's first. Zucchelli is a graduate of the Polimoda School of Fashion Design in Florence (1988), although he previously attended courses for two years at the Architecture University, also in Florence. Prior to being recruited by Calvin Klein, he spent two years as menswear designer for Jil Sander, then a spell as designer at Romeo Gigli. Born on June 4 1965, he grew up near the Italian coastal town of La Spezia. Zucchelli recalls that his first glimpse into the world of Calvin Klein was provided in 1982, with a men's underwear advertisement that starred Olympic pole-vault athlete Tom Hintnaus. Zucchelli's designs encapsulate the spirit of Calvin Klein's sexy, American philosophy, an aesthetic inspired by the human form and the idea of designing clothes that relate directly to the body in a sophisticated and effortless manner. The simplicity and purity of the brand's design roots is a discipline in itself, one that Zucchelli deploys with a certain European panache, and an inherent sense of sophisticated cool that has not only met with critical acclaim, but is an honest continuation of the Calvin Klein brand philosophy. Zucchelli lives and works in New York City.

Als Calvin Klein sich 2003 zurückzog, übernahm Italo Zucchelli den Posten des Design Directors für die Herrenkollektionen, nachdem er vier Saisons lang eng mit Klein persönlich zusammengearbeitet hatte. Zucchellis Debüt war die 2003 präsentierte Kollektion Frühjahr/Sommer 2004. Zucchelli ist Absolvent der Polimoda Schule für Modedesign in Florenz (1988), studierte zuvor jedoch ebenfalls in Florenz zwei Jahre lang Architektur. Bevor er von Calvin Klein engagiert wurde, hatte er zwei Jahre lang Herrenmode für Jil Sander entworfen und anschließend als Designer bei Romeo Gigli gearbeitet. Geboren wurde er am 4. Juni 1965, aufgewachsen ist er in der Nähe der italienischen Hafenstadt La Spezia. Zucchelli erinnert sich, dass er den ersten Eindruck von der Welt Calvin Kleins einer Werbung für Herrenunterwäsche von 1982 verdankte, die den olympischen Stabhochspringer Tom Hintnaus zeigte. Zucchellis

Entwürfe verkörpern den Geist von Calvin Kleins verführerischer amerikanischer Philosophie; eine Ästhetik, die vom menschlichen Körper inspiriert ist und von der Vorstellung, Mode zu designen, die auf raffinierte und zugleich mühelose Weise in unmittelbarem Bezug zum Körper steht. Die Schlichtheit und Reinheit der designerischen Ursprünge des Labels sind eine Disziplin für sich, die Zucchelli mit einer gewissen europäischen Überlegenheit absolviert. Dazu kommt sein angeborenes Gespür für exquisite Coolness, die nicht nur für Lob bei den Kritikern sorgte, sondern echte Kontinuität in der Markenphilosophie von Calvin Klein bedeutet. Zucchelli lebt und arbeitet in New York.

Depuis que Calvin Klein a pris sa retraite en 2003, Italo Zucchelli assume le rôle de directeur de la création des collections pour homme de la marque, après quatre saisons de collaboration directe avec Klein. Présentée en 2003, la collection printemps/été 2004 est la première signée par Zucchelli. Bien qu'il ait également suivi des études d'architecture à l'université de Florence, Italo Zucchelli est diplômé de la Polimoda School of Fashion Design de la même ville (1988). Avant d'être recruté par Calvin Klein, il passe deux ans chez Jil Sander en tant que styliste pour homme, puis travaille pendant une brève période pour Romeo Gigli. Né le 4 juin 1965, il grandit près de la ville côtière italienne de La Spezia. Zucchelli découvre pour la première fois l'univers de Calvin Klein en 1982, grâce à une publicité de sous-vêtements pour homme de la marque où apparaît le champion olympique de saut à la perche Tom Hintnaus. Les créations de Zucchelli réussissent à saisir la philosophie américaine et sexy propre à l'esprit Calvin Klein ; son esthétique s'inspire de la forme humaine, et de l'idée qui consiste à créer de manière sophistiquée et facile des vêtements qui entretiennent une relation directe avec le corps. La simplicité et la pureté des racines créatives de la marque sont une véritable discipline en soi, que Zucchelli déploie avec son panache très européen et son sens inné du cool sophistiqué, lequel est non seulement plébiscité par la critique, mais constitue également une continuation honnête de la philosophie Calvin Klein. Zucchelli vit et travaille à New York.

DAVID LAMB

PORTRAIT COURTESY ITALO ZUCCHELLI. PHOTOGRAPHY BEN DUNBAR-BRUNTON. STYLING SIMON FOXTON. MODEL DOMINIQUE HOLLINGTON. FEBRUARY 2006

TO STAY INFORMED ABOUT UPCOMING TASCHEN TITLES, PLEASE REQUEST OUR MAGAZINE
AT WWW.TASCHEN.COM/MAGAZINE OR WRITE TO TASCHEN, HOHENZOLLERNRING 53,
D-50672 COLOGNE, GERMANY, CONTACT@TASCHEN.COM. WE WILL BE HAPPY TO SEND YOU
A FREE COPY OF OUR MAGAZINE, WHICH IS FILLED WITH INFORMATION ABOUT ALL OF OUR BOOKS.

EDITOR: TERRY JONES
MANAGING EDITORS: DOMINIQUE FENN, KAREN HODKINSON
DESIGN: MATTHEW HAWKER
FASHION DIRECTOR: EDWARD ENNINFUL
FASHION EDITORS: ERIKA KURIHARA, CAROLINE NEWELL
EDITORIAL ASSISTANCE: BEN REARDON, HOLLY SHACKLETON
DESIGN ASSISTANCE: KEVIN WONG
EXECUTIVE DIRECTOR: TRICIA JONES

WRITERS:
JAMES ANDERSON
LEE CARTER
SIMON CHILVERS
LAUREN COCHRANE
PETER DE POTTER
AIMEE FARRELL
JO-ANN FURNISS
LIZ HANCOCK
KAREN HODKINSON
MARK HOOPER
JAMIE HUCKBODY
TERRY JONES
DAVID LAMB
AVRIL MAIR
TERRY NEWMAN
MAX PEARMAIN
BEN REARDON
MARCUS ROSS
SUSIE RUSHTON
HOLLY SHACKLETON
SKYE SHERWIN
JAMES SHERWOOD
JOSH SIMS
DAVID VASCOTT
GLENN WALDRON
NANCY WATERS

EDITORIAL COORDINATION: SIMONE PHILIPPI, COLOGNE
PRODUCTION COORDINATION: UTE WACHENDORF, COLOGNE

GERMAN TRANSLATION: HENRIETTE ZELTNER, MUNICH
FRENCH TRANSLATION: CLAIRE LE BRETON, PARIS

PRINTED IN CHINA
ISBN 978-3-8365-3614-1